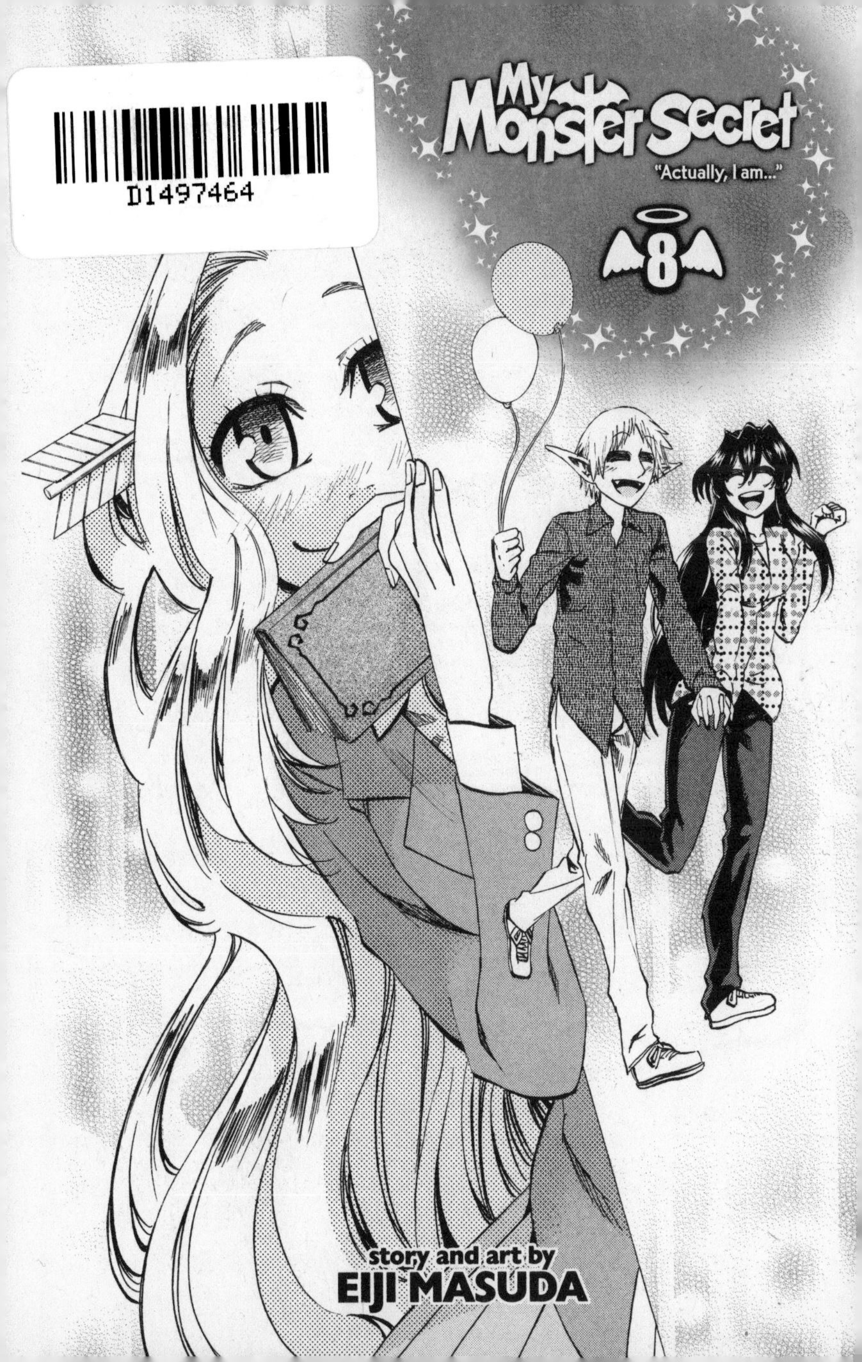
My Monster Secret
"Actually, I am..."
8
story and art by
EIJI MASUDA

My Monster Secret

"Actually, I am..."

Story & Character

After school one day, Kuromine Asahi opened the door to his classroom to confess his love to his crush Shiragami Youko...and discovered that she's actually a vampire! His goal was to tell Shiragami that he loved her, but he instead resolved to keep her secret--as a friend. It means they can continue to go to school together, but their problems are only beginning...

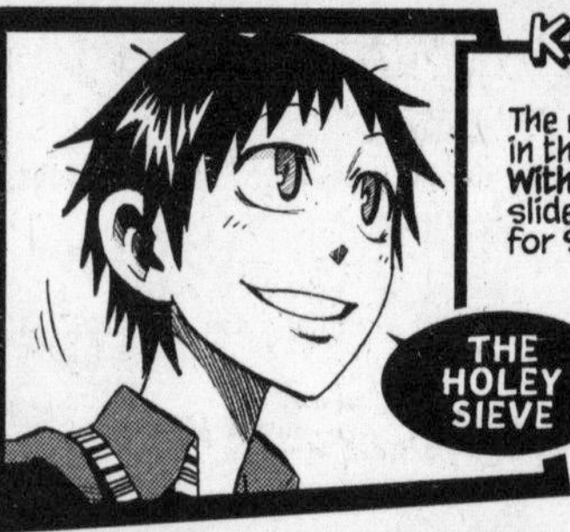
THE HOLEY SIEVE

KUROMINE ASAHI

The man with the worst poker face in the world, he's known as **The Sieve With A Hole In It**...because secrets slide right out of him. Has feelings for Shiragami-san.

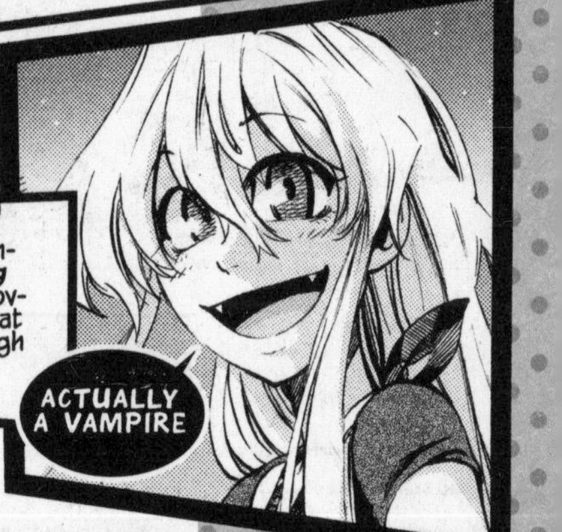
ACTUALLY A VAMPIRE

SHIRAGAMI YOUKO

She's attending a human high school under the condition that she'll ***stop going immediately*** if her true identity is discovered. She's managed to hide the fact that she's a vampire and is living a normal high school life, somehow!

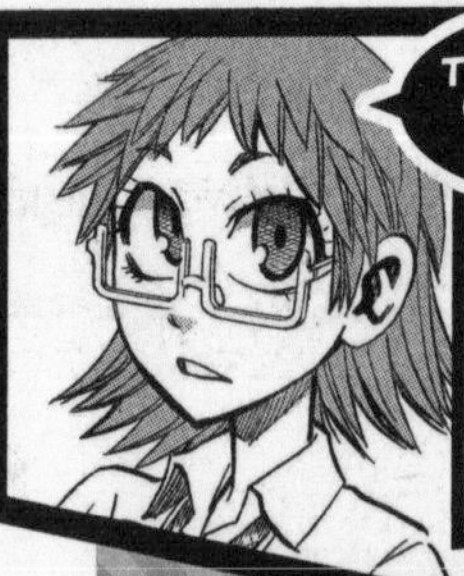
THE QUEEN OF PURE EVIL

AKEMI MIKAN

Editor-in-chief of the school newspaper and a childhood friend of Asahi's. Her favorite pair of glasses has become the **Goddess of Fortune, Fuku-chan.** In love with Asahi.

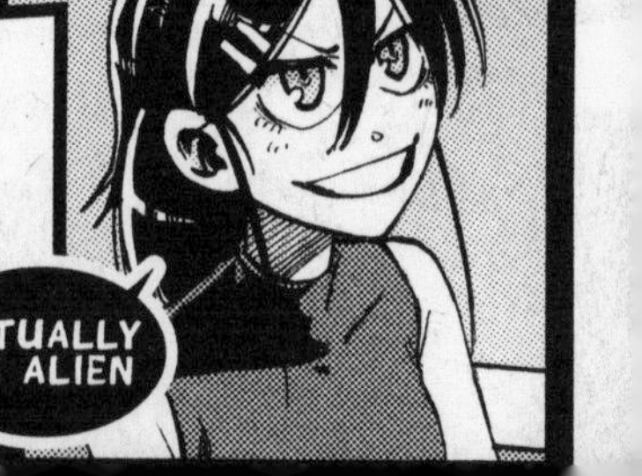
ACTUALLY AN ALIEN

AIZAWA NAGISA

Currently investigating Earth as a class representative, she once mercilessly tore Asahi to shreds before he could confess his love, but she now harbors an unrequited crush on him. Her true (tiny) form emerges from the screw-shaped cockpit on her head. Her brother **Aizawa Ryo** is also staying on Earth.

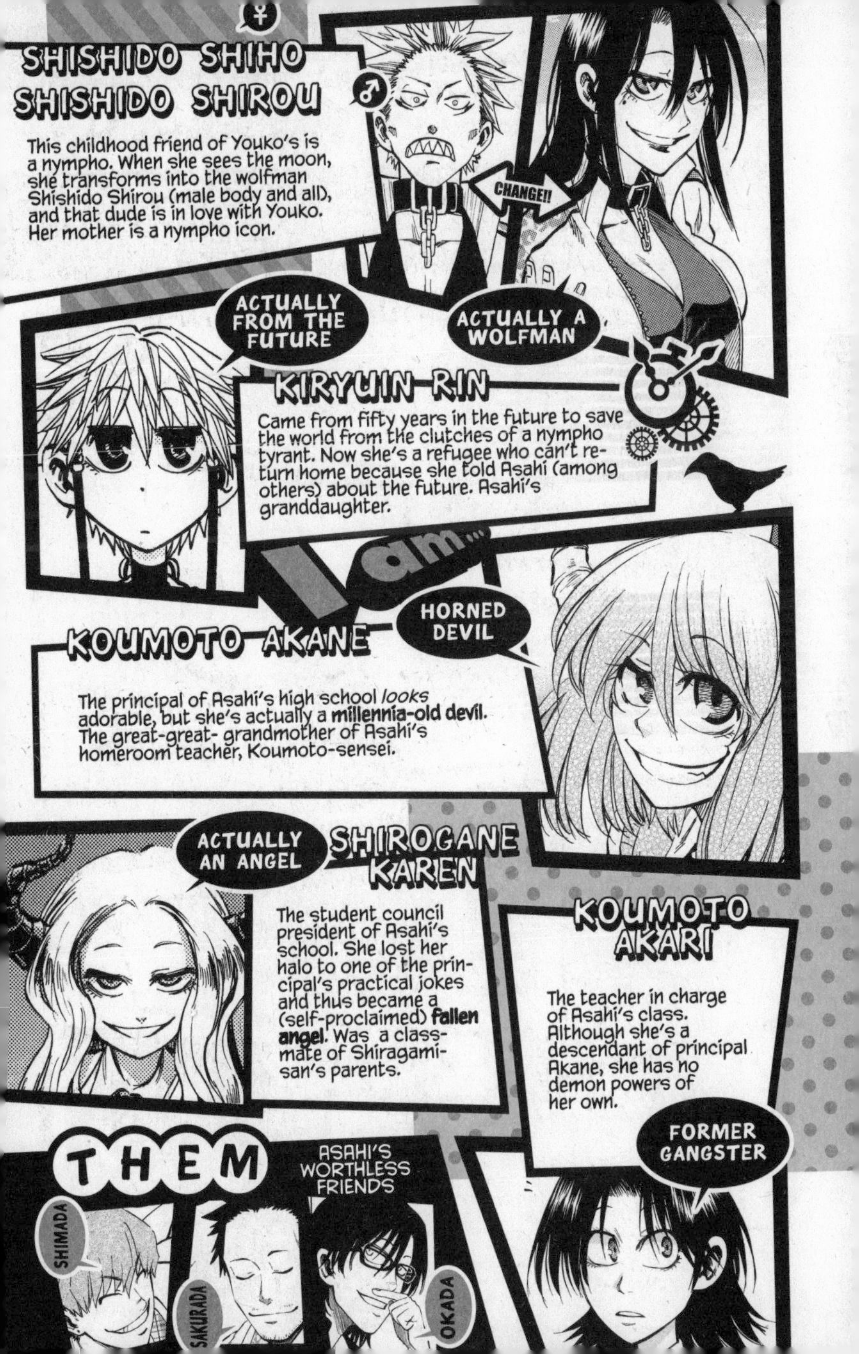
SHISHIDO SHIHO
SHISHIDO SHIROU
This childhood friend of Youko's is a nympho. When she sees the moon, she transforms into the wolfman Shishido Shirou (male body and all), and that dude is in love with Youko. Her mother is a nympho icon.
CHANGE!!
ACTUALLY A WOLFMAN
ACTUALLY FROM THE FUTURE
KIRYUIN RIN
Came from fifty years in the future to save the world from the clutches of a nympho tyrant. Now she's a refugee who can't return home because she told Asahi (among others) about the future. Asahi's granddaughter.
I am...
HORNED DEVIL
KOUMOTO AKANE
The principal of Asahi's high school *looks* adorable, but she's actually a **millennia-old devil**. The great-great- grandmother of Asahi's homeroom teacher, Koumoto-sensei.
KOUMOTO AKARI
The teacher in charge of Asahi's class. Although she's a descendant of principal Akane, she has no demon powers of her own.
ACTUALLY AN ANGEL
SHIROGANE KAREN
The student council president of Asahi's school. She lost her halo to one of the principal's practical jokes and thus became a (self-proclaimed) **fallen angel**. Was a classmate of Shiragami-san's parents.
FORMER GANGSTER
ASAHI'S WORTHLESS FRIENDS
THEM
OKADA
SAKURADA
SHIMADA

SEVEN SEAS ENTERTAINMENT PRESENTS

My Monster Secret

"Actually, I am..."

story and art by Eiji Masuda

VOLUME 8

TRANSLATION
Alethea and Athena Nibley

ADAPTATION
Lianne Sentar

LETTERING AND LAYOUT
Annaliese Christman

LOGO DESIGN
Karis Page

COVER DESIGN
Nicky Lim

PROOFREADER
Shanti Whitesides
Danielle King

ASSISTANT EDITOR
Jenn Grunigen

PRODUCTION ASSISTANT
CK Russell

PRODUCTION MANAGER
Lissa Pattillo

EDITOR IN CHIEF
Adam Arnold

PUBLISHER
Jason DeAngelis

JITSUHA WATASHIHA Volume 8
© EIJI MASUDA 2014
Originally published in Japan in 2014 by Akita Publishing Co., Ltd.
English translation rights arranged with Akita Publishing Co., Ltd.
through TOHAN CORPORATION, Tokyo.

Seven Seas books may be purchased in bulk for promotional, educational, or
business use. Please contact your local bookseller or the Macmillan Corporate
and Premium Sales Department at 1-800-221-7945, extension 5442, or by
e-mail at MacmillanSpecialMarkets@macmillan.com.

Seven Seas and the Seven Seas logo are trademarks of
Seven Seas Entertainment, LLC. All rights reserved.

ISBN: 978-1-626925-81-6

Printed in Canada

First Printing: November 2017

10 9 8 7 6 5 4 3 2 1

FOLLOW US ONLINE: *www.gomanga.com*

READING DIRECTIONS

This book reads from **right to left**, Japanese style.
If this is your first time reading manga, you start
reading from the top right panel on each page and
take it from there. If you get lost, just follow the
numbered diagram here. It may seem backwards at
first, but you'll get the hang of it! Have fun!!

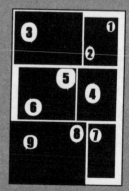

Chapter 62: "Let's Play with Angel Feathers!"

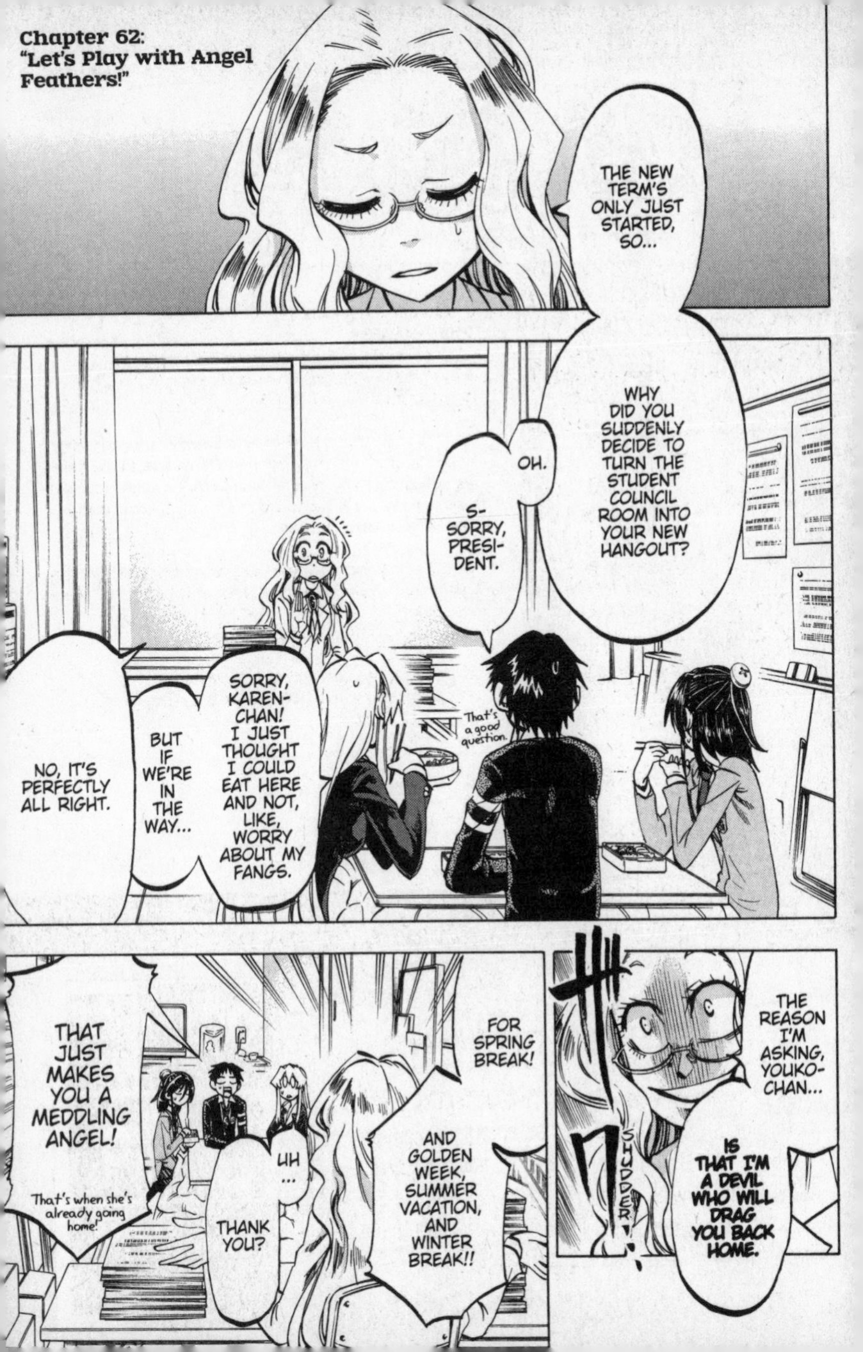
THE NEW TERM'S ONLY JUST STARTED, SO...
WHY DID YOU SUDDENLY DECIDE TO TURN THE STUDENT COUNCIL ROOM INTO YOUR NEW HANGOUT?
OH.
S-SORRY, PRESIDENT.
That's a good question.
SORRY, KAREN-CHAN! I JUST THOUGHT I COULD EAT HERE AND NOT, LIKE, WORRY ABOUT MY FANGS.
BUT IF WE'RE IN THE WAY...
NO, IT'S PERFECTLY ALL RIGHT.
THE REASON I'M ASKING, YOUKO-CHAN...
SHUDDER
IS THAT I'M A DEVIL WHO WILL DRAG YOU BACK HOME.
FOR SPRING BREAK!
AND GOLDEN WEEK, SUMMER VACATION, AND WINTER BREAK!!
UH...
THANK YOU?
THAT JUST MAKES YOU A MEDDLING ANGEL!
That's when she's already going home!

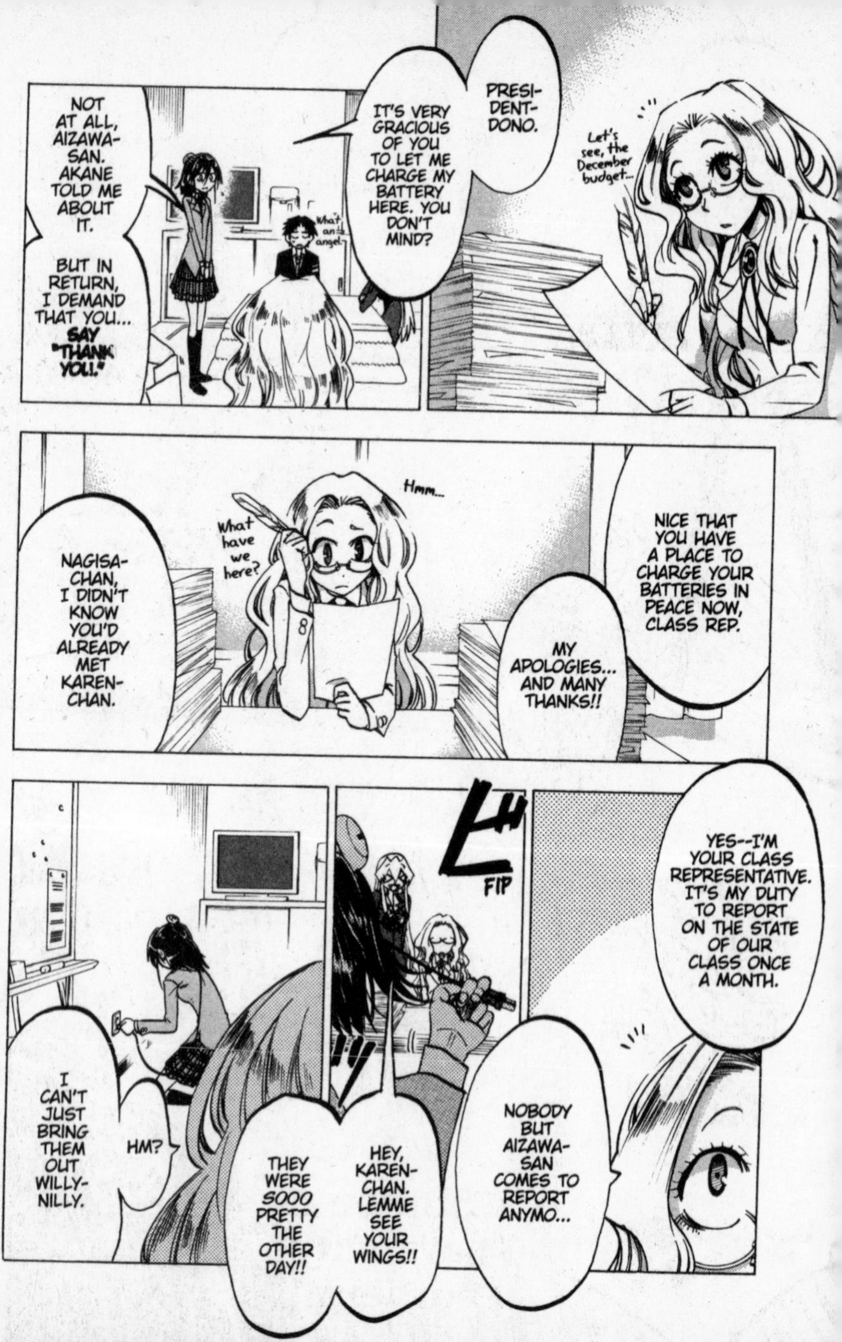

Let's see, the December budget...
PRESI-DENT-DONO.
IT'S VERY GRACIOUS OF YOU TO LET ME CHARGE MY BATTERY HERE. YOU DON'T MIND?
What an angel.
NOT AT ALL, AIZAWA-SAN. AKANE TOLD ME ABOUT IT.
BUT IN RETURN, I DEMAND THAT YOU... SAY "THANK YOU!"
NICE THAT YOU HAVE A PLACE TO CHARGE YOUR BATTERIES IN PEACE NOW, CLASS REP.
MY APOLOGIES... AND MANY THANKS!!
Hmm...
What have we here?
NAGISA-CHAN, I DIDN'T KNOW YOU'D ALREADY MET KAREN-CHAN.
YES--I'M YOUR CLASS REPRESENTATIVE. IT'S MY DUTY TO REPORT ON THE STATE OF OUR CLASS ONCE A MONTH.
NOBODY BUT AIZAWA-SAN COMES TO REPORT ANYMO...
FIP
HEY, KAREN-CHAN. LEMME SEE YOUR WINGS!!
THEY WERE SOOO PRETTY THE OTHER DAY!!
HM?
I CAN'T JUST BRING THEM OUT WILLY-NILLY.

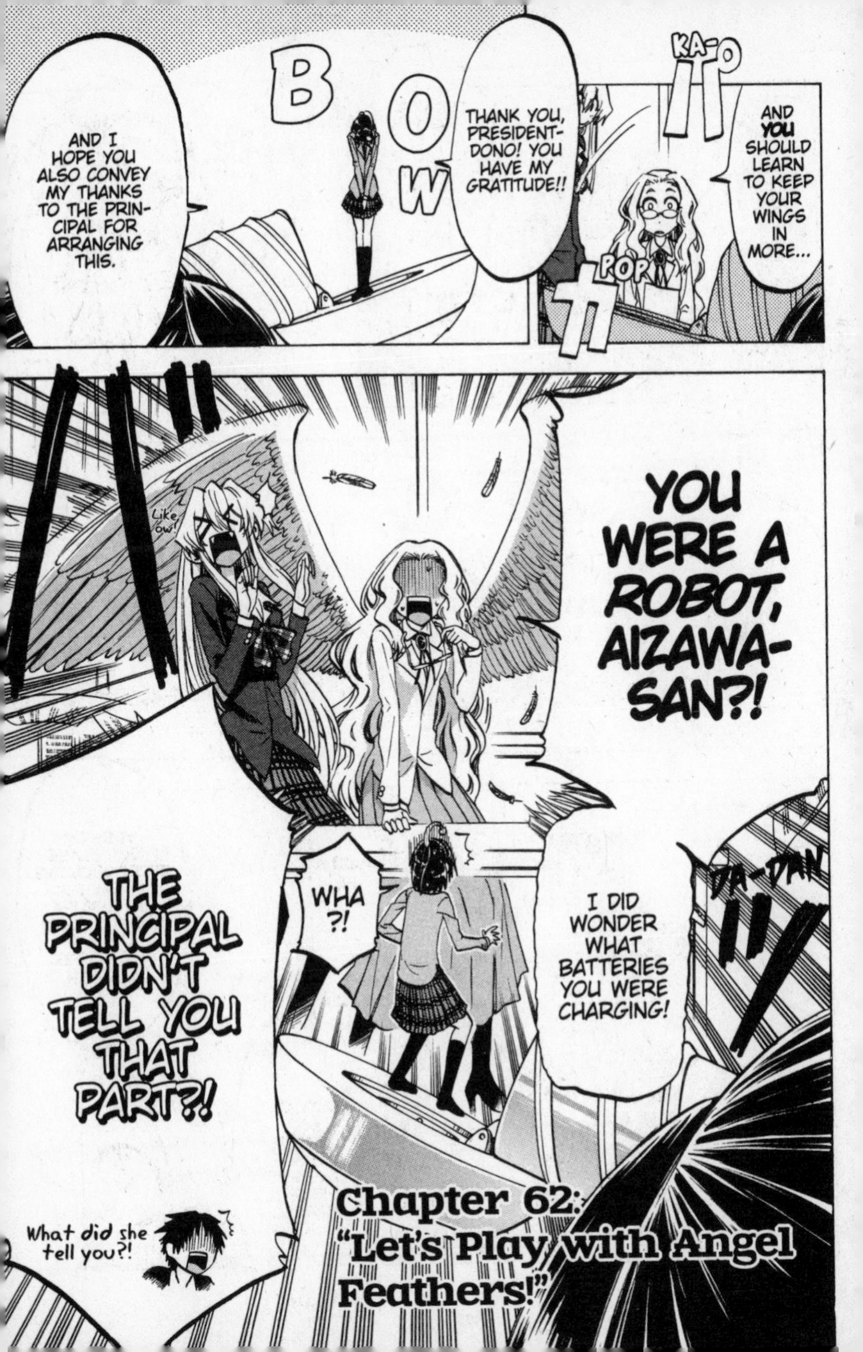
KA-O
AND YOU SHOULD LEARN TO KEEP YOUR WINGS IN MORE...
POP
THANK YOU, PRESIDENT-DONO! YOU HAVE MY GRATITUDE!!
BOW
AND I HOPE YOU ALSO CONVEY MY THANKS TO THE PRINCIPAL FOR ARRANGING THIS.
YOU WERE A ROBOT, AIZAWA-SAN?!
Like, ow!
DA-DAN
I DID WONDER WHAT BATTERIES YOU WERE CHARGING!
WHA ?!
THE PRINCIPAL DIDN'T TELL YOU THAT PART?!
What did she tell you?!

Chapter 62: "Let's Play with Angel Feathers!"

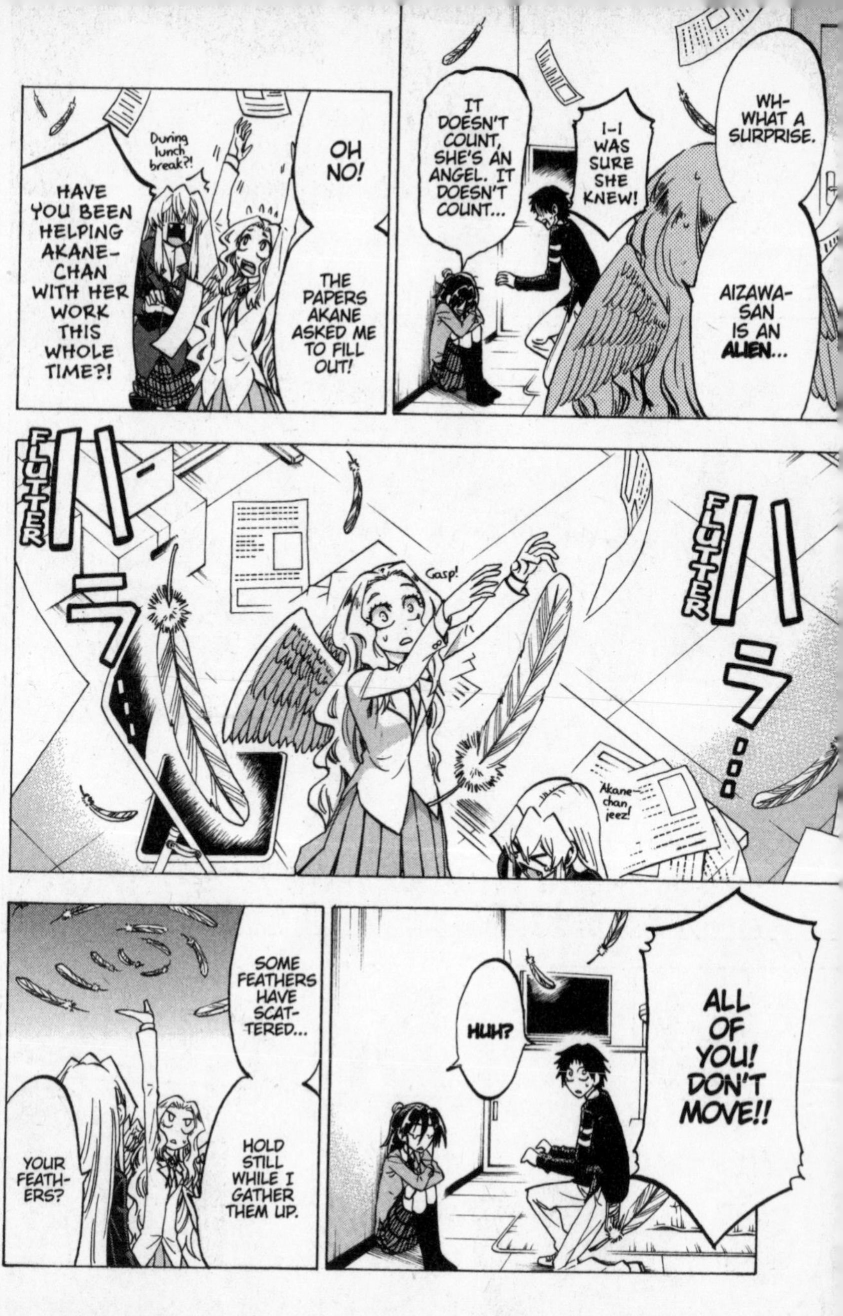
WH-WHAT A SURPRISE.
AIZAWA-SAN IS AN ALIEN...
I-I WAS SURE SHE KNEW!
IT DOESN'T COUNT, SHE'S AN ANGEL. IT DOESN'T COUNT...
OH NO!
THE PAPERS AKANE ASKED ME TO FILL OUT!
During lunch break?!
HAVE YOU BEEN HELPING AKANE-CHAN WITH HER WORK THIS WHOLE TIME?!
FLUTTER
ハラ...
FLUTTER
ハラ
Gasp!
Akane-chan jeez!
ALL OF YOU! DON'T MOVE!!
HUH?
SOME FEATHERS HAVE SCATTERED...
HOLD STILL WHILE I GATHER THEM UP.
YOUR FEATHERS?

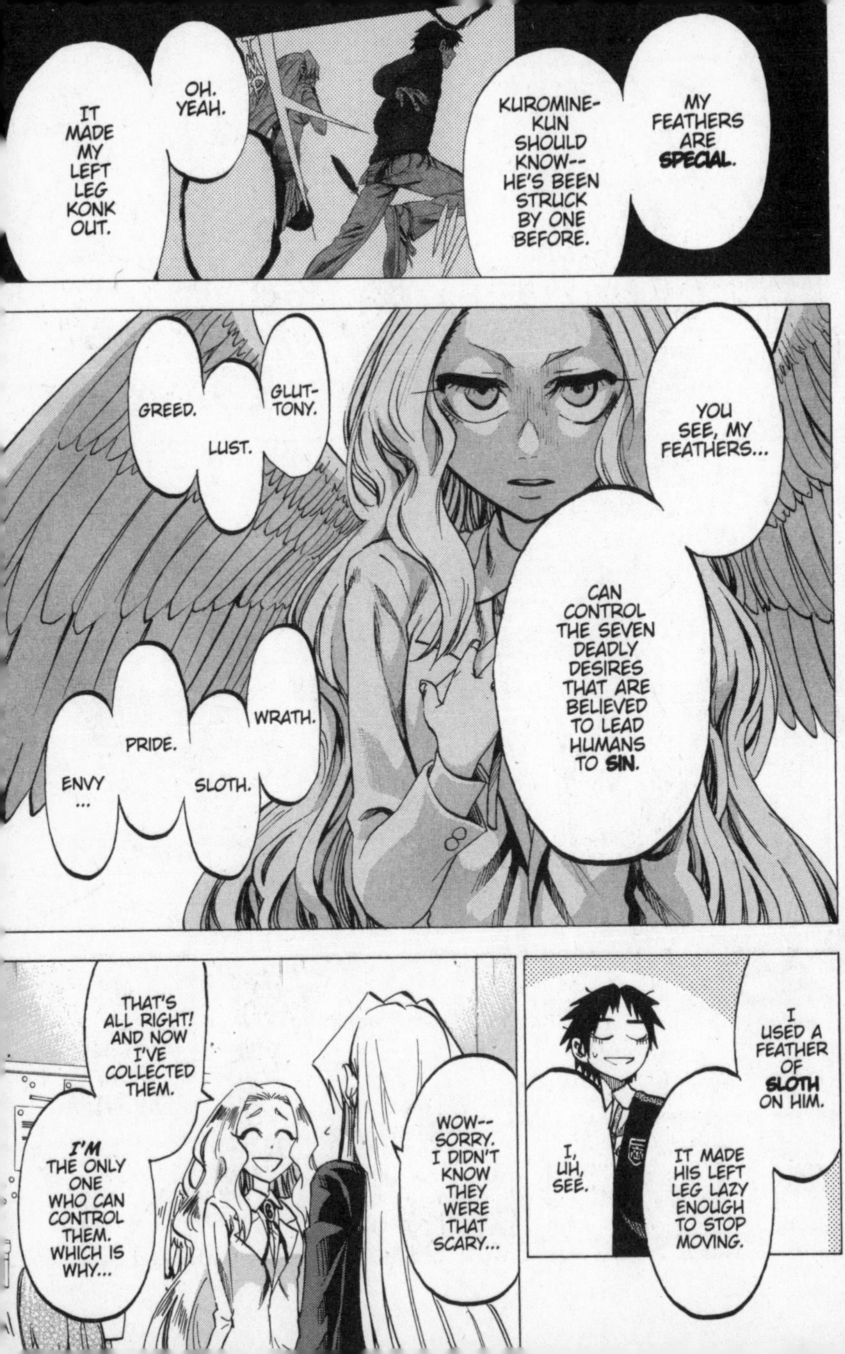
MY FEATHERS ARE **SPECIAL**.
KUROMINE-KUN SHOULD KNOW-- HE'S BEEN STRUCK BY ONE BEFORE.
OH. YEAH.
IT MADE MY LEFT LEG KONK OUT.
YOU SEE, MY FEATHERS...
CAN CONTROL THE SEVEN DEADLY DESIRES THAT ARE BELIEVED TO LEAD HUMANS TO **SIN**.
GLUTTONY.
GREED.
LUST.
WRATH.
PRIDE.
SLOTH.
ENVY...
I USED A FEATHER OF **SLOTH** ON HIM.
IT MADE HIS LEFT LEG LAZY ENOUGH TO STOP MOVING.
I, UH, SEE.
WOW-- SORRY. I DIDN'T KNOW THEY WERE THAT SCARY...
THAT'S ALL RIGHT! AND NOW I'VE COLLECTED THEM.
I'M THE ONLY ONE WHO CAN CONTROL THEM. WHICH IS WHY...

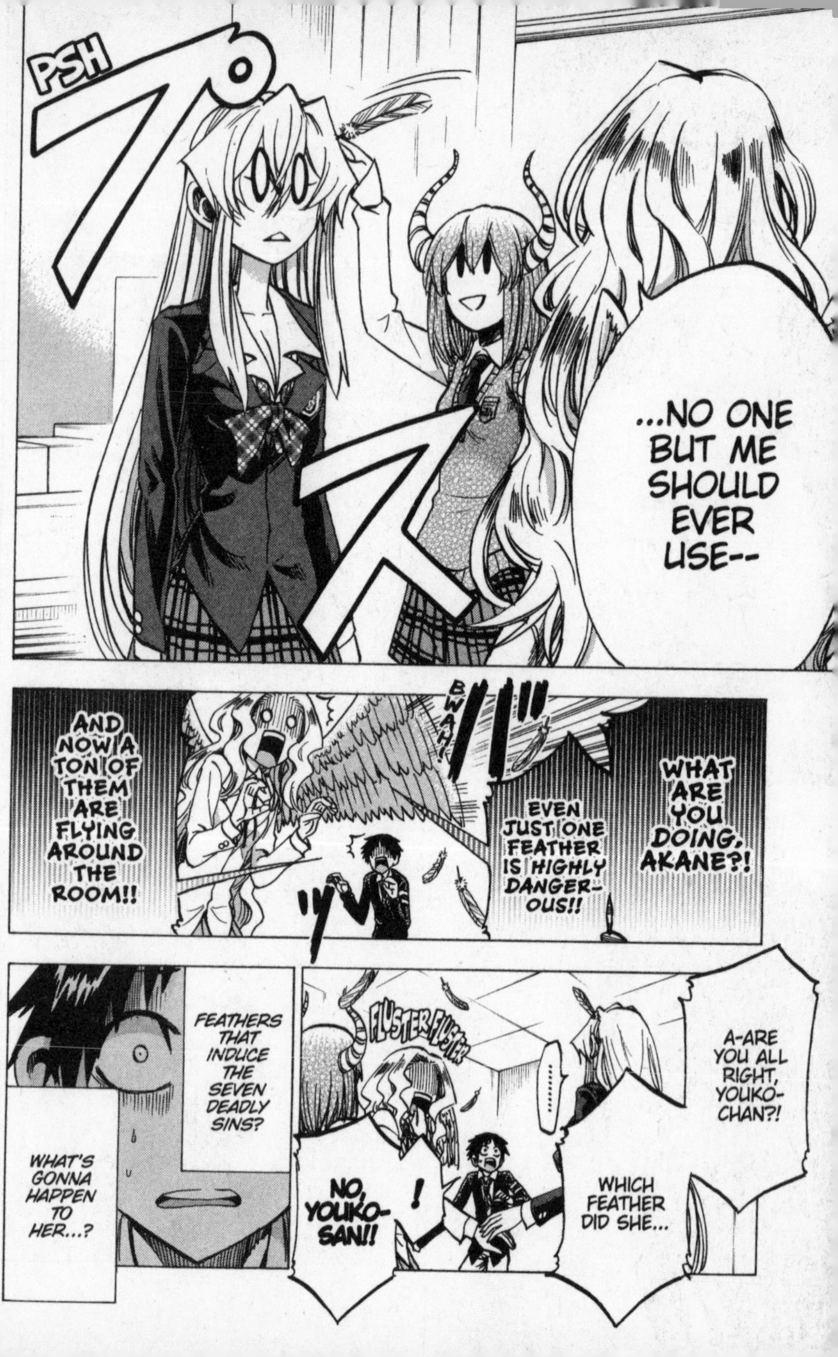
...NO ONE BUT ME SHOULD EVER USE--
PSH
WHAT ARE YOU DOING, AKANE?!
BWAH!
EVEN JUST ONE FEATHER IS HIGHLY DANGER-OUS!!
AND NOW A TON OF THEM ARE FLYING AROUND THE ROOM!!
A-ARE YOU ALL RIGHT, YOUKO-CHAN?!
....
FLUSTER FLUSTER
WHICH FEATHER DID SHE...
!
NO, YOUKO-SAN!!
FEATHERS THAT INDUCE THE SEVEN DEADLY SINS?
WHAT'S GONNA HAPPEN TO HER...?

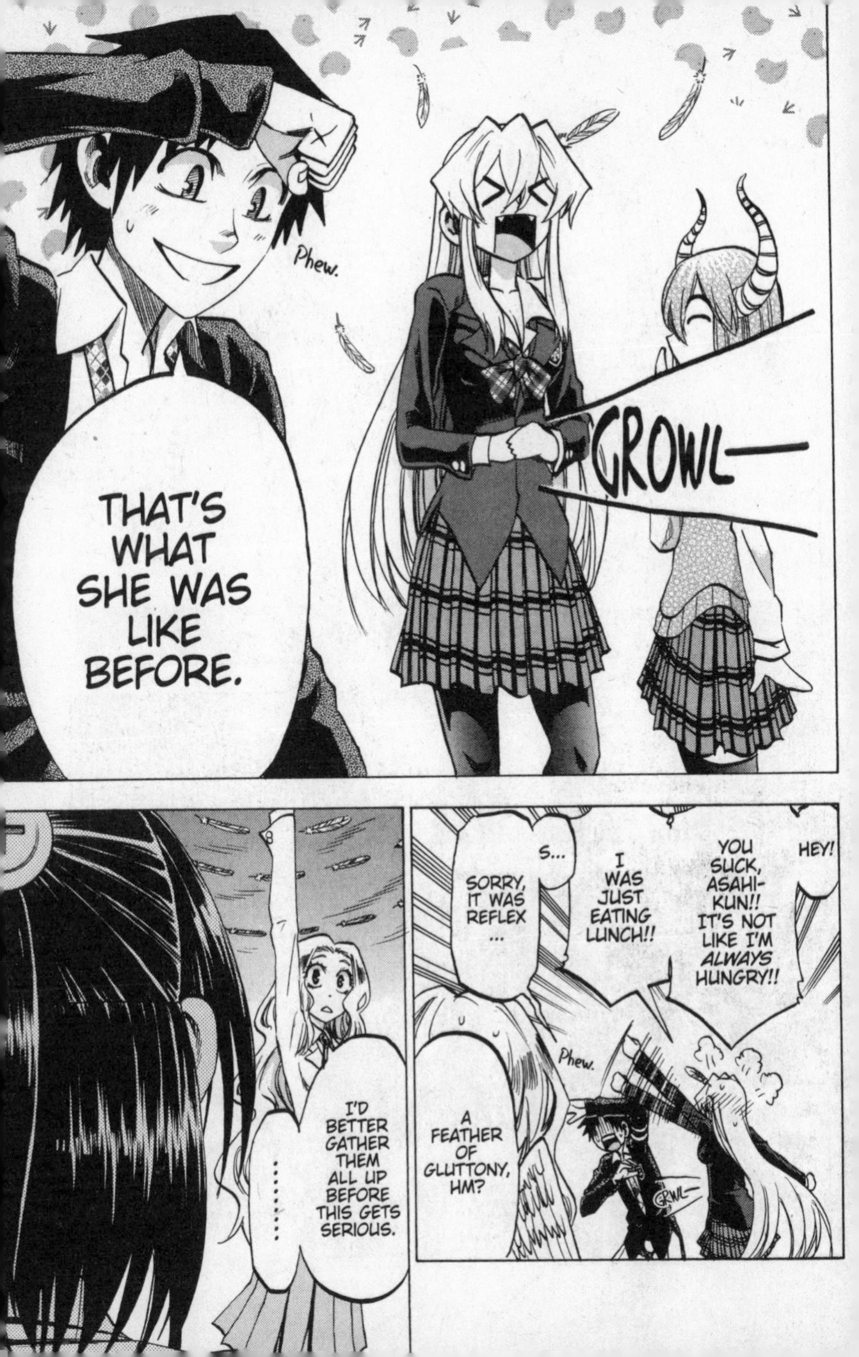
Phew.
GROWL—
THAT'S WHAT SHE WAS LIKE BEFORE.
HEY!
YOU SUCK, ASAHI-KUN!! IT'S NOT LIKE I'M ALWAYS HUNGRY!!
I WAS JUST EATING LUNCH!!
S...
SORRY, IT WAS REFLEX...
Phew.
GRWL—
A FEATHER OF GLUTTONY, HM?
......
I'D BETTER GATHER THEM ALL UP BEFORE THIS GETS SERIOUS.

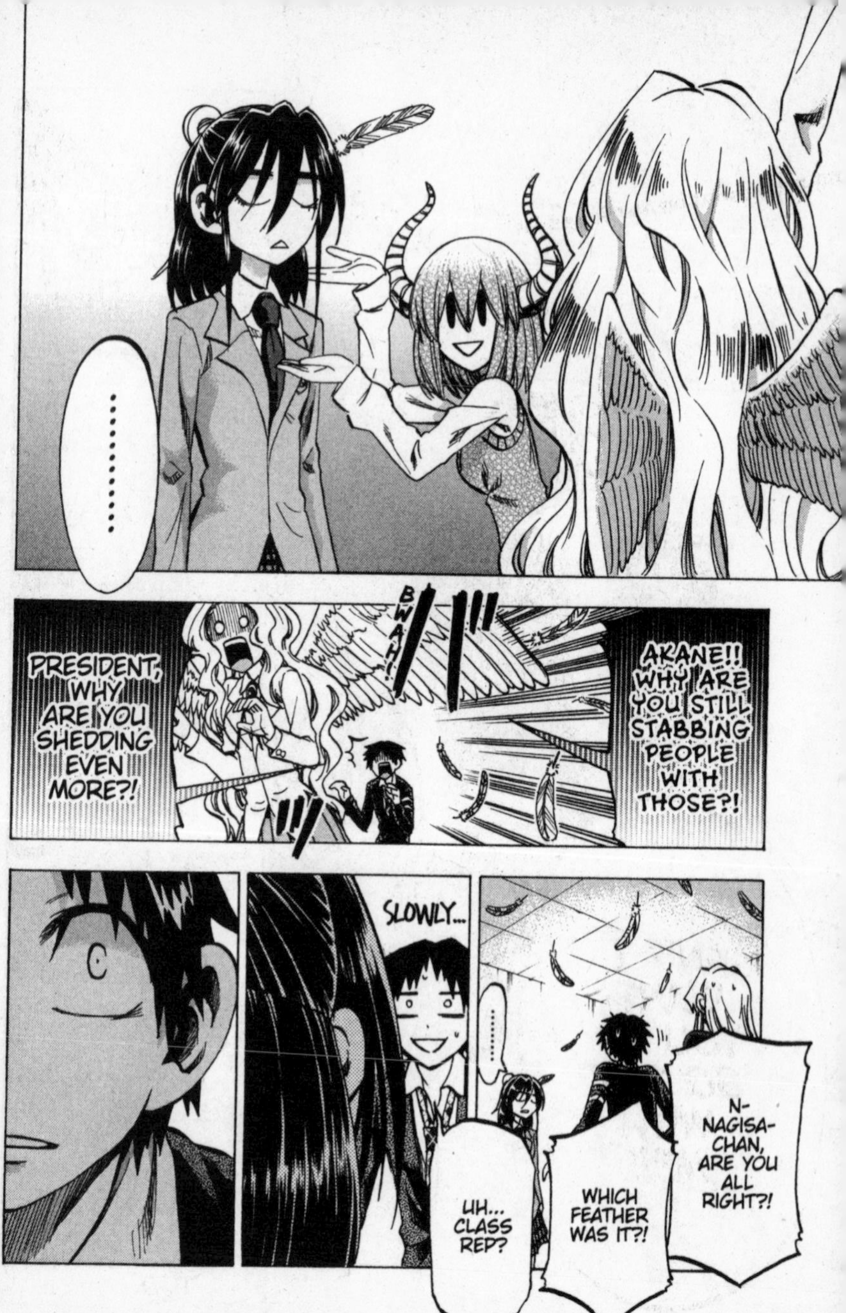
……
AKANE!! WHY ARE YOU STILL STABBING PEOPLE WITH THOSE?!
BWAH!!
PRESIDENT, WHY ARE YOU SHEDDING EVEN MORE?!
N-NAGISA-CHAN, ARE YOU ALL RIGHT?!
WHICH FEATHER WAS IT?!
……
UH... CLASS REP?
SLOWLY...

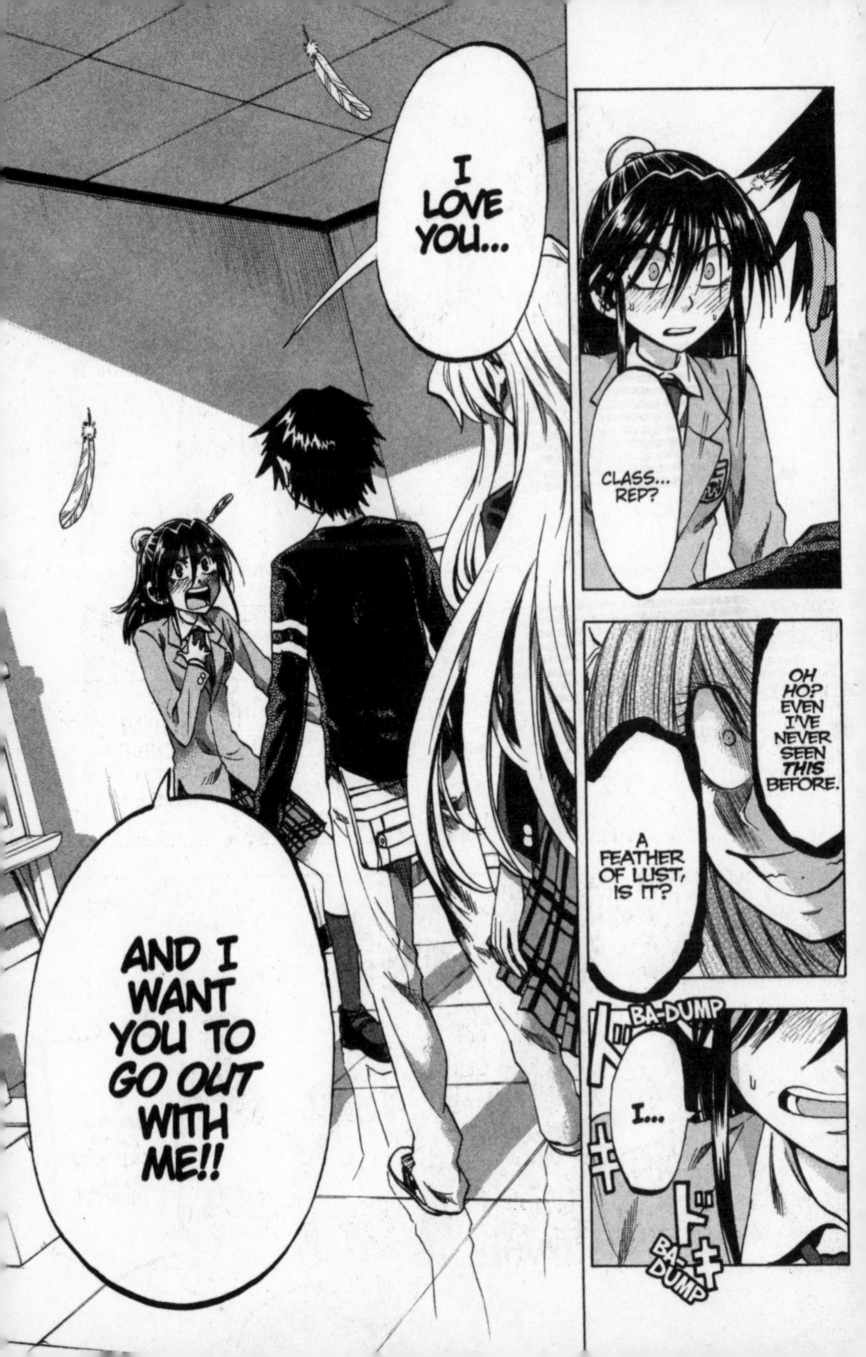
CLASS... REP?
OH HO? EVEN I'VE NEVER SEEN THIS BEFORE.
A FEATHER OF LUST, IS IT?
BA-DUMP
I...
BA-DUMP
I LOVE YOU...
AND I WANT YOU TO GO OUT WITH ME!!

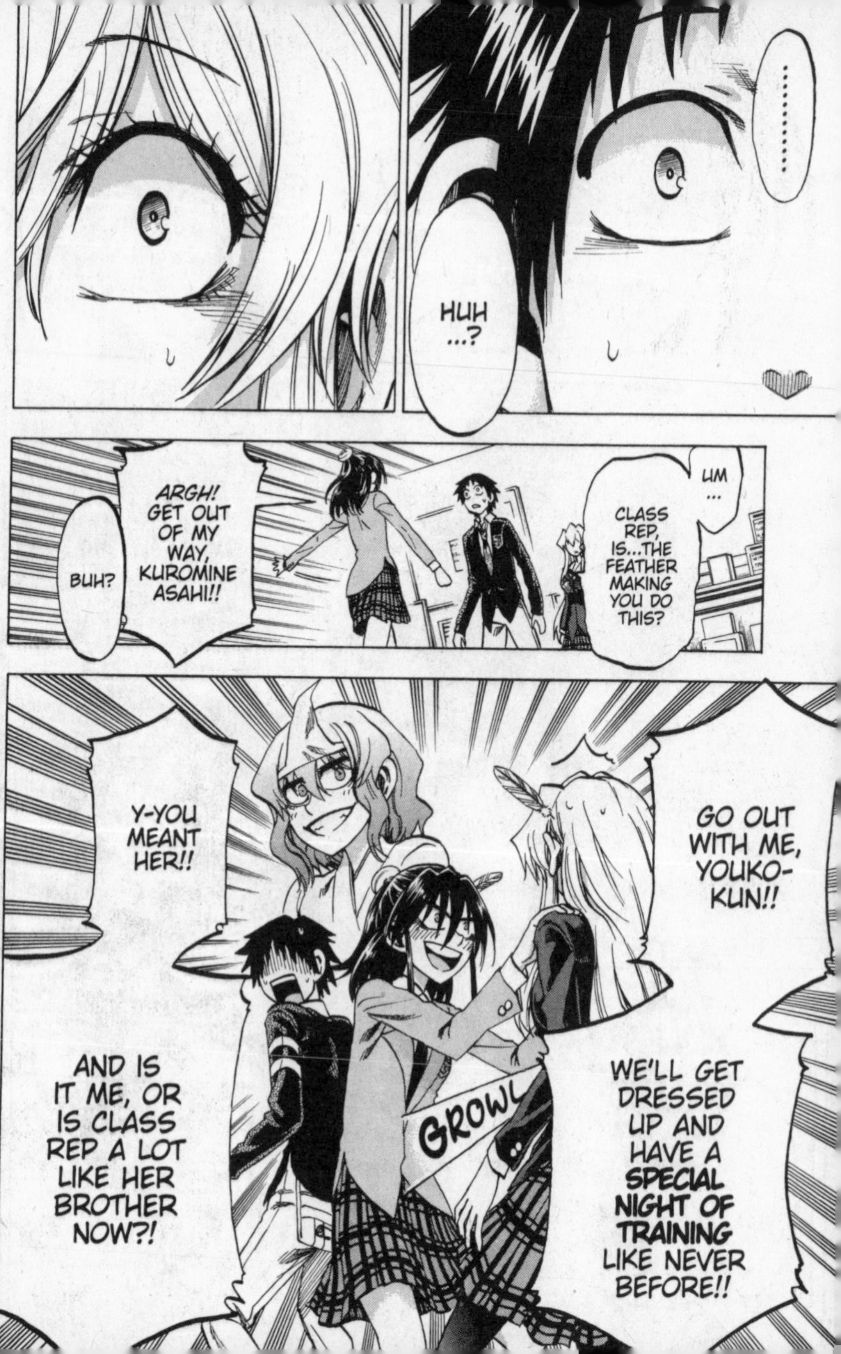
……
HUH ...?
UM ...
CLASS REP, IS...THE FEATHER MAKING YOU DO THIS?
ARGH! GET OUT OF MY WAY, KUROMINE ASAHI!!
BUH?
GO OUT WITH ME, YOUKO-KUN!!
Y-YOU MEANT HER!!
WE'LL GET DRESSED UP AND HAVE A **SPECIAL NIGHT OF TRAINING** LIKE NEVER BEFORE!!
GROWL
AND IS IT ME, OR IS CLASS REP A LOT LIKE HER BROTHER NOW?!

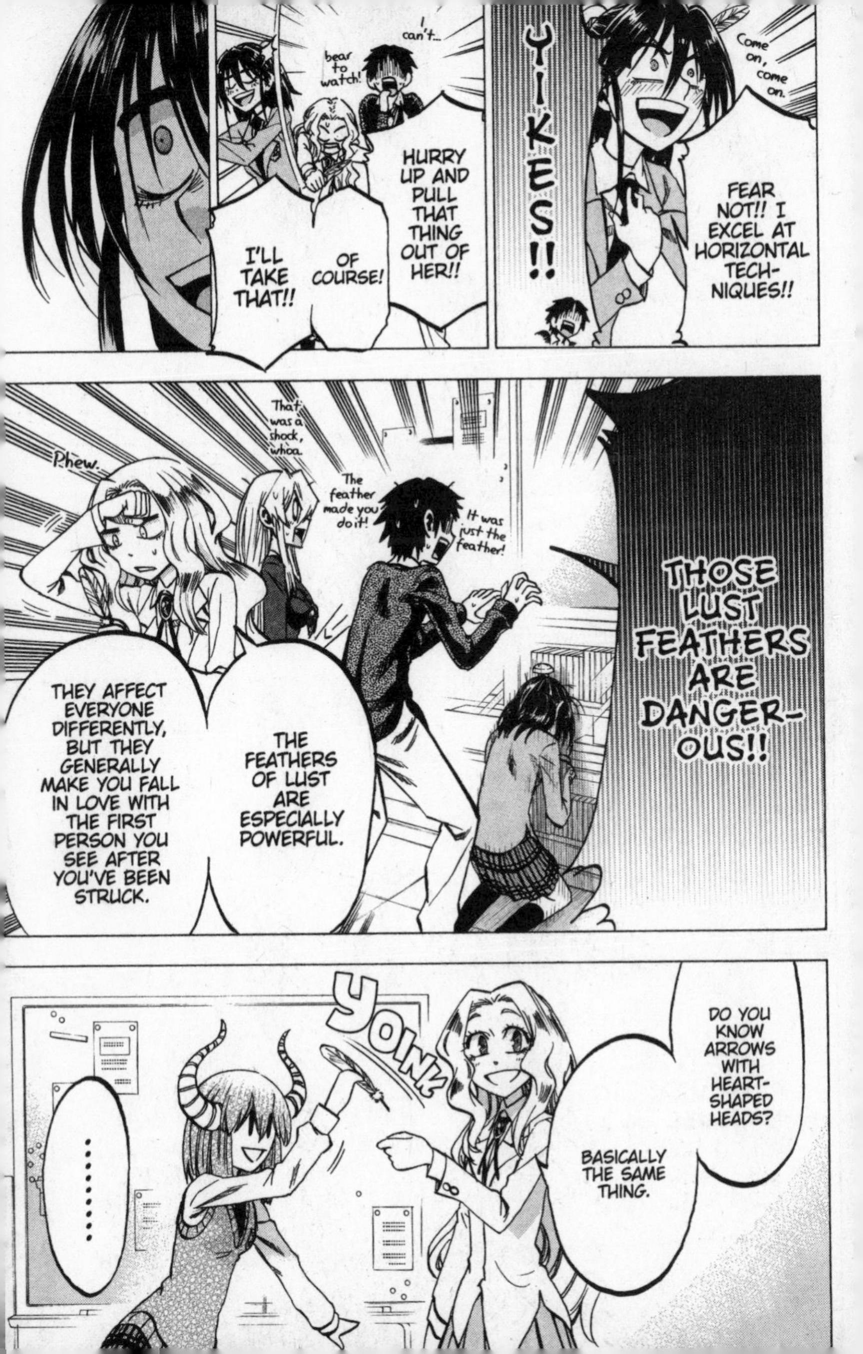
Come on, come on.
FEAR NOT!! I EXCEL AT HORIZONTAL TECH-NIQUES!!
YIKES!!
I can't... bear to watch!
HURRY UP AND PULL THAT THING OUT OF HER!!
OF COURSE!
I'LL TAKE THAT!!
THOSE LUST FEATHERS ARE DANGER-OUS!!
It was just the feather!
The feather made you do it!
That was a shock, whoa.
Phew.
THE FEATHERS OF LUST ARE ESPECIALLY POWERFUL.
THEY AFFECT EVERYONE DIFFERENTLY, BUT THEY GENERALLY MAKE YOU FALL IN LOVE WITH THE FIRST PERSON YOU SEE AFTER YOU'VE BEEN STRUCK.
DO YOU KNOW ARROWS WITH HEART-SHAPED HEADS?
BASICALLY THE SAME THING.
YOINK
....

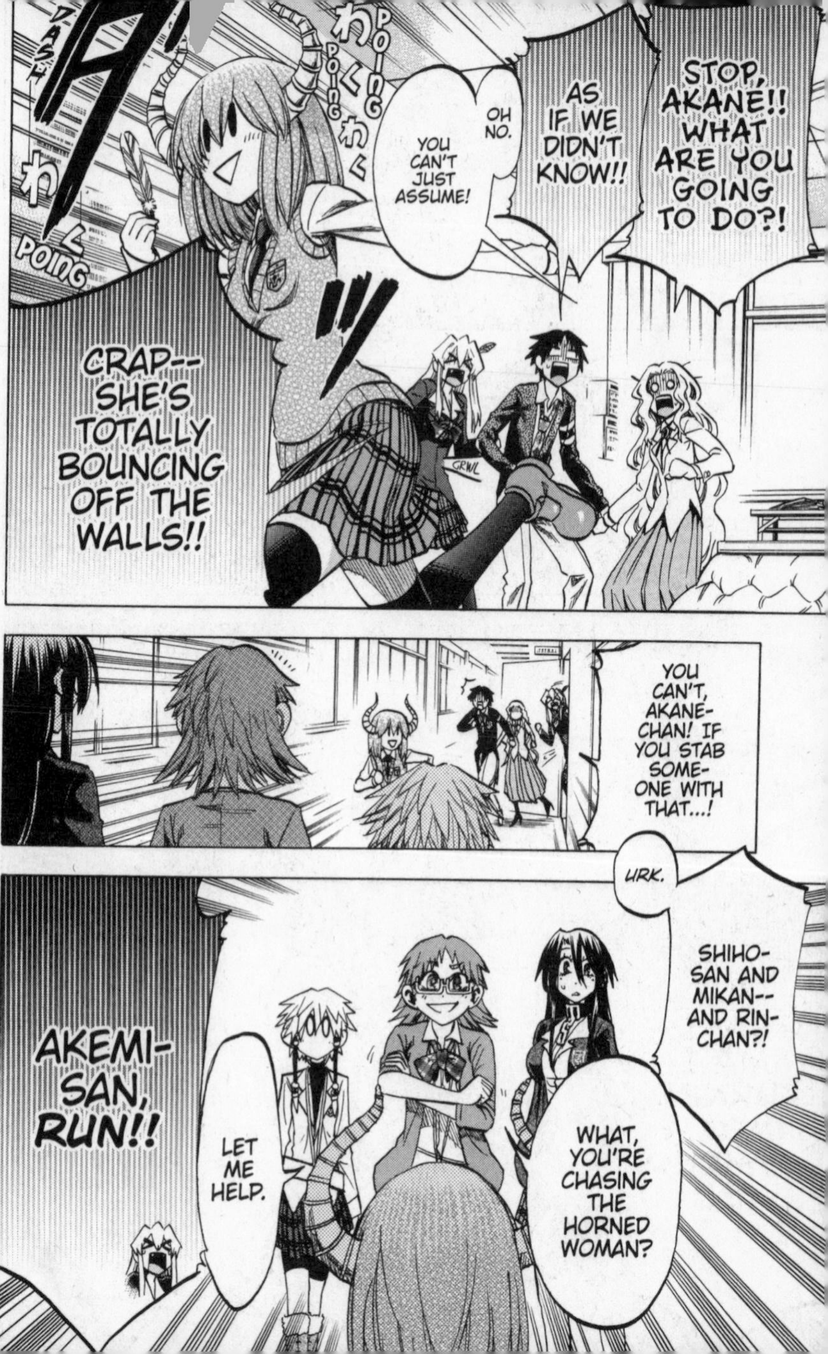
STOP, AKANE!! WHAT ARE YOU GOING TO DO?!
AS IF WE DIDN'T KNOW!!
OH NO.
YOU CAN'T JUST ASSUME!
POING POING
わくわく
DASH
わく
POING
CRAP-- SHE'S TOTALLY BOUNCING OFF THE WALLS!!
GRWL
YOU CAN'T, AKANE-CHAN! IF YOU STAB SOME-ONE WITH THAT...!
URK.
SHIHO-SAN AND MIKAN-- AND RIN-CHAN?!
WHAT, YOU'RE CHASING THE HORNED WOMAN?
LET ME HELP.
AKEMI-SAN, RUN!!

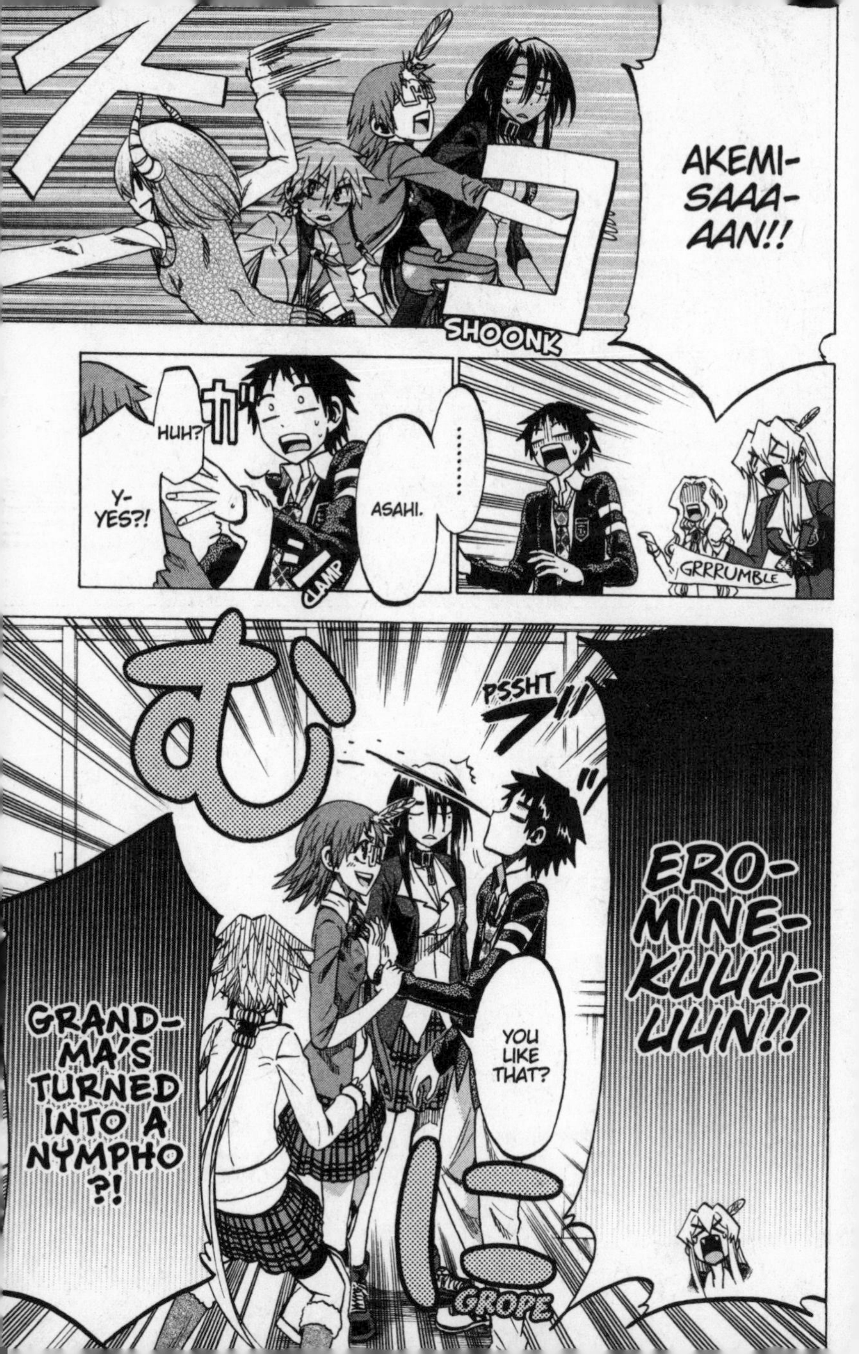
AKEMI-SAAAA-AAN!!
SHOONK
GRRRUMBLE
....
ASAHI.
HUH?
Y-YES?!
CLAMP
PSSHT
ERO-MINE-KUUU-UUN!!
YOU LIKE THAT?
GROPE
GRAND-MA'S TURNED INTO A NYMPHO ?!

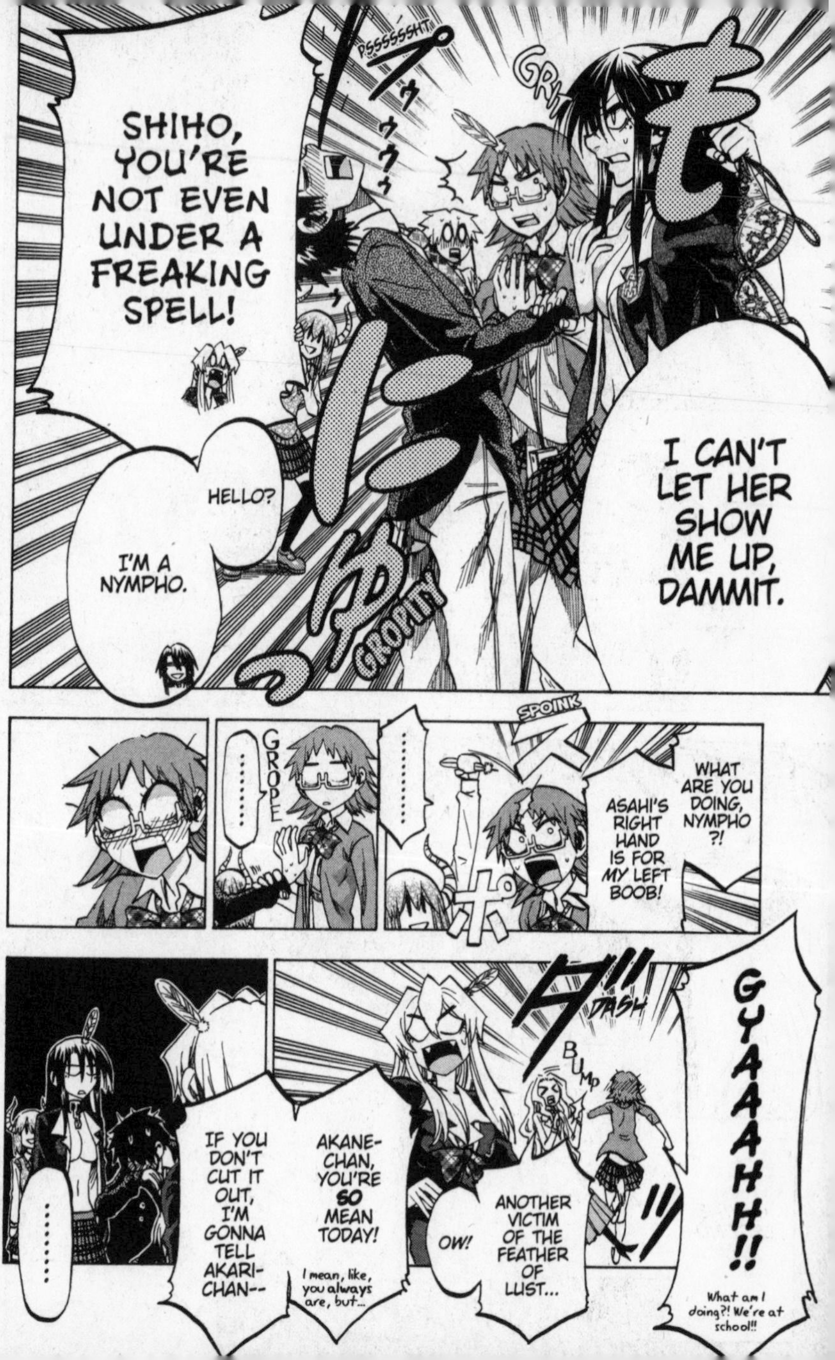
GRY
PSSSSSSHT
I CAN'T LET HER SHOW ME UP, DAMMIT.
SHIHO, YOU'RE NOT EVEN UNDER A FREAKING SPELL!
HELLO?
I'M A NYMPHO.
GROPITY
SPOINK
WHAT ARE YOU DOING, NYMPHO?!
ASAHI'S RIGHT HAND IS FOR MY LEFT BOOB!
......
GROPE
......
DASH
GYAAAAHH!!
What am I doing?! We're at school!!
BUMP
ANOTHER VICTIM OF THE FEATHER OF LUST...
OW!
AKANE-CHAN, YOU'RE **SO** MEAN TODAY!
I mean, like, you always are, but...
IF YOU DON'T CUT IT OUT, I'M GONNA TELL AKARI-CHAN--
......

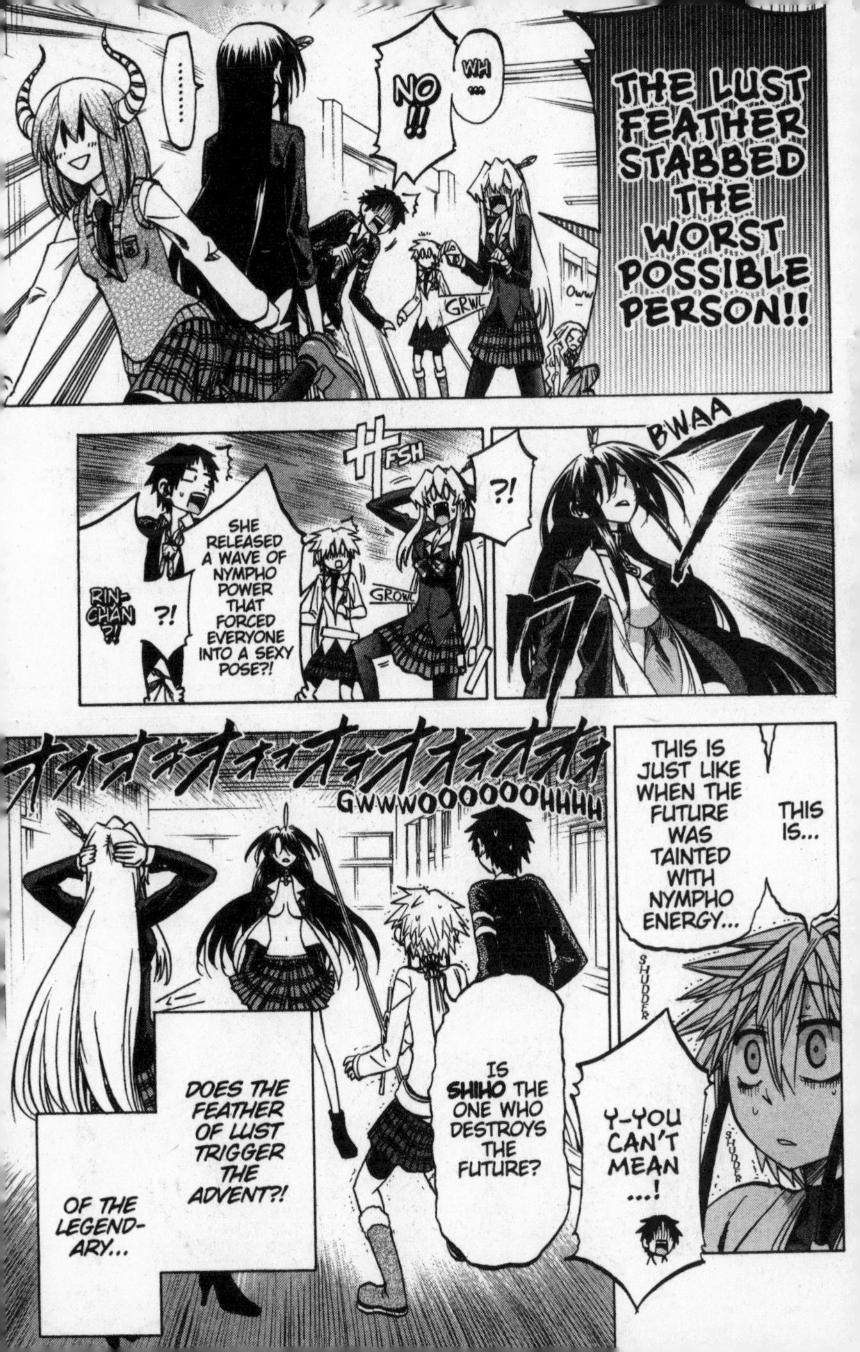

THE LUST FEATHER STABBED THE WORST POSSIBLE PERSON!!
WH ...
NO!!
......
Oww ...
GRWL
BWAA
?!
FSH
SHE RELEASED A WAVE OF NYMPHO POWER THAT FORCED EVERYONE INTO A SEXY POSE?!
GROWL
?!
RIN-CHAN ?!
THIS IS...
THIS IS JUST LIKE WHEN THE FUTURE WAS TAINTED WITH NYMPHO ENERGY...
SHUDDER
Y-YOU CAN'T MEAN ...!
SHUDDER
GWWWOOOOOOHHHH
IS SHIHO THE ONE WHO DESTROYS THE FUTURE?
DOES THE FEATHER OF LUST TRIGGER THE ADVENT?!
OF THE LEGEND-ARY...

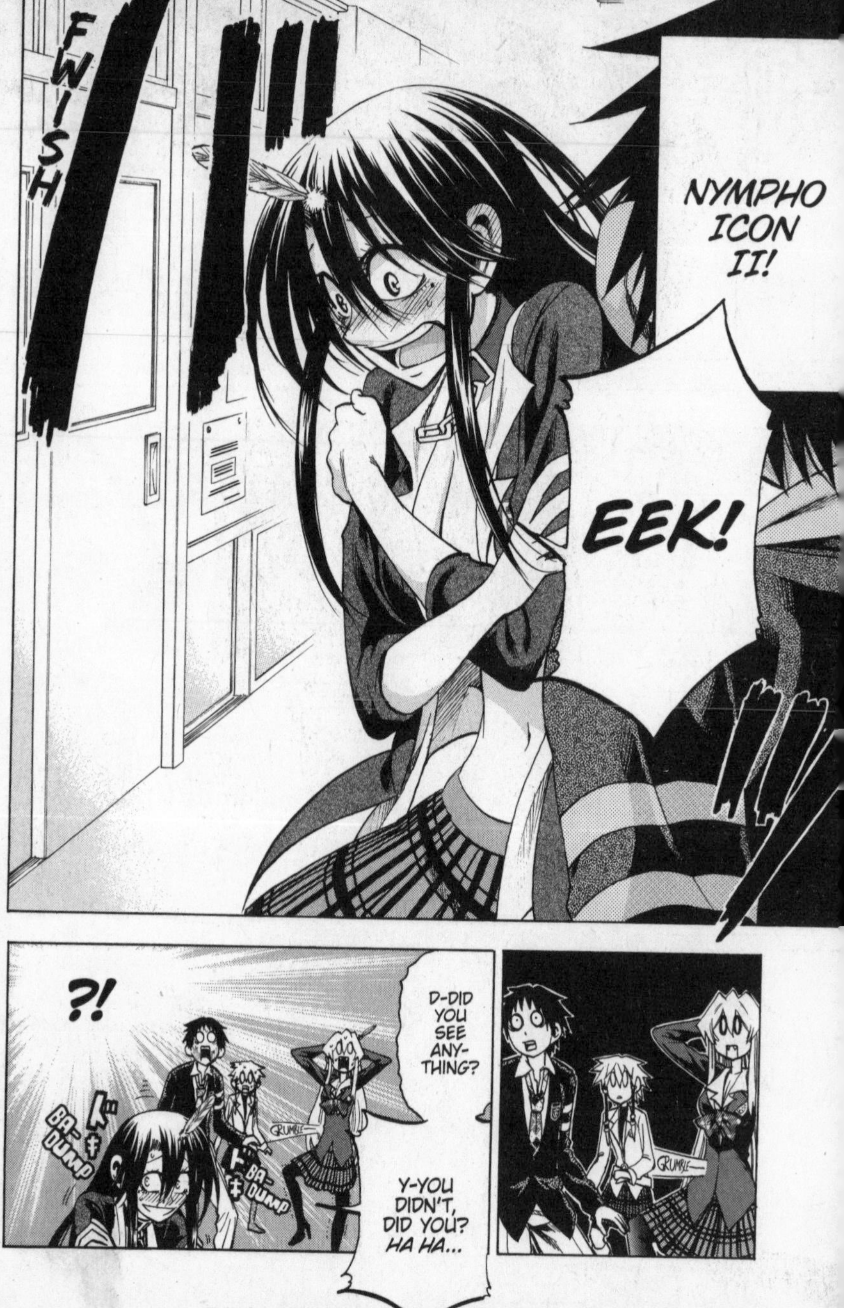
NYMPHO ICON II!
EEK!
FWISH
GRUMBLE
D-DID YOU SEE ANYTHING?
Y-YOU DIDN'T, DID YOU? HA HA...
?!
GRUMBLE
ドキ
BA-DUMP
ドキ
BA-DUMP

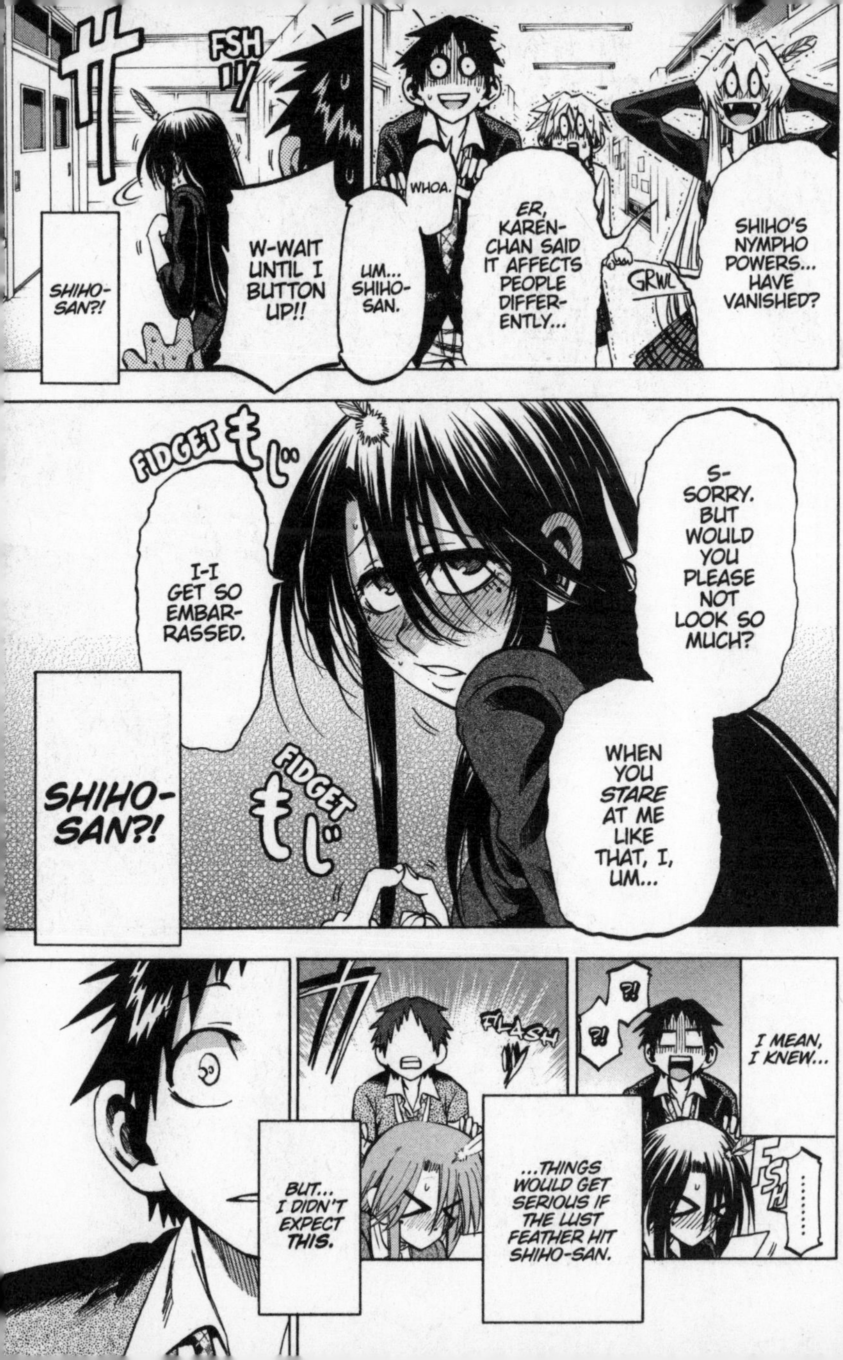
SHIHO'S NYMPHO POWERS... HAVE VANISHED?
GRWL
ER, KAREN-CHAN SAID IT AFFECTS PEOPLE DIFFERENTLY...
WHOA.
UM... SHIHO-SAN.
W-WAIT UNTIL I BUTTON UP!!
FSH
SHIHO-SAN?!
S-SORRY. BUT WOULD YOU PLEASE NOT LOOK SO MUCH?
WHEN YOU STARE AT ME LIKE THAT, I, UM...
FIDGET もじ
I-I GET SO EMBARRASSED.
FIDGET もじ
SHIHO-SAN?!
I MEAN, I KNEW...
?!
?!
FSH
......
...THINGS WOULD GET SERIOUS IF THE LUST FEATHER HIT SHIHO-SAN.
FLASH
BUT... I DIDN'T EXPECT THIS.

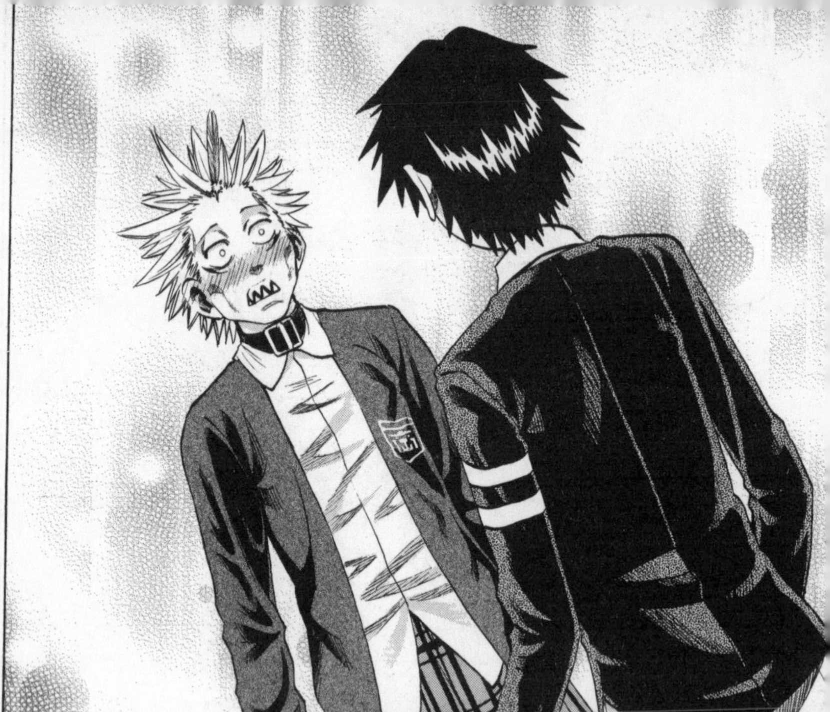

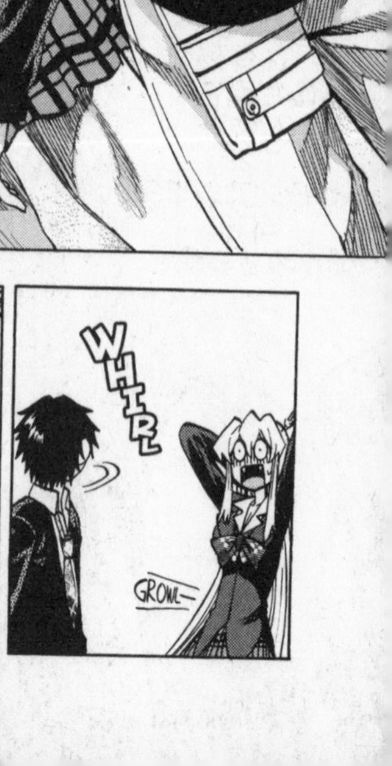
WHIRL
GROWL

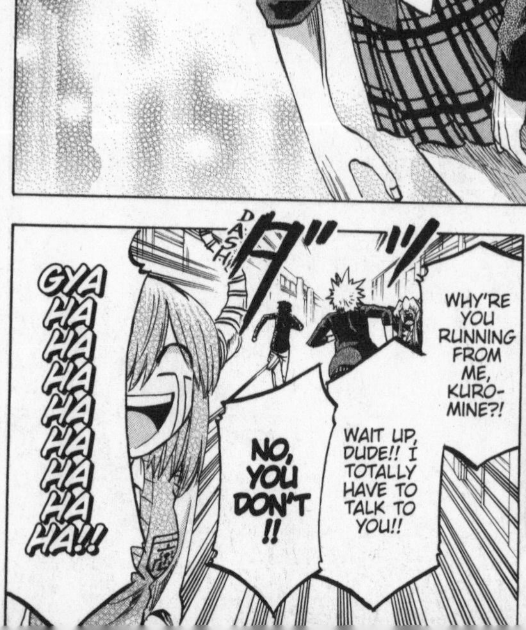
DASH
WHY'RE YOU RUNNING FROM ME, KURO-MINE?!
WAIT UP, DUDE!! I TOTALLY HAVE TO TALK TO YOU!!
NO, YOU DON'T!!
GYAHAHAHAHAHAHAHAHAHAHA!!

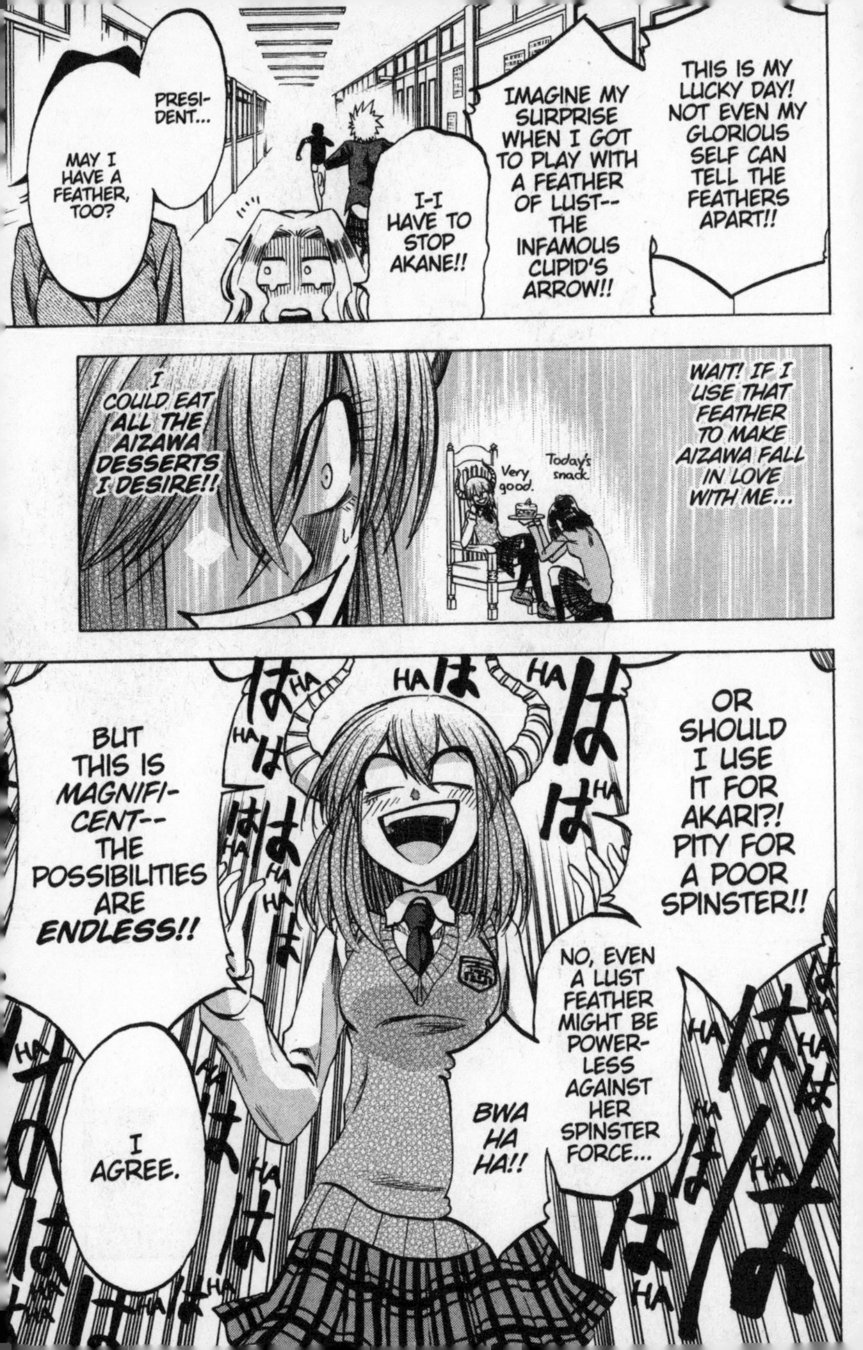
THIS IS MY LUCKY DAY! NOT EVEN MY GLORIOUS SELF CAN TELL THE FEATHERS APART!!
IMAGINE MY SURPRISE WHEN I GOT TO PLAY WITH A FEATHER OF LUST-- THE INFAMOUS CUPID'S ARROW!!
I-I HAVE TO STOP AKANE!!
PRESI-DENT...
MAY I HAVE A FEATHER, TOO?
WAIT! IF I USE THAT FEATHER TO MAKE AIZAWA FALL IN LOVE WITH ME...
Today's snack.
Very good.
I COULD EAT ALL THE AIZAWA DESSERTS I DESIRE!!
OR SHOULD I USE IT FOR AKARI?! PITY FOR A POOR SPINSTER!!
NO, EVEN A LUST FEATHER MIGHT BE POWER-LESS AGAINST HER SPINSTER FORCE...
BWA HA HA!!
BUT THIS IS MAGNIFI-CENT-- THE POSSIBILITIES ARE ENDLESS!!
I AGREE.

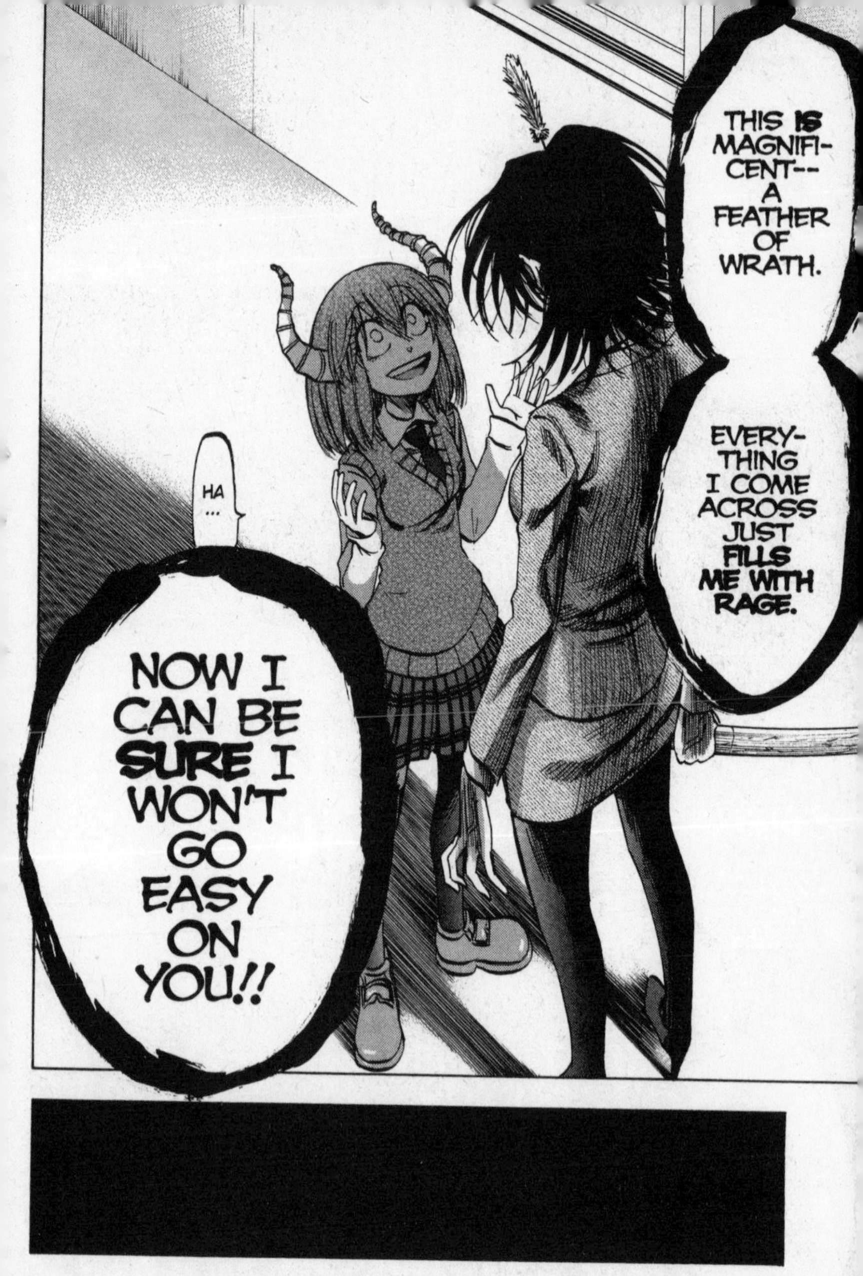
THIS IS MAGNIFICENT-- A FEATHER OF WRATH.
EVERYTHING I COME ACROSS JUST FILLS ME WITH RAGE.
HA...
NOW I CAN BE SURE I WON'T GO EASY ON YOU!!

[redacted]

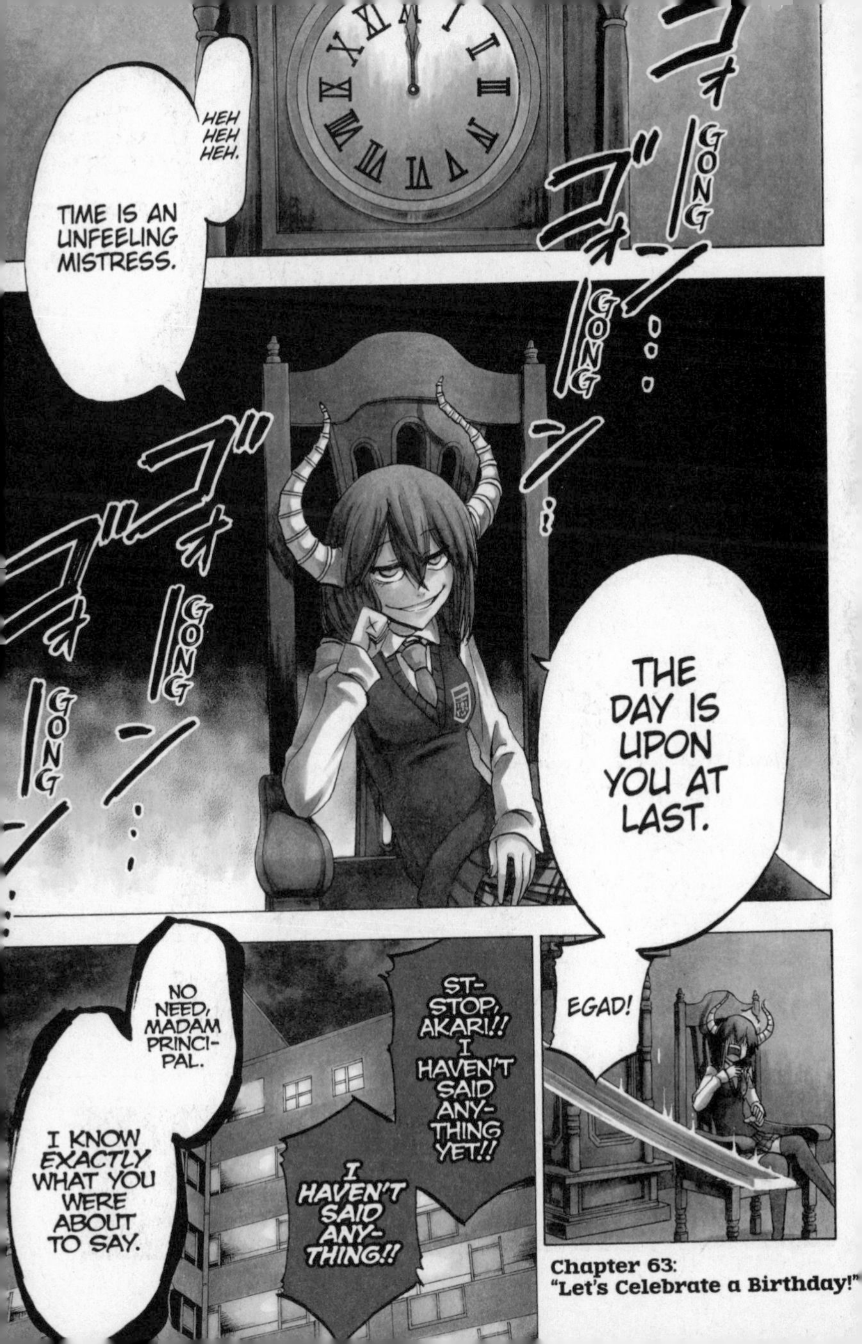
HEH HEH HEH.
TIME IS AN UNFEELING MISTRESS.
GONG
GONG
GONG
GONG
THE DAY IS UPON YOU AT LAST.
EGAD!
ST-STOP, AKARI!! I HAVEN'T SAID ANYTHING YET!!
NO NEED, MADAM PRINCIPAL.
I KNOW *EXACTLY* WHAT YOU WERE ABOUT TO SAY.
I HAVEN'T SAID ANYTHING!!

Chapter 63: "Let's Celebrate a Birthday!"

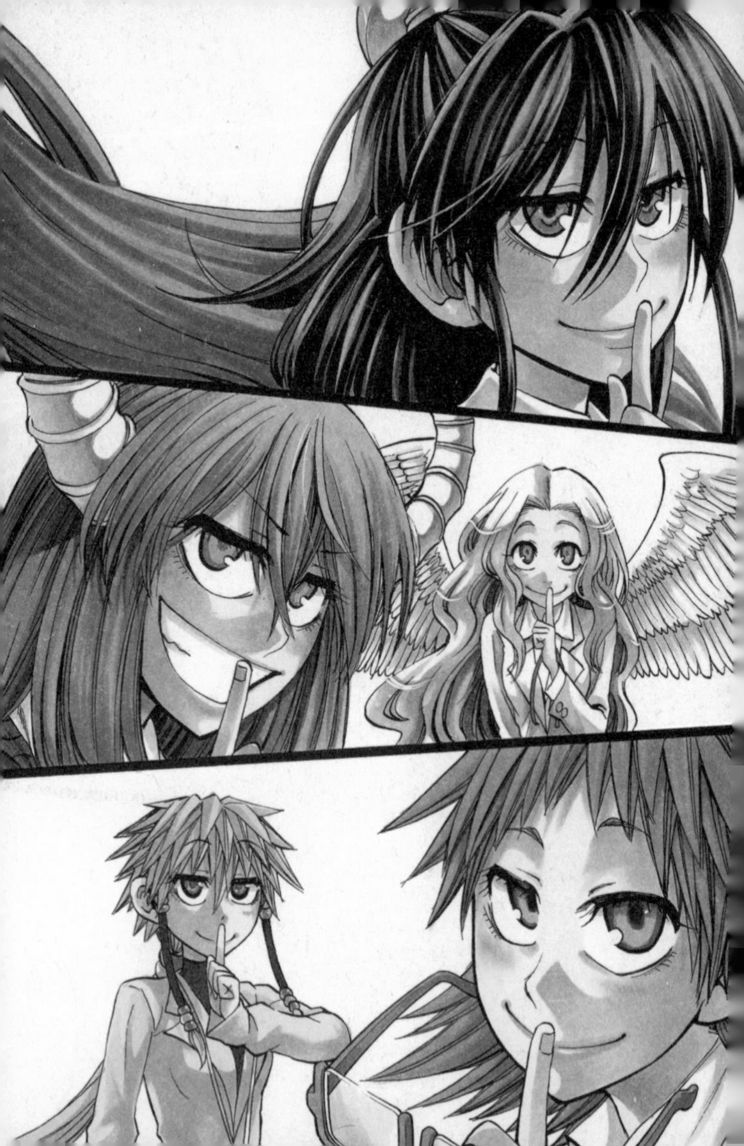

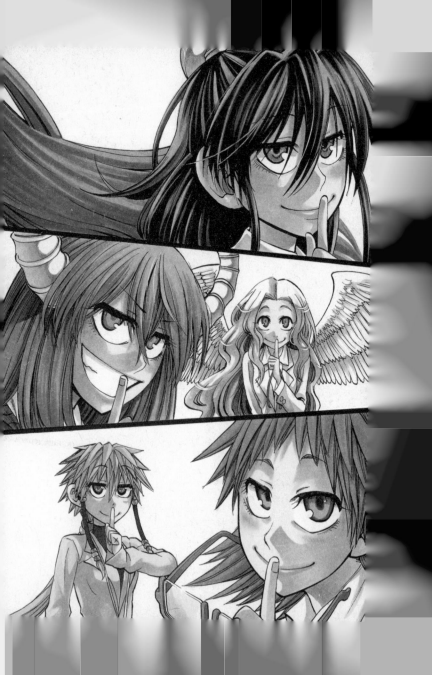

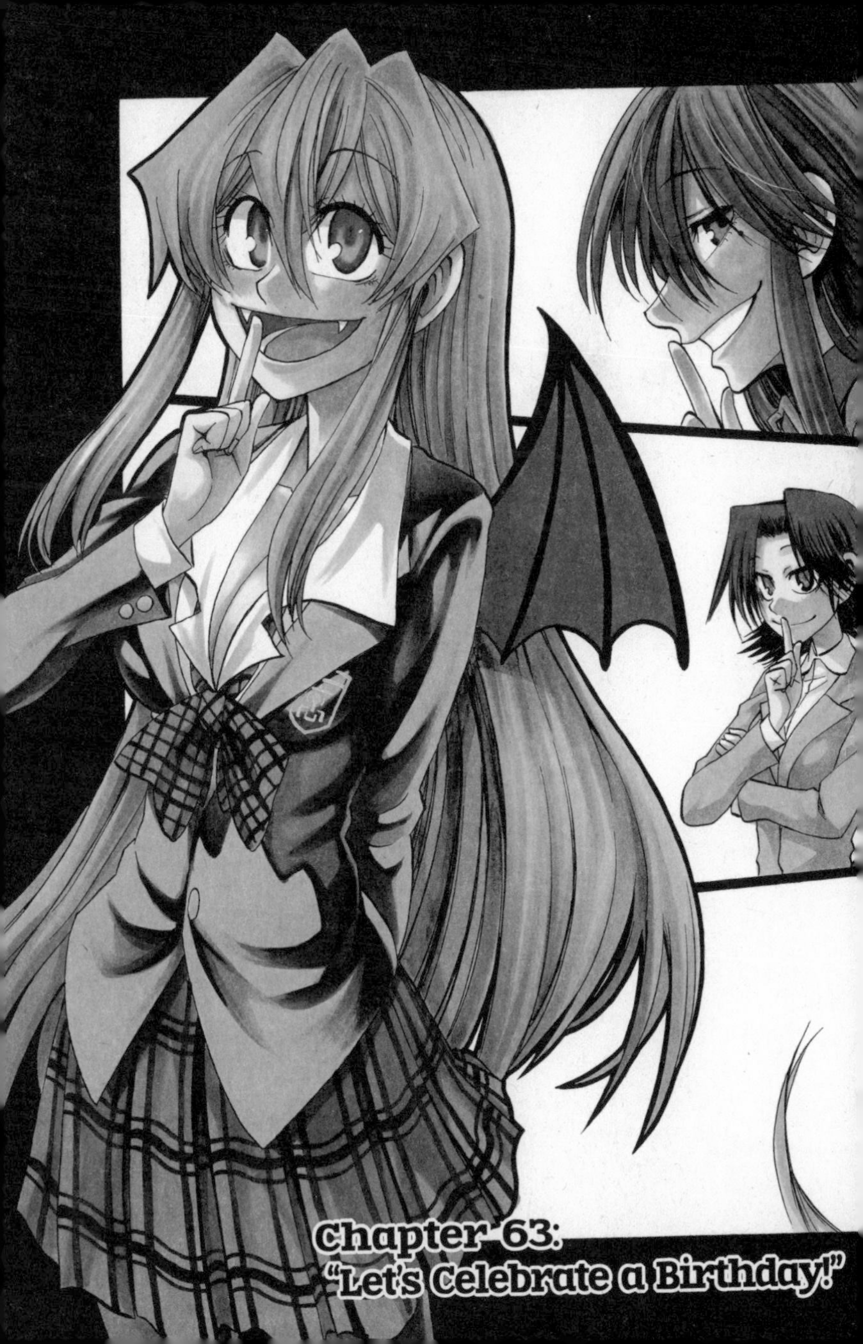
Chapter 63:
"Let's Celebrate a Birthday!"

TOP SECRET

My Monster Secret 8

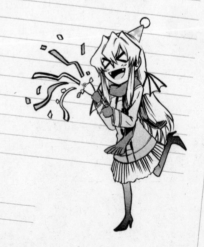

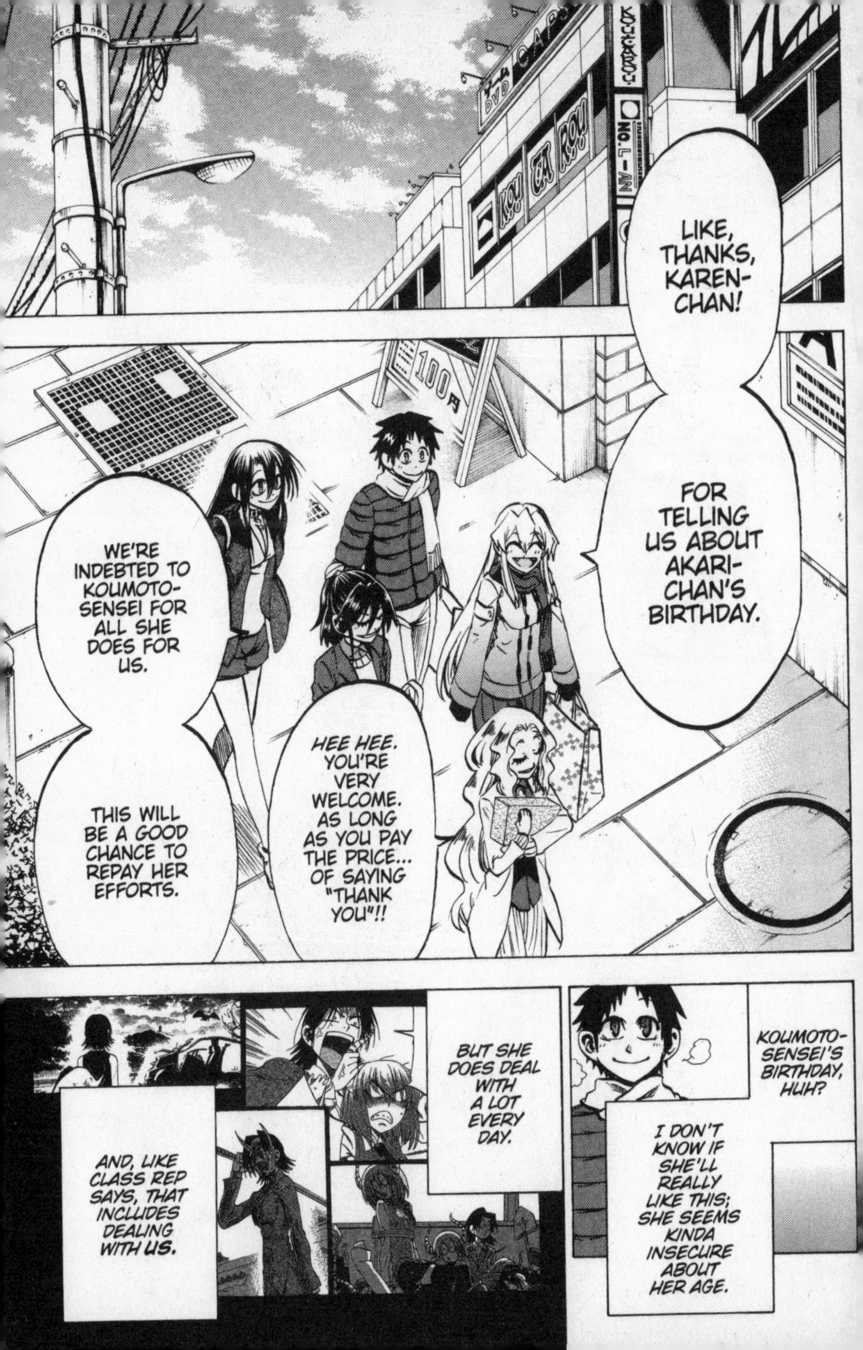
DVD
100円
LIKE, THANKS, KAREN-CHAN!
FOR TELLING US ABOUT AKARI-CHAN'S BIRTHDAY.
HEE HEE. YOU'RE VERY WELCOME. AS LONG AS YOU PAY THE PRICE... OF SAYING "THANK YOU"!!
WE'RE INDEBTED TO KOUMOTO-SENSEI FOR ALL SHE DOES FOR US.
THIS WILL BE A GOOD CHANCE TO REPAY HER EFFORTS.
KOUMOTO-SENSEI'S BIRTHDAY, HUH?
I DON'T KNOW IF SHE'LL REALLY LIKE THIS; SHE SEEMS KINDA INSECURE ABOUT HER AGE.
BUT SHE DOES DEAL WITH A LOT EVERY DAY.
AND, LIKE CLASS REP SAYS, THAT INCLUDES DEALING WITH US.

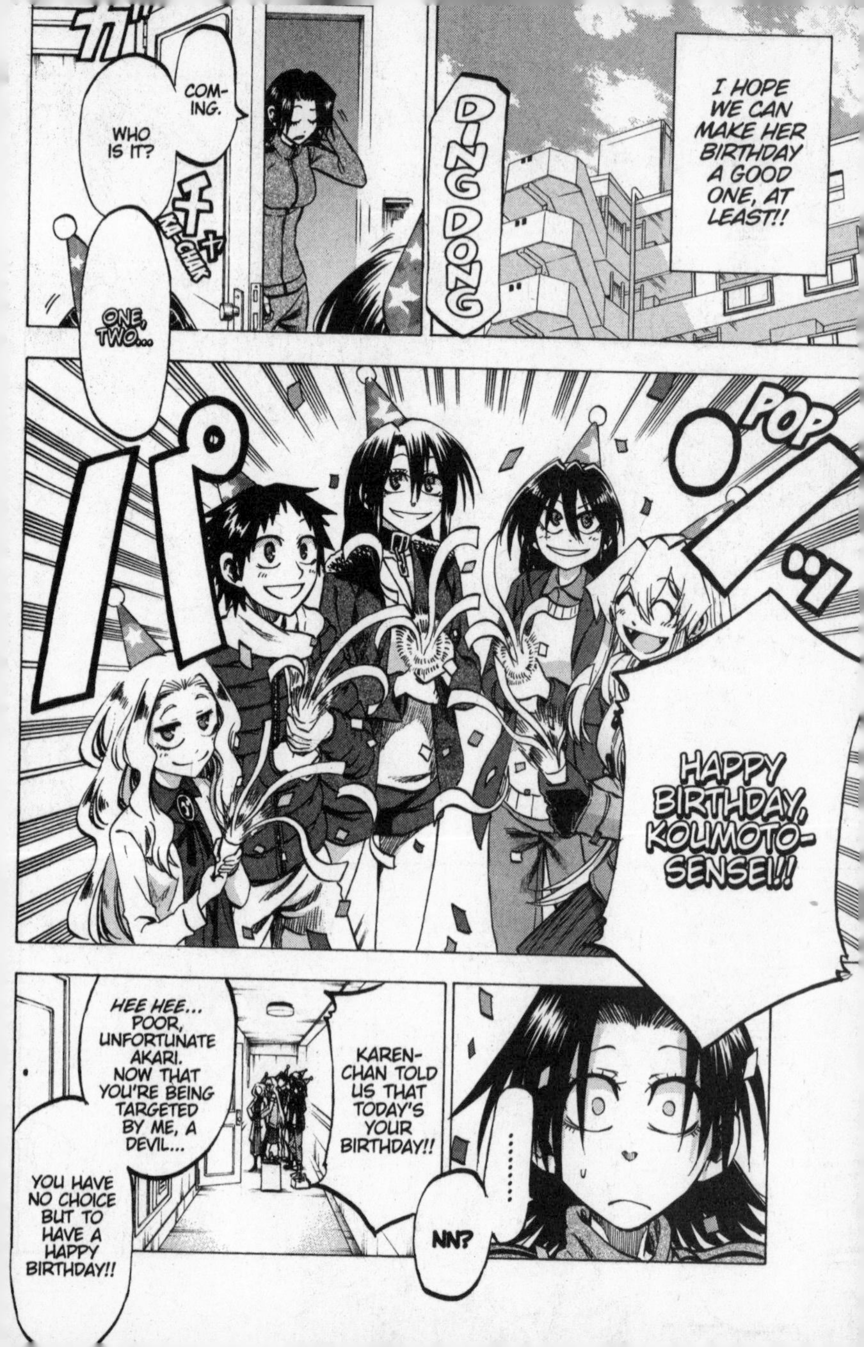
I HOPE WE CAN MAKE HER BIRTHDAY A GOOD ONE, AT LEAST!!
DING DONG
COMING.
WHO IS IT?
KA-CHAK
ONE, TWO...
POP
HAPPY BIRTHDAY, KOUMOTO-SENSEI!!
......
NN?
KAREN-CHAN TOLD US THAT TODAY'S YOUR BIRTHDAY!!
HEE HEE... POOR, UNFORTUNATE AKARI. NOW THAT YOU'RE BEING TARGETED BY ME, A DEVIL...
YOU HAVE NO CHOICE BUT TO HAVE A HAPPY BIRTHDAY!!

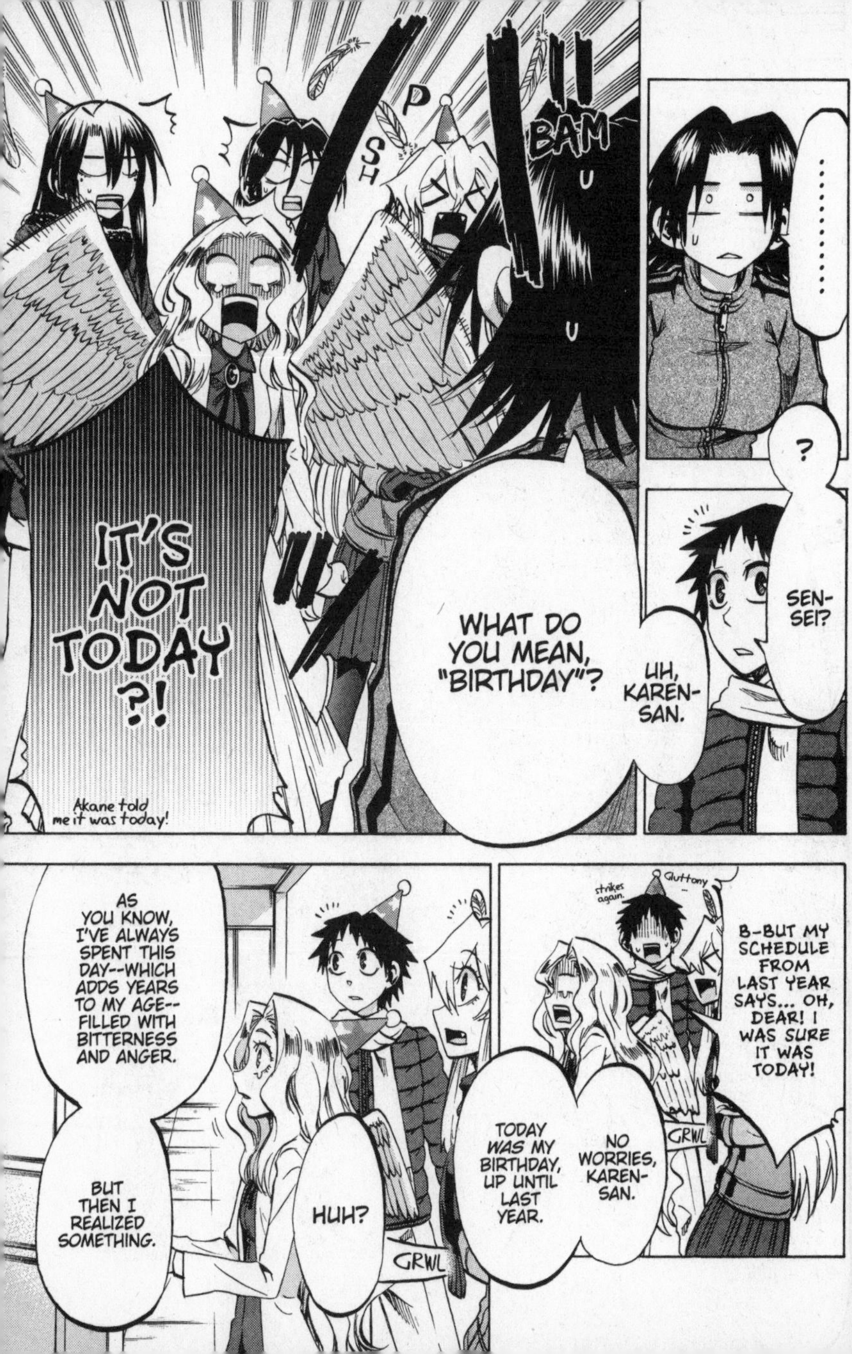
......
?
SEN-SEI?
UH, KAREN-SAN.
WHAT DO YOU MEAN, "BIRTHDAY"?
BAM
PSH
IT'S NOT TODAY ?!
Akane told me it was today!
Gluttony— strikes again.
B-BUT MY SCHEDULE FROM LAST YEAR SAYS... OH, DEAR! I WAS SURE IT WAS TODAY!
NO WORRIES, KAREN-SAN.
TODAY *WAS* MY BIRTHDAY, UP UNTIL LAST YEAR.
GRWL
AS YOU KNOW, I'VE ALWAYS SPENT THIS DAY--WHICH ADDS YEARS TO MY AGE--FILLED WITH BITTERNESS AND ANGER.
HUH?
BUT THEN I REALIZED SOMETHING.
GRWL

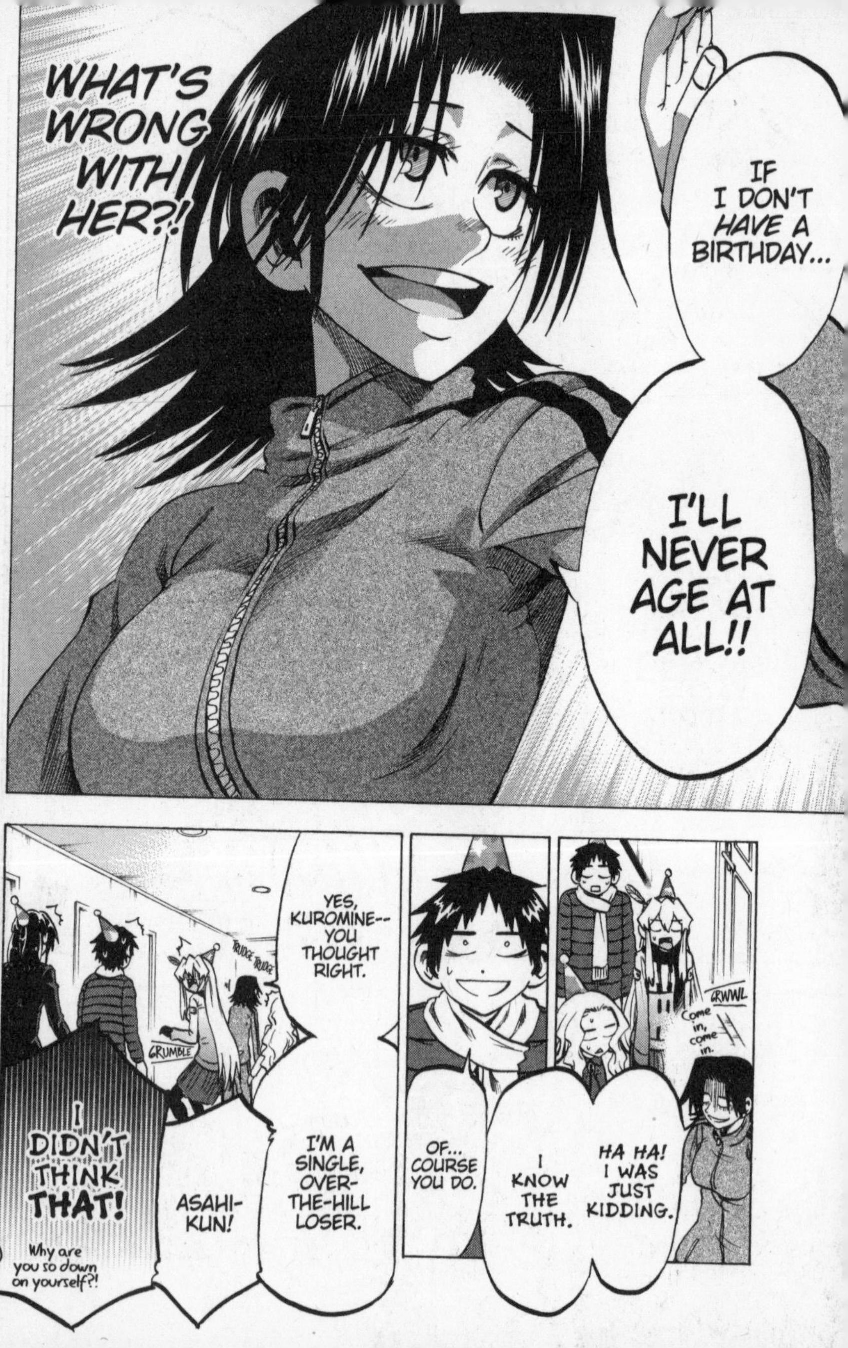
IF I DON'T *HAVE* A BIRTHDAY...
I'LL NEVER AGE AT ALL!!
WHAT'S WRONG WITH HER?!
GRWWL
Come in, come in.
HA HA! I WAS JUST KIDDING.
I KNOW THE TRUTH.
OF... COURSE YOU DO.
YES, KUROMINE-- YOU THOUGHT RIGHT.
I'M A SINGLE, OVER-THE-HILL LOSER.
ASAHI-KUN!
TRUDGE TRUDGE
GRUMBLE
I DIDN'T THINK THAT!
Why are you so down on yourself?!

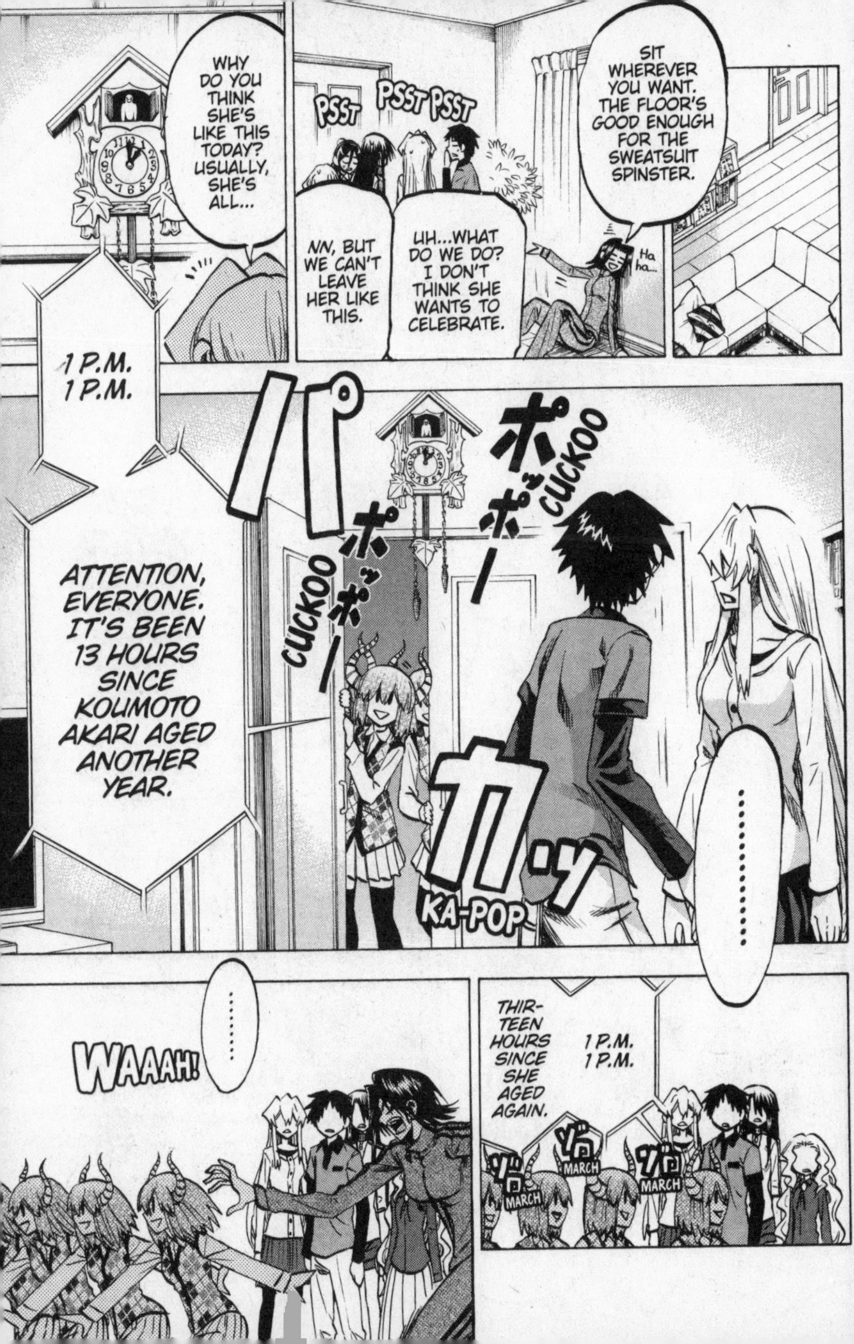
SIT WHEREVER YOU WANT. THE FLOOR'S GOOD ENOUGH FOR THE SWEATSUIT SPINSTER.
Ha ha...
PSST PSST
PSST
UH...WHAT DO WE DO? I DON'T THINK SHE WANTS TO CELEBRATE.
NN, BUT WE CAN'T LEAVE HER LIKE THIS.
WHY DO YOU THINK SHE'S LIKE THIS TODAY? USUALLY, SHE'S ALL...
1 P.M. 1 P.M.
ポッポー
CUCKOO
パ
ポッポー
CUCKOO
......
カッ
KA-POP
ATTENTION, EVERYONE. IT'S BEEN 13 HOURS SINCE KOUMOTO AKARI AGED ANOTHER YEAR.
1 P.M. 1 P.M.
THIRTEEN HOURS SINCE SHE AGED AGAIN.
ゾロ
MARCH
ゾロ
MARCH
ゾロ
MARCH
......
WAAAH!

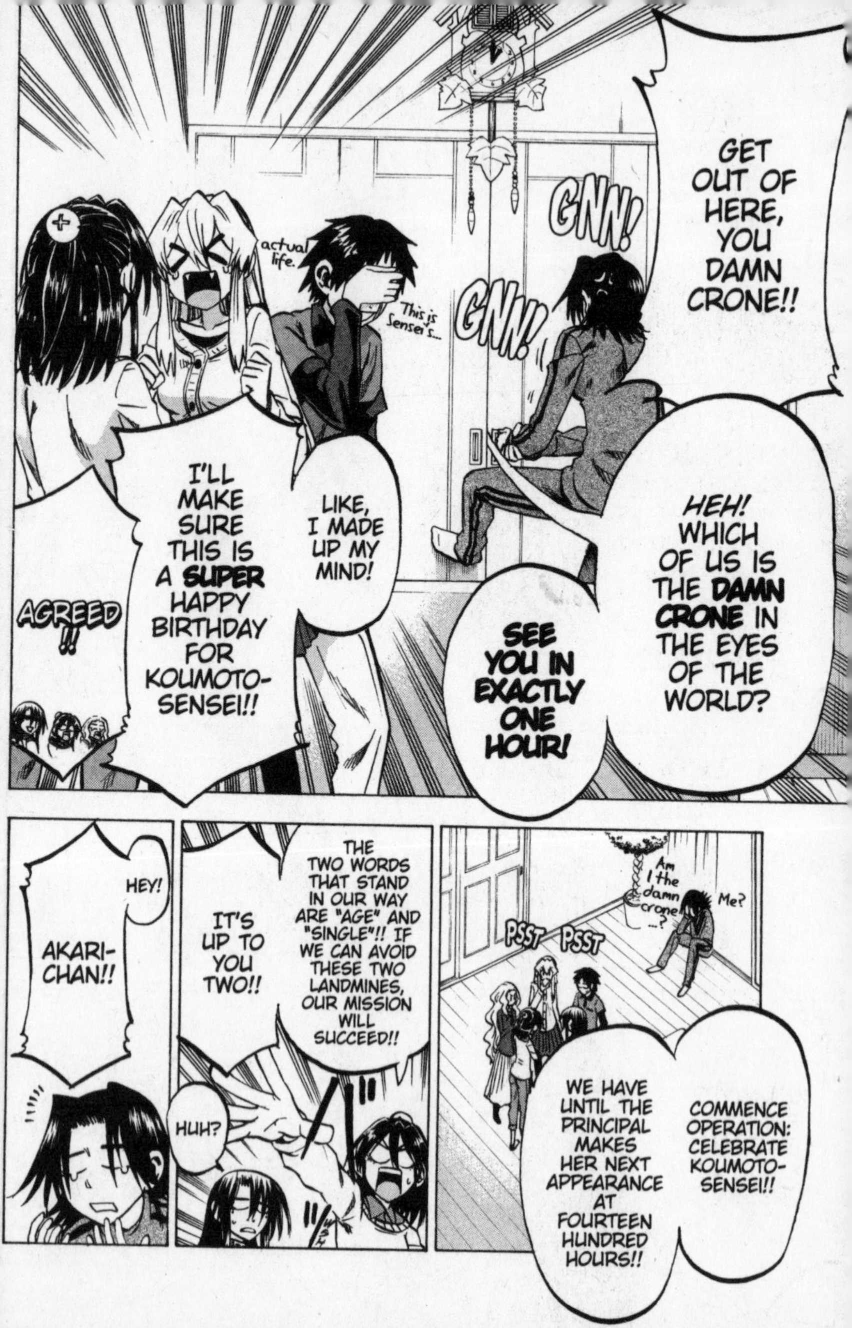
GET OUT OF HERE, YOU DAMN CRONE!!
GNN!
GNN!
HEH! WHICH OF US IS THE DAMN CRONE IN THE EYES OF THE WORLD?
SEE YOU IN EXACTLY ONE HOUR!
This is Sensei's... actual life.
LIKE, I MADE UP MY MIND!
I'LL MAKE SURE THIS IS A SUPER HAPPY BIRTHDAY FOR KOUMOTO-SENSEI!!
AGREED!!
Am I the damn crone...?
Me?
PSST
PSST
COMMENCE OPERATION: CELEBRATE KOUMOTO-SENSEI!!
WE HAVE UNTIL THE PRINCIPAL MAKES HER NEXT APPEARANCE AT FOURTEEN HUNDRED HOURS!!
THE TWO WORDS THAT STAND IN OUR WAY ARE "AGE" AND "SINGLE"!! IF WE CAN AVOID THESE TWO LANDMINES, OUR MISSION WILL SUCCEED!!
IT'S UP TO YOU TWO!!
HUH?
HEY!
AKARI-CHAN!!

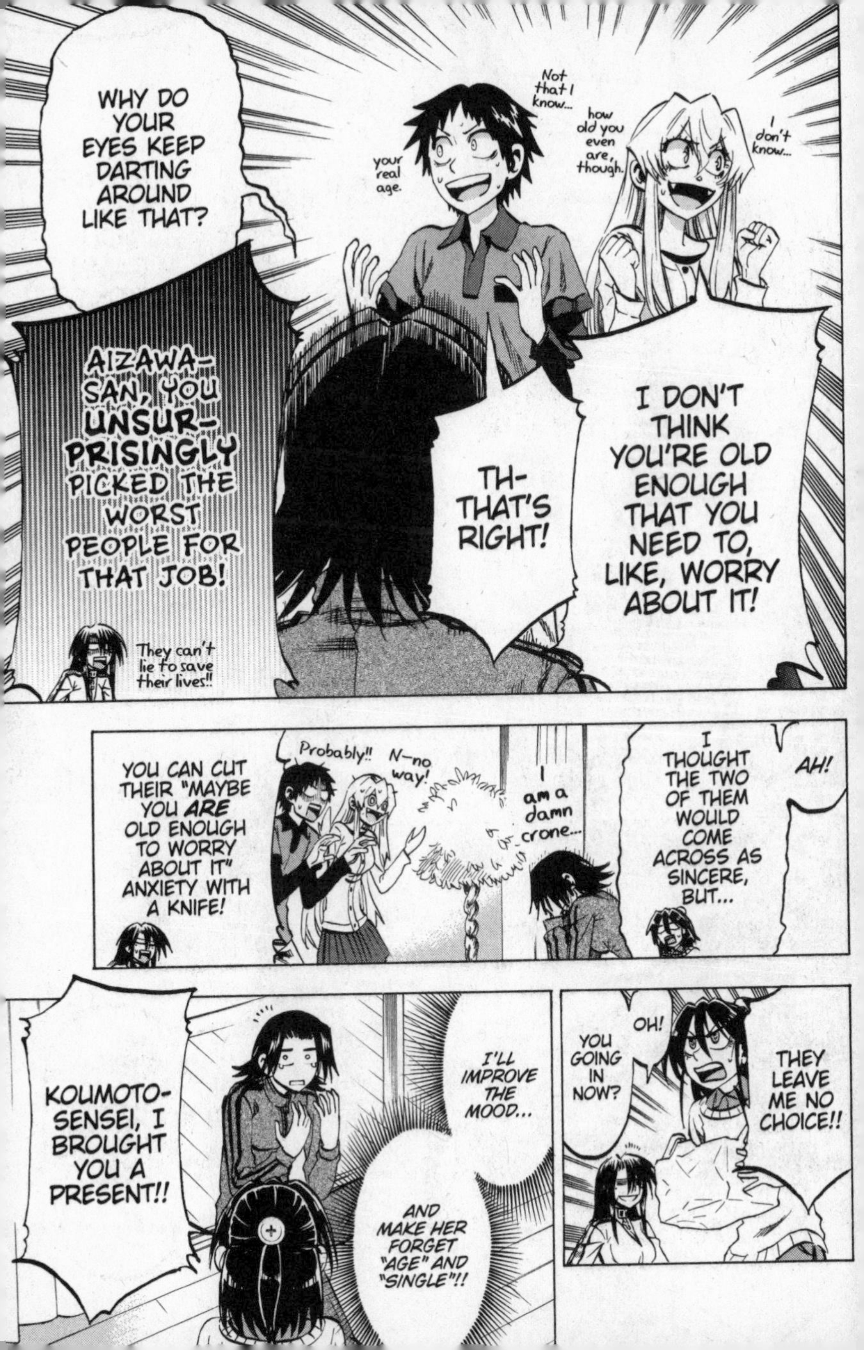
I don't know...
how old you even are, though.
Not that I know...
your real age.
WHY DO YOUR EYES KEEP DARTING AROUND LIKE THAT?
I DON'T THINK YOU'RE OLD ENOUGH THAT YOU NEED TO, LIKE, WORRY ABOUT IT!
TH-THAT'S RIGHT!
AIZAWA-SAN, YOU **UNSURPRISINGLY** PICKED THE WORST PEOPLE FOR THAT JOB!
They can't lie to save their lives!!
AH!
I THOUGHT THE TWO OF THEM WOULD COME ACROSS AS SINCERE, BUT...
I am a damn crone...
N-no way!
Probably!!
YOU CAN CUT THEIR "MAYBE YOU *ARE* OLD ENOUGH TO WORRY ABOUT IT" ANXIETY WITH A KNIFE!
THEY LEAVE ME NO CHOICE!!
OH!
YOU GOING IN NOW?
I'LL IMPROVE THE MOOD...
AND MAKE HER FORGET "AGE" AND "SINGLE"!!
KOUMOTO-SENSEI, I BROUGHT YOU A PRESENT!!

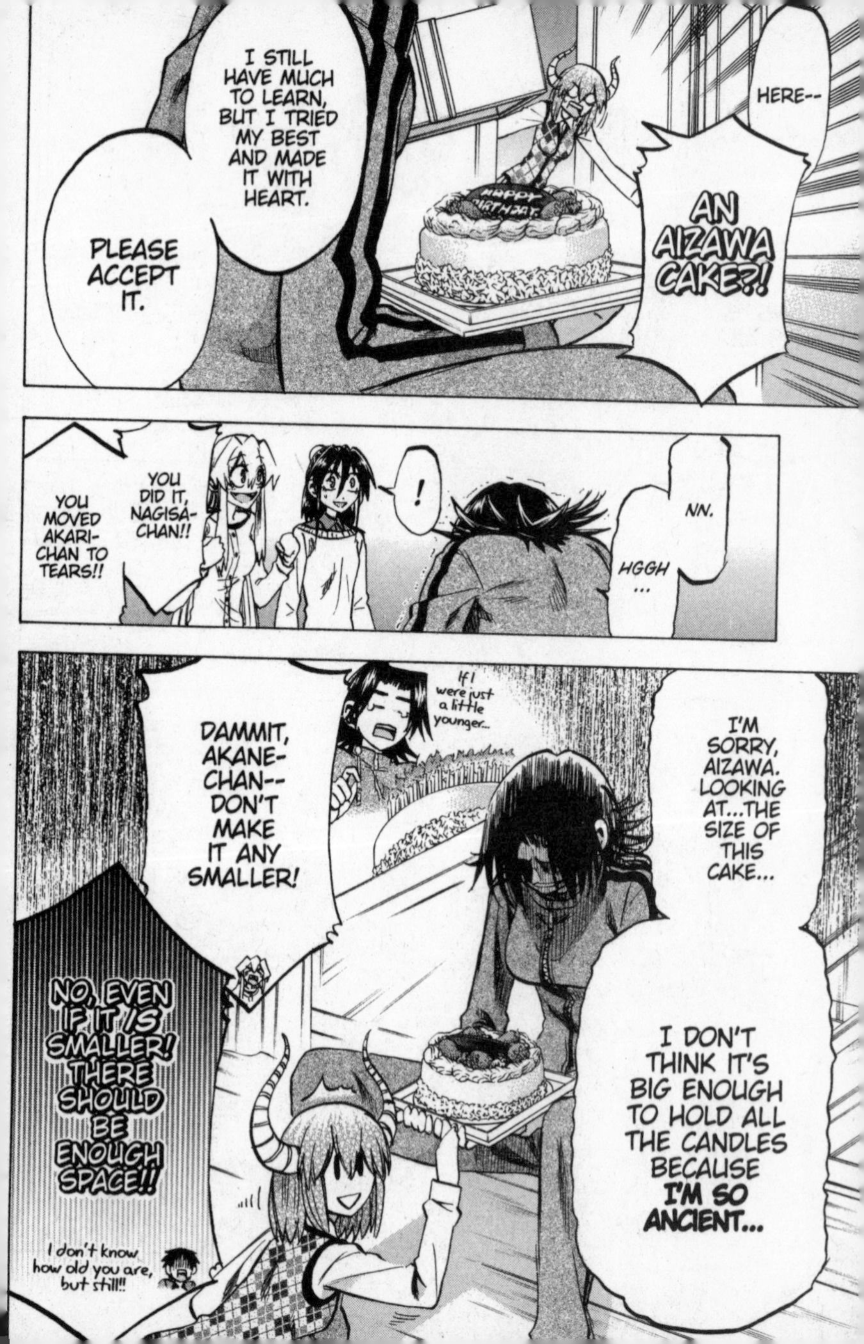
HERE--
AN AIZAWA CAKE?!
I STILL HAVE MUCH TO LEARN, BUT I TRIED MY BEST AND MADE IT WITH HEART.
PLEASE ACCEPT IT.
NN.
HGGH...
!
YOU DID IT, NAGISA-CHAN!!
YOU MOVED AKARI-CHAN TO TEARS!!
I'M SORRY, AIZAWA. LOOKING AT...THE SIZE OF THIS CAKE...
I DON'T THINK IT'S BIG ENOUGH TO HOLD ALL THE CANDLES BECAUSE **I'M SO ANCIENT...**
If I were just a little younger...
DAMMIT, AKANE-CHAN-- DON'T MAKE IT ANY SMALLER!
NO, EVEN IF IT *IS* SMALLER! THERE SHOULD BE ENOUGH SPACE!!
I don't know how old you are, but still!!

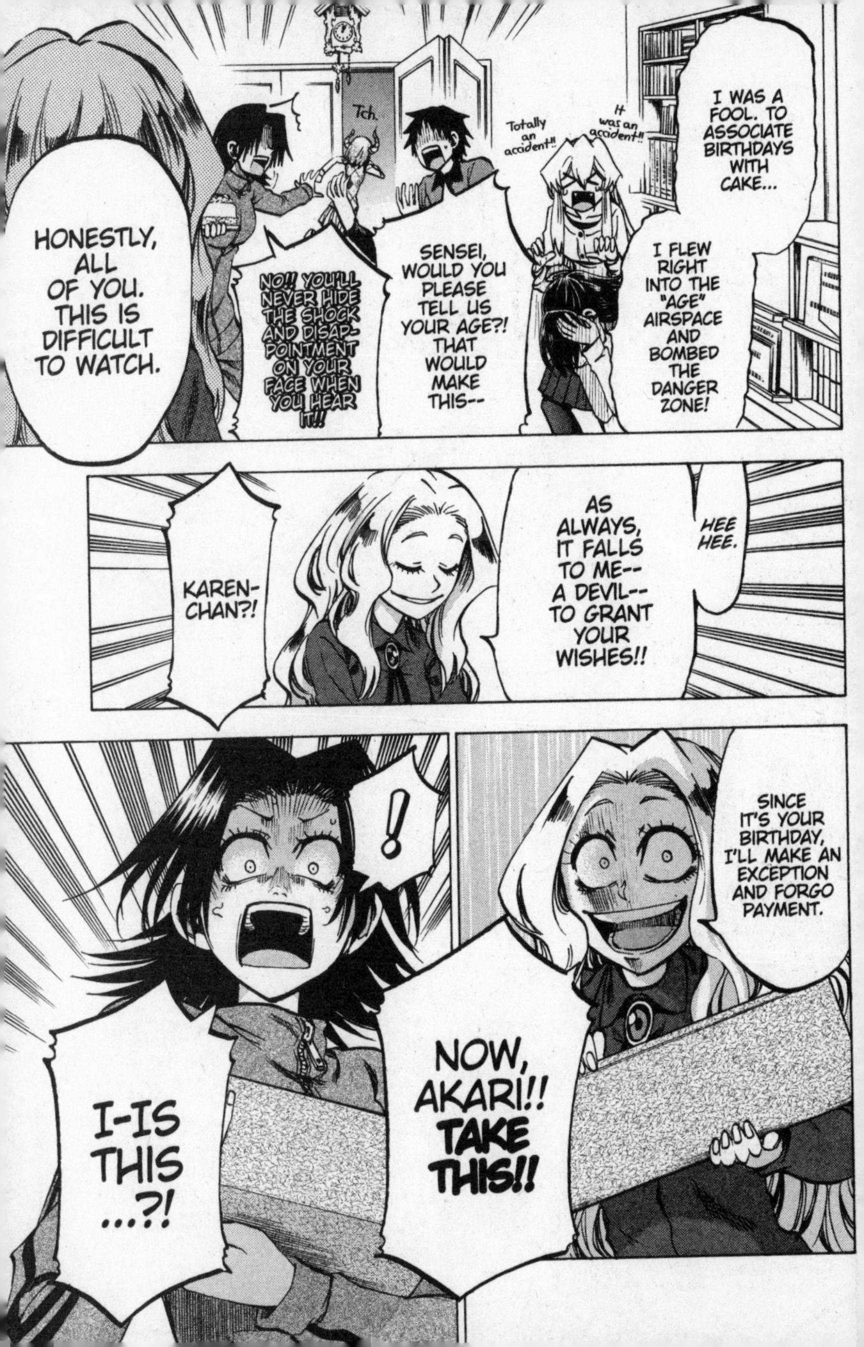
I WAS A FOOL. TO ASSOCIATE BIRTHDAYS WITH CAKE...
I FLEW RIGHT INTO THE "AGE" AIRSPACE AND BOMBED THE DANGER ZONE!
It was an accident!!
Totally an accident!!
SENSEI, WOULD YOU PLEASE TELL US YOUR AGE?! THAT WOULD MAKE THIS--
Tch.
NO!! YOU'LL NEVER HIDE THE SHOCK AND DISAPPOINTMENT ON YOUR FACE WHEN YOU HEAR IT!!
HONESTLY, ALL OF YOU. THIS IS DIFFICULT TO WATCH.
HEE HEE.
AS ALWAYS, IT FALLS TO ME-- A DEVIL-- TO GRANT YOUR WISHES!!
KAREN-CHAN?!
SINCE IT'S YOUR BIRTHDAY, I'LL MAKE AN EXCEPTION AND FORGO PAYMENT.
NOW, AKARI!! TAKE THIS!!
!
I-IS THIS ...?!

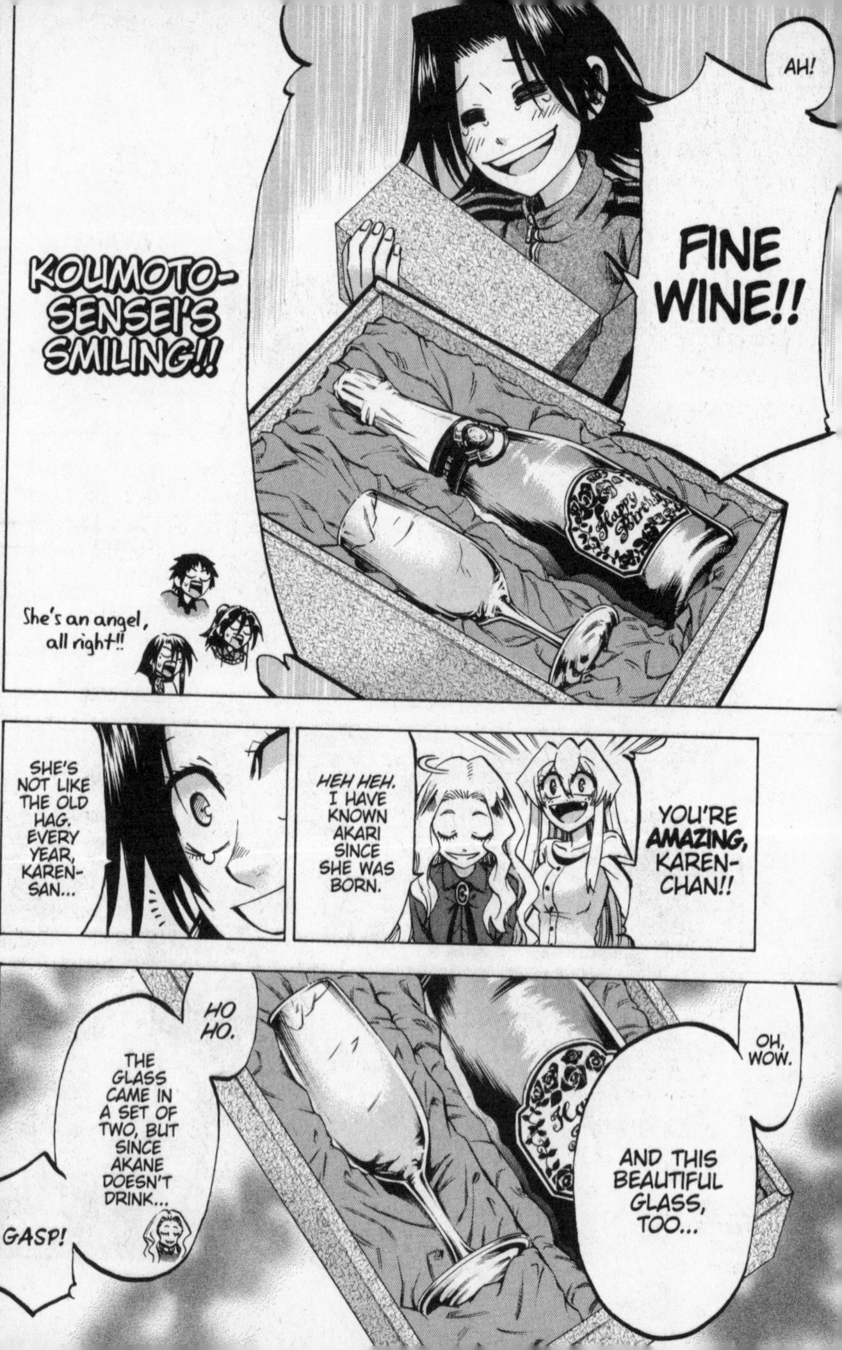
AH!
FINE WINE!!
KOUMOTO-SENSEI'S SMILING!!
She's an angel, all right!!
YOU'RE AMAZING, KAREN-CHAN!!
HEH HEH. I HAVE KNOWN AKARI SINCE SHE WAS BORN.
SHE'S NOT LIKE THE OLD HAG. EVERY YEAR, KAREN-SAN...
OH, WOW.
AND THIS BEAUTIFUL GLASS, TOO...
HO HO.
THE GLASS CAME IN A SET OF TWO, BUT SINCE AKANE DOESN'T DRINK...
GASP!

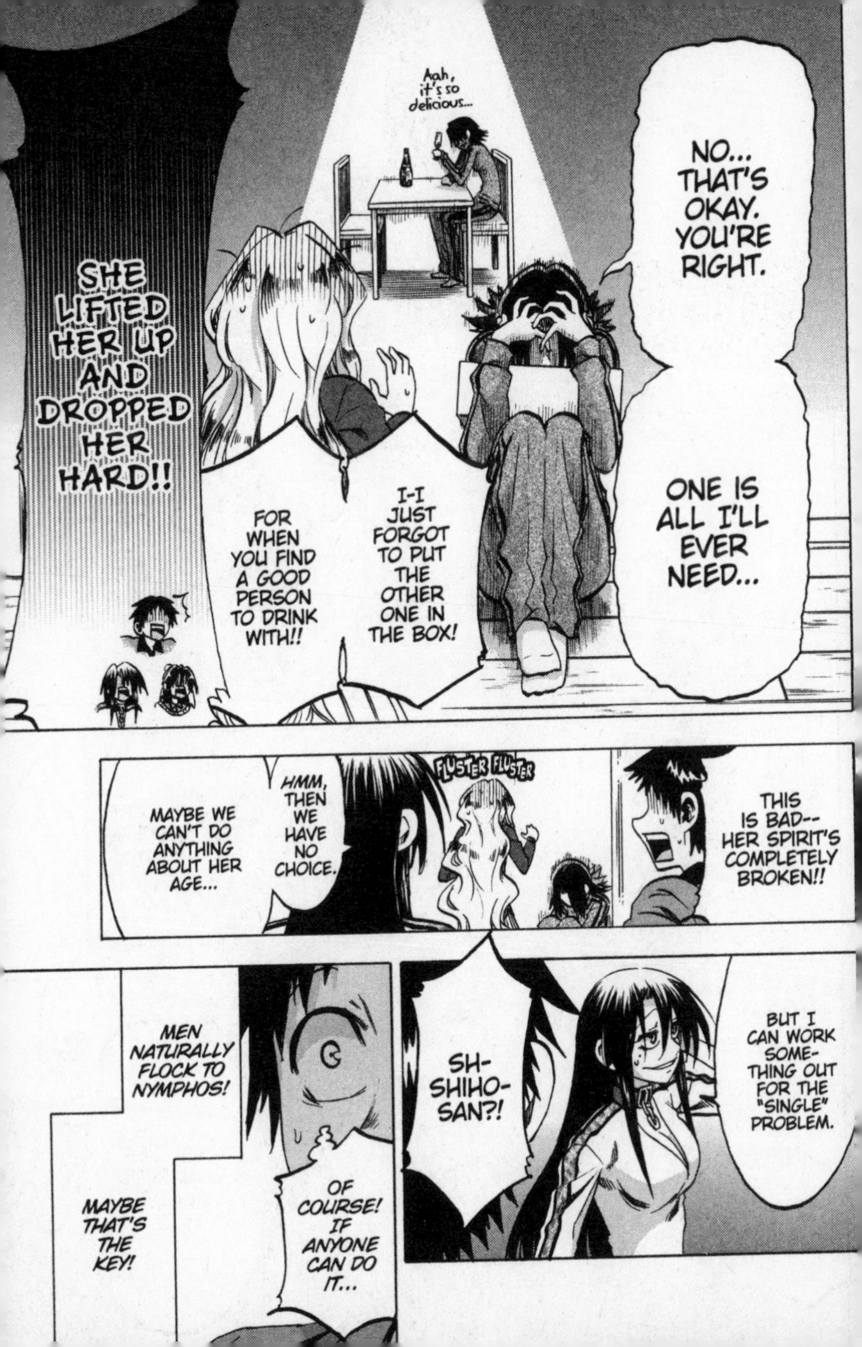
NO... THAT'S OKAY. YOU'RE RIGHT.
ONE IS ALL I'LL EVER NEED...
Aah, it's so delicious...
I-I JUST FORGOT TO PUT THE OTHER ONE IN THE BOX!
FOR WHEN YOU FIND A GOOD PERSON TO DRINK WITH!!
SHE LIFTED HER UP AND DROPPED HER HARD!!
THIS IS BAD-- HER SPIRIT'S COMPLETELY BROKEN!!
FLUSTER FLUSTER
HMM, THEN WE HAVE NO CHOICE.
MAYBE WE CAN'T DO ANYTHING ABOUT HER AGE...
BUT I CAN WORK SOME-THING OUT FOR THE "SINGLE" PROBLEM.
SH-SHIHO-SAN?!
OF COURSE! IF ANYONE CAN DO IT...
MEN NATURALLY FLOCK TO NYMPHOS!
MAYBE THAT'S THE KEY!

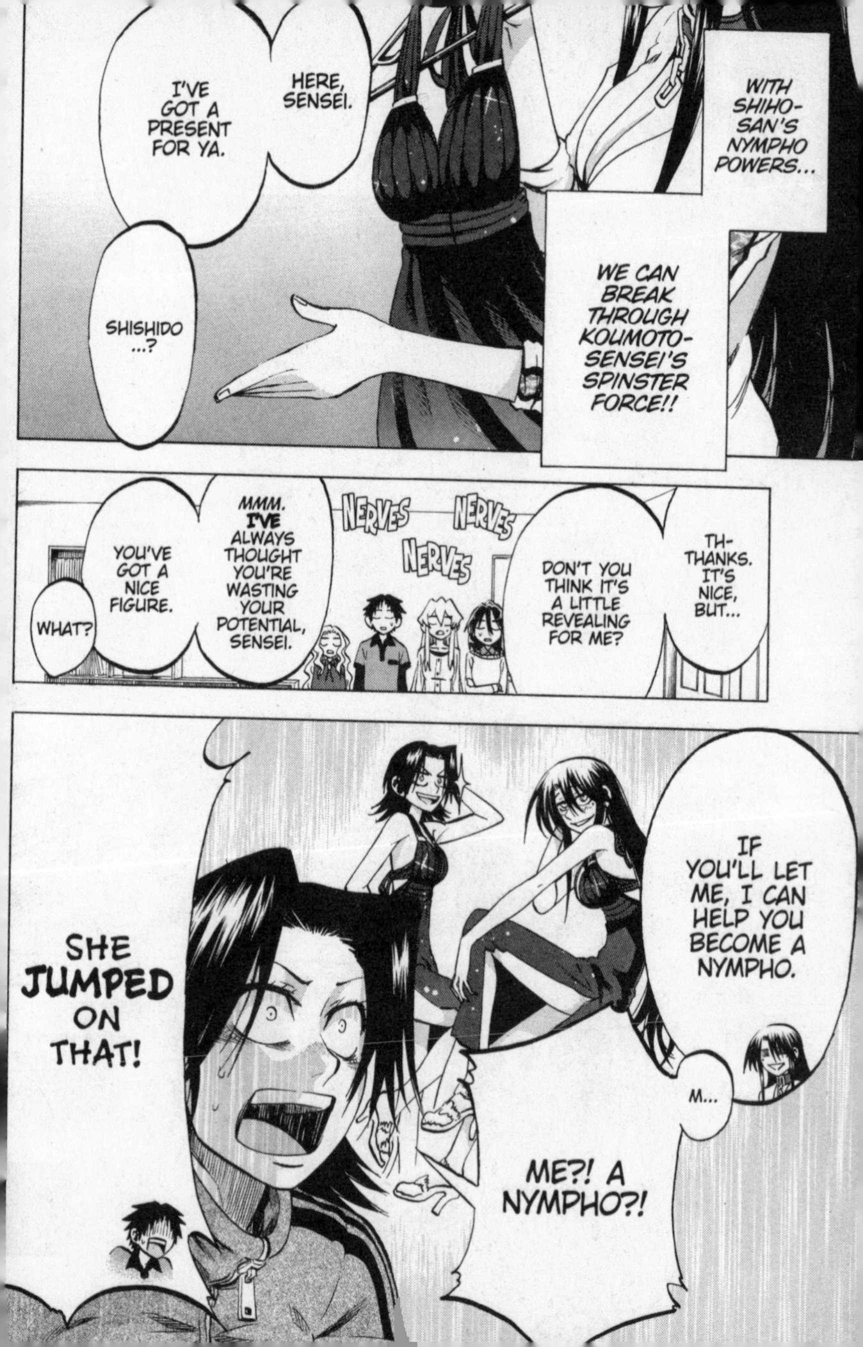
WITH SHIHO-SAN'S NYMPHO POWERS...
WE CAN BREAK THROUGH KOUMOTO-SENSEI'S SPINSTER FORCE!!
HERE, SENSEI.
I'VE GOT A PRESENT FOR YA.
SHISHIDO ...?
TH-THANKS. IT'S NICE, BUT...
DON'T YOU THINK IT'S A LITTLE REVEALING FOR ME?
NERVES
NERVES
NERVES
MMM. I'VE ALWAYS THOUGHT YOU'RE WASTING YOUR POTENTIAL, SENSEI.
YOU'VE GOT A NICE FIGURE.
WHAT?
IF YOU'LL LET ME, I CAN HELP YOU BECOME A NYMPHO.
M...
ME?! A NYMPHO?!
SHE JUMPED ON THAT!

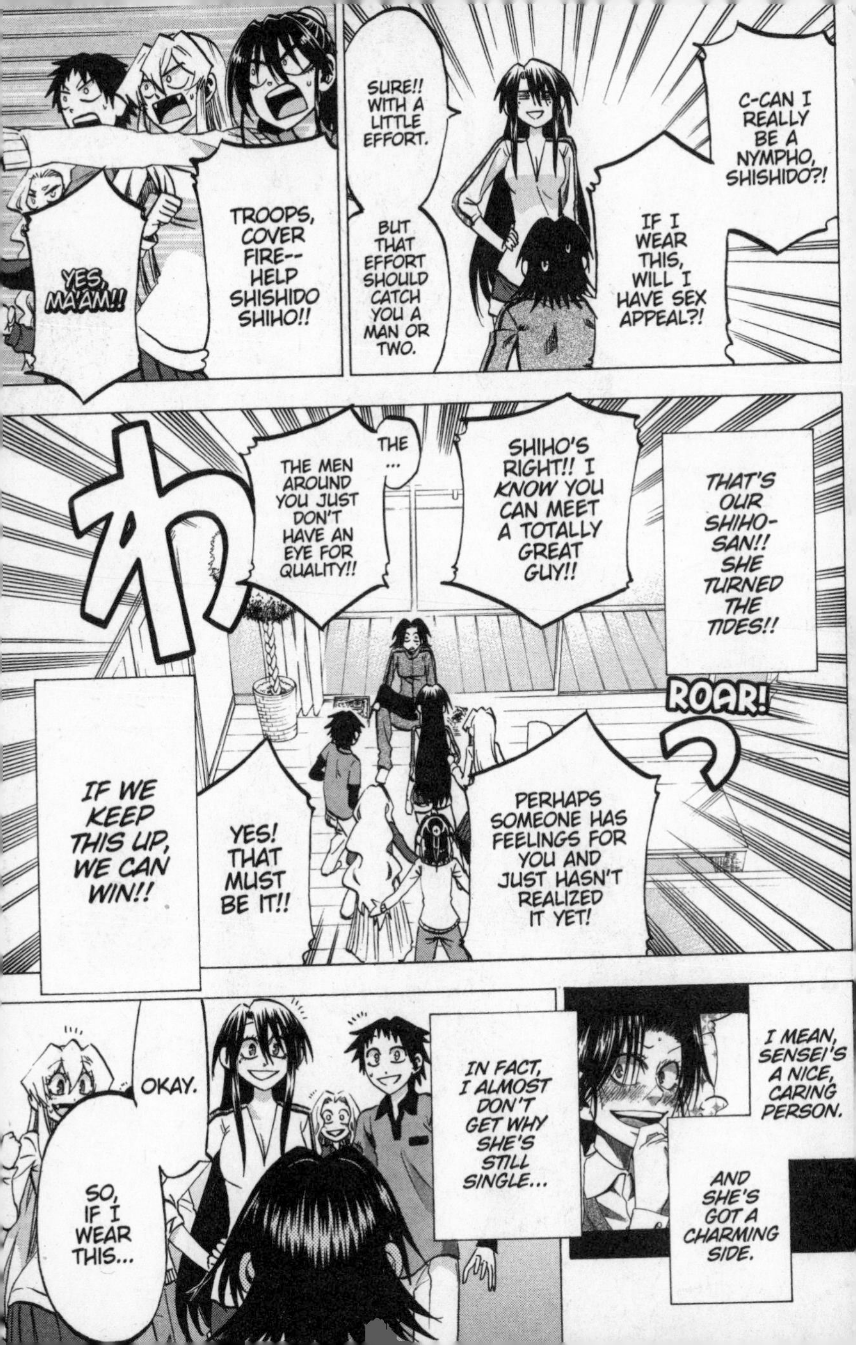
C-CAN I REALLY BE A NYMPHO, SHISHIDO?!
IF I WEAR THIS, WILL I HAVE SEX APPEAL?!
SURE!! WITH A LITTLE EFFORT.
BUT THAT EFFORT SHOULD CATCH YOU A MAN OR TWO.
TROOPS, COVER FIRE-- HELP SHISHIDO SHIHO!!
YES, MA'AM!!
THAT'S OUR SHIHO-SAN!! SHE TURNED THE TIDES!!
SHIHO'S RIGHT!! I KNOW YOU CAN MEET A TOTALLY GREAT GUY!!
THE ...
THE MEN AROUND YOU JUST DON'T HAVE AN EYE FOR QUALITY!!
ROAR!
PERHAPS SOMEONE HAS FEELINGS FOR YOU AND JUST HASN'T REALIZED IT YET!
YES! THAT MUST BE IT!!
IF WE KEEP THIS UP, WE CAN WIN!!
I MEAN, SENSEI'S A NICE, CARING PERSON.
AND SHE'S GOT A CHARMING SIDE.
IN FACT, I ALMOST DON'T GET WHY SHE'S STILL SINGLE...
OKAY.
SO, IF I WEAR THIS...

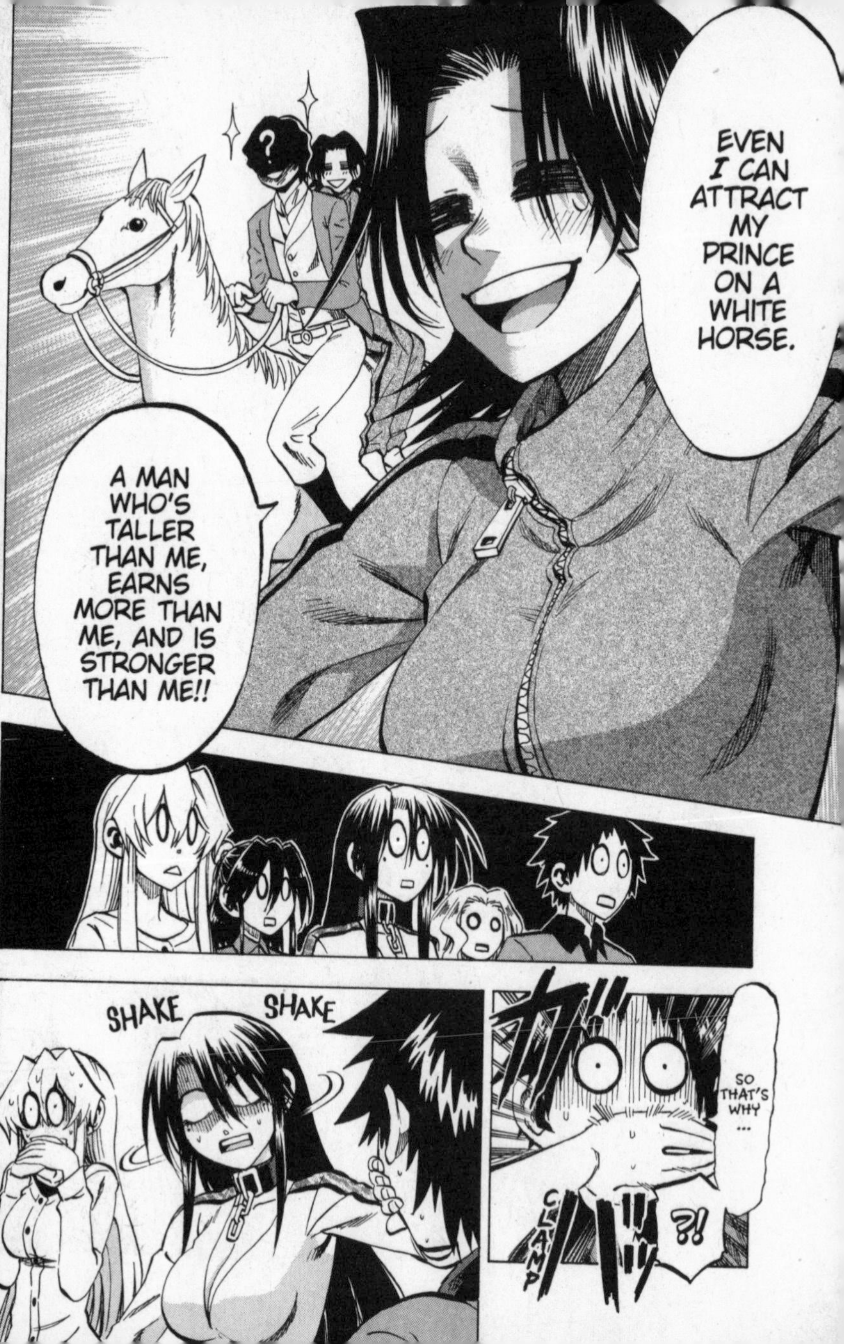
EVEN I CAN ATTRACT MY PRINCE ON A WHITE HORSE.
A MAN WHO'S TALLER THAN ME, EARNS MORE THAN ME, AND IS STRONGER THAN ME!!
SO THAT'S WHY...
?!
CLAMP
SHAKE
SHAKE

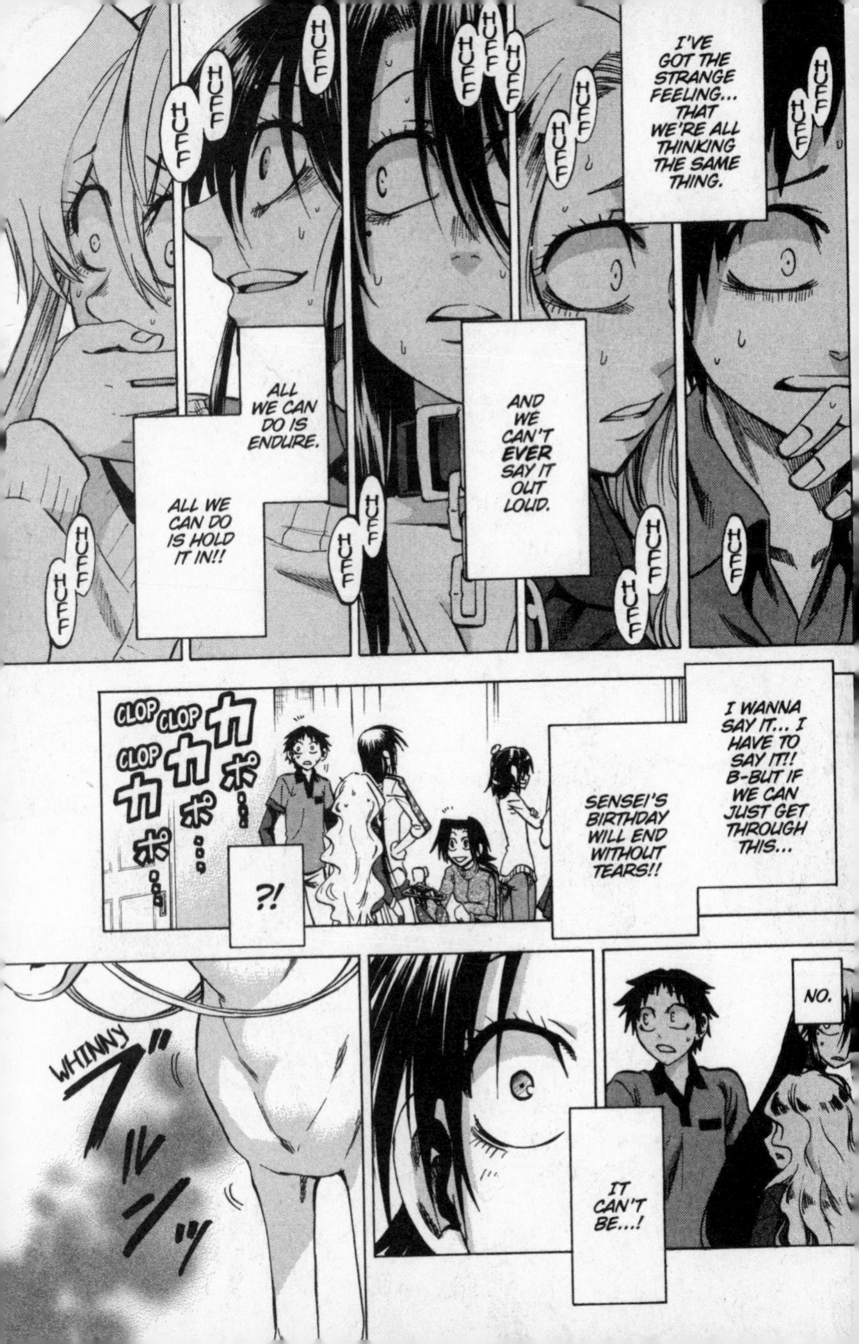
I'VE GOT THE STRANGE FEELING... THAT WE'RE ALL THINKING THE SAME THING.
HUFF
HUFF
HUFF
HUFF
HUFF
HUFF
HUFF
HUFF
HUFF
HUFF
AND WE CAN'T EVER SAY IT OUT LOUD.
HUFF
HUFF
HUFF
HUFF
ALL WE CAN DO IS ENDURE.
ALL WE CAN DO IS HOLD IT IN!!
HUFF
HUFF
I WANNA SAY IT... I HAVE TO SAY IT!! B-BUT IF WE CAN JUST GET THROUGH THIS...
SENSEI'S BIRTHDAY WILL END WITHOUT TEARS!!
?!
CLOP CLOP CLOP
カポ…カポ…カポ…
NO.
IT CAN'T BE...!
WHINNY
ブルンッ

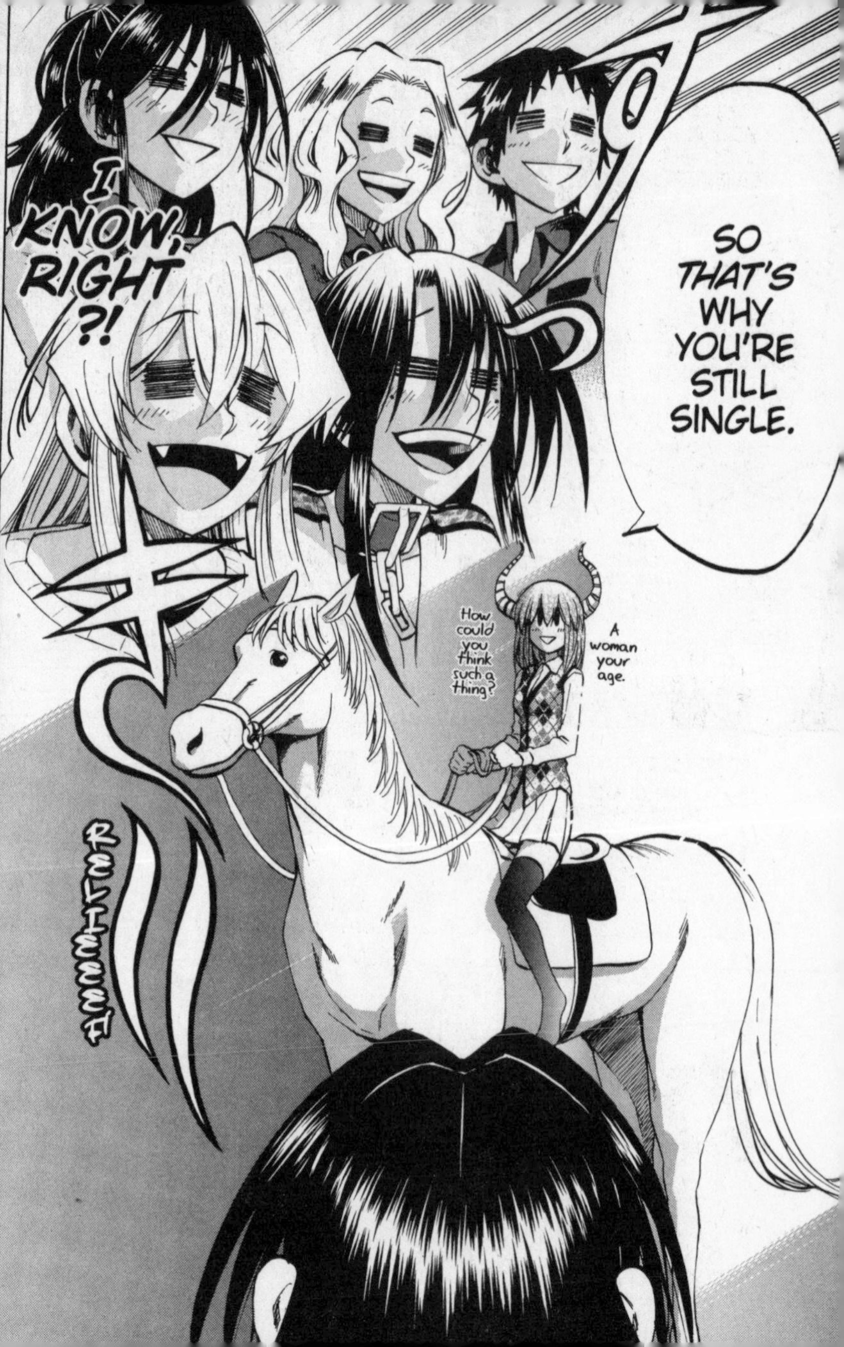
SO THAT'S WHY YOU'RE STILL SINGLE.
A woman your age.
How could you think such a thing?
I KNOW, RIGHT?!
RELIEEEEF

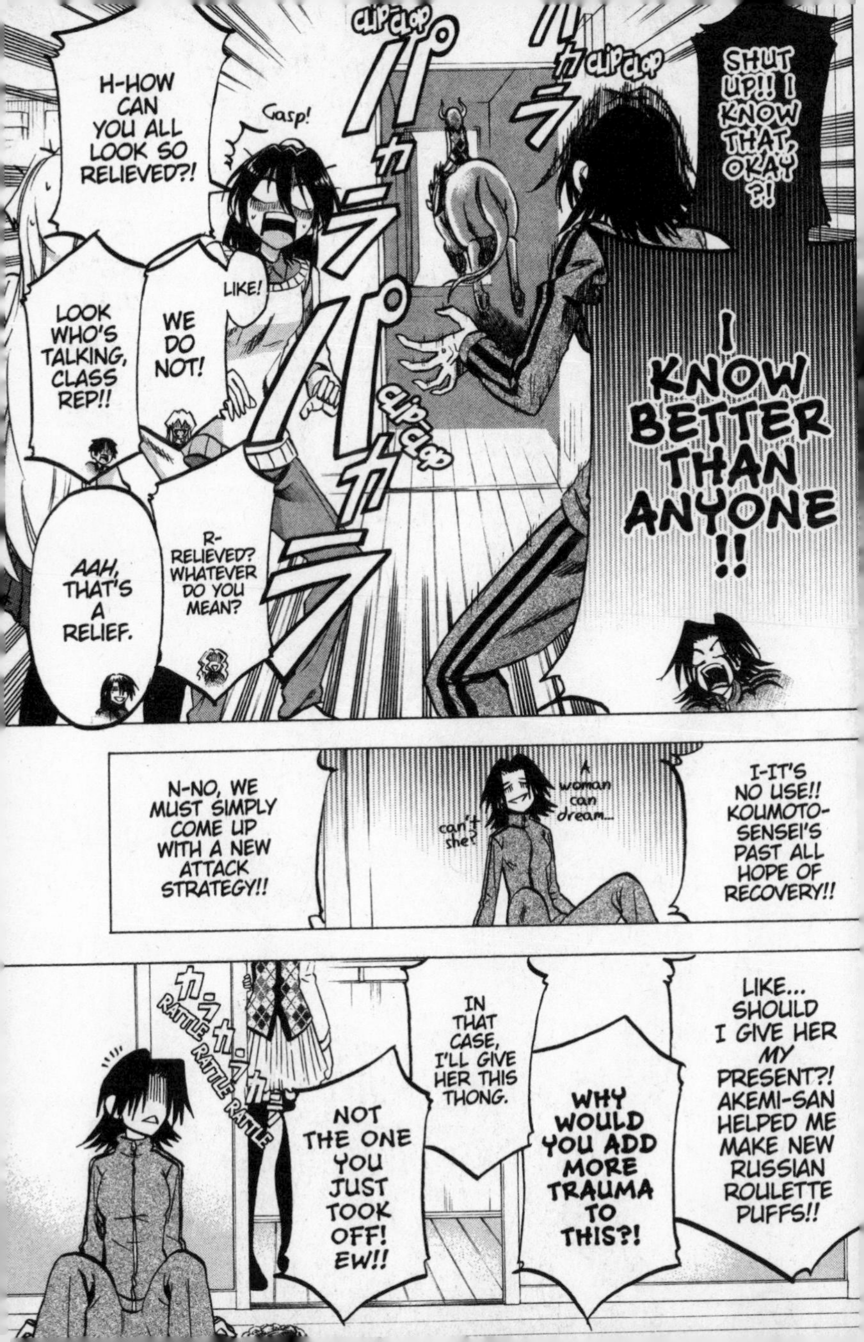
SHUT UP!! I KNOW THAT, OKAY?!
I KNOW BETTER THAN ANYONE!!
CLIP-CLOP
CLIP-CLOP
パカラ
パカラ
CLIP-CLOP
H-HOW CAN YOU ALL LOOK SO RELIEVED?!
Gasp!
LIKE!
WE DO NOT!
LOOK WHO'S TALKING, CLASS REP!!
R-RELIEVED? WHATEVER DO YOU MEAN?
AAH, THAT'S A RELIEF.
I-IT'S NO USE!! KOUMOTO-SENSEI'S PAST ALL HOPE OF RECOVERY!!
A woman can dream...
can't she?
N-NO, WE MUST SIMPLY COME UP WITH A NEW ATTACK STRATEGY!!
LIKE... SHOULD I GIVE HER *MY* PRESENT?! AKEMI-SAN HELPED ME MAKE NEW RUSSIAN ROULETTE PUFFS!!
WHY WOULD YOU ADD MORE TRAUMA TO THIS?!
IN THAT CASE, I'LL GIVE HER THIS THONG.
NOT THE ONE YOU JUST TOOK OFF! EW!!
カラカラカ
RATTLE RATTLE RATTLE

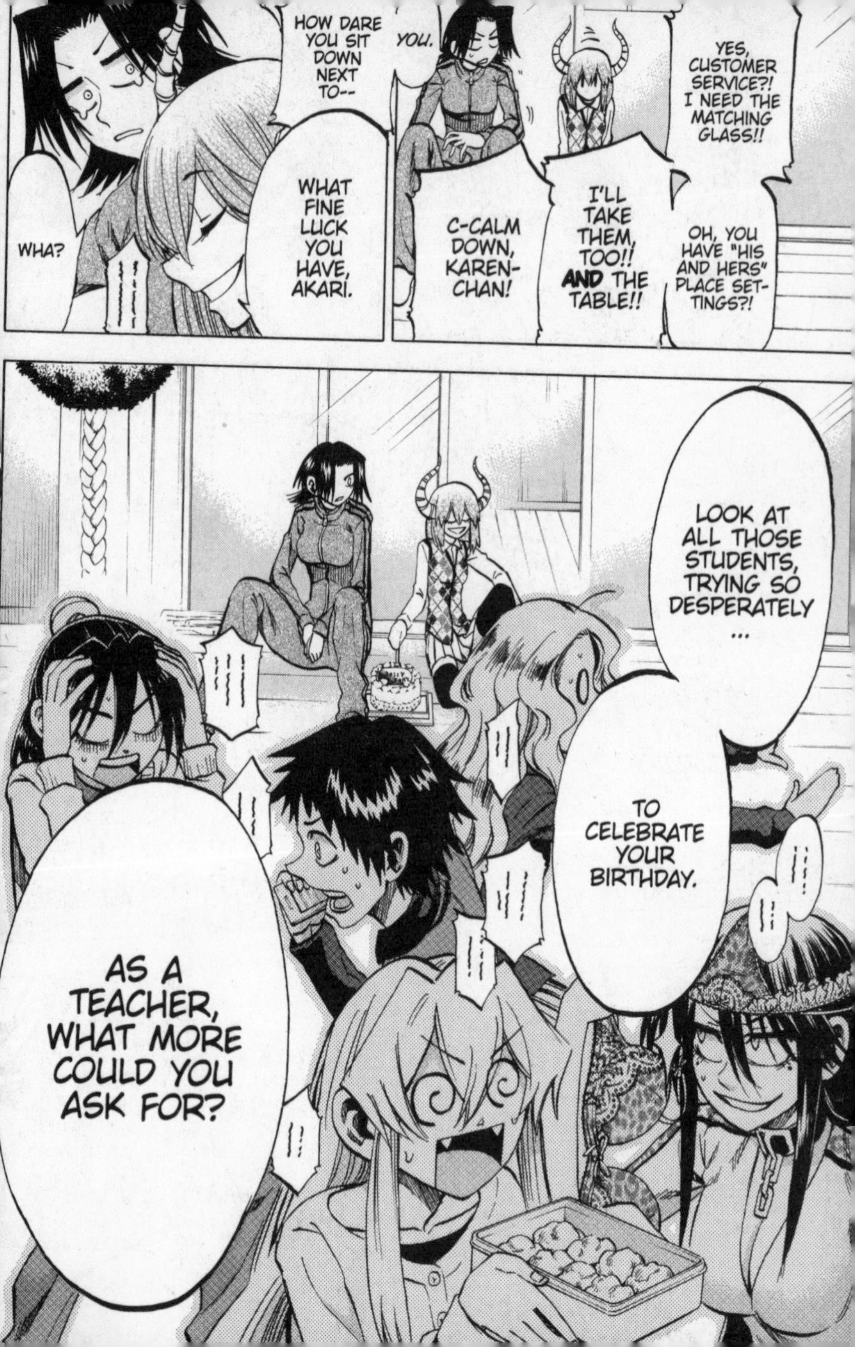

YES, CUSTOMER SERVICE?! I NEED THE MATCHING GLASS!!
OH, YOU HAVE "HIS AND HERS" PLACE SETTINGS?!
I'LL TAKE THEM, TOO!! **AND** THE TABLE!!
C-CALM DOWN, KAREN-CHAN!
HOW DARE YOU SIT DOWN NEXT TO--
YOU.
WHAT FINE LUCK YOU HAVE, AKARI.
WHA?
LOOK AT ALL THOSE STUDENTS, TRYING SO DESPERATELY...
TO CELEBRATE YOUR BIRTHDAY.
AS A TEACHER, WHAT MORE COULD YOU ASK FOR?

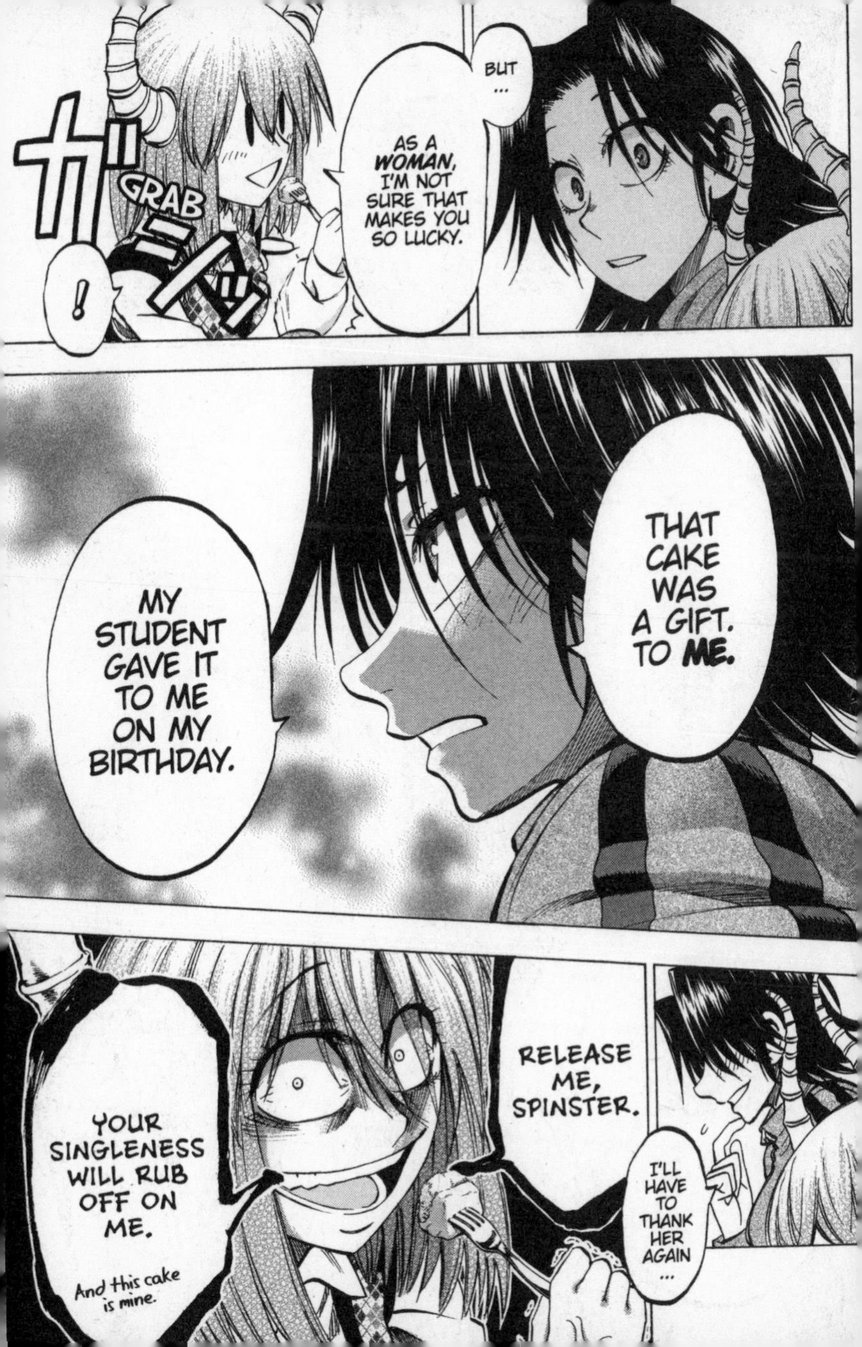
BUT ...
AS A *WOMAN,* I'M NOT SURE THAT MAKES YOU SO LUCKY.
ガッ
GRAB
!
THAT CAKE WAS A GIFT. TO **ME.**
MY STUDENT GAVE IT TO ME ON MY BIRTHDAY.
I'LL HAVE TO THANK HER AGAIN ...
RELEASE ME, SPINSTER.
YOUR SINGLENESS WILL RUB OFF ON ME.
And this cake is mine.

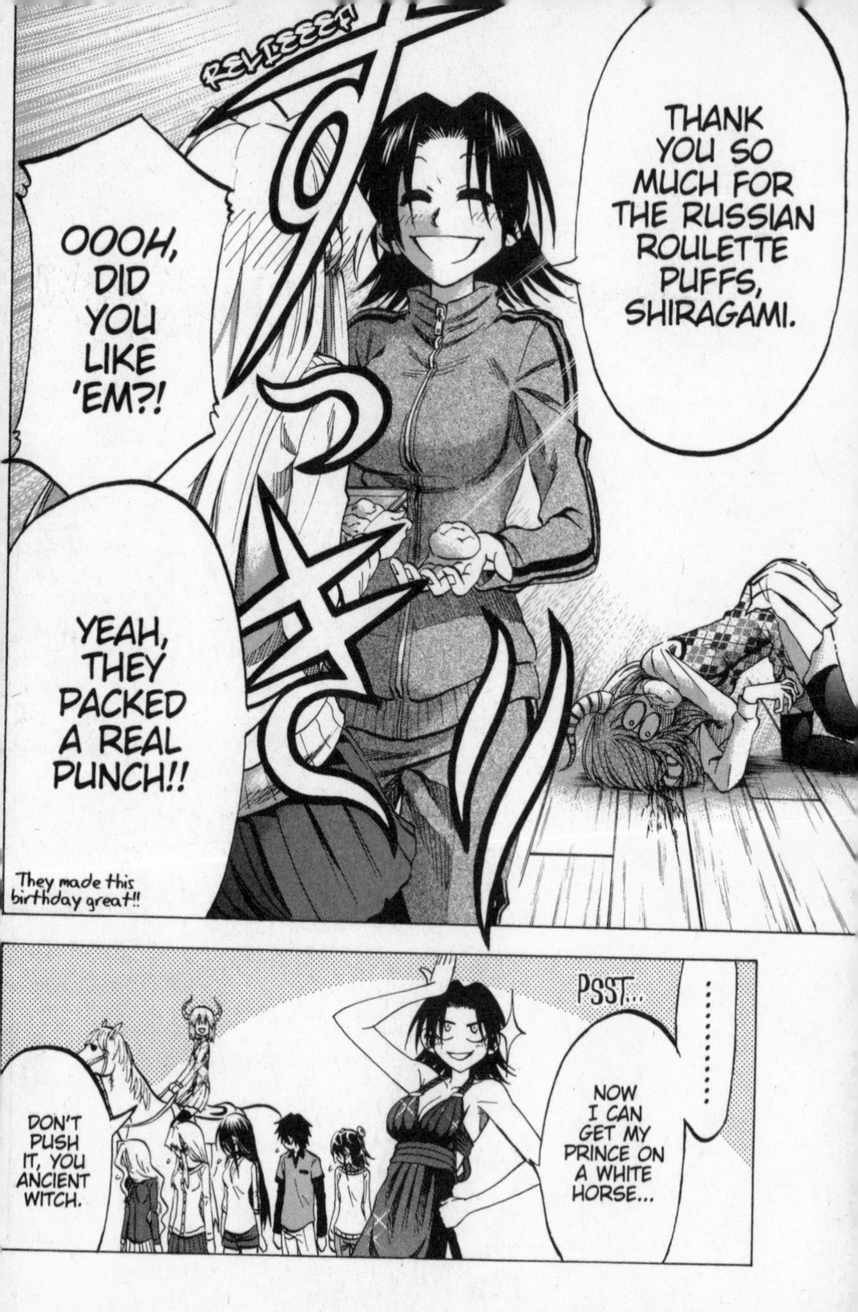
RELIEEEF!
THANK YOU SO MUCH FOR THE RUSSIAN ROULETTE PUFFS, SHIRAGAMI.
OOOH, DID YOU LIKE 'EM?!
YEAH, THEY PACKED A REAL PUNCH!!
They made this birthday great!!
PSST...
......
NOW I CAN GET MY PRINCE ON A WHITE HORSE...
DON'T PUSH IT, YOU ANCIENT WITCH.

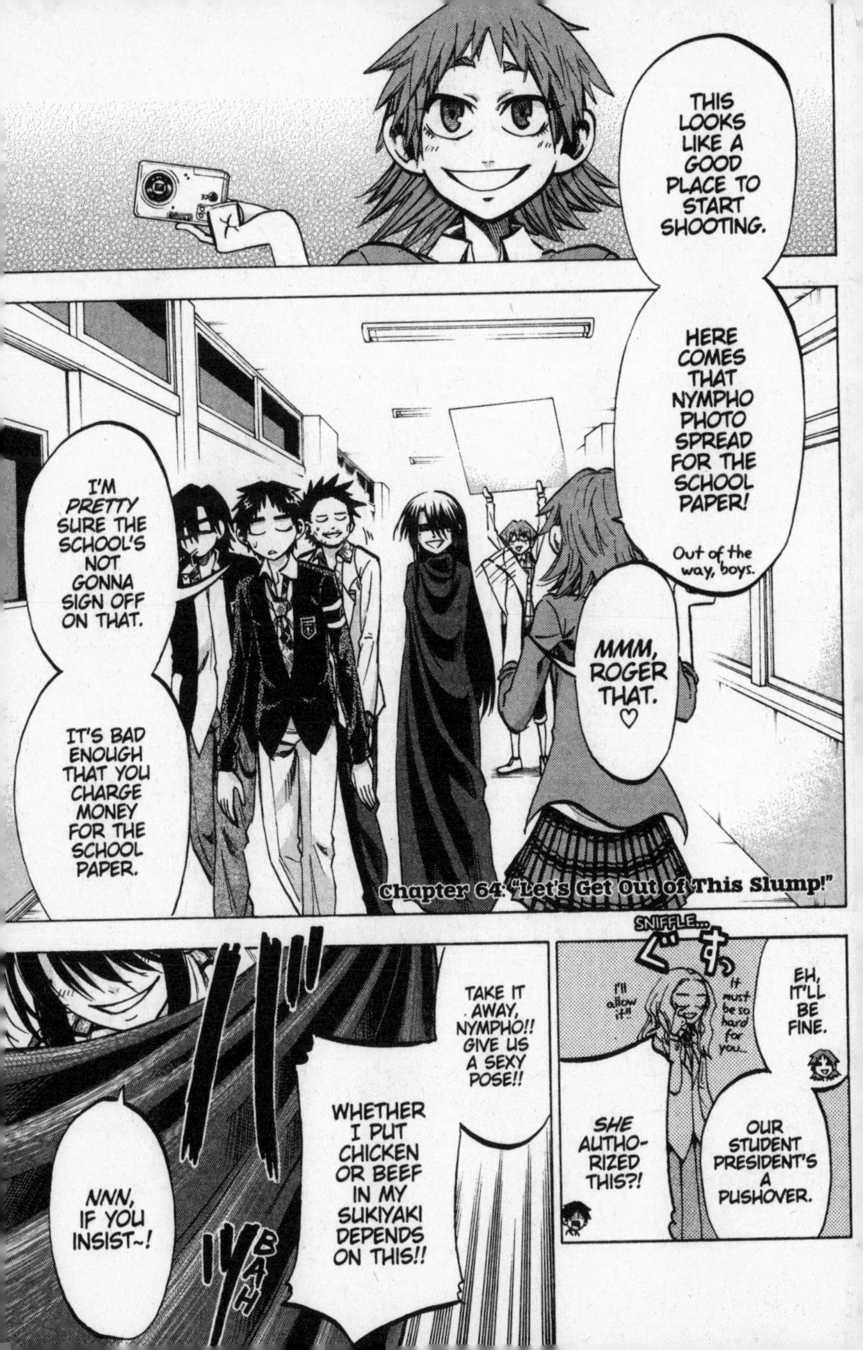
THIS LOOKS LIKE A GOOD PLACE TO START SHOOTING.
HERE COMES THAT NYMPHO PHOTO SPREAD FOR THE SCHOOL PAPER!
Out of the way, boys.
MMM, ROGER THAT. ♡
I'M *PRETTY* SURE THE SCHOOL'S NOT GONNA SIGN OFF ON THAT.
IT'S BAD ENOUGH THAT YOU CHARGE MONEY FOR THE SCHOOL PAPER.
Chapter 64: "Let's Get Out of This Slump!"
SNIFFLE...
EH, IT'LL BE FINE.
It must be so hard for you...
I'll allow it!!
OUR STUDENT PRESIDENT'S A PUSHOVER.
SHE AUTHORIZED THIS?!
TAKE IT AWAY, NYMPHO!! GIVE US A SEXY POSE!!
WHETHER I PUT CHICKEN OR BEEF IN MY SUKIYAKI DEPENDS ON THIS!!
NNN, IF YOU INSIST~!
BAH

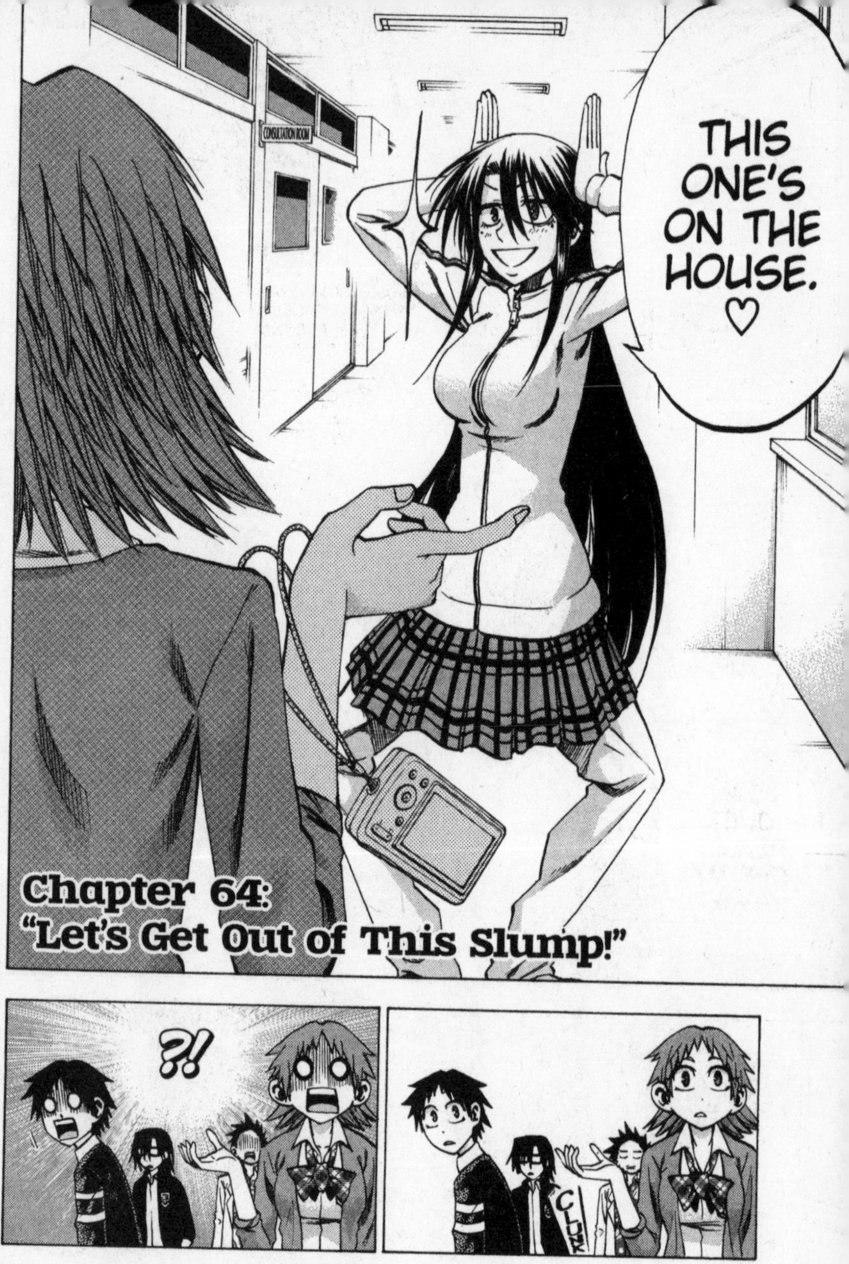
THIS ONE'S ON THE HOUSE. ♡
Chapter 64:
"Let's Get Out of This Slump!"
CLUNK
?!

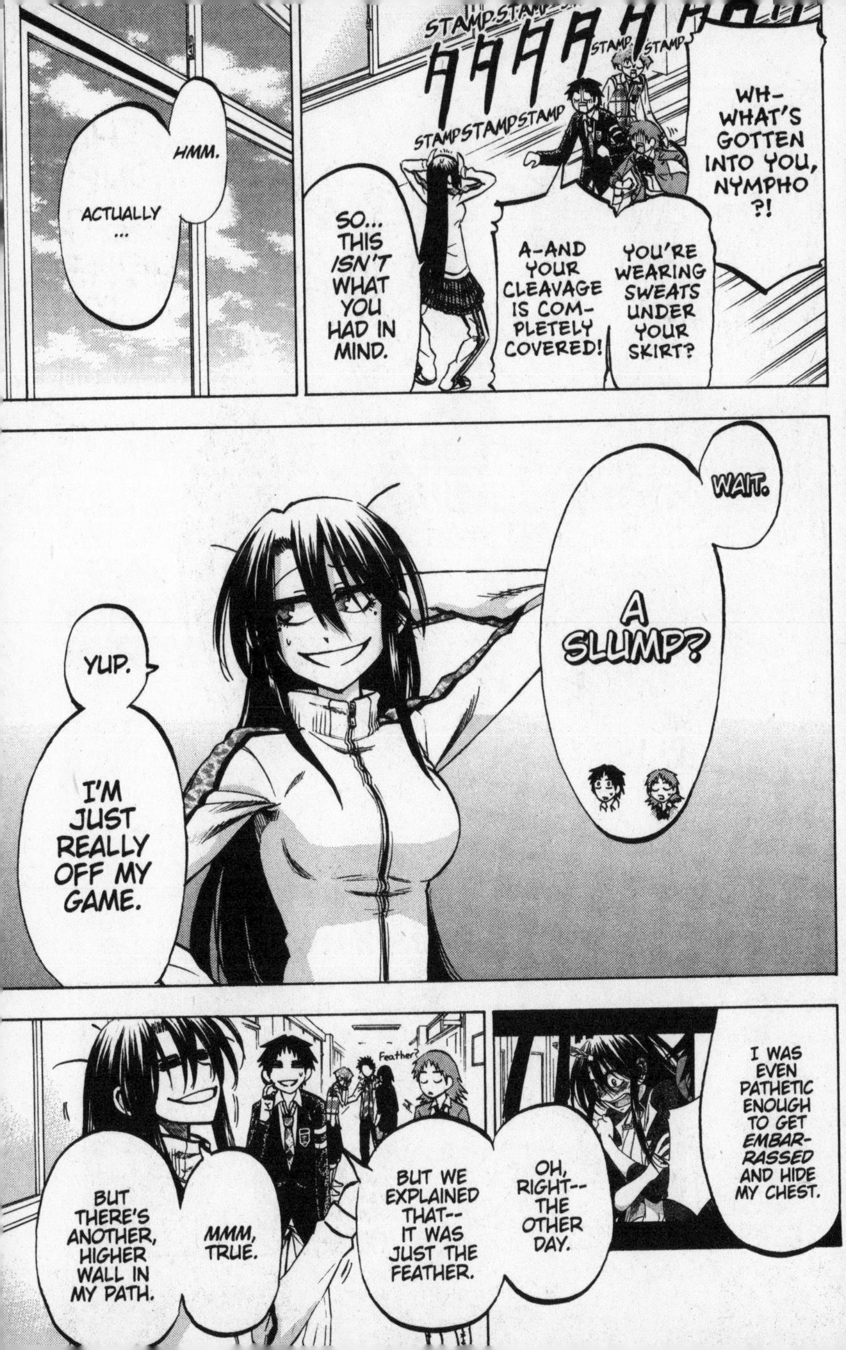
STAMPSTAMP
タタタタ
STAMP STAMP
WH-WHAT'S GOTTEN INTO YOU, NYMPHO?!
YOU'RE WEARING SWEATS UNDER YOUR SKIRT?
A-AND YOUR CLEAVAGE IS COMPLETELY COVERED!
SO... THIS ISN'T WHAT YOU HAD IN MIND.
STAMPSTAMPSTAMP
HMM.
ACTUALLY...
WAIT.
A SLLUMP?
YUP.
I'M JUST REALLY OFF MY GAME.
I WAS EVEN PATHETIC ENOUGH TO GET EMBARRASSED AND HIDE MY CHEST.
OH, RIGHT-- THE OTHER DAY.
BUT WE EXPLAINED THAT-- IT WAS JUST THE FEATHER.
Feather?
MMM, TRUE.
BUT THERE'S ANOTHER, HIGHER WALL IN MY PATH.

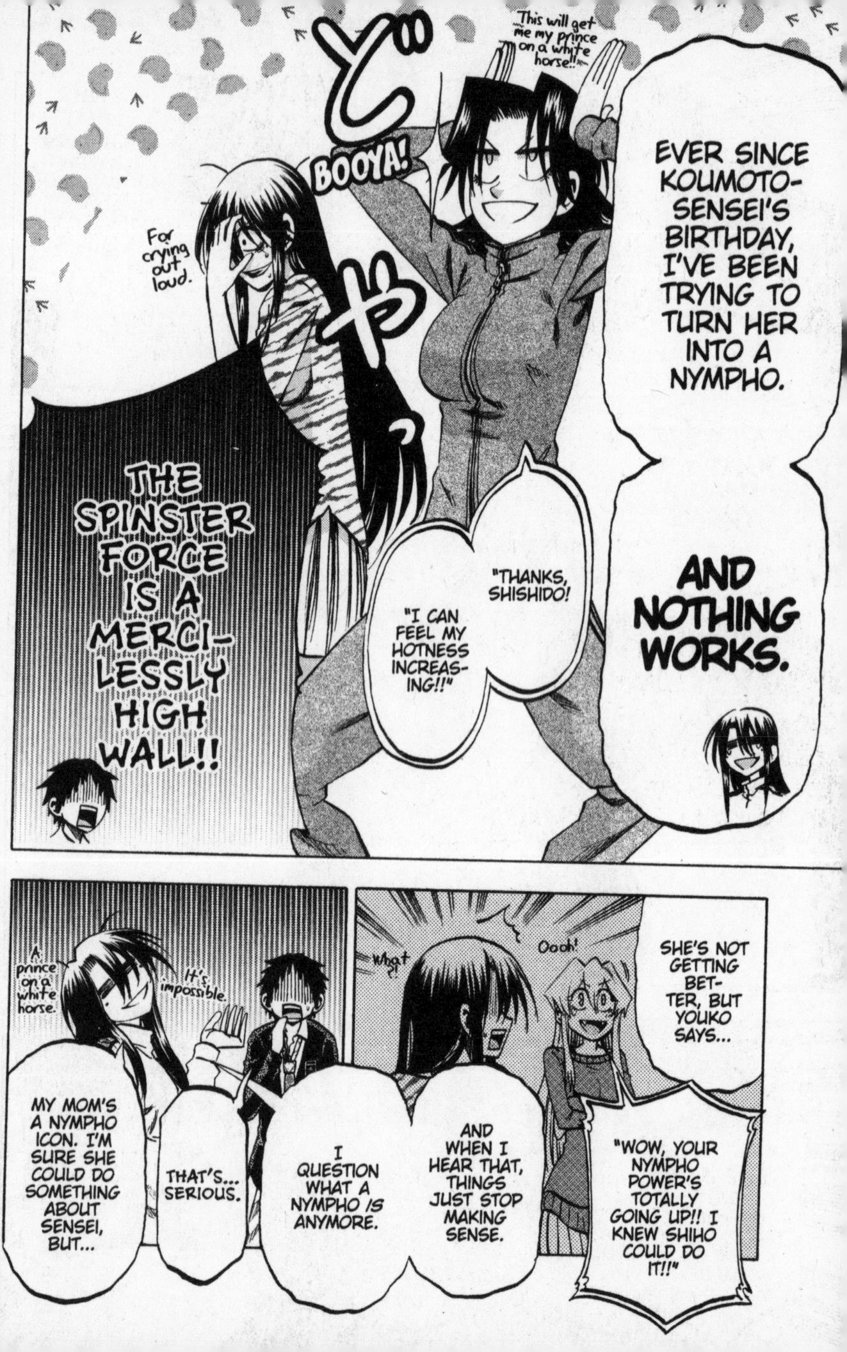
EVER SINCE KOUMOTO-SENSEI'S BIRTHDAY, I'VE BEEN TRYING TO TURN HER INTO A NYMPHO.
AND NOTHING WORKS.
...This will get me my prince on a white horse!!
どや
BOOYA!
"THANKS, SHISHIDO!
"I CAN FEEL MY HOTNESS INCREAS-ING!!"
For crying out loud.
THE SPINSTER FORCE IS A MERCI-LESSLY HIGH WALL!!
SHE'S NOT GETTING BET-TER, BUT YOUKO SAYS...
"WOW, YOUR NYMPHO POWER'S TOTALLY GOING UP!! I KNEW SHIHO COULD DO IT!!"
Oooh!
What?
AND WHEN I HEAR THAT, THINGS JUST STOP MAKING SENSE.
I QUESTION WHAT A NYMPHO *IS* ANYMORE.
It's impossible.
A prince on a white horse.
THAT'S... SERIOUS.
MY MOM'S A NYMPHO ICON. I'M SURE SHE COULD DO SOMETHING ABOUT SENSEI, BUT...

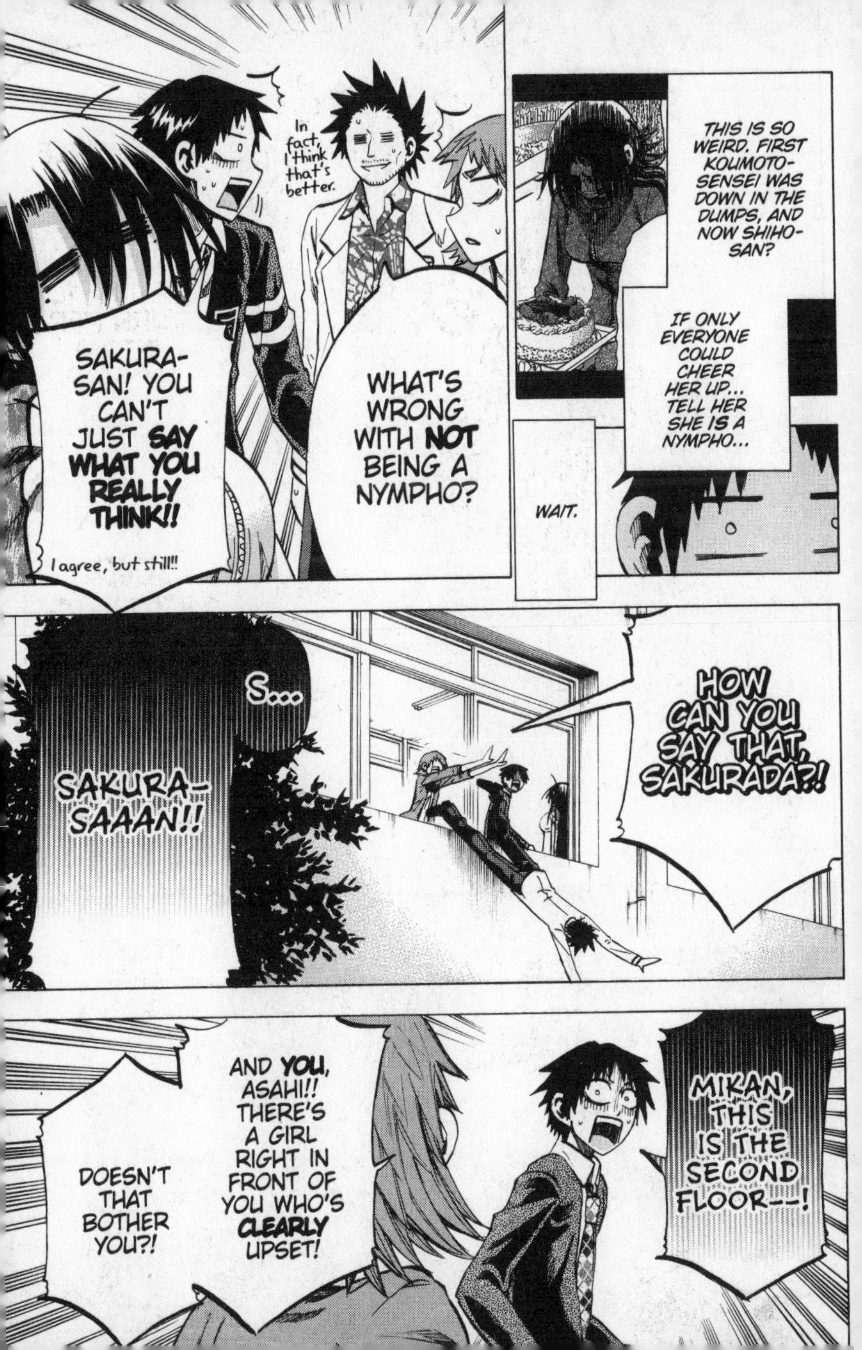

THIS IS SO WEIRD. FIRST KOUMOTO-SENSEI WAS DOWN IN THE DUMPS, AND NOW SHIHO-SAN?
IF ONLY EVERYONE COULD CHEER HER UP... TELL HER SHE IS A NYMPHO...
WAIT.
WHAT'S WRONG WITH NOT BEING A NYMPHO?
In fact, I think that's better.
SAKURA-SAN! YOU CAN'T JUST SAY WHAT YOU REALLY THINK!!
I agree, but still!!
HOW CAN YOU SAY THAT, SAKURADA?!
S...
SAKURA-SAAAN!!
MIKAN, THIS IS THE SECOND FLOOR--!
AND YOU, ASAHI!! THERE'S A GIRL RIGHT IN FRONT OF YOU WHO'S CLEARLY UPSET!
DOESN'T THAT BOTHER YOU?!

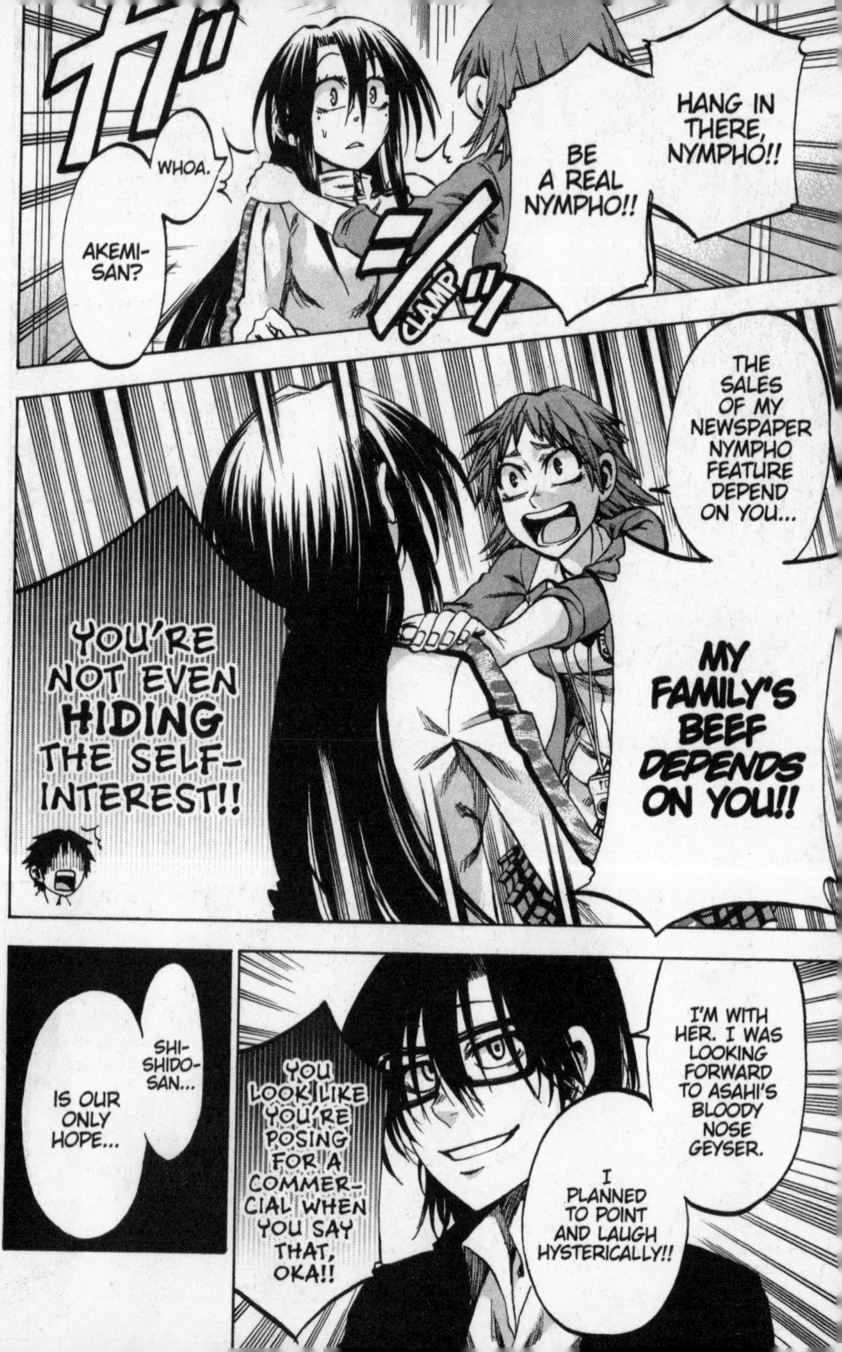
HANG IN THERE, NYMPHO!!
BE A REAL NYMPHO!!
CLAMP
WHOA.
AKEMI-SAN?
THE SALES OF MY NEWSPAPER NYMPHO FEATURE DEPEND ON YOU...
MY FAMILY'S BEEF DEPENDS ON YOU!!
YOU'RE NOT EVEN HIDING THE SELF-INTEREST!!
I'M WITH HER. I WAS LOOKING FORWARD TO ASAHI'S BLOODY NOSE GEYSER.
I PLANNED TO POINT AND LAUGH HYSTERICALLY!!
YOU LOOK LIKE YOU'RE POSING FOR A COMMERCIAL WHEN YOU SAY THAT, OKA!!
SHI-SHIDO-SAN...
IS OUR ONLY HOPE...

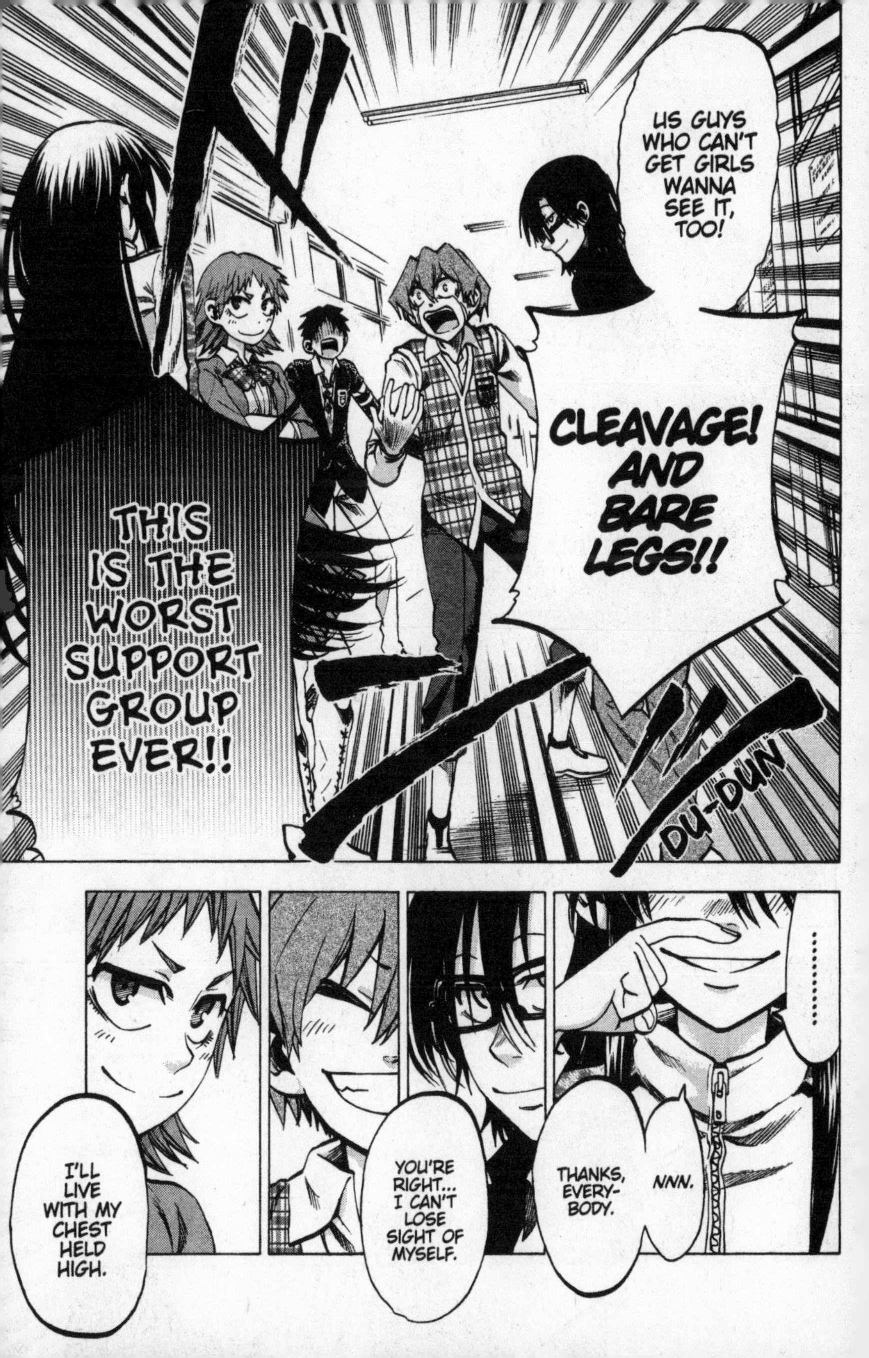
US GUYS WHO CAN'T GET GIRLS WANNA SEE IT, TOO!
CLEAVAGE! AND BARE LEGS!!
DU-DUN
THIS IS THE WORST SUPPORT GROUP EVER!!
......
NNN.
THANKS, EVERY-BODY.
YOU'RE RIGHT... I CAN'T LOSE SIGHT OF MYSELF.
I'LL LIVE WITH MY CHEST HELD HIGH.

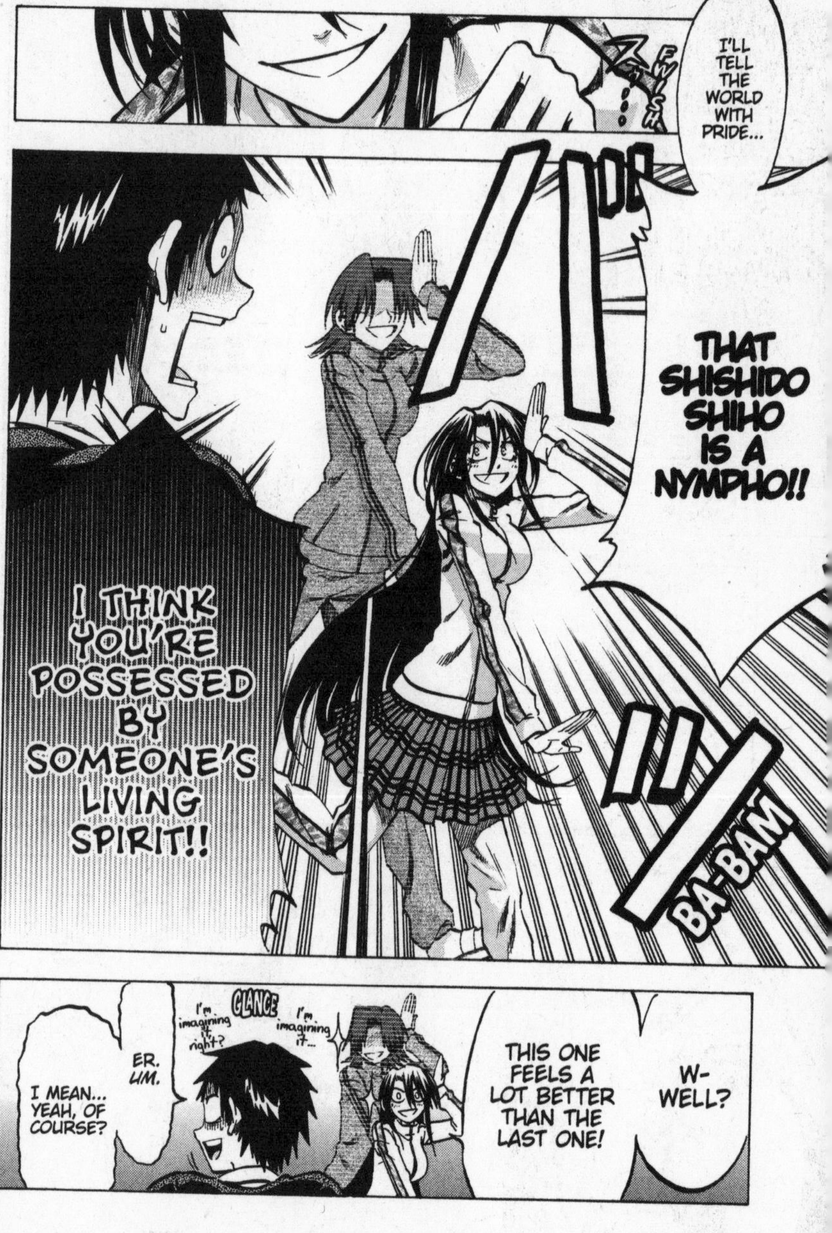
I'LL TELL THE WORLD WITH PRIDE...
FWISH
THAT SHISHIDO SHIHO IS A NYMPHO!!
BA-BAM
I THINK YOU'RE POSSESSED BY SOMEONE'S LIVING SPIRIT!!
W-WELL?
THIS ONE FEELS A LOT BETTER THAN THE LAST ONE!
I'm imagining it...
GLANCE
I'm imagining it, right?
ER. UM.
I MEAN... YEAH, OF COURSE?

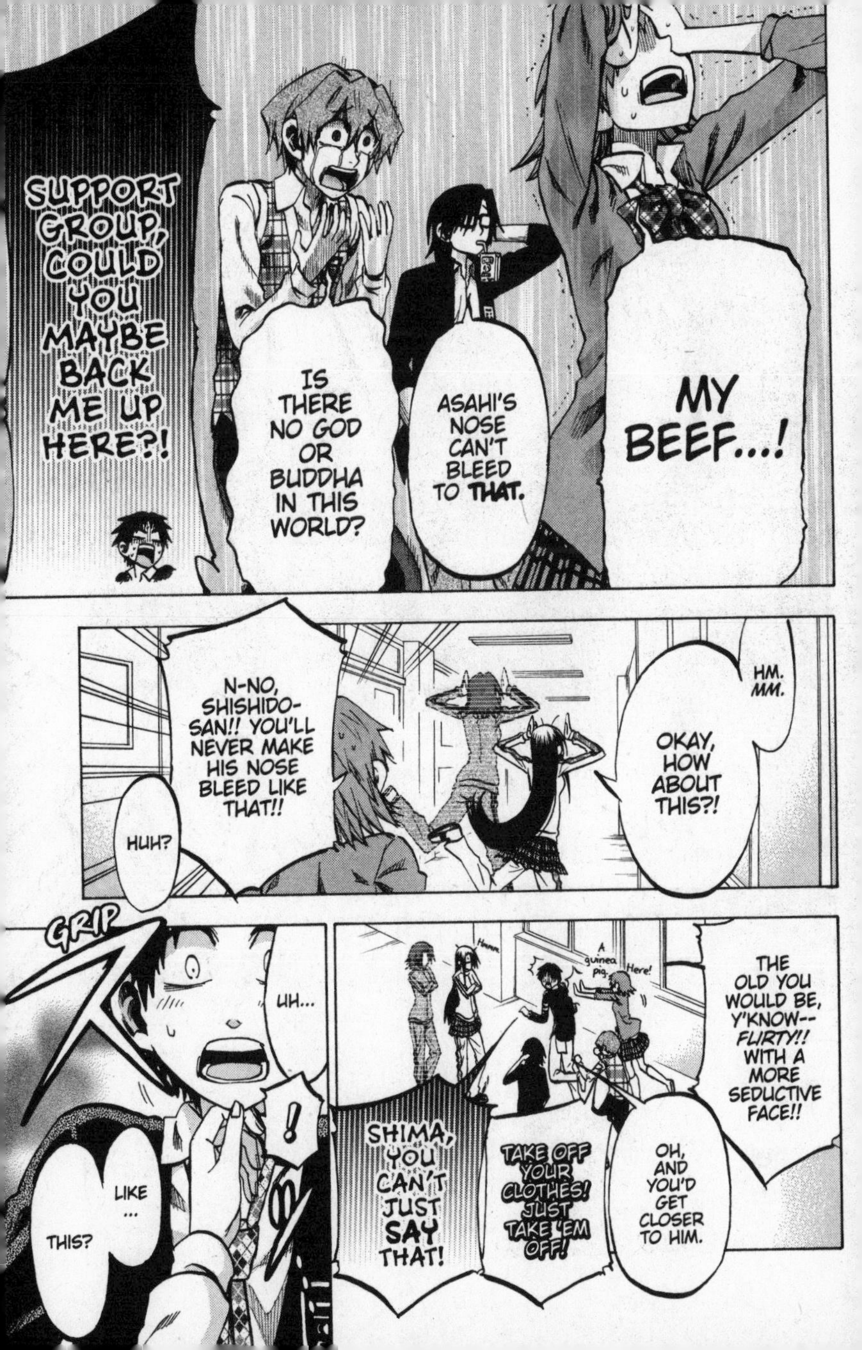
MY BEEF...!
ASAHI'S NOSE CAN'T BLEED TO THAT.
IS THERE NO GOD OR BUDDHA IN THIS WORLD?
SUPPORT GROUP, COULD YOU MAYBE BACK ME UP HERE?!
HM. MM.
OKAY, HOW ABOUT THIS?!
N-NO, SHISHIDO-SAN!! YOU'LL NEVER MAKE HIS NOSE BLEED LIKE THAT!!
HUH?
THE OLD YOU WOULD BE, Y'KNOW-- FLIRTY!! WITH A MORE SEDUCTIVE FACE!!
Here!
A guinea pig.
Hmmm
OH, AND YOU'D GET CLOSER TO HIM.
TAKE OFF YOUR CLOTHES! JUST TAKE 'EM OFF!
SHIMA, YOU CAN'T JUST SAY THAT!
GRIP
UH...
!
LIKE ... THIS?

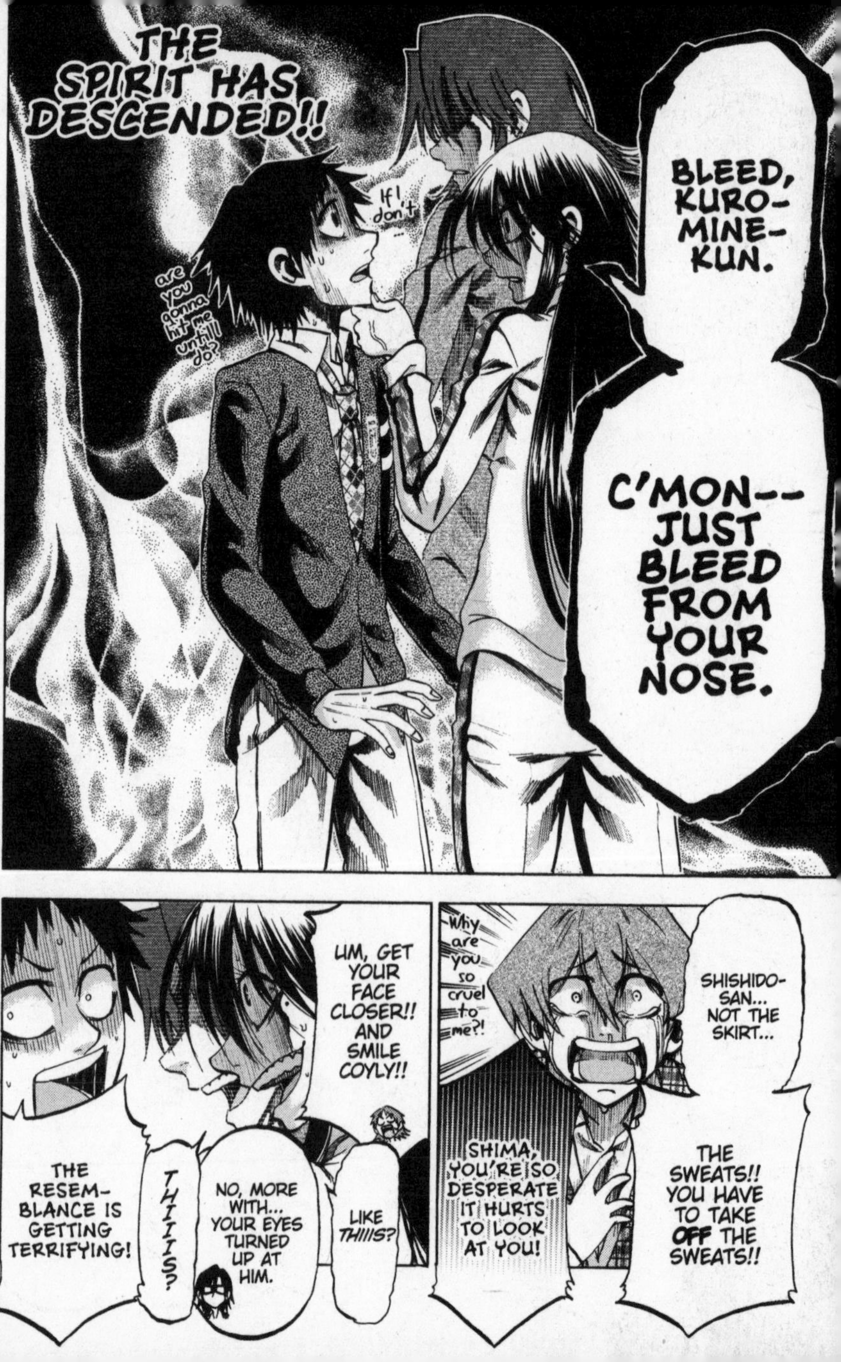
BLEED, KURO-MINE-KUN.
If I don't...
are you gonna hit me until I do?
C'MON-- JUST BLEED FROM YOUR NOSE.
THE SPIRIT HAS DESCENDED!!
SHISHIDO-SAN... NOT THE SKIRT...
Why are you so cruel to me?!
THE SWEATS!! YOU HAVE TO TAKE OFF THE SWEATS!!
SHIMA, YOU'RE SO DESPERATE IT HURTS TO LOOK AT YOU!
UM, GET YOUR FACE CLOSER!! AND SMILE COYLY!!
LIKE THIIIS?
NO, MORE WITH... YOUR EYES TURNED UP AT HIM.
THIIIS?
THE RESEM-BLANCE IS GETTING TERRIFYING!

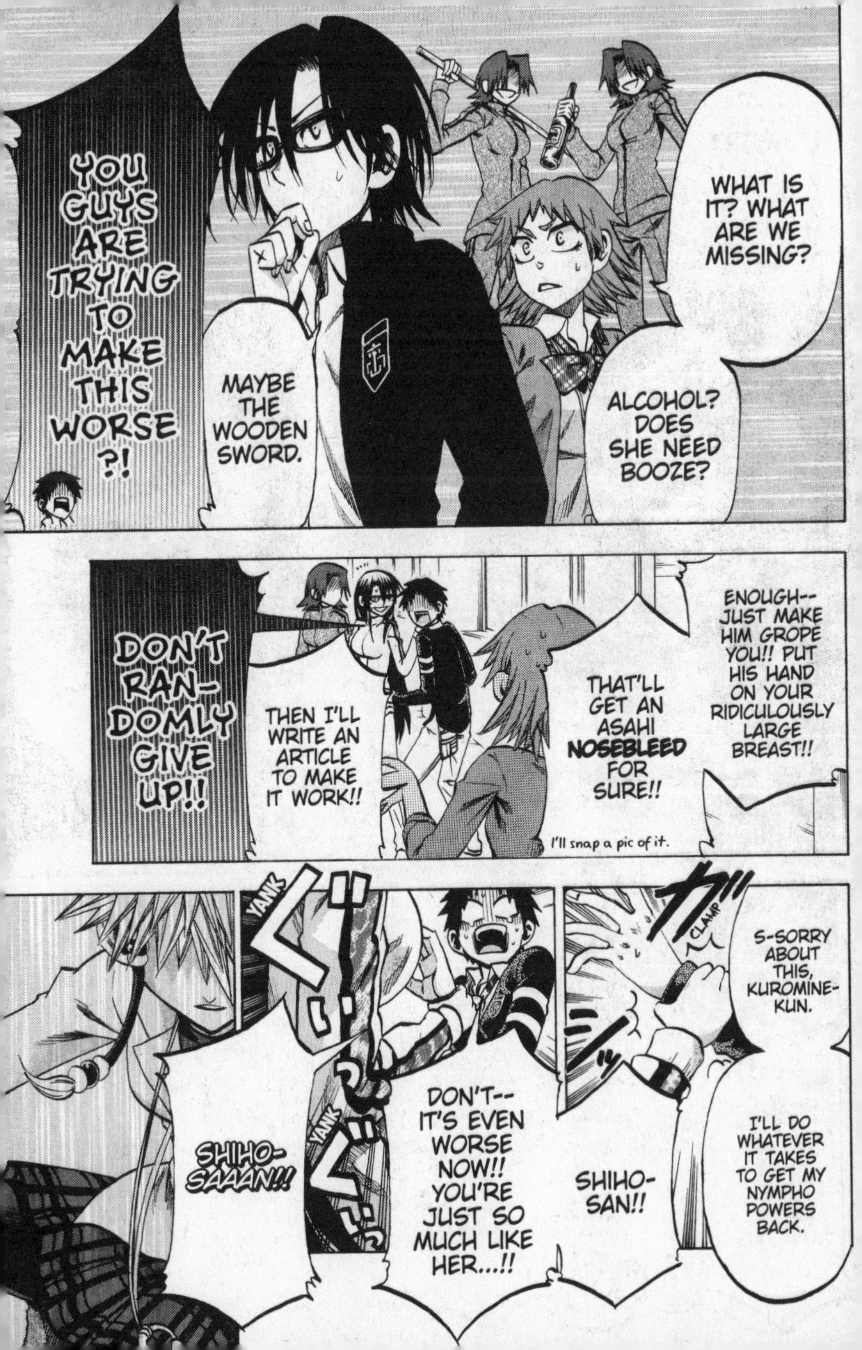
WHAT IS IT? WHAT ARE WE MISSING?
ALCOHOL? DOES SHE NEED BOOZE?
MAYBE THE WOODEN SWORD.
YOU GUYS ARE TRYING TO MAKE THIS WORSE?!
ENOUGH--JUST MAKE HIM GROPE YOU!! PUT HIS HAND ON YOUR RIDICULOUSLY LARGE BREAST!!
THAT'LL GET AN ASAHI **NOSEBLEED** FOR SURE!!
I'll snap a pic of it.
THEN I'LL WRITE AN ARTICLE TO MAKE IT WORK!!
DON'T RAN-DOMLY GIVE UP!!
CLAMP
S-SORRY ABOUT THIS, KUROMINE-KUN.
I'LL DO WHATEVER IT TAKES TO GET MY NYMPHO POWERS BACK.
SHIHO-SAN!!
DON'T--IT'S EVEN WORSE NOW!! YOU'RE JUST SO MUCH LIKE HER...!!
YANK
YANK
SHIHO-SAAAN!!

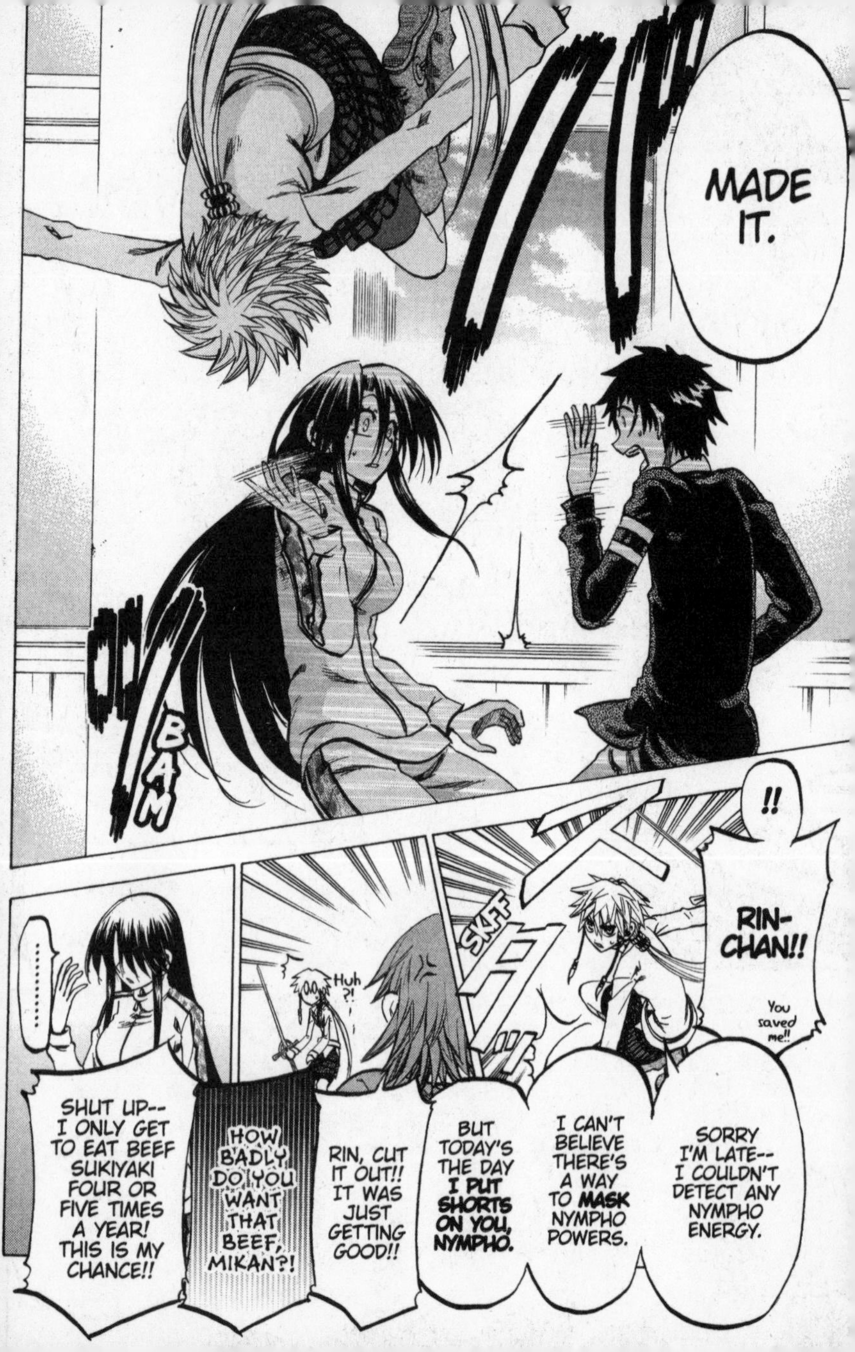
MADE IT.
BAM
!!
RIN-CHAN!!
You saved me!!
SKFF
SORRY I'M LATE-- I COULDN'T DETECT ANY NYMPHO ENERGY.
I CAN'T BELIEVE THERE'S A WAY TO MASK NYMPHO POWERS.
BUT TODAY'S THE DAY I PUT SHORTS ON YOU, NYMPHO.
Huh?!
RIN, CUT IT OUT!! IT WAS JUST GETTING GOOD!!
HOW BADLY DO YOU WANT THAT BEEF, MIKAN?!
......
SHUT UP-- I ONLY GET TO EAT BEEF SUKIYAKI FOUR OR FIVE TIMES A YEAR! THIS IS MY CHANCE!!

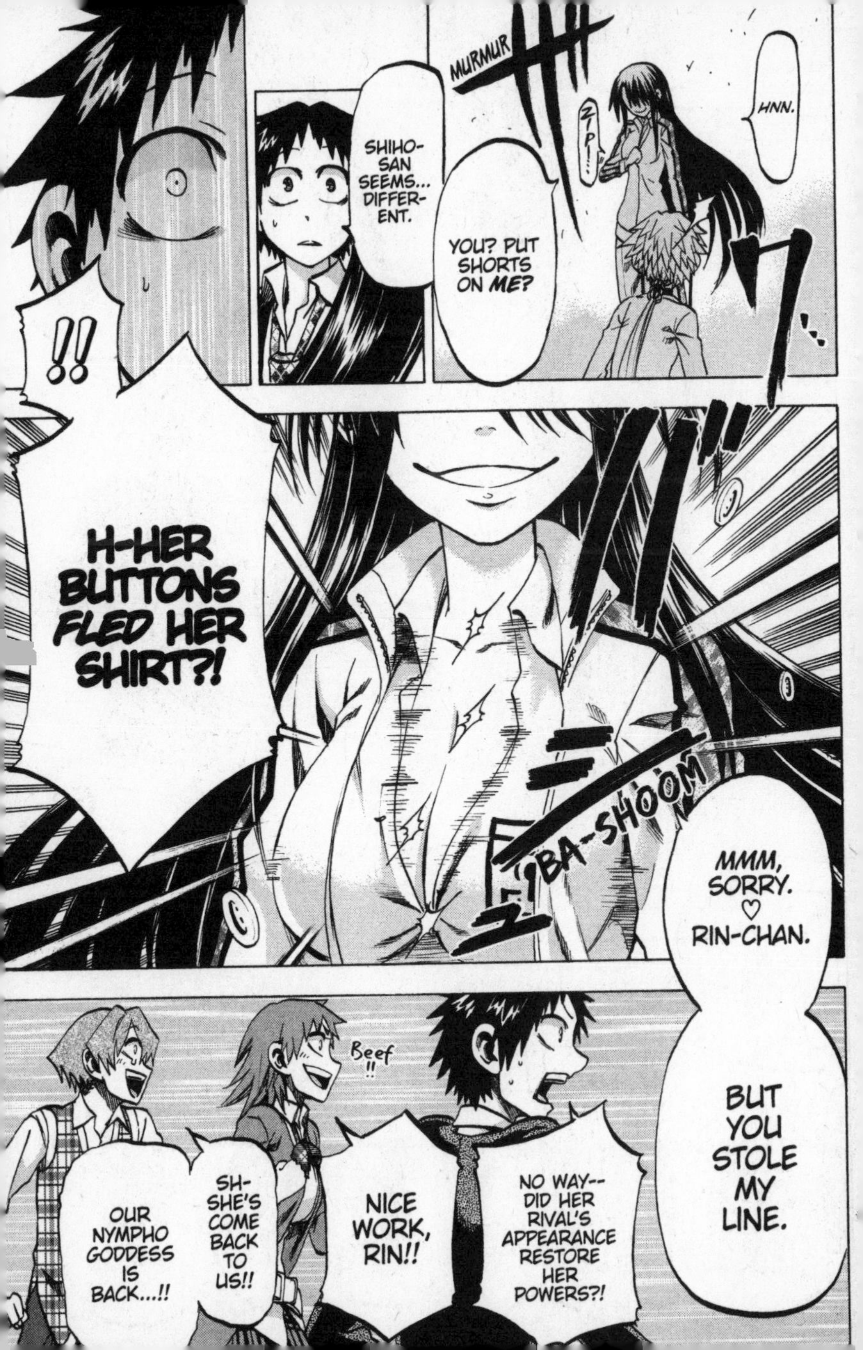
HNN.
ZIP!...
MURMUR
...
YOU? PUT SHORTS ON *ME*?
SHIHO-SAN SEEMS... DIFFERENT.
!!
MMM, SORRY. ♡ RIN-CHAN.
BA-SHOOM
H-HER BUTTONS FLED HER SHIRT?!
BUT YOU STOLE MY LINE.
NO WAY-- DID HER RIVAL'S APPEARANCE RESTORE HER POWERS?!
Beef!!
NICE WORK, RIN!!
SH-SHE'S COME BACK TO US!!
OUR NYMPHO GODDESS IS BACK...!!

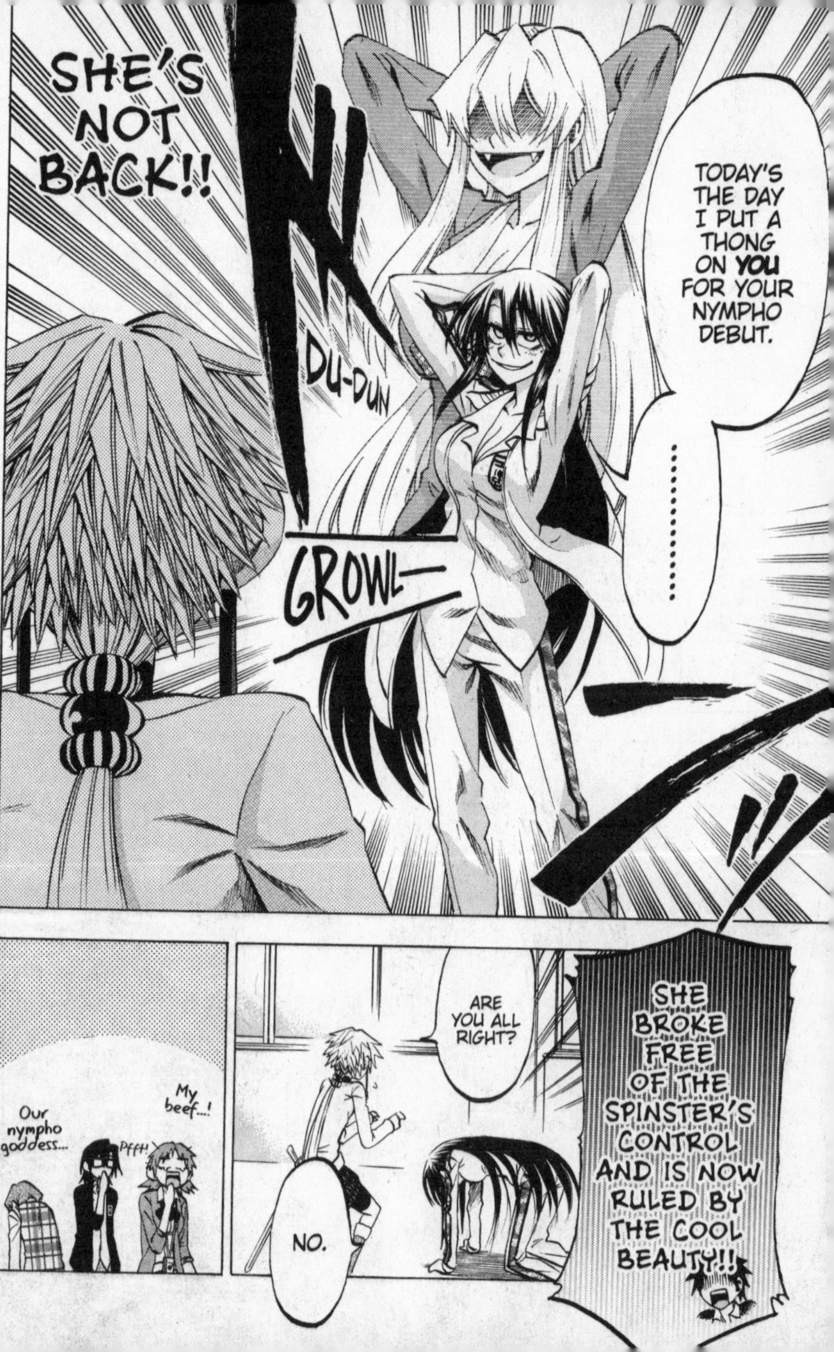
TODAY'S THE DAY I PUT A THONG ON **YOU** FOR YOUR NYMPHO DEBUT.
......
DU-DUN
GROWL—
SHE'S NOT BACK!!
SHE BROKE FREE OF THE SPINSTER'S CONTROL AND IS NOW RULED BY THE COOL BEAUTY!!
ARE YOU ALL RIGHT?
NO.
My beef...!
Pfft!
Our nympho goddess...

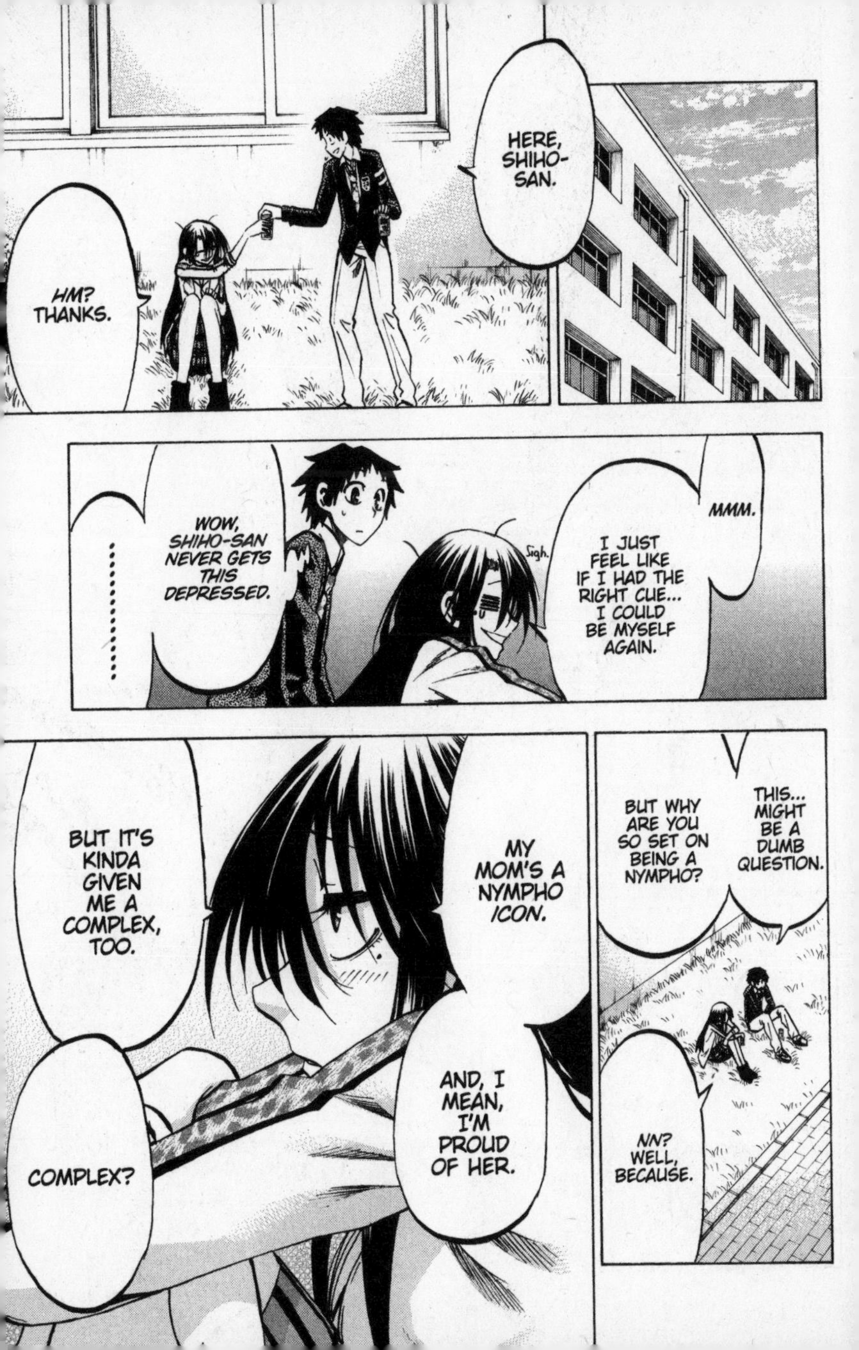
HERE, SHIHO-SAN.
HM? THANKS.
MMM.
I JUST FEEL LIKE IF I HAD THE RIGHT CUE... I COULD BE MYSELF AGAIN.
Sigh.
WOW, SHIHO-SAN NEVER GETS THIS DEPRESSED.
....
THIS... MIGHT BE A DUMB QUESTION.
BUT WHY ARE YOU SO SET ON BEING A NYMPHO?
NN? WELL, BECAUSE.
MY MOM'S A NYMPHO ICON.
AND, I MEAN, I'M PROUD OF HER.
BUT IT'S KINDA GIVEN ME A COMPLEX, TOO.
COMPLEX?

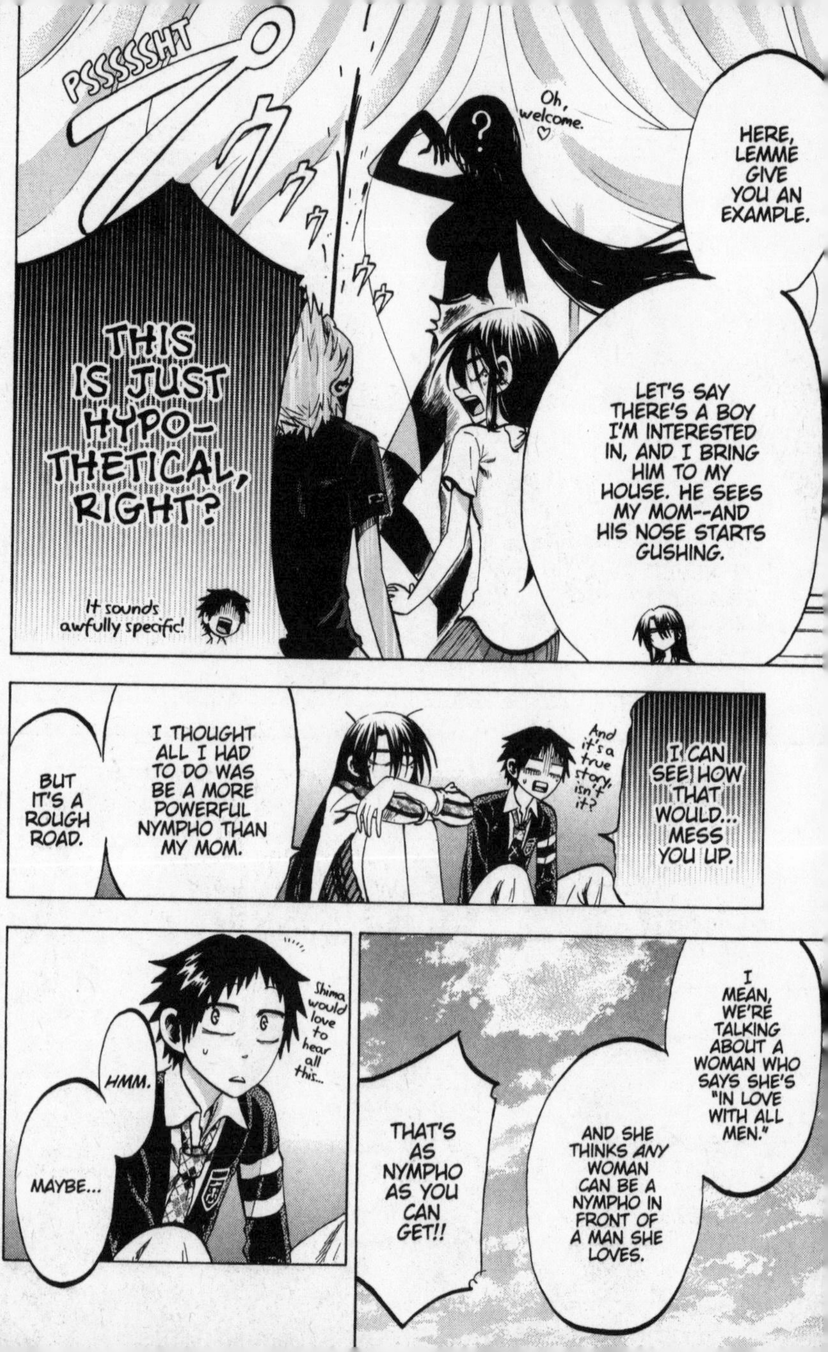
HERE, LEMME GIVE YOU AN EXAMPLE.
LET'S SAY THERE'S A BOY I'M INTERESTED IN, AND I BRING HIM TO MY HOUSE. HE SEES MY MOM--AND HIS NOSE STARTS GUSHING.
Oh, welcome.
PSSSSSHT
THIS IS JUST HYPO-THETICAL, RIGHT?
It sounds awfully specific!
I CAN SEE HOW THAT WOULD... MESS YOU UP.
And it's a true story, isn't it?
I THOUGHT ALL I HAD TO DO WAS BE A MORE POWERFUL NYMPHO THAN MY MOM.
BUT IT'S A ROUGH ROAD.
I MEAN, WE'RE TALKING ABOUT A WOMAN WHO SAYS SHE'S "IN LOVE WITH ALL MEN."
AND SHE THINKS *ANY* WOMAN CAN BE A NYMPHO IN FRONT OF A MAN SHE LOVES.
THAT'S AS NYMPHO AS YOU CAN GET!!
Shima would love to hear all this...
HMM.
MAYBE...

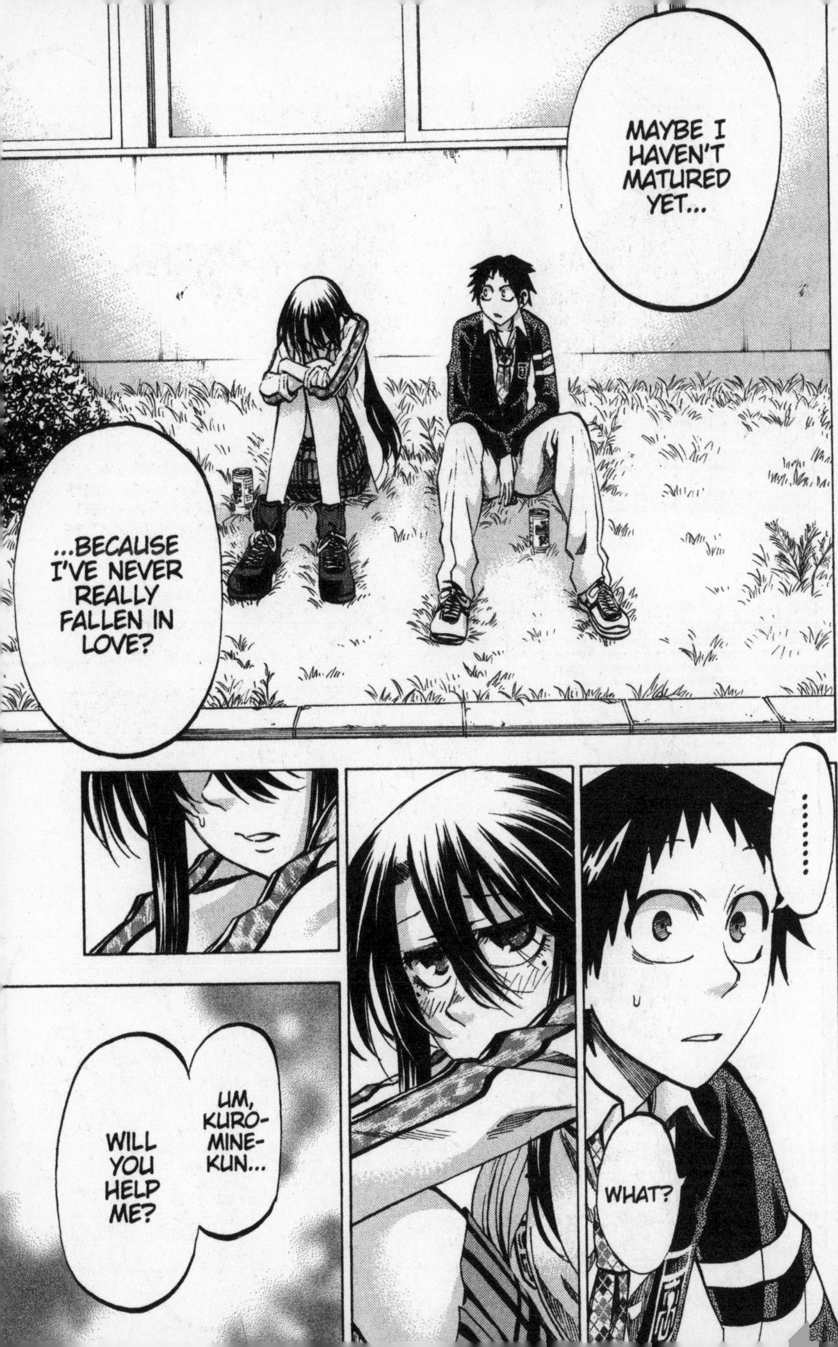
MAYBE I HAVEN'T MATURED YET...
...BECAUSE I'VE NEVER REALLY FALLEN IN LOVE?
....
WHAT?
UM, KURO-MINE-KUN...
WILL YOU HELP ME?

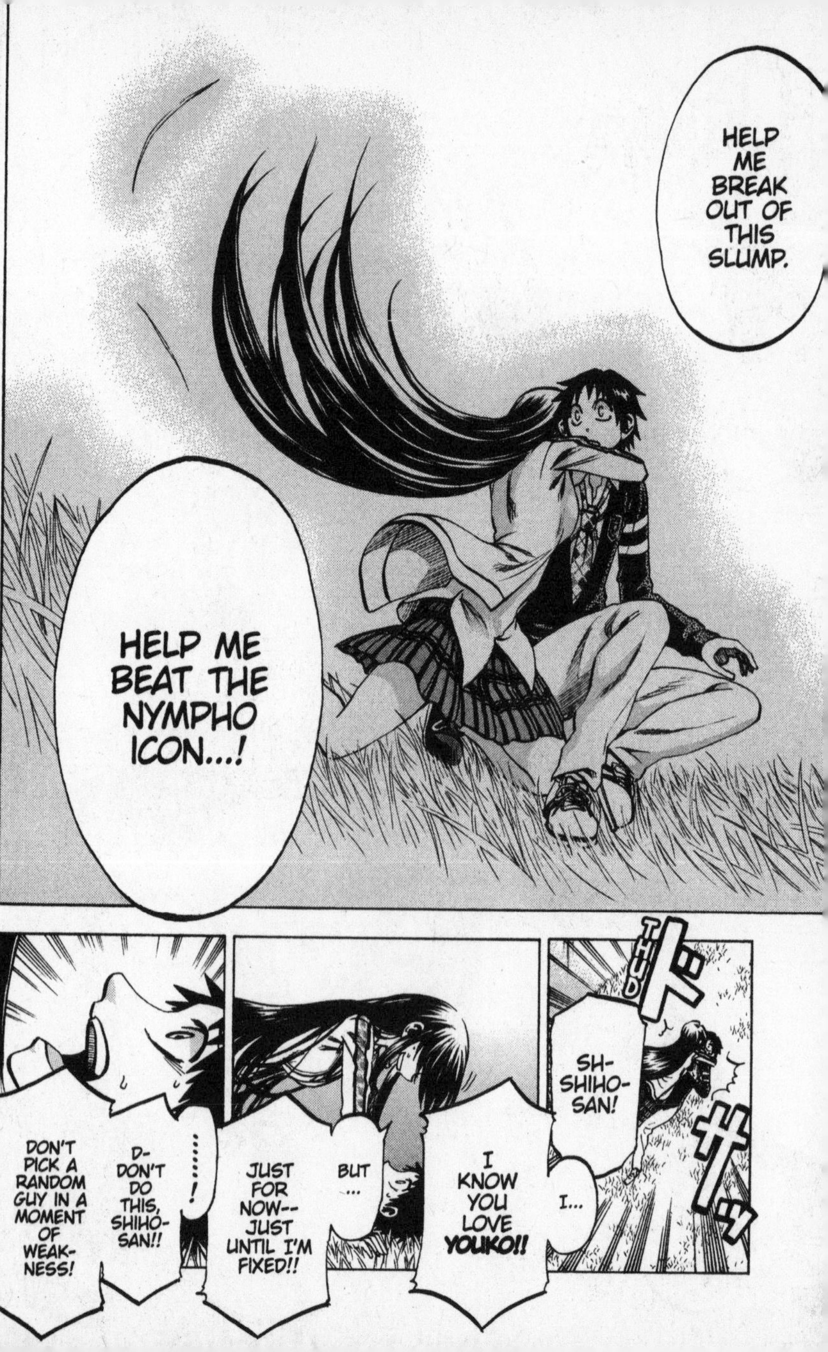
HELP ME BREAK OUT OF THIS SLUMP.
HELP ME BEAT THE NYMPHO ICON...!
THUD
SH-SHIHO-SAN!
I...
I KNOW YOU LOVE YOUKO!!
BUT ...
JUST FOR NOW-- JUST UNTIL I'M FIXED!!
......!
D-DON'T DO THIS, SHIHO-SAN!!
DON'T PICK A RANDOM GUY IN A MOMENT OF WEAK-NESS!

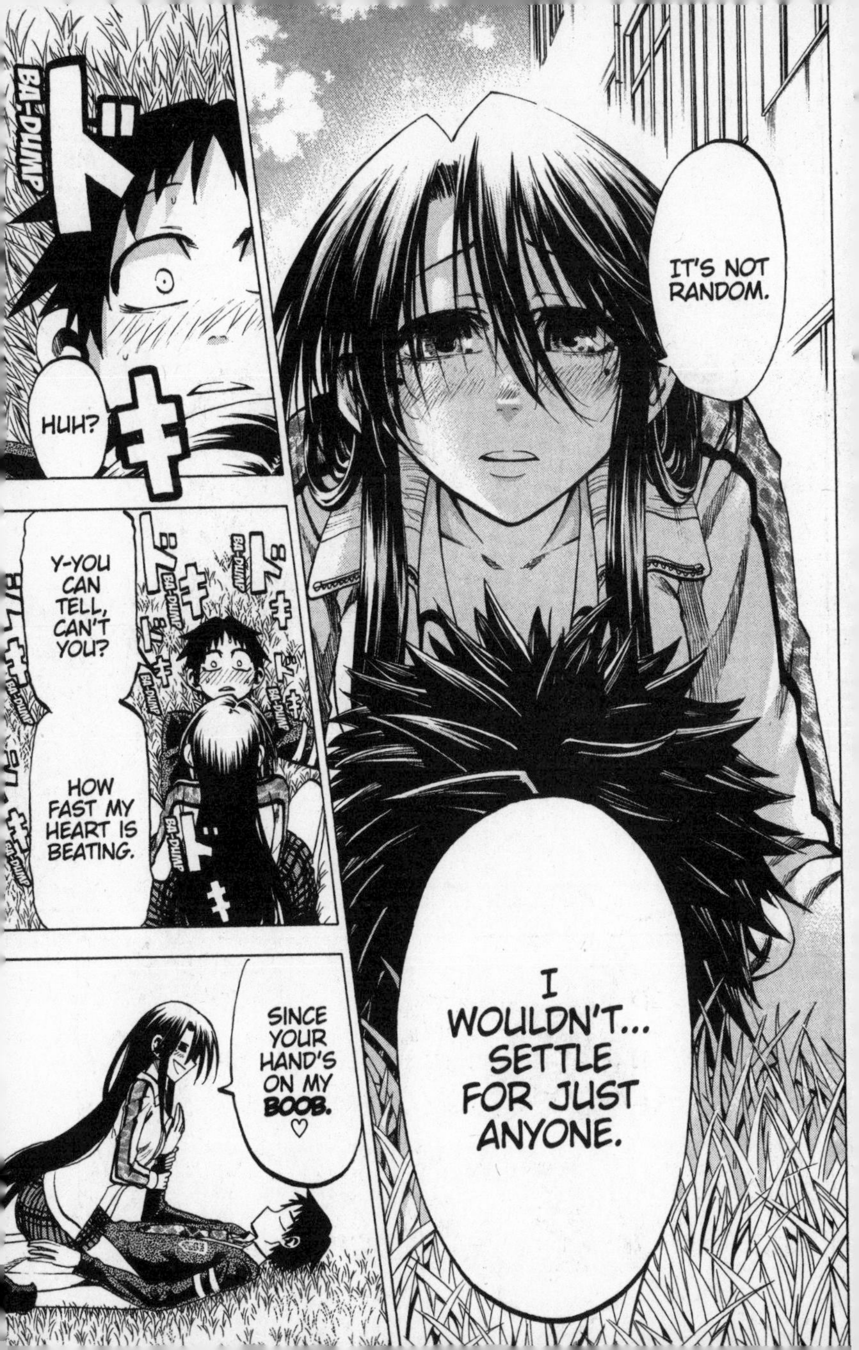
IT'S NOT RANDOM.
I WOULDN'T... SETTLE FOR JUST ANYONE.
BA-DUMP
HUH?
Y-YOU CAN TELL, CAN'T YOU?
HOW FAST MY HEART IS BEATING.
BA-DUMP
BA-DUMP
BA-DUMP
BA-DUMP
BA-DUMP
BA-DUMP
SINCE YOUR HAND'S ON MY **BOOB.** ♡

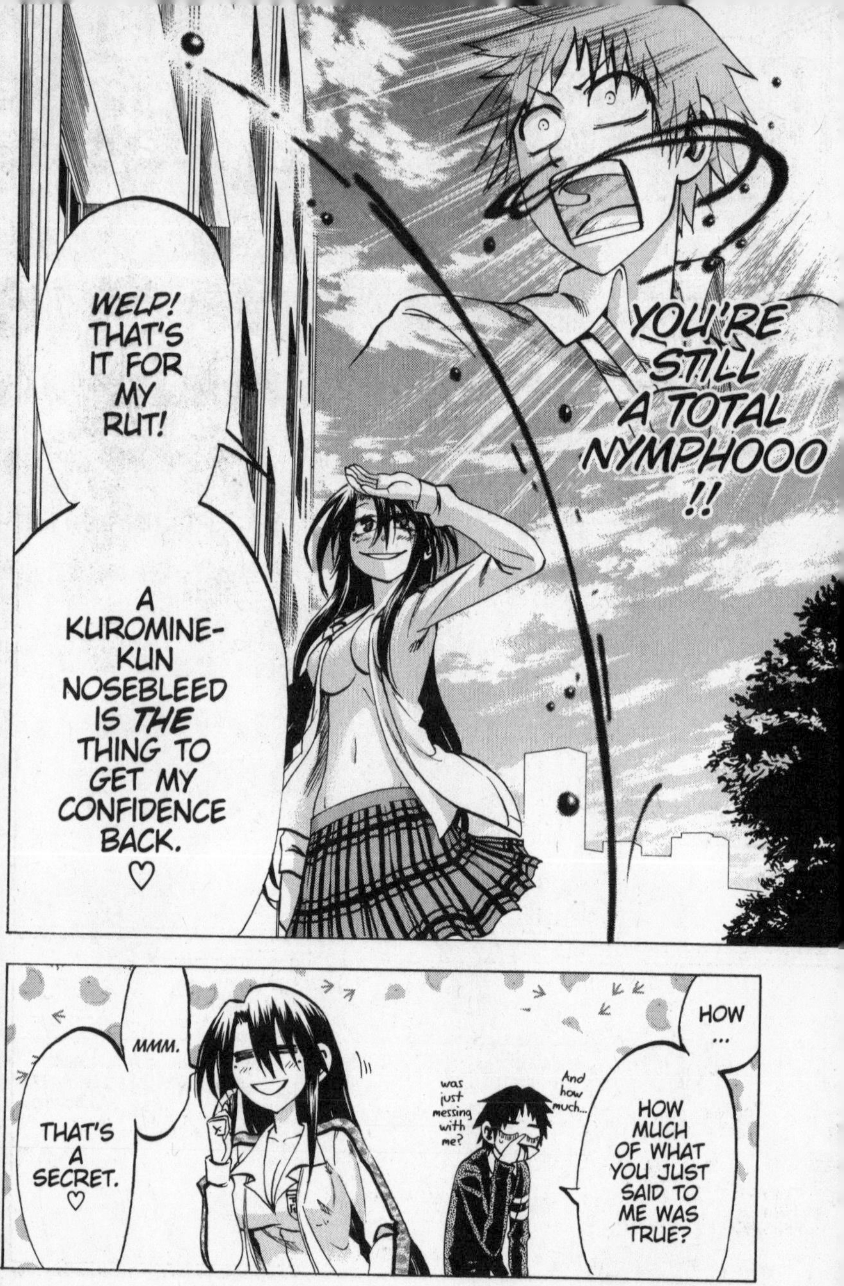
YOU'RE STILL A TOTAL NYMPHOOO !!
WELP! THAT'S IT FOR MY RUT!
A KUROMINE-KUN NOSEBLEED IS *THE* THING TO GET MY CONFIDENCE BACK. ♡
HOW ...
HOW MUCH OF WHAT YOU JUST SAID TO ME WAS TRUE?
And how much...
was just messing with me?
MMM.
THAT'S A SECRET. ♡

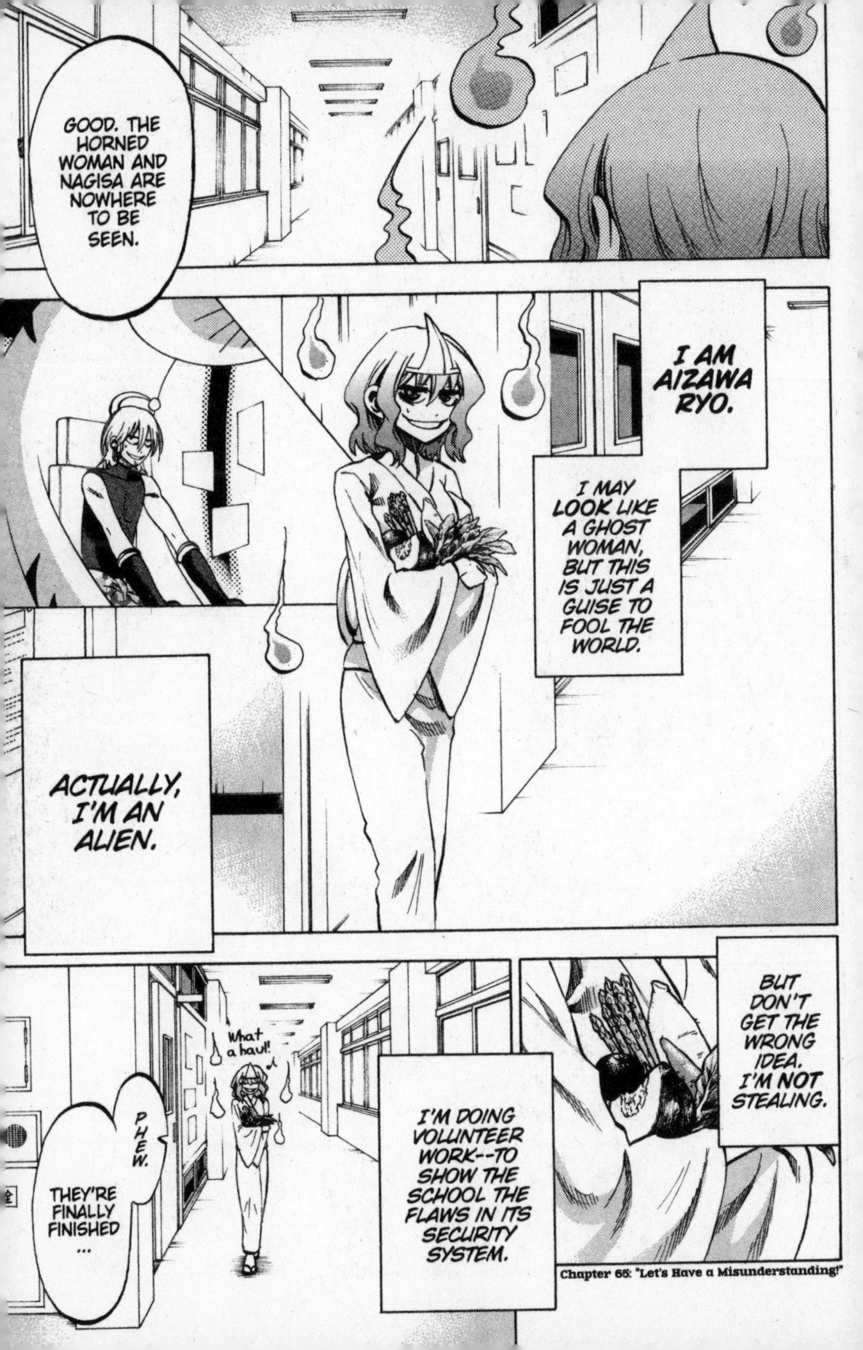

GOOD. THE HORNED WOMAN AND NAGISA ARE NOWHERE TO BE SEEN.
I AM AIZAWA RYO.
I MAY LOOK LIKE A GHOST WOMAN, BUT THIS IS JUST A GUISE TO FOOL THE WORLD.
ACTUALLY, I'M AN ALIEN.
BUT DON'T GET THE WRONG IDEA. I'M NOT STEALING.
I'M DOING VOLUNTEER WORK--TO SHOW THE SCHOOL THE FLAWS IN ITS SECURITY SYSTEM.
What a haul!
PHEW.
THEY'RE FINALLY FINISHED...

Chapter 65: "Let's Have a Misunderstanding!"

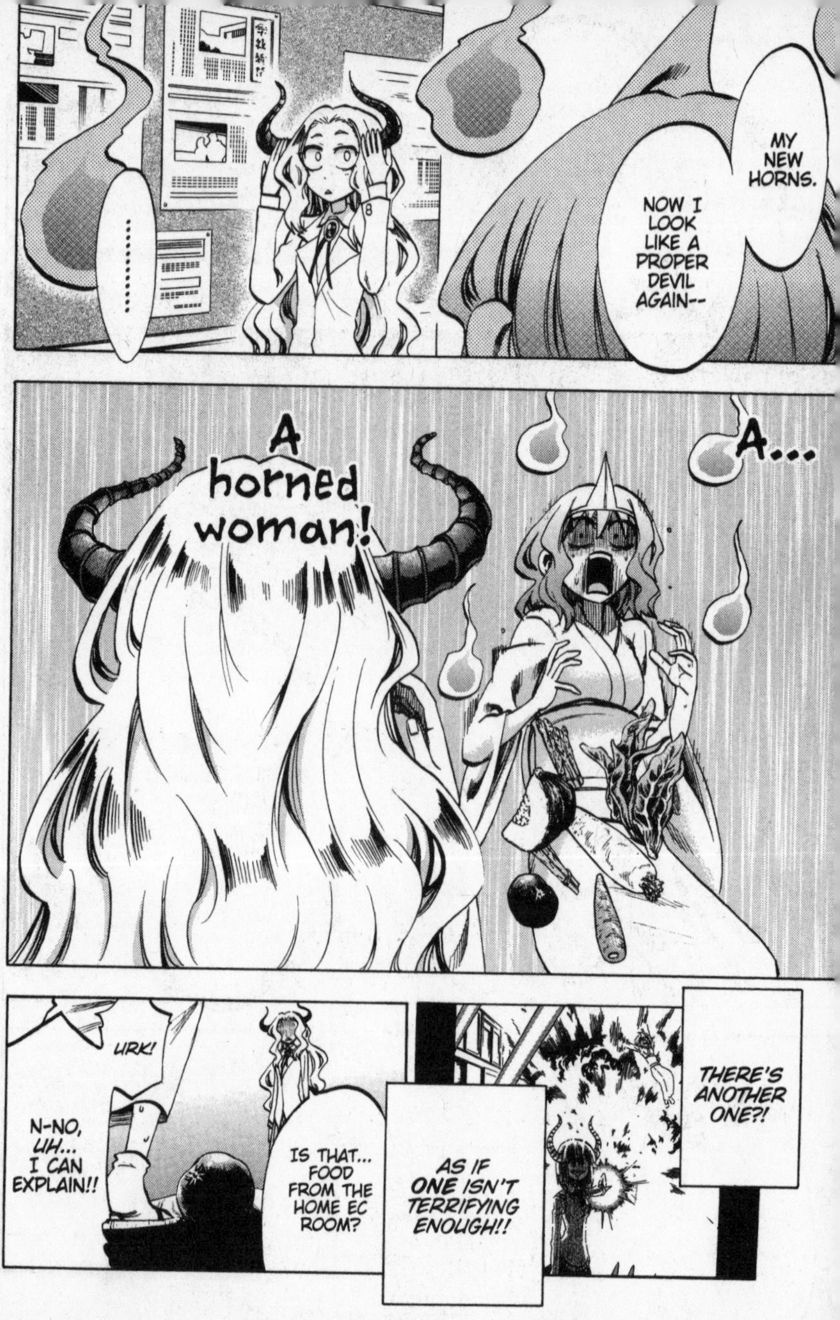
MY NEW HORNS.
NOW I LOOK LIKE A PROPER DEVIL AGAIN--
......
A...
A horned woman!
THERE'S ANOTHER ONE?!
AS IF ONE ISN'T TERRIFYING ENOUGH!!
IS THAT... FOOD FROM THE HOME EC ROOM?
URK!
N-NO, UH... I CAN EXPLAIN!!

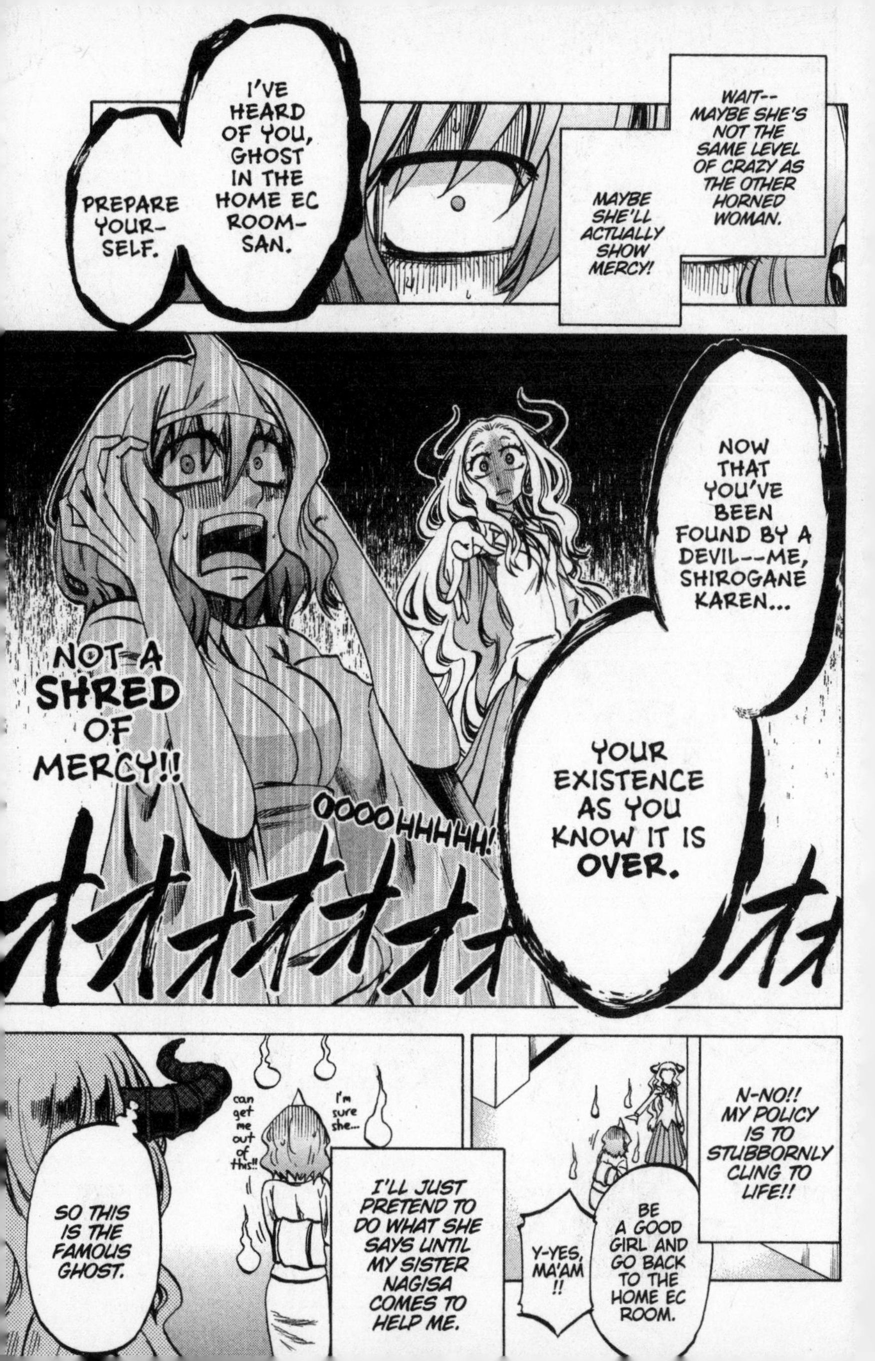
WAIT-- MAYBE SHE'S NOT THE SAME LEVEL OF CRAZY AS THE OTHER HORNED WOMAN.
MAYBE SHE'LL ACTUALLY SHOW MERCY!
I'VE HEARD OF YOU, GHOST IN THE HOME EC ROOM-SAN.
PREPARE YOURSELF.
NOW THAT YOU'VE BEEN FOUND BY A DEVIL--ME, SHIROGANE KAREN...
YOUR EXISTENCE AS YOU KNOW IT IS **OVER.**
OOOOHHHHH!
NOT A **SHRED** OF MERCY!!
N-NO!! MY POLICY IS TO STUBBORNLY CLING TO LIFE!!
BE A GOOD GIRL AND GO BACK TO THE HOME EC ROOM.
Y-YES, MA'AM!!
I'LL JUST PRETEND TO DO WHAT SHE SAYS UNTIL MY SISTER NAGISA COMES TO HELP ME.
I'm sure she...
can get me out of this!!
SO THIS IS THE FAMOUS GHOST.

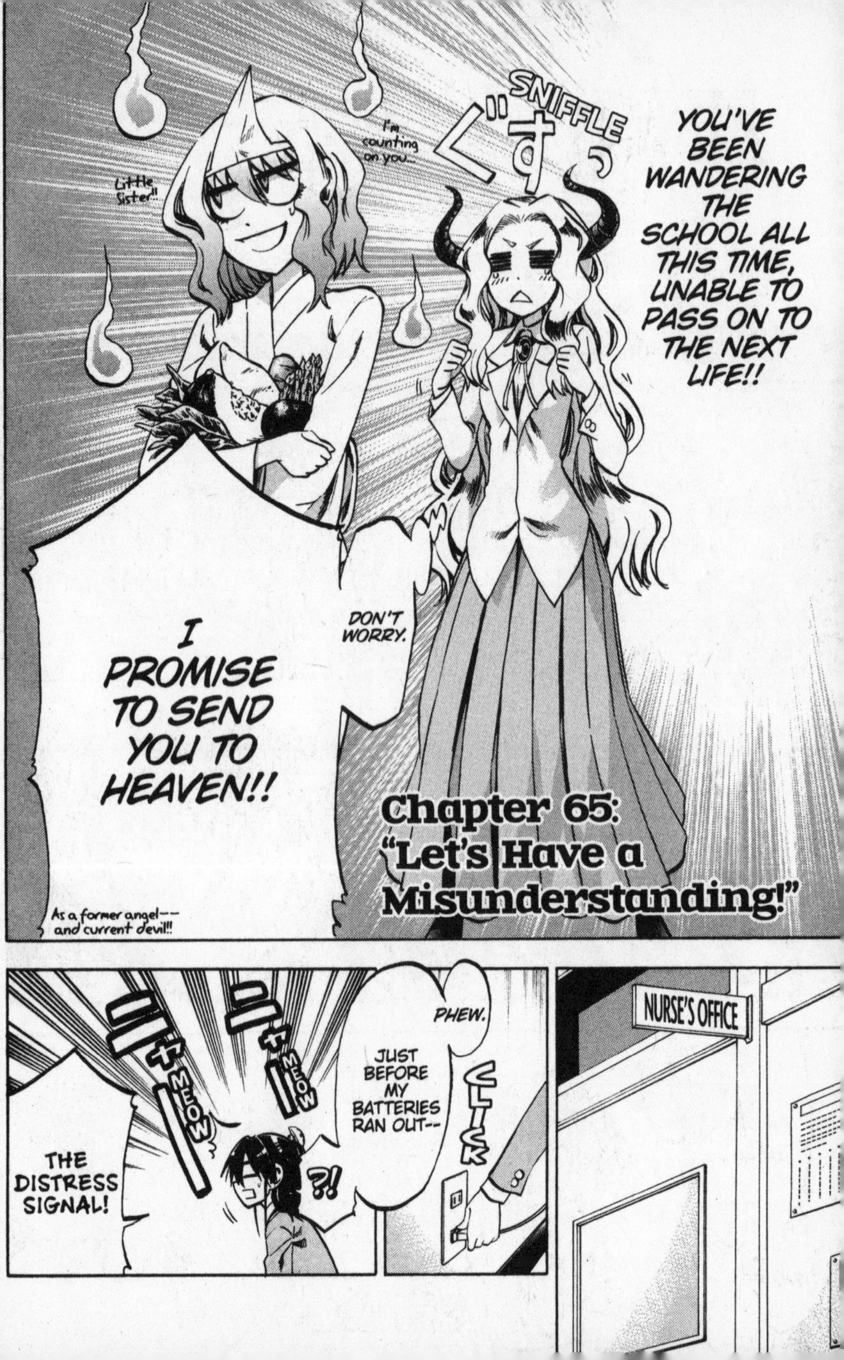

ぐすっ
SNIFFLE
YOU'VE BEEN WANDERING THE SCHOOL ALL THIS TIME, UNABLE TO PASS ON TO THE NEXT LIFE!!
I'm counting on you...
Little Sister!!
DON'T WORRY.
I PROMISE TO SEND YOU TO HEAVEN!!
Chapter 65: "Let's Have a Misunderstanding!"
As a former angel-- and current devil!!
NURSE'S OFFICE
PHEW.
JUST BEFORE MY BATTERIES RAN OUT--
CLICK
MEOW
MEOW
THE DISTRESS SIGNAL!
?!

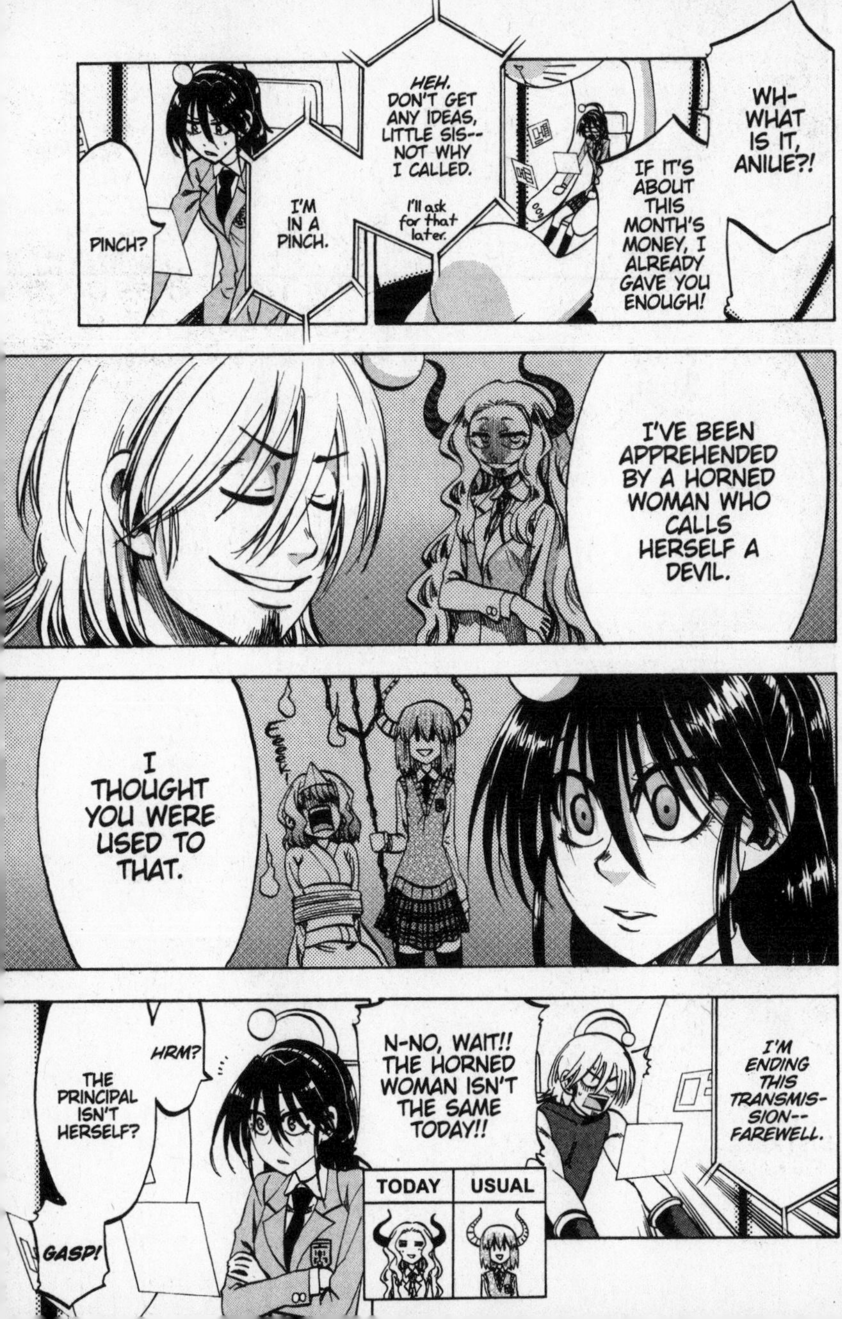
WH-WHAT IS IT, ANIUE?!
IF IT'S ABOUT THIS MONTH'S MONEY, I ALREADY GAVE YOU ENOUGH!
HEH. DON'T GET ANY IDEAS, LITTLE SIS-- NOT WHY I CALLED.
I'll ask for that later.
I'M IN A PINCH.
PINCH?
I'VE BEEN APPREHENDED BY A HORNED WOMAN WHO CALLS HERSELF A DEVIL.
I THOUGHT YOU WERE USED TO THAT.
I'M ENDING THIS TRANSMIS-SION--FAREWELL.
N-NO, WAIT!! THE HORNED WOMAN ISN'T THE SAME TODAY!!
TODAY
USUAL
HRM?
THE PRINCIPAL ISN'T HERSELF?
GASP!

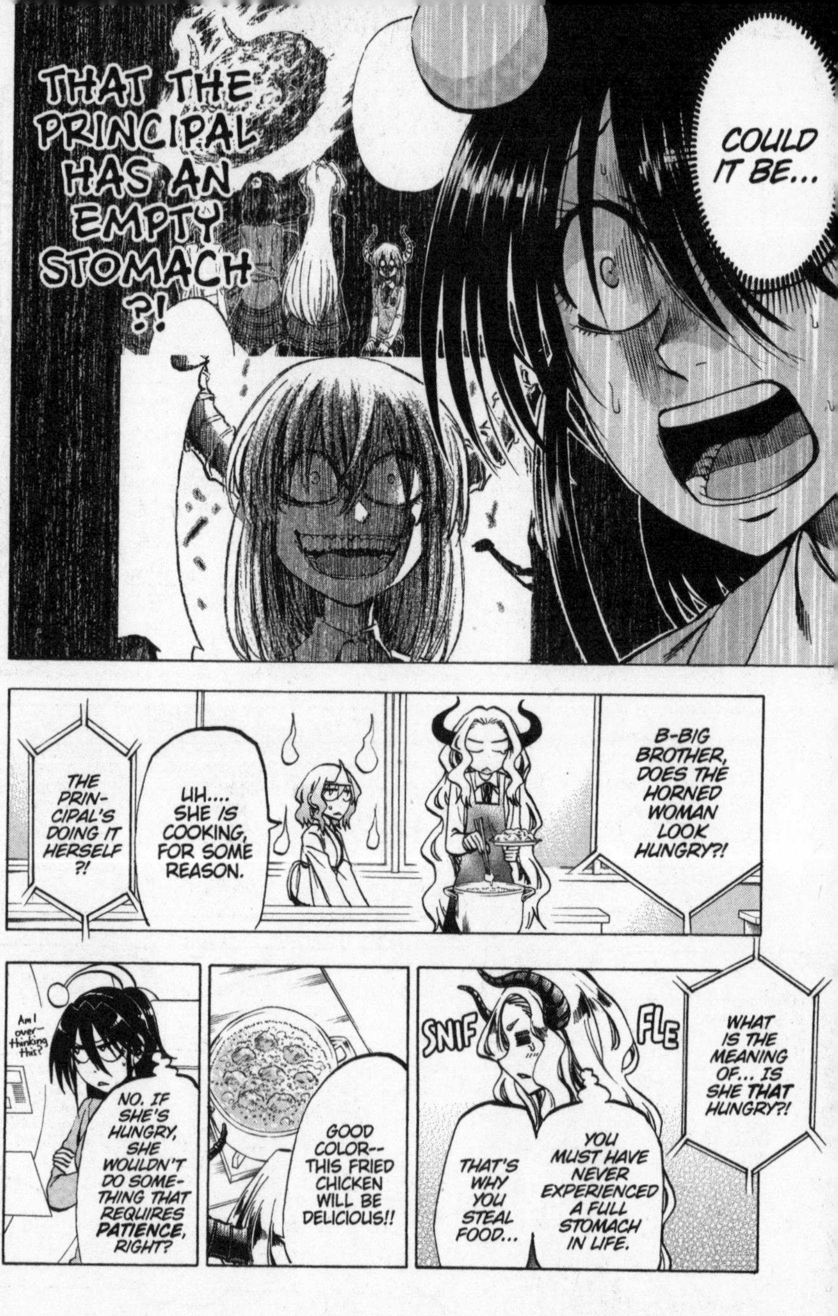
COULD IT BE...
THAT THE PRINCIPAL HAS AN EMPTY STOMACH ?!
B-BIG BROTHER, DOES THE HORNED WOMAN LOOK HUNGRY?!
UH.... SHE IS COOKING, FOR SOME REASON.
THE PRINCIPAL'S DOING IT HERSELF ?!
WHAT IS THE MEANING OF... IS SHE THAT HUNGRY?!
SNIF FLE
YOU MUST HAVE NEVER EXPERIENCED A FULL STOMACH IN LIFE.
THAT'S WHY YOU STEAL FOOD...
GOOD COLOR-- THIS FRIED CHICKEN WILL BE DELICIOUS!!
Am I over-thinking this?
NO. IF SHE'S HUNGRY, SHE WOULDN'T DO SOME-THING THAT REQUIRES PATIENCE, RIGHT?

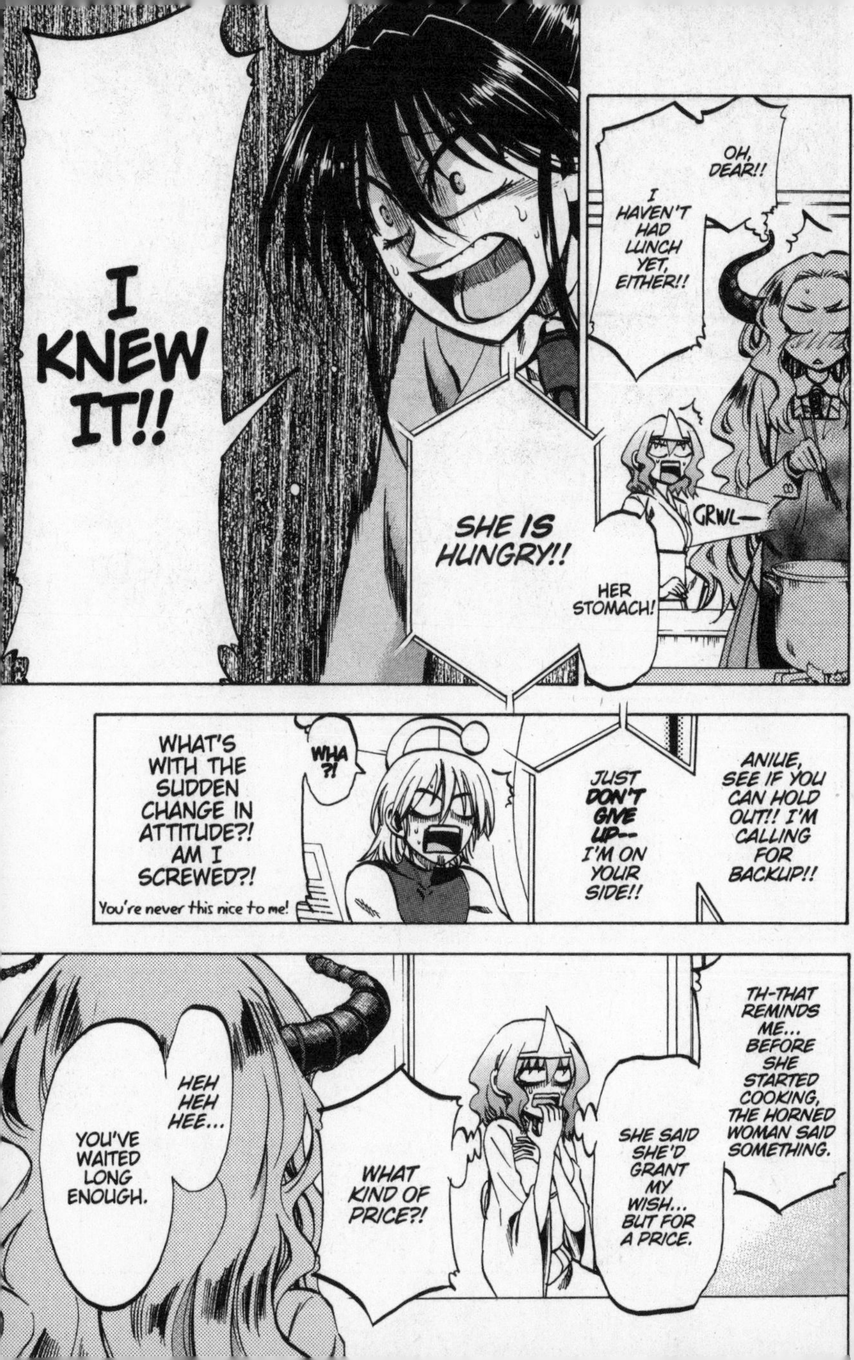
OH, DEAR!!
I HAVEN'T HAD LUNCH YET, EITHER!!
GRWL—
SHE IS HUNGRY!!
HER STOMACH!
I KNEW IT!!
ANIUE, SEE IF YOU CAN HOLD OUT!! I'M CALLING FOR BACKUP!!
JUST DON'T GIVE UP-- I'M ON YOUR SIDE!!
WHA ?!
WHAT'S WITH THE SUDDEN CHANGE IN ATTITUDE?! AM I SCREWED?!
You're never this nice to me!
TH-THAT REMINDS ME... BEFORE SHE STARTED COOKING, THE HORNED WOMAN SAID SOMETHING.
SHE SAID SHE'D GRANT MY WISH... BUT FOR A PRICE.
WHAT KIND OF PRICE?!
HEH HEH HEE...
YOU'VE WAITED LONG ENOUGH.

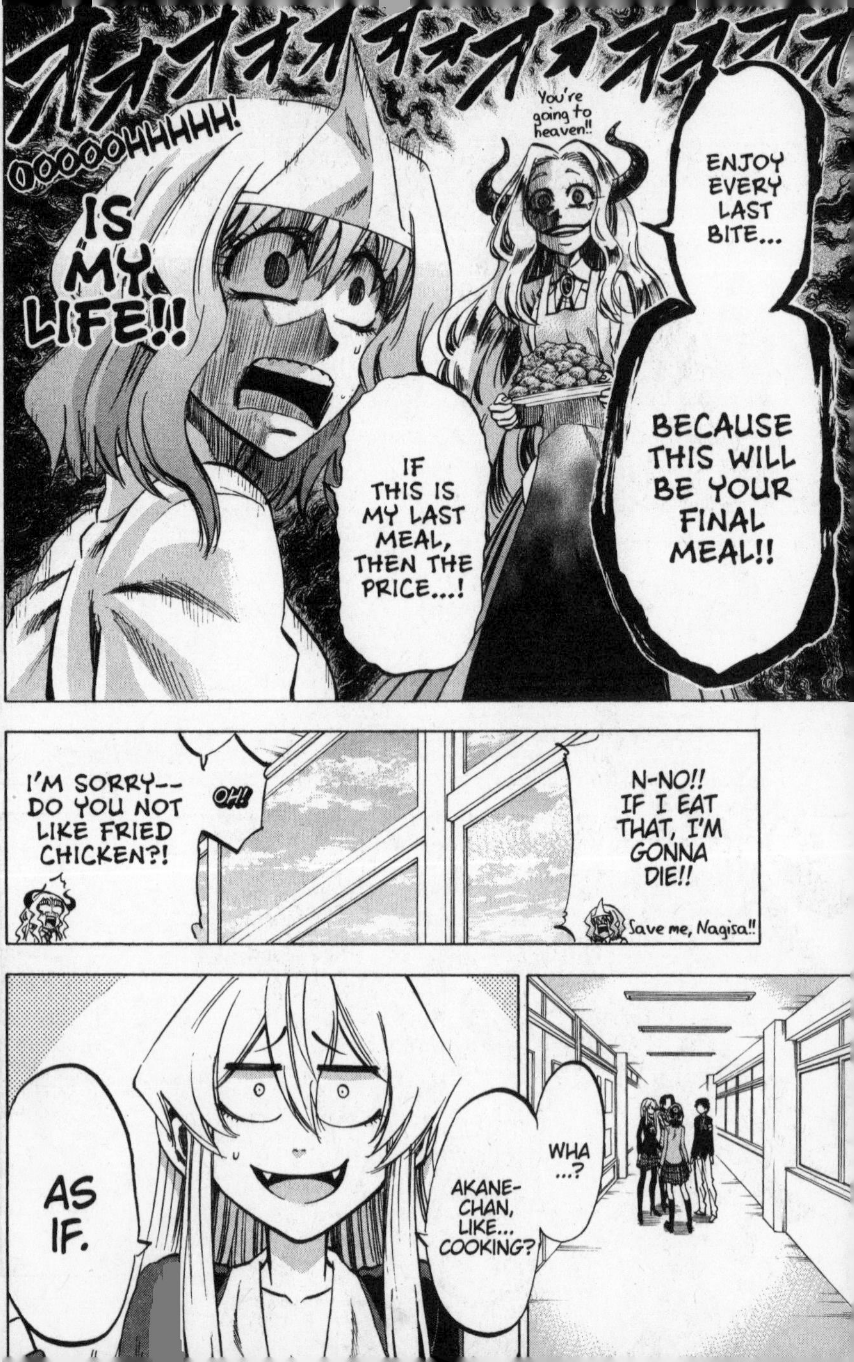
ENJOY EVERY LAST BITE...
BECAUSE THIS WILL BE YOUR FINAL MEAL!!
You're going to heaven!!
IF THIS IS MY LAST MEAL, THEN THE PRICE...!
IS MY LIFE!!
OOOOOHHHHH!
N-NO!! IF I EAT THAT, I'M GONNA DIE!!
Save me, Nagisa!!
OH!
I'M SORRY-- DO YOU NOT LIKE FRIED CHICKEN?!
WHA ...?
AKANE-CHAN, LIKE... COOKING?
AS IF.

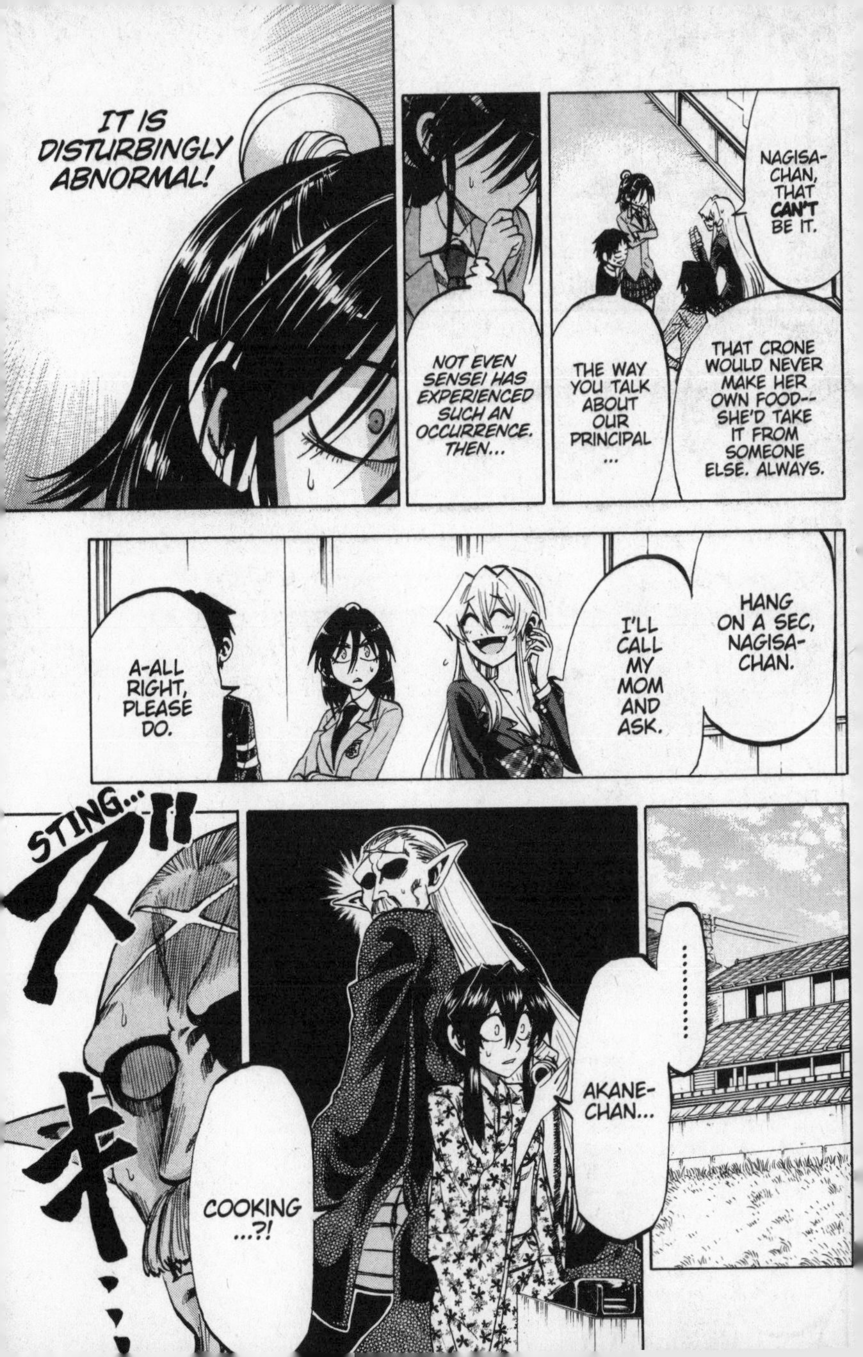
NAGISA-CHAN, THAT **CAN'T** BE IT.
THAT CRONE WOULD NEVER MAKE HER OWN FOOD--SHE'D TAKE IT FROM SOMEONE ELSE. ALWAYS.
THE WAY YOU TALK ABOUT OUR PRINCIPAL...
NOT EVEN SENSEI HAS EXPERIENCED SUCH AN OCCURRENCE. THEN...
IT IS DISTURBINGLY ABNORMAL!
HANG ON A SEC, NAGISA-CHAN.
I'LL CALL MY MOM AND ASK.
A-ALL RIGHT, PLEASE DO.
......
AKANE-CHAN...
COOKING...?!
STING...!!

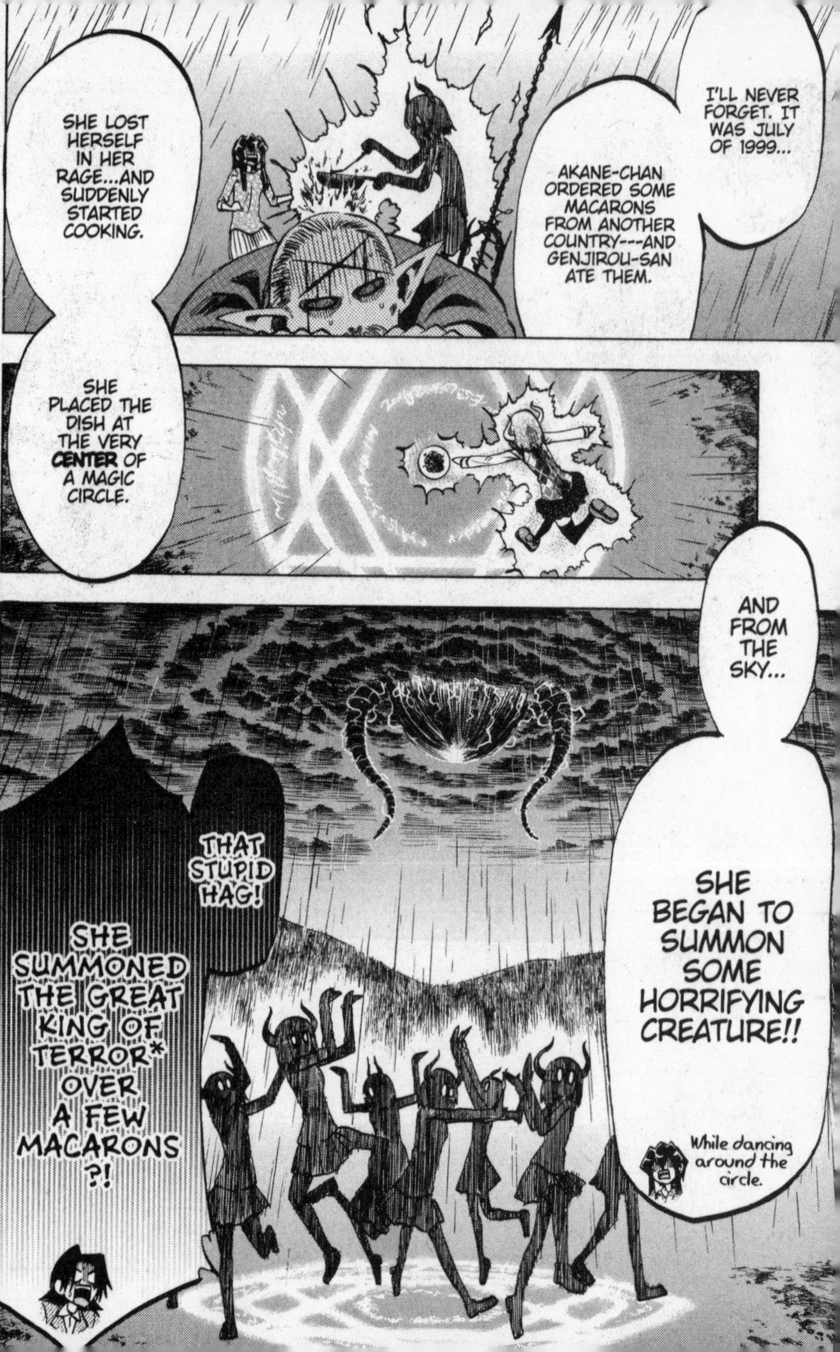
I'LL NEVER FORGET. IT WAS JULY OF 1999...
AKANE-CHAN ORDERED SOME MACARONS FROM ANOTHER COUNTRY---AND GENJIROU-SAN ATE THEM.
SHE LOST HERSELF IN HER RAGE...AND SUDDENLY STARTED COOKING.
SHE PLACED THE DISH AT THE VERY CENTER OF A MAGIC CIRCLE.
AND FROM THE SKY...
SHE BEGAN TO SUMMON SOME HORRIFYING CREATURE!!
While dancing around the circle.
THAT STUPID HAG!
SHE SUMMONED THE GREAT KING OF TERROR* OVER A FEW MACARONS ?!

...which stated that a great king of terror would come from the sky in the seventh month of 1999.

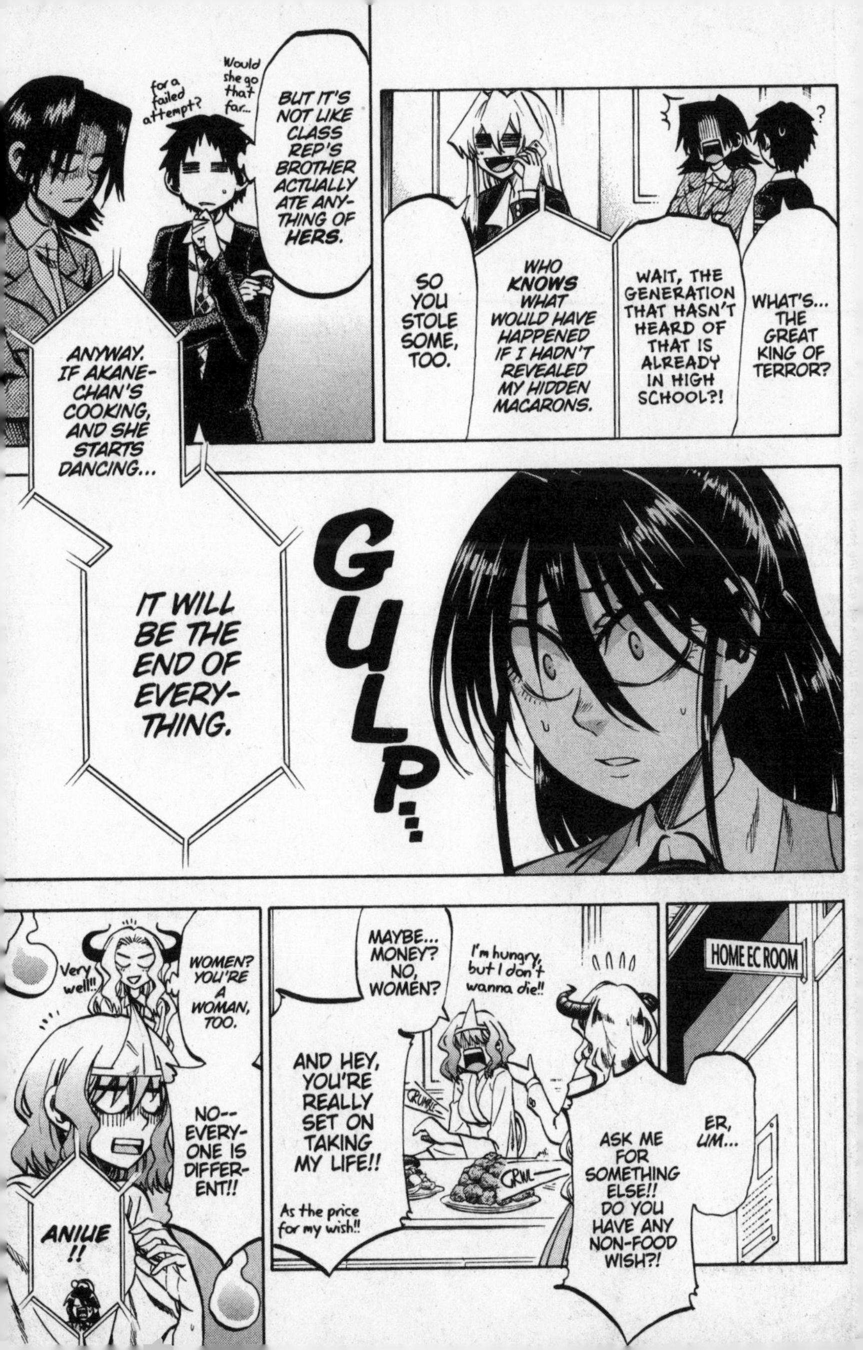
WHAT'S... THE GREAT KING OF TERROR?
WAIT, THE GENERATION THAT HASN'T HEARD OF THAT IS ALREADY IN HIGH SCHOOL?!
WHO KNOWS WHAT WOULD HAVE HAPPENED IF I HADN'T REVEALED MY HIDDEN MACARONS.
SO YOU STOLE SOME, TOO.
BUT IT'S NOT LIKE CLASS REP'S BROTHER ACTUALLY ATE ANYTHING OF HERS.
Would she go that far...
for a failed attempt?
ANYWAY. IF AKANE-CHAN'S COOKING, AND SHE STARTS DANCING...
IT WILL BE THE END OF EVERYTHING.
GULP...
HOME EC ROOM
ER, UM...
ASK ME FOR SOMETHING ELSE!! DO YOU HAVE ANY NON-FOOD WISH?!
I'm hungry, but I don't wanna die!!
MAYBE... MONEY? NO, WOMEN?
GRUMBLE
GRWL
AND HEY, YOU'RE REALLY SET ON TAKING MY LIFE!!
As the price for my wish!!
WOMEN? YOU'RE A WOMAN, TOO.
Very well!!
NO-- EVERYONE IS DIFFERENT!!
ANIUE!!

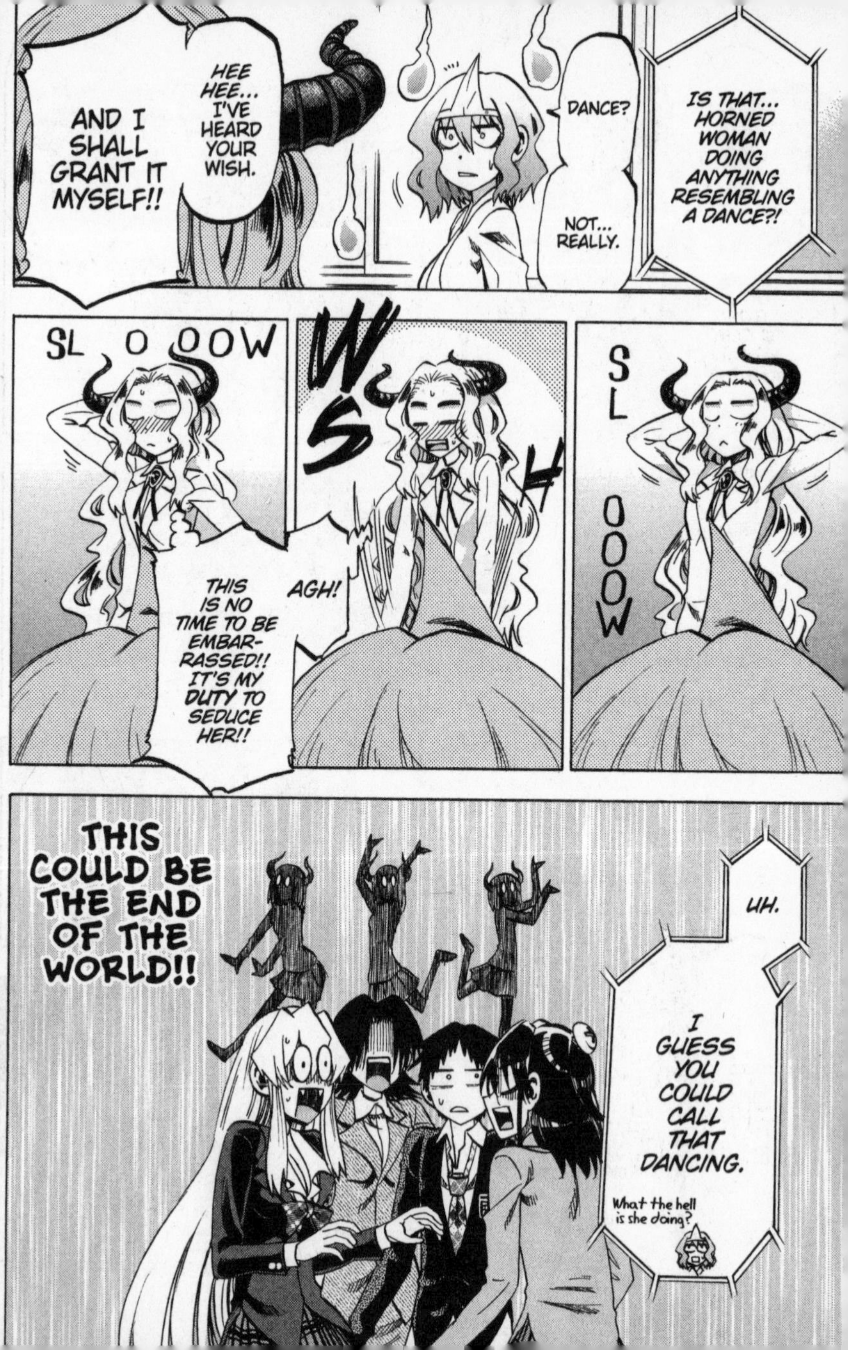

IS THAT... HORNED WOMAN DOING ANYTHING RESEMBLING A DANCE?!
DANCE?
NOT... REALLY.
HEE HEE... I'VE HEARD YOUR WISH.
AND I SHALL GRANT IT MYSELF!!
SLOOOOW
WSH
AGH!
SL O OOW
THIS IS NO TIME TO BE EMBARRASSED!! IT'S MY DUTY TO SEDUCE HER!!
UH.
I GUESS YOU COULD CALL THAT DANCING.
What the hell is she doing?
THIS COULD BE THE END OF THE WORLD!!

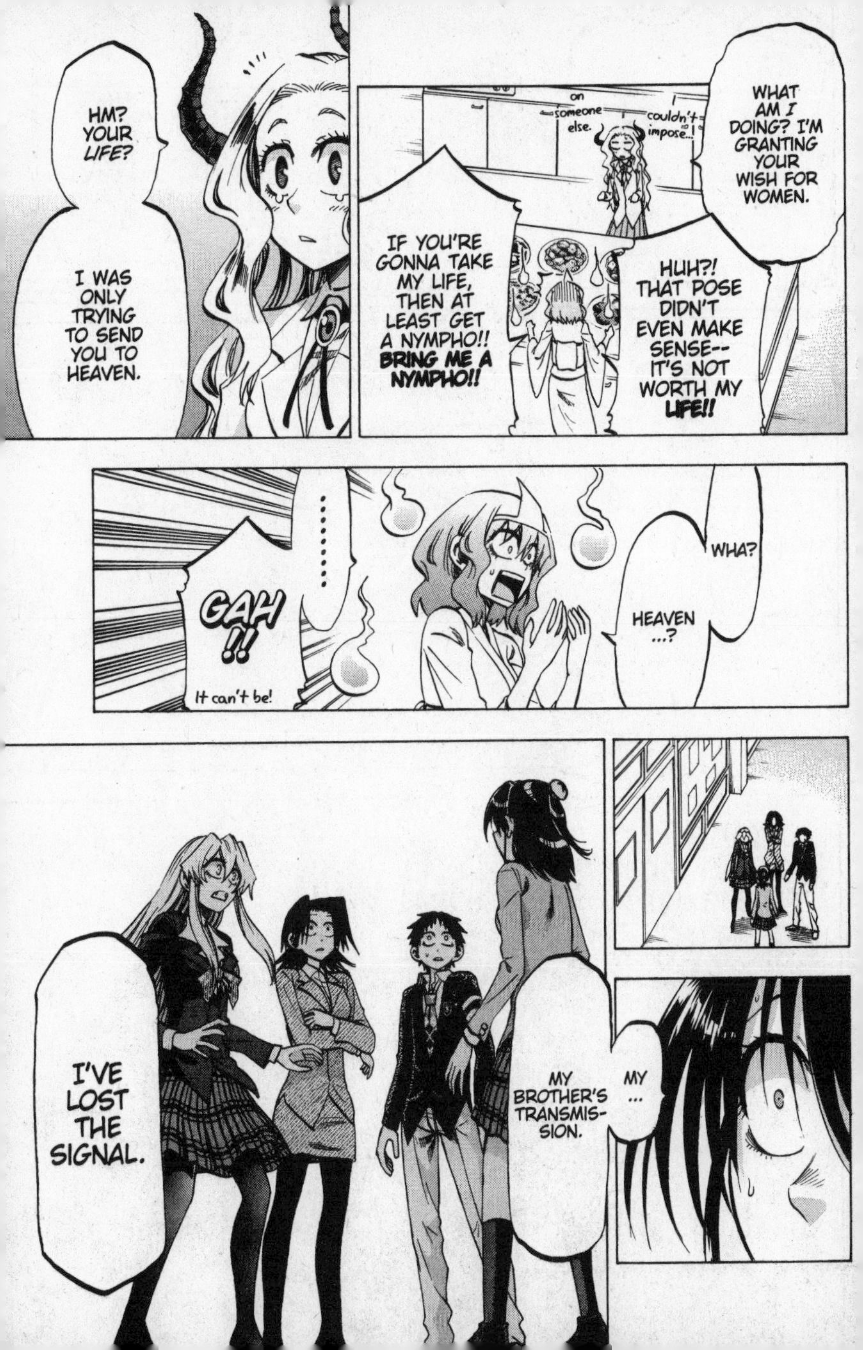
WHAT AM I DOING? I'M GRANTING YOUR WISH FOR WOMEN.
I couldn't impose... on someone else.
HUH?! THAT POSE DIDN'T EVEN MAKE SENSE-- IT'S NOT WORTH MY LIFE!!
IF YOU'RE GONNA TAKE MY LIFE, THEN AT LEAST GET A NYMPHO!! BRING ME A NYMPHO!!
HM? YOUR LIFE?
I WAS ONLY TRYING TO SEND YOU TO HEAVEN.
WHA?
HEAVEN ...?
......
GAH !!
It can't be!
MY ...
MY BROTHER'S TRANSMISSION.
I'VE LOST THE SIGNAL.

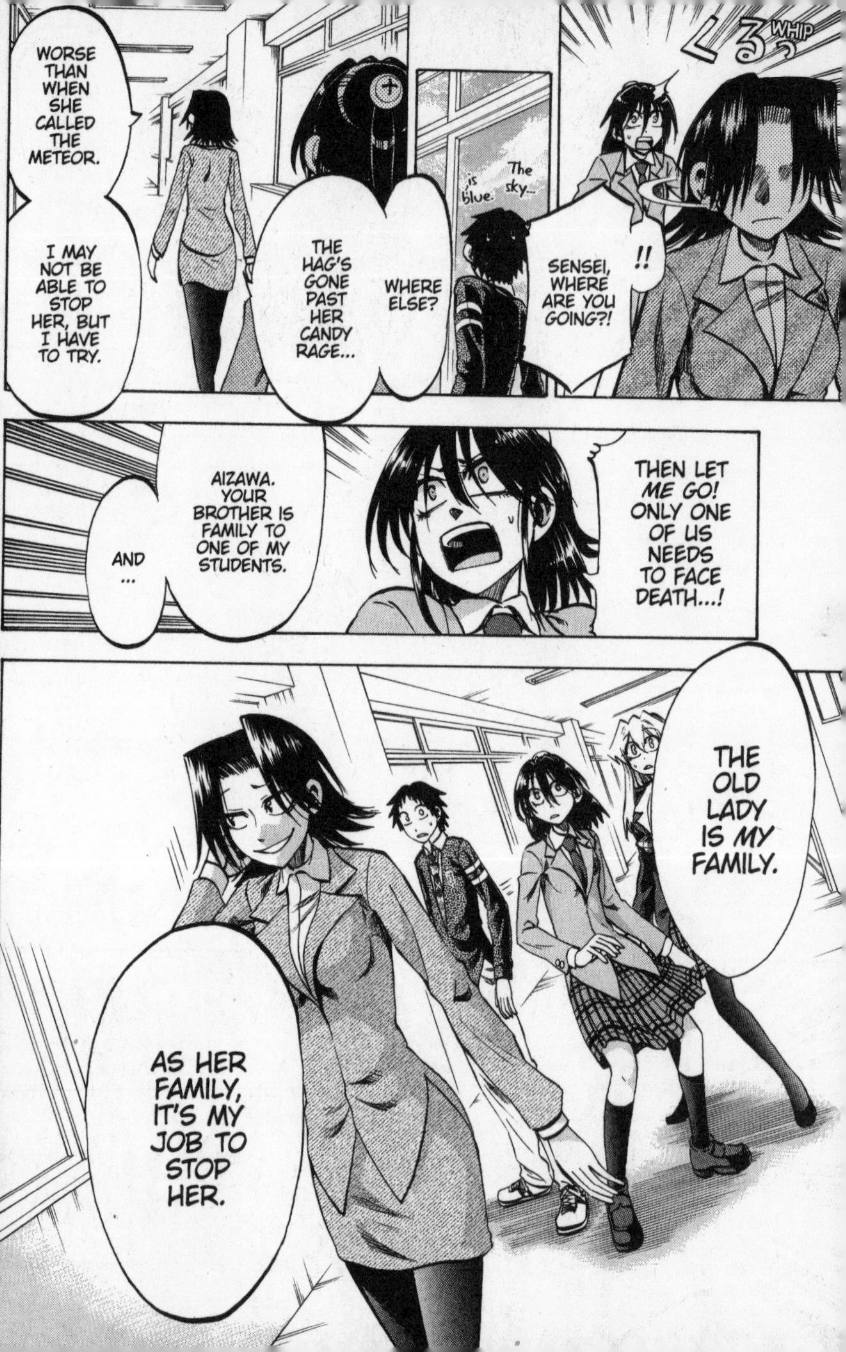
くるっ WHIP
!!
SENSEI, WHERE ARE YOU GOING?!
The sky... is blue.
WHERE ELSE?
THE HAG'S GONE PAST HER CANDY RAGE...
WORSE THAN WHEN SHE CALLED THE METEOR.
I MAY NOT BE ABLE TO STOP HER, BUT I HAVE TO TRY.
THEN LET *ME GO!* ONLY ONE OF US NEEDS TO FACE DEATH...!
AIZAWA. YOUR BROTHER IS FAMILY TO ONE OF MY STUDENTS.
AND ...
THE OLD LADY IS *MY* FAMILY.
AS HER FAMILY, IT'S MY JOB TO STOP HER.

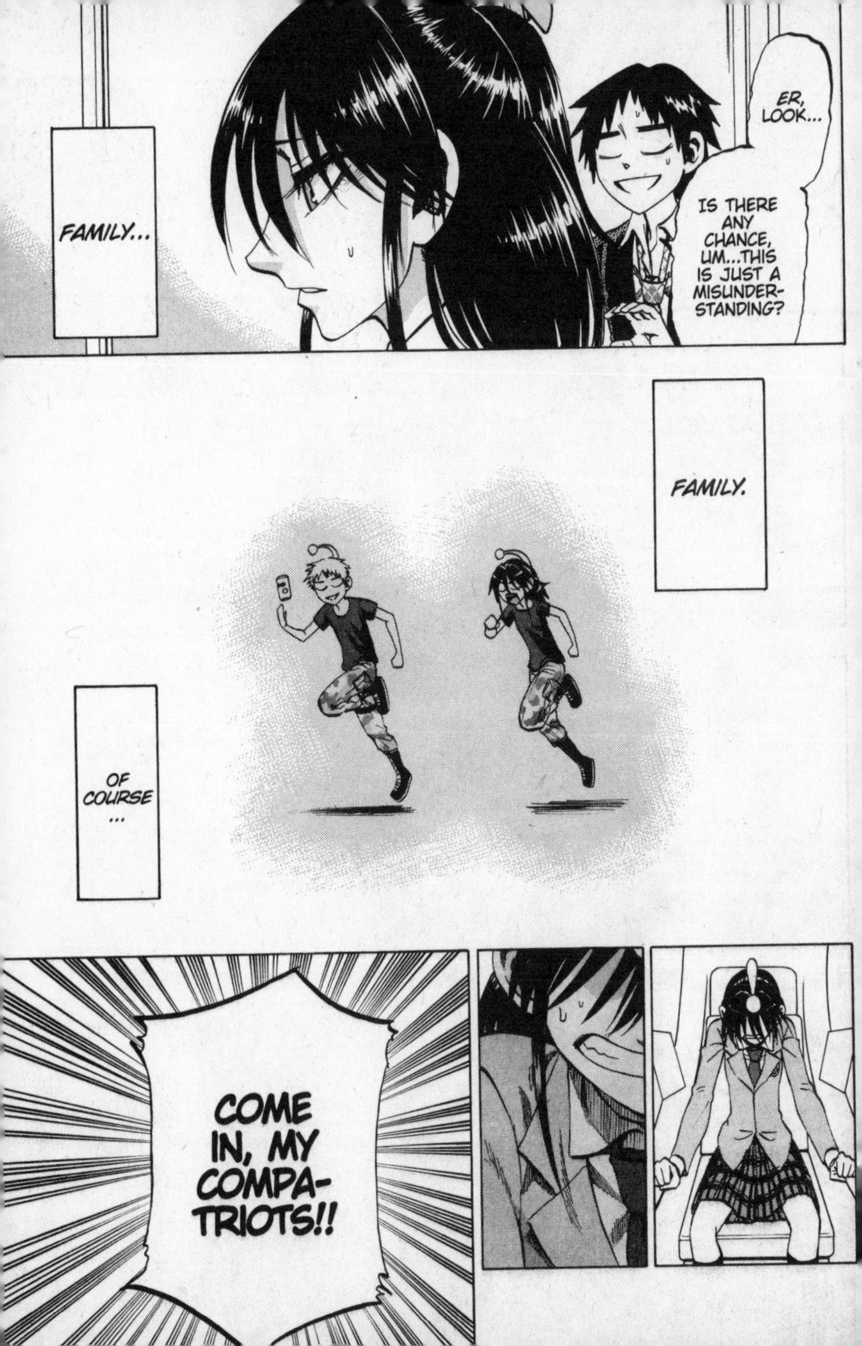
ER, LOOK...
IS THERE ANY CHANCE, UM...THIS IS JUST A MISUNDERSTANDING?
FAMILY...
FAMILY.
OF COURSE ...
COME IN, MY COMPATRIOTS!!

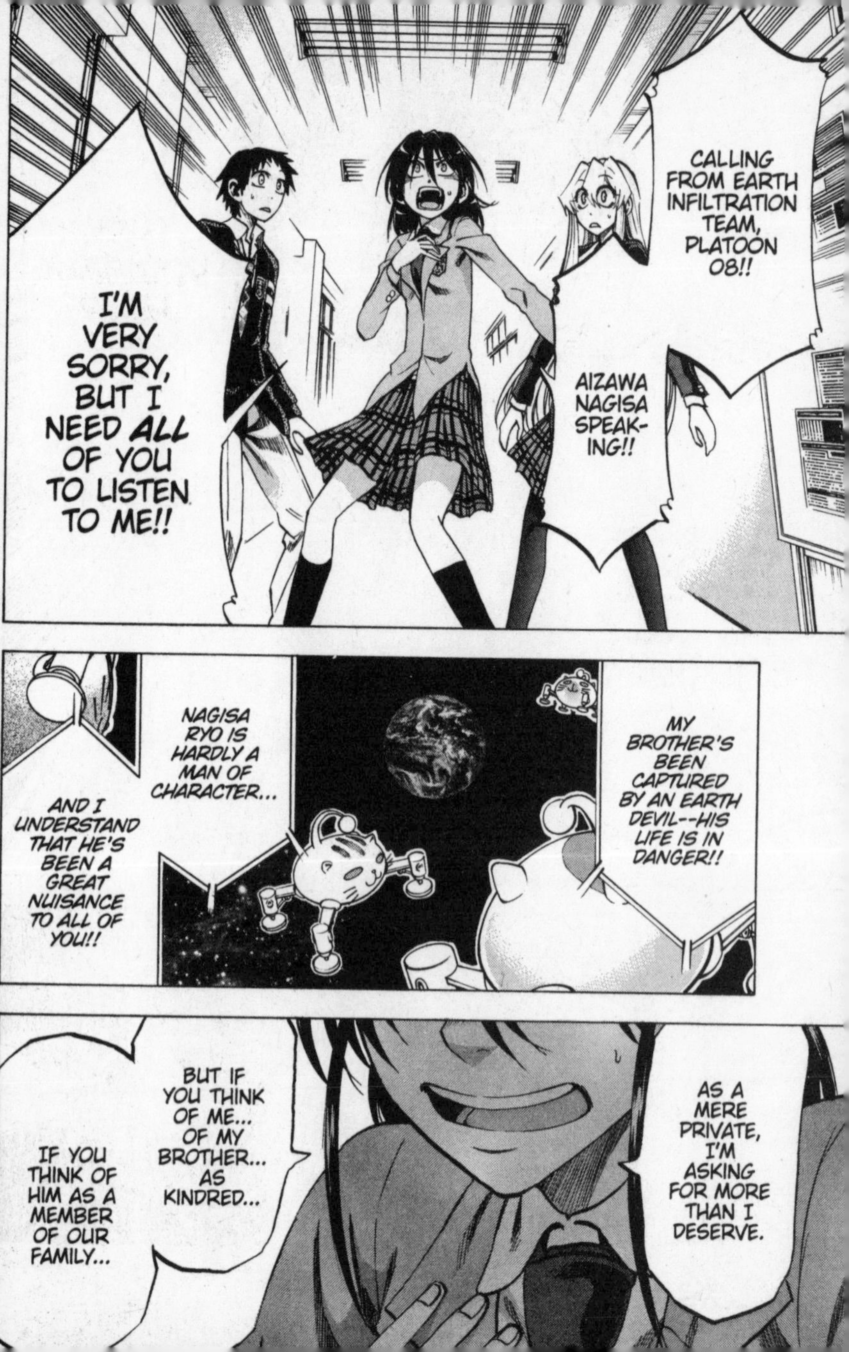
CALLING FROM EARTH INFILTRATION TEAM, PLATOON 08!!
AIZAWA NAGISA SPEAKING!!
I'M VERY SORRY, BUT I NEED ALL OF YOU TO LISTEN TO ME!!
MY BROTHER'S BEEN CAPTURED BY AN EARTH DEVIL--HIS LIFE IS IN DANGER!!
NAGISA RYO IS HARDLY A MAN OF CHARACTER...
AND I UNDERSTAND THAT HE'S BEEN A GREAT NUISANCE TO ALL OF YOU!!
AS A MERE PRIVATE, I'M ASKING FOR MORE THAN I DESERVE.
BUT IF YOU THINK OF ME... OF MY BROTHER... AS KINDRED...
IF YOU THINK OF HIM AS A MEMBER OF OUR FAMILY...

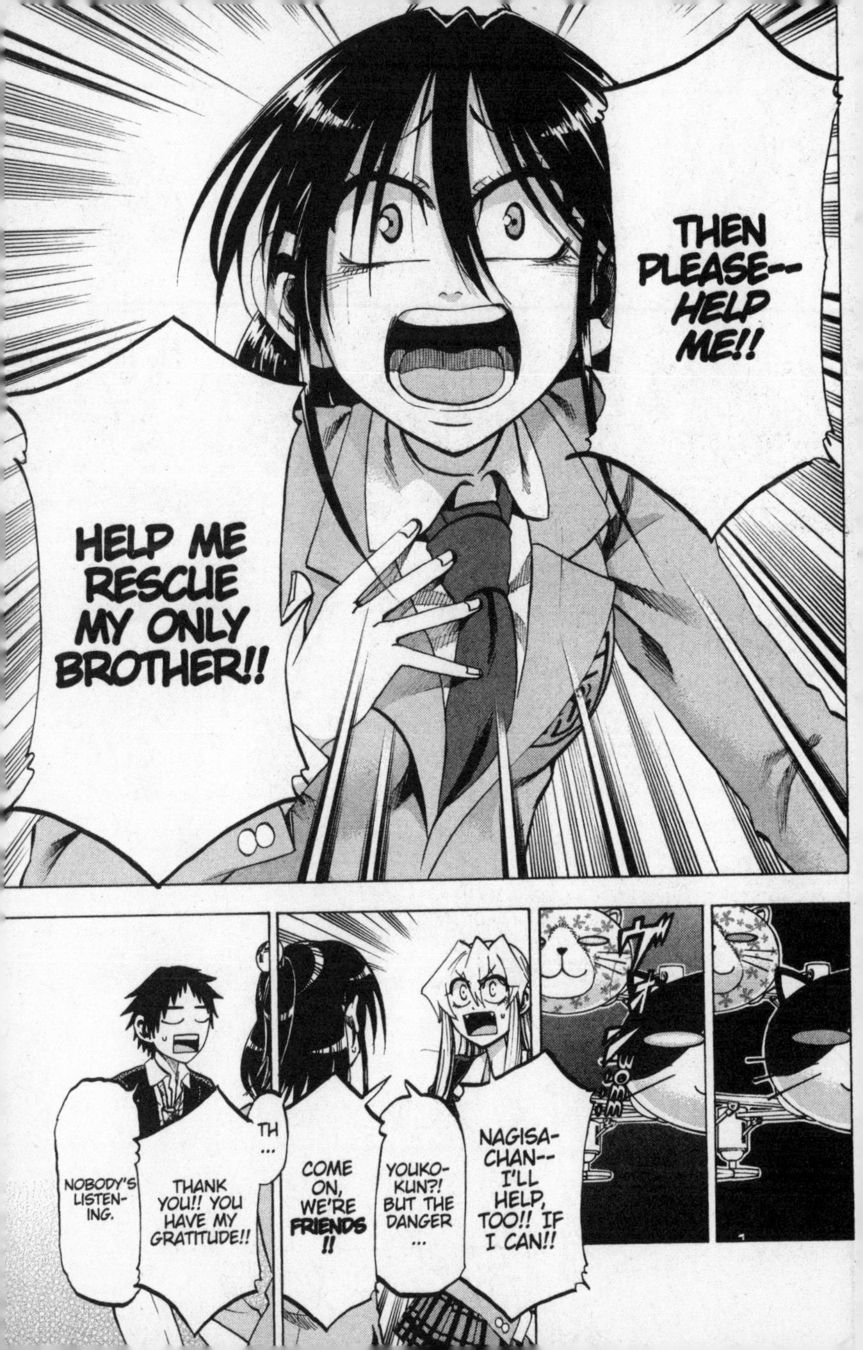
THEN PLEASE-- HELP ME!!
HELP ME RESCUE MY ONLY BROTHER!!
NAGISA-CHAN-- I'LL HELP, TOO!! IF I CAN!!
YOUKO-KUN?! BUT THE DANGER ...
COME ON, WE'RE FRIENDS !!
TH ...
THANK YOU!! YOU HAVE MY GRATITUDE!!
NOBODY'S LISTEN-ING.

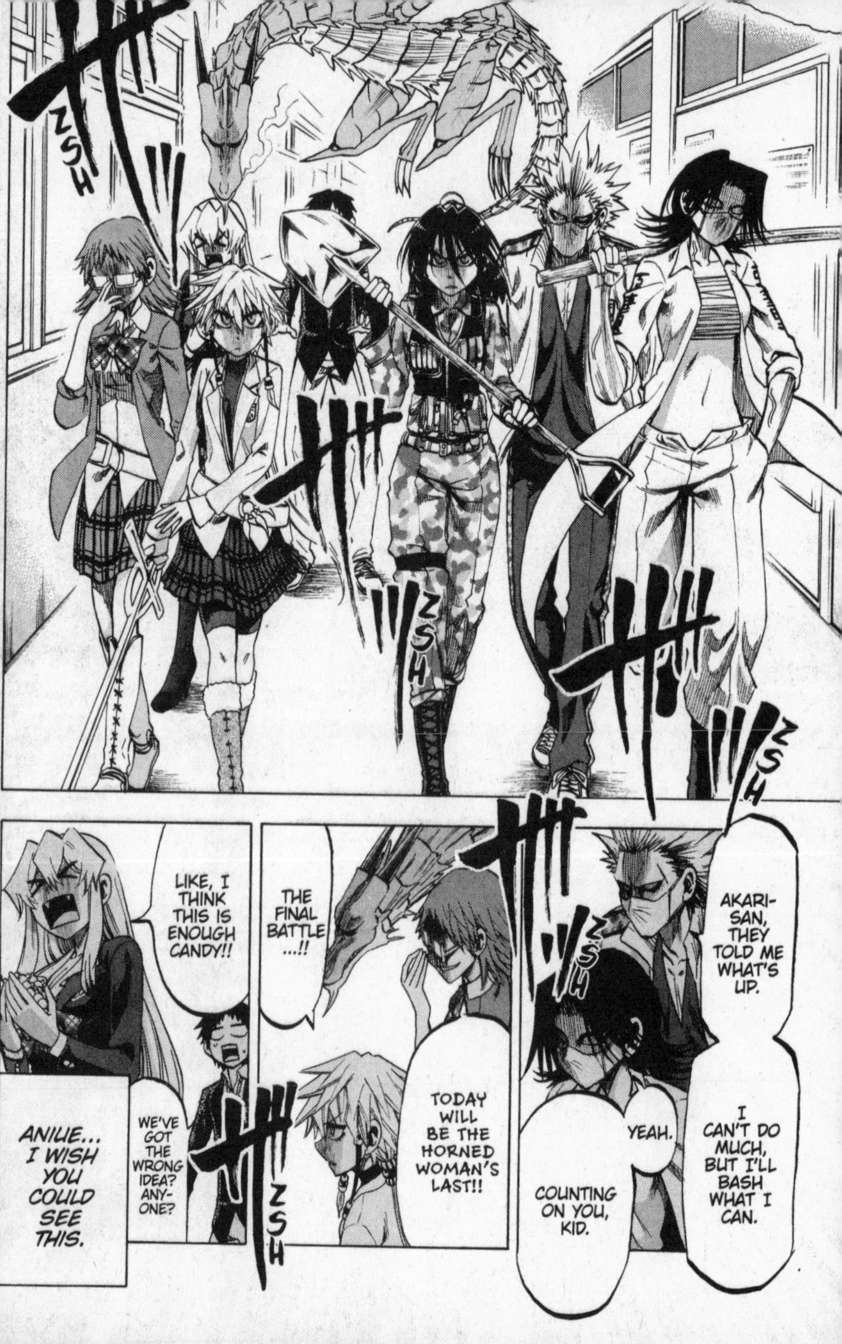
ZSH
ZSH
ZSH
ZSH
AKARI-SAN, THEY TOLD ME WHAT'S UP.
ZSH
I CAN'T DO MUCH, BUT I'LL BASH WHAT I CAN.
YEAH.
COUNTING ON YOU, KID.
THE FINAL BATTLE ...!!
TODAY WILL BE THE HORNED WOMAN'S LAST!!
ZSH
LIKE, I THINK THIS IS ENOUGH CANDY!!
WE'VE GOT THE WRONG IDEA? ANYONE?
ANIUE... I WISH YOU COULD SEE THIS.

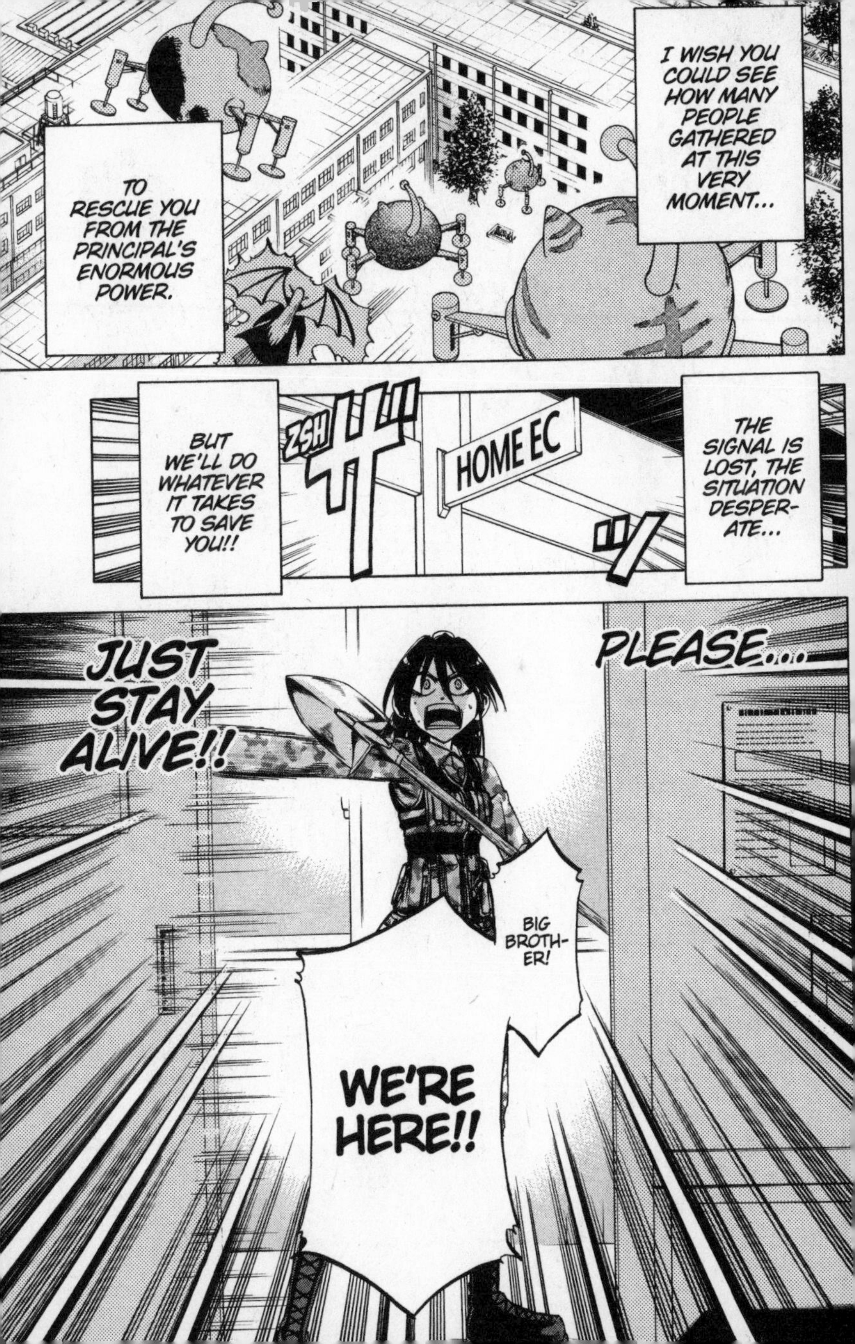
I WISH YOU COULD SEE HOW MANY PEOPLE GATHERED AT THIS VERY MOMENT...
TO RESCUE YOU FROM THE PRINCIPAL'S ENORMOUS POWER.
THE SIGNAL IS LOST, THE SITUATION DESPER-ATE...
HOME EC
ZSH
BUT WE'LL DO WHATEVER IT TAKES TO SAVE YOU!!
PLEASE...
JUST STAY ALIVE!!
BIG BROTH-ER!
WE'RE HERE!!

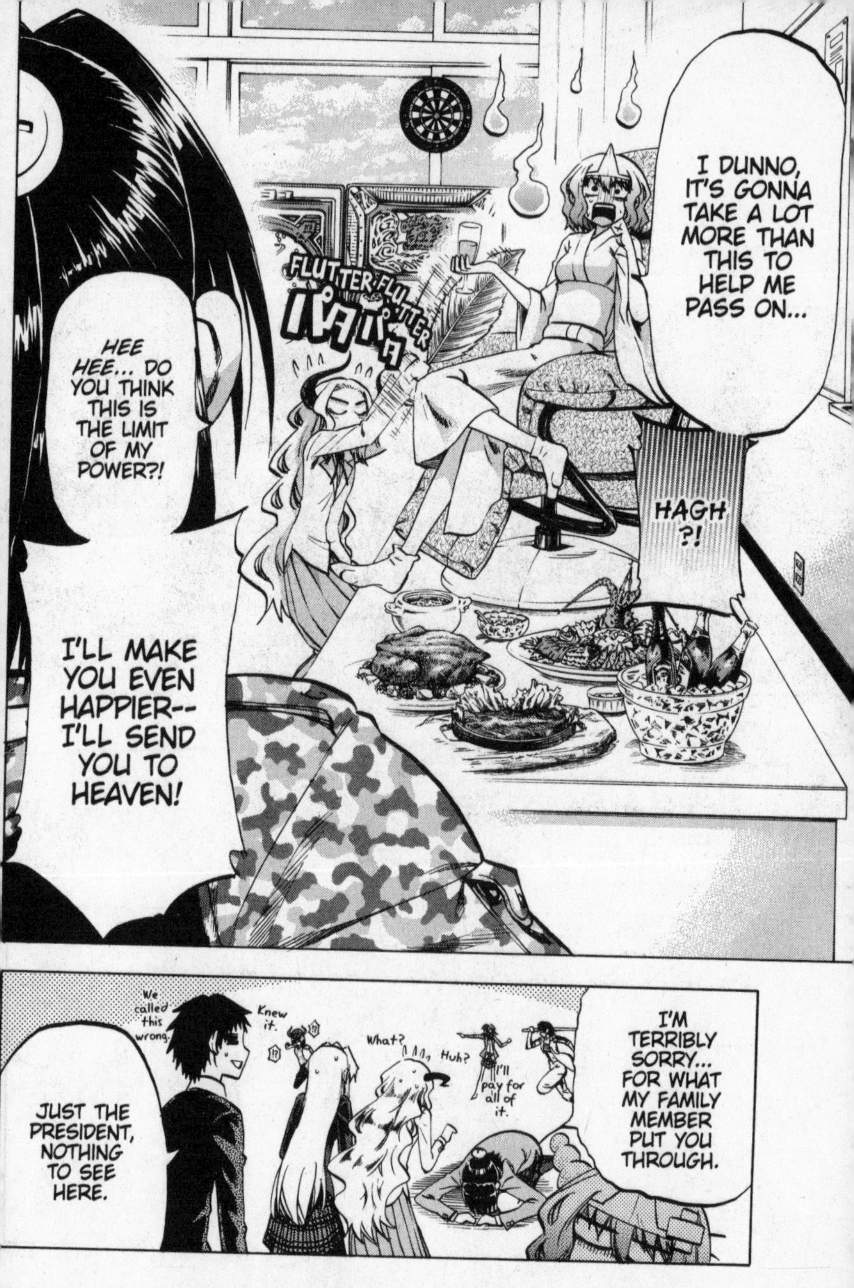
I DUNNO, IT'S GONNA TAKE A LOT MORE THAN THIS TO HELP ME PASS ON...
HAGH ?!
FLUTTER FLUTTER
パタパタ
HEE HEE... DO YOU THINK THIS IS THE LIMIT OF MY POWER?!
I'LL MAKE YOU EVEN HAPPIER-- I'LL SEND YOU TO HEAVEN!
I'M TERRIBLY SORRY... FOR WHAT MY FAMILY MEMBER PUT YOU THROUGH.
I'll pay for all of it.
Huh?
What?
Knew it.
We called this wrong.
JUST THE PRESIDENT, NOTHING TO SEE HERE.

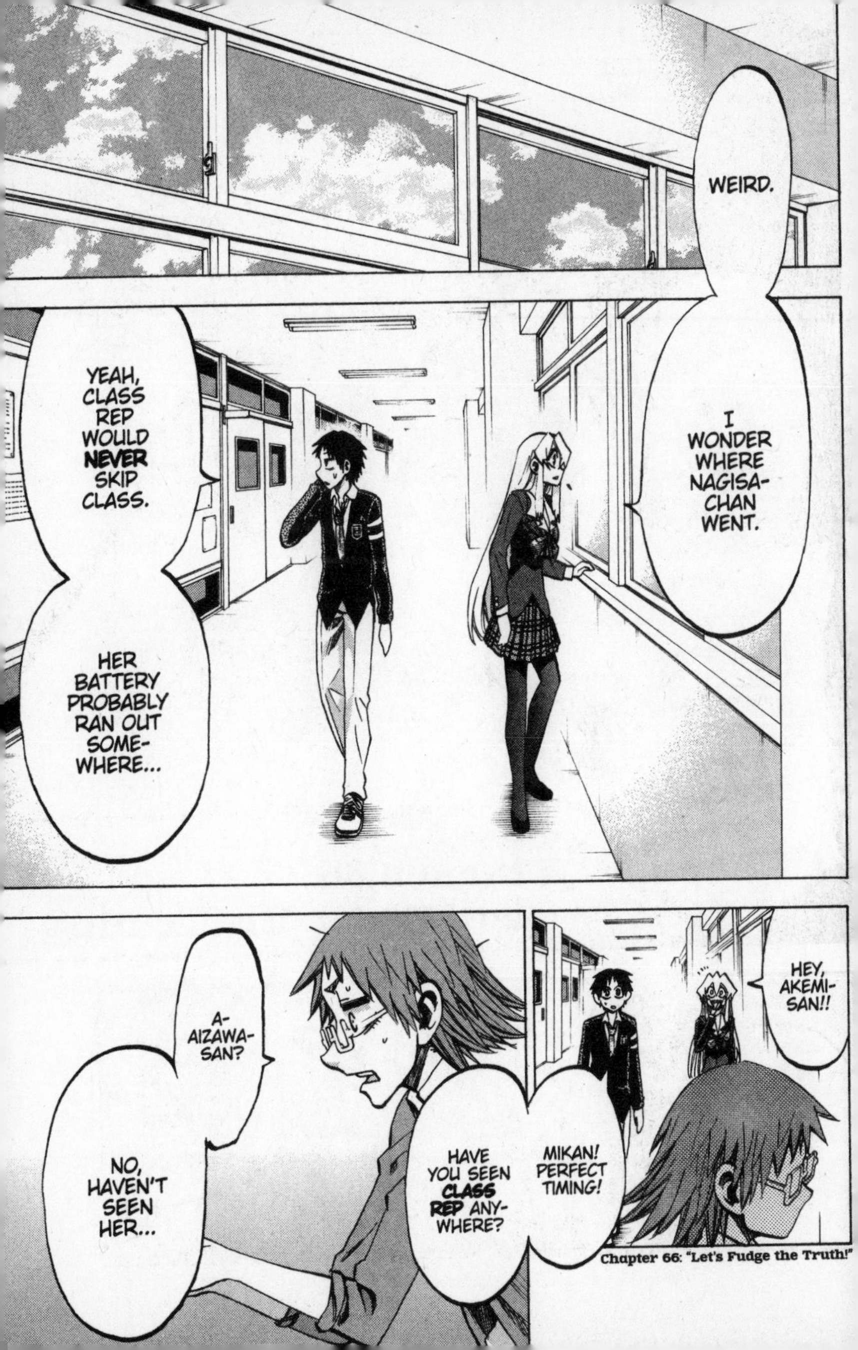
WEIRD.
I WONDER WHERE NAGISA-CHAN WENT.
YEAH, CLASS REP WOULD NEVER SKIP CLASS.
HER BATTERY PROBABLY RAN OUT SOME-WHERE...
HEY, AKEMI-SAN!!
MIKAN! PERFECT TIMING!
HAVE YOU SEEN CLASS REP ANY-WHERE?
A-AIZAWA-SAN?
NO, HAVEN'T SEEN HER...
Chapter 66: "Let's Fudge the Truth!"

Chapter 66: "Let's Fudge the Truth!"

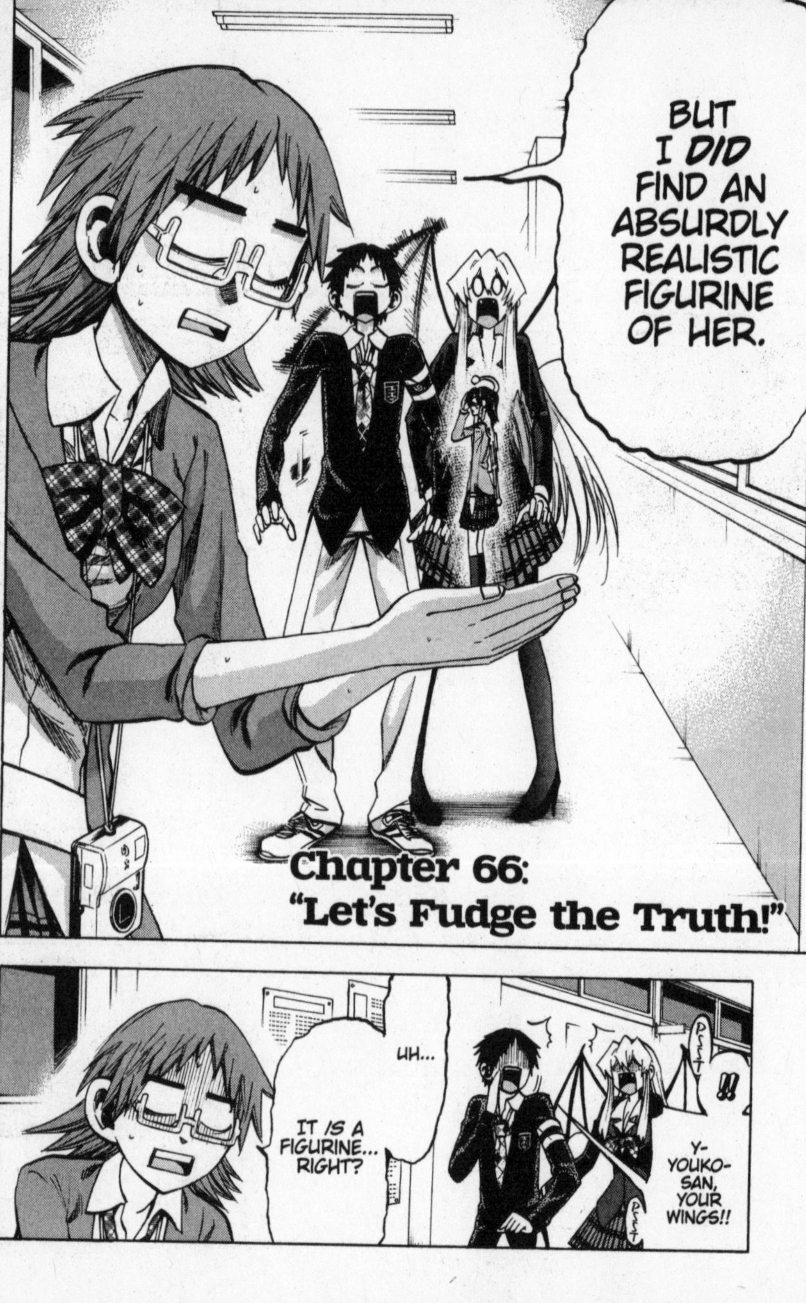

BUT I *DID* FIND AN ABSURDLY REALISTIC FIGURINE OF HER.
PSST
!!
Y-YOUKO-SAN, YOUR WINGS!!
PSST
UH...
IT *IS* A FIGURINE... RIGHT?

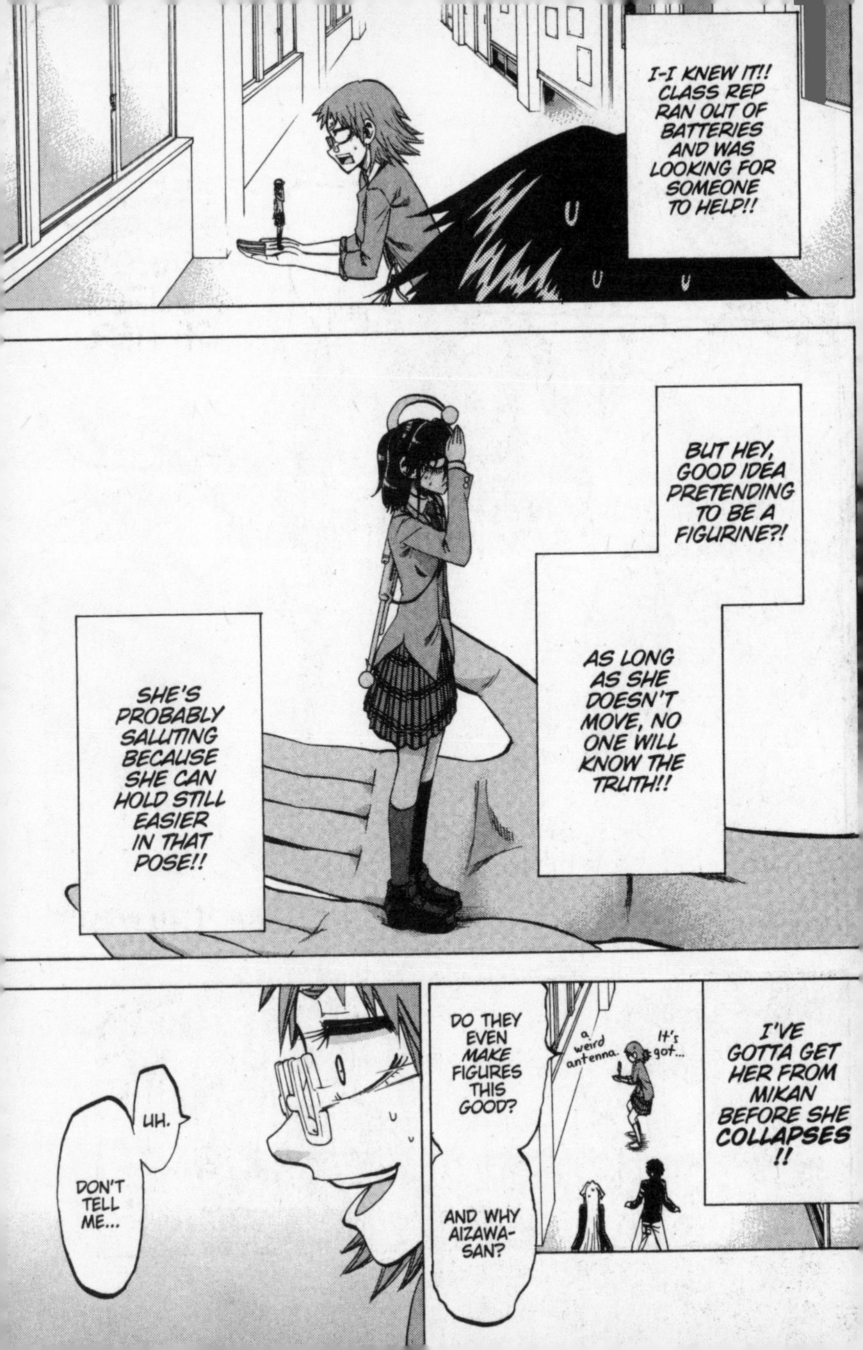
I-I KNEW IT!! CLASS REP RAN OUT OF BATTERIES AND WAS LOOKING FOR SOMEONE TO HELP!!
BUT HEY, GOOD IDEA PRETENDING TO BE A FIGURINE?!
AS LONG AS SHE DOESN'T MOVE, NO ONE WILL KNOW THE TRUTH!!
SHE'S PROBABLY SALUTING BECAUSE SHE CAN HOLD STILL EASIER IN THAT POSE!!
I'VE GOTTA GET HER FROM MIKAN BEFORE SHE COLLAPSES!!
It's got...
a weird antenna.
DO THEY EVEN MAKE FIGURES THIS GOOD?
AND WHY AIZAWA-SAN?
UH.
DON'T TELL ME...

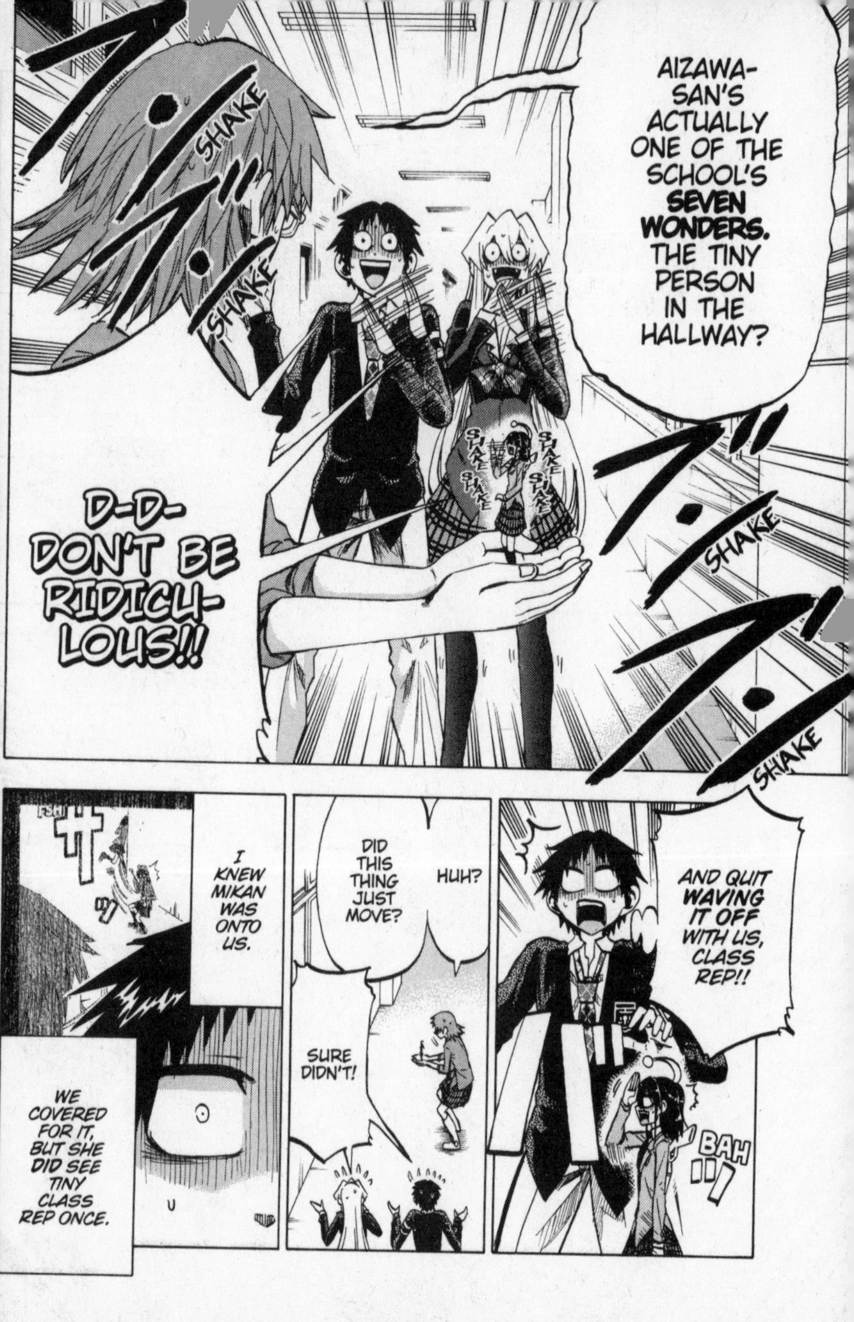
AIZAWA-SAN'S ACTUALLY ONE OF THE SCHOOL'S **SEVEN WONDERS.** THE TINY PERSON IN THE HALLWAY?
SHAKE
SHAKE
SHAKE SHAKE
SHAKE SHAKE
SHAKE
SHAKE
D-D-DON'T BE RIDICULOUS!!
AND QUIT **WAVING** IT OFF WITH US, CLASS REP!!
BAH
HUH?
DID THIS THING JUST MOVE?
SURE DIDN'T!
FSH
I KNEW MIKAN WAS ONTO US.
WE COVERED FOR IT, BUT SHE DID SEE TINY CLASS REP ONCE.

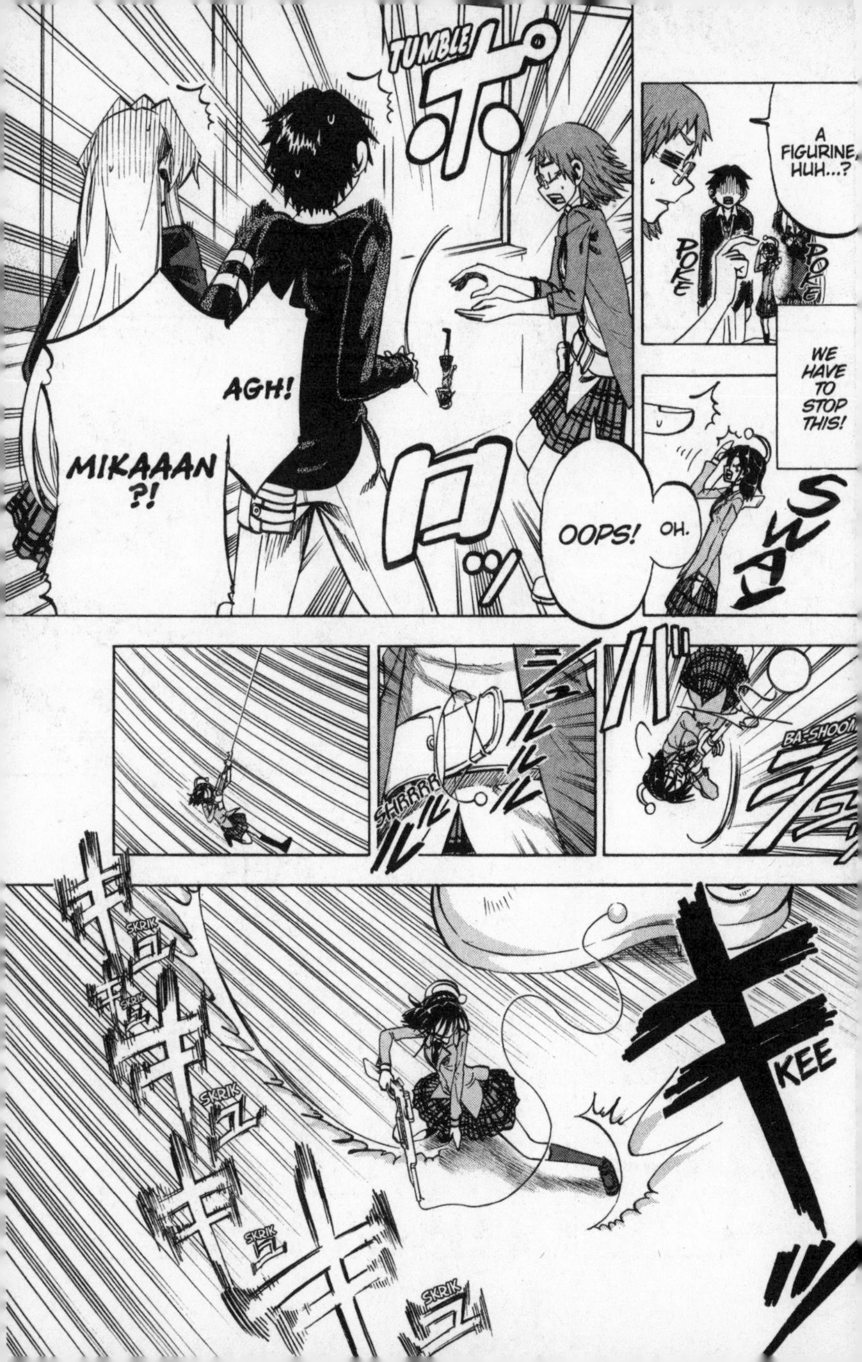
A FIGURINE, HUH...?
POKE
POKE
WE HAVE TO STOP THIS!
SWAY
OH.
OOPS!
TUMBLE
AGH!
MIKAAAN ?!
BA-SHOOM
SHRRRR
KEE
SKRIK
SKRIK
SKRIK
SKRIK
SKRIK

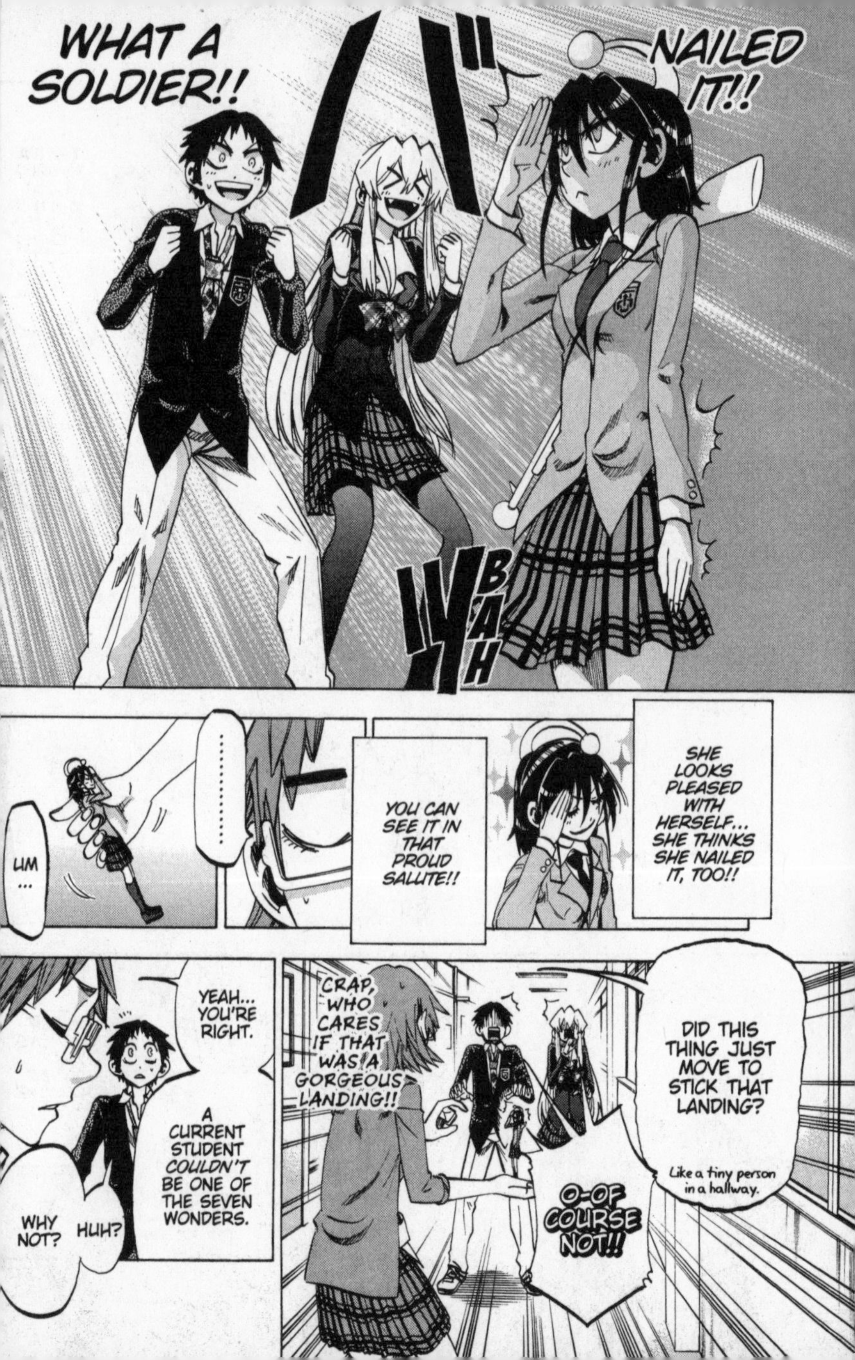
NAILED IT!!
WHAT A SOLDIER!!
BAH
SHE LOOKS PLEASED WITH HERSELF... SHE THINKS SHE NAILED IT, TOO!!
YOU CAN SEE IT IN THAT PROUD SALUTE!!
......
UM ...
DID THIS THING JUST MOVE TO STICK THAT LANDING?
Like a tiny person in a hallway.
O-OF COURSE NOT!!
CRAP, WHO CARES IF THAT WAS A GORGEOUS LANDING!!
YEAH... YOU'RE RIGHT.
A CURRENT STUDENT COULDN'T BE ONE OF THE SEVEN WONDERS.
HUH?
WHY NOT?

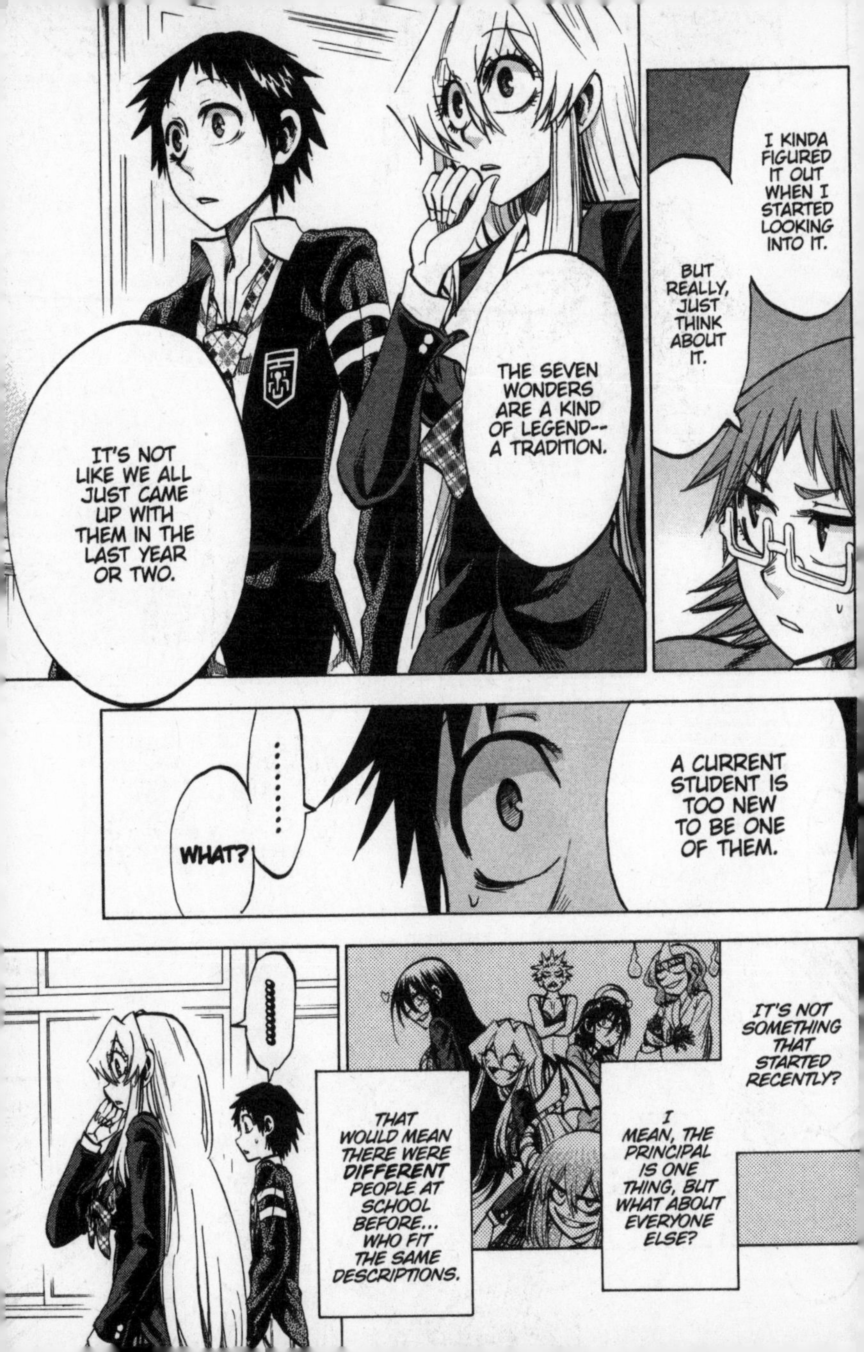
I KINDA FIGURED IT OUT WHEN I STARTED LOOKING INTO IT.
BUT REALLY, JUST THINK ABOUT IT.
THE SEVEN WONDERS ARE A KIND OF LEGEND-- A TRADITION.
IT'S NOT LIKE WE ALL JUST CAME UP WITH THEM IN THE LAST YEAR OR TWO.
A CURRENT STUDENT IS TOO NEW TO BE ONE OF THEM.
......
WHAT?
IT'S NOT SOMETHING THAT STARTED RECENTLY?
I MEAN, THE PRINCIPAL IS ONE THING, BUT WHAT ABOUT EVERYONE ELSE?
THAT WOULD MEAN THERE WERE DIFFERENT PEOPLE AT SCHOOL BEFORE... WHO FIT THE SAME DESCRIPTIONS.
....

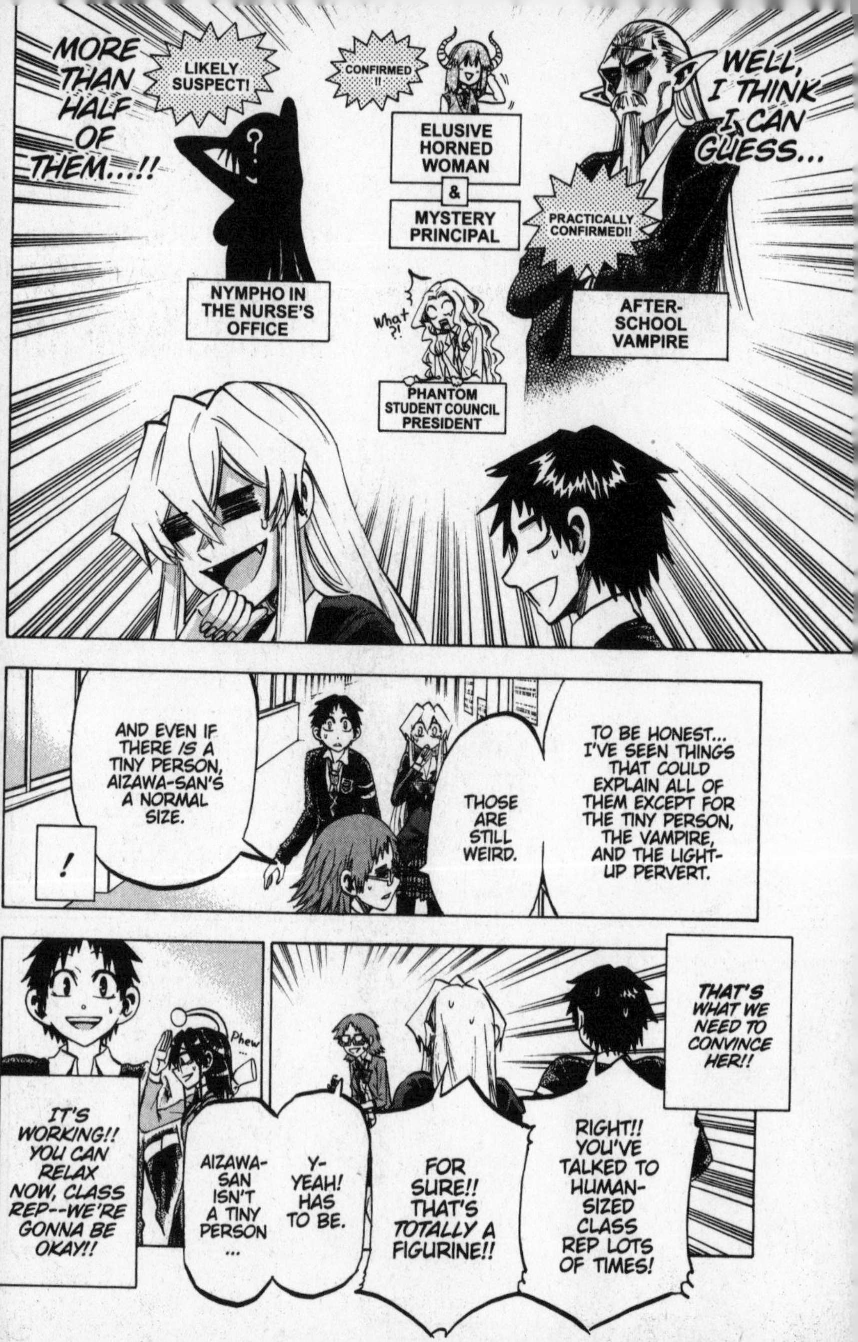
WELL, I THINK I CAN GUESS...
PRACTICALLY CONFIRMED!!
AFTER-SCHOOL VAMPIRE
CONFIRMED !!
ELUSIVE HORNED WOMAN
&
MYSTERY PRINCIPAL
What?!
PHANTOM STUDENT COUNCIL PRESIDENT
LIKELY SUSPECT!
NYMPHO IN THE NURSE'S OFFICE
MORE THAN HALF OF THEM...!!
TO BE HONEST... I'VE SEEN THINGS THAT COULD EXPLAIN ALL OF THEM EXCEPT FOR THE TINY PERSON, THE VAMPIRE, AND THE LIGHT-UP PERVERT.
THOSE ARE STILL WEIRD.
AND EVEN IF THERE *IS* A TINY PERSON, AIZAWA-SAN'S A NORMAL SIZE.
!
THAT'S WHAT WE NEED TO CONVINCE HER!!
RIGHT!! YOU'VE TALKED TO HUMAN-SIZED CLASS REP LOTS OF TIMES!
FOR SURE!! THAT'S *TOTALLY* A FIGURINE!!
Y-YEAH! HAS TO BE.
AIZAWA-SAN ISN'T A TINY PERSON ...
Phew
IT'S WORKING!! YOU CAN RELAX NOW, CLASS REP--WE'RE GONNA BE OKAY!!

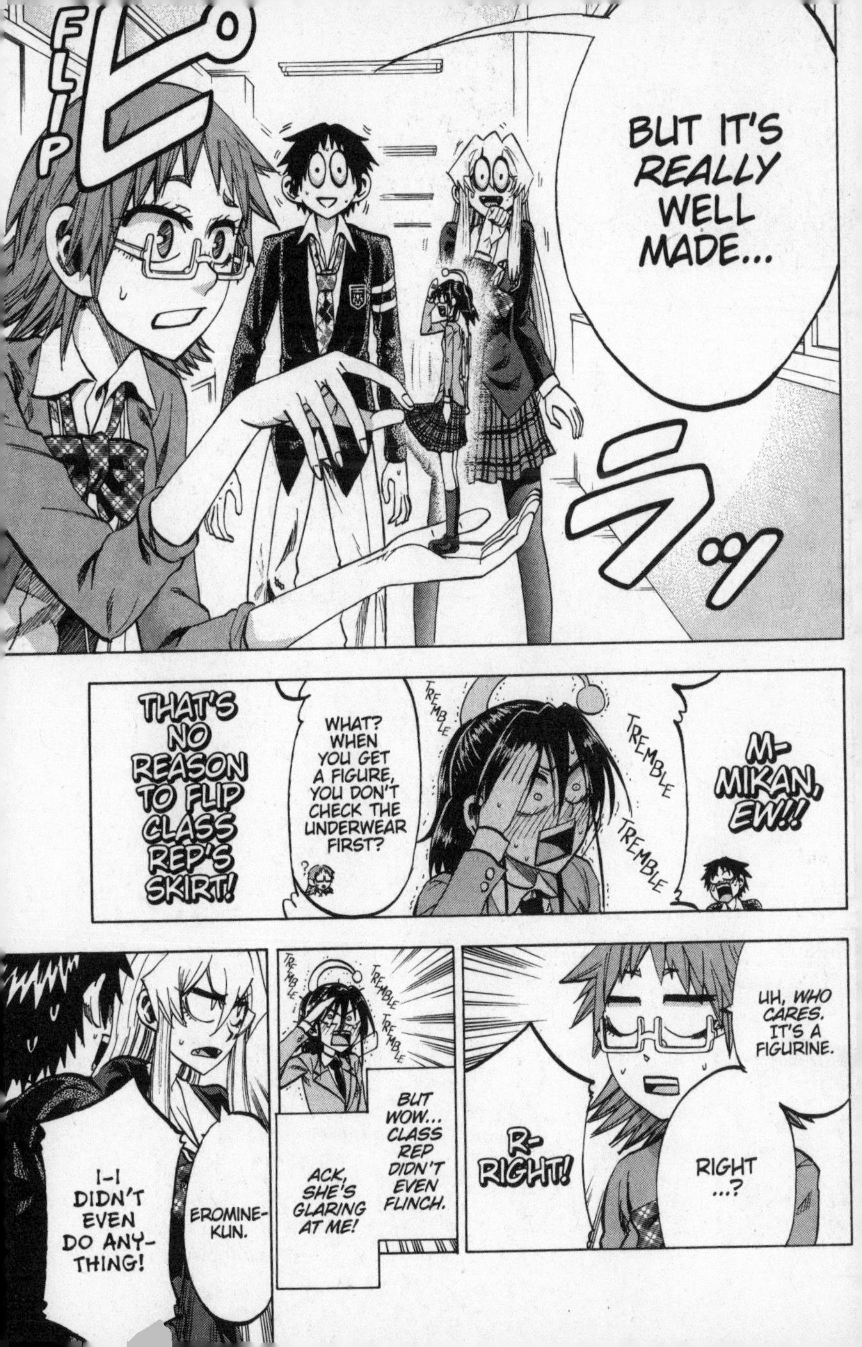
BUT IT'S REALLY WELL MADE...
ラッ
FLIP
ピ
M-MIKAN, EW!!
TREMBLE
TREMBLE
TREMBLE
WHAT? WHEN YOU GET A FIGURE, YOU DON'T CHECK THE UNDERWEAR FIRST?
THAT'S NO REASON TO FLIP CLASS REP'S SKIRT!
UH, WHO CARES. IT'S A FIGURINE.
RIGHT ...?
R-RIGHT!
TREMBLE
TREMBLE
TREMBLE
TREMBLE
BUT WOW... CLASS REP DIDN'T EVEN FLINCH.
ACK, SHE'S GLARING AT ME!
EROMINE-KUN.
I-I DIDN'T EVEN DO ANYTHING!

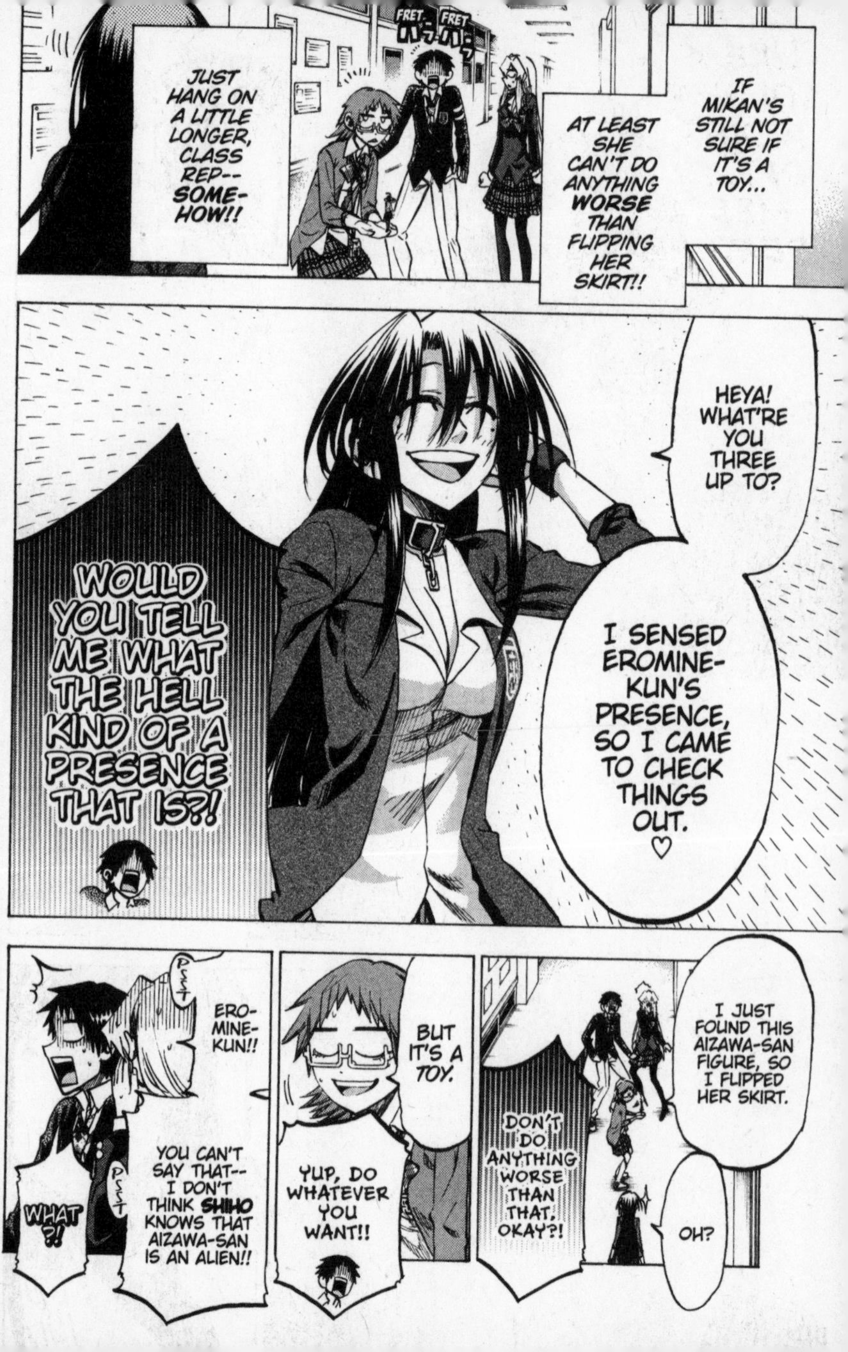
IF MIKAN'S STILL NOT SURE IF IT'S A TOY...
AT LEAST SHE CAN'T DO ANYTHING WORSE THAN FLIPPING HER SKIRT!!
FRET FRET
JUST HANG ON A LITTLE LONGER, CLASS REP-- SOMEHOW!!
HEYA! WHAT'RE YOU THREE UP TO?
I SENSED EROMINE-KUN'S PRESENCE, SO I CAME TO CHECK THINGS OUT. ♡
WOULD YOU TELL ME WHAT THE HELL KIND OF A PRESENCE THAT IS?!
I JUST FOUND THIS AIZAWA-SAN FIGURE, SO I FLIPPED HER SKIRT.
OH?
DON'T DO ANYTHING WORSE THAN THAT, OKAY?!
BUT IT'S A TOY.
YUP, DO WHATEVER YOU WANT!!
PSST
ERO-MINE-KUN!!
YOU CAN'T SAY THAT-- I DON'T THINK SHIHO KNOWS THAT AIZAWA-SAN IS AN ALIEN!!
PSST
WHAT?!

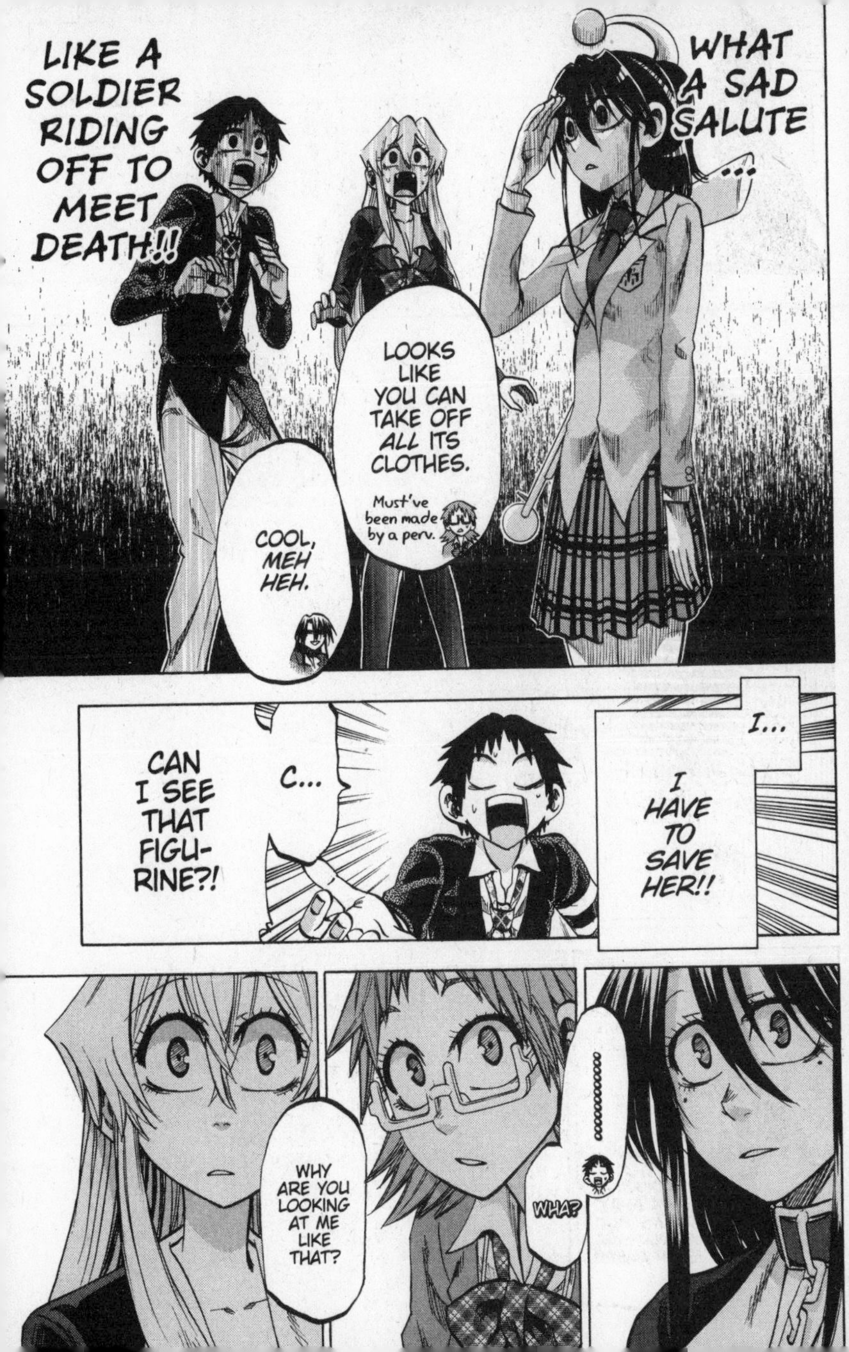
WHAT A SAD SALUTE ...
LIKE A SOLDIER RIDING OFF TO MEET DEATH!!
LOOKS LIKE YOU CAN TAKE OFF ALL ITS CLOTHES.
Must've been made by a perv.
COOL, MEH HEH.
I...
I HAVE TO SAVE HER!!
C...
CAN I SEE THAT FIGU-RINE?!
....
WHA?
WHY ARE YOU LOOKING AT ME LIKE THAT?

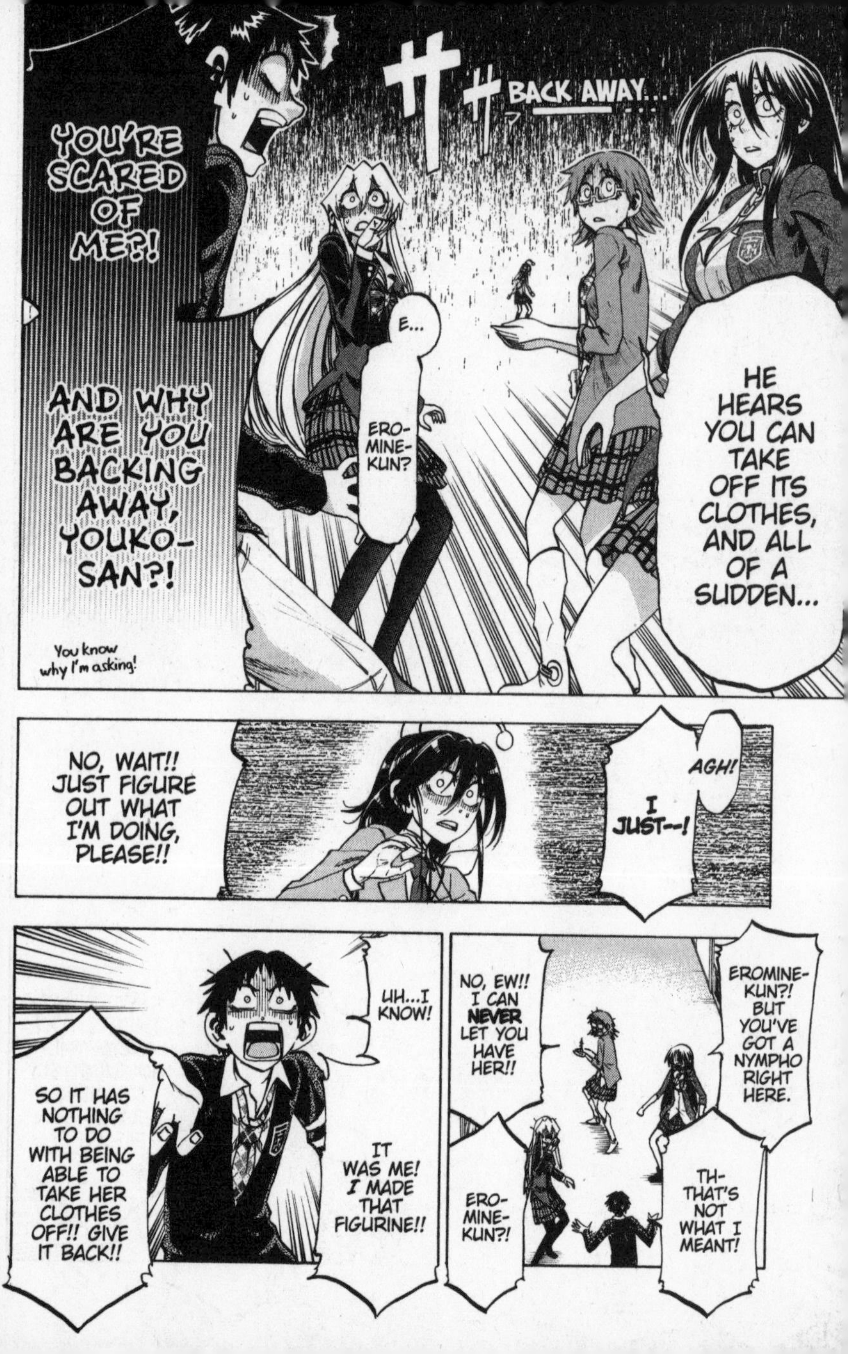
BACK AWAY...
HE HEARS YOU CAN TAKE OFF ITS CLOTHES, AND ALL OF A SUDDEN...
E... ERO-MINE-KUN?
YOU'RE SCARED OF ME?!
AND WHY ARE YOU BACKING AWAY, YOUKO-SAN?!
You know why I'm asking!
AGH! I JUST--!
NO, WAIT!! JUST FIGURE OUT WHAT I'M DOING, PLEASE!!
EROMINE-KUN?! BUT YOU'VE GOT A NYMPHO RIGHT HERE.
NO, EW!! I CAN NEVER LET YOU HAVE HER!!
TH-THAT'S NOT WHAT I MEANT!
ERO-MINE-KUN?!
UH...I KNOW!
IT WAS ME! I MADE THAT FIGURINE!!
SO IT HAS NOTHING TO DO WITH BEING ABLE TO TAKE HER CLOTHES OFF!! GIVE IT BACK!!

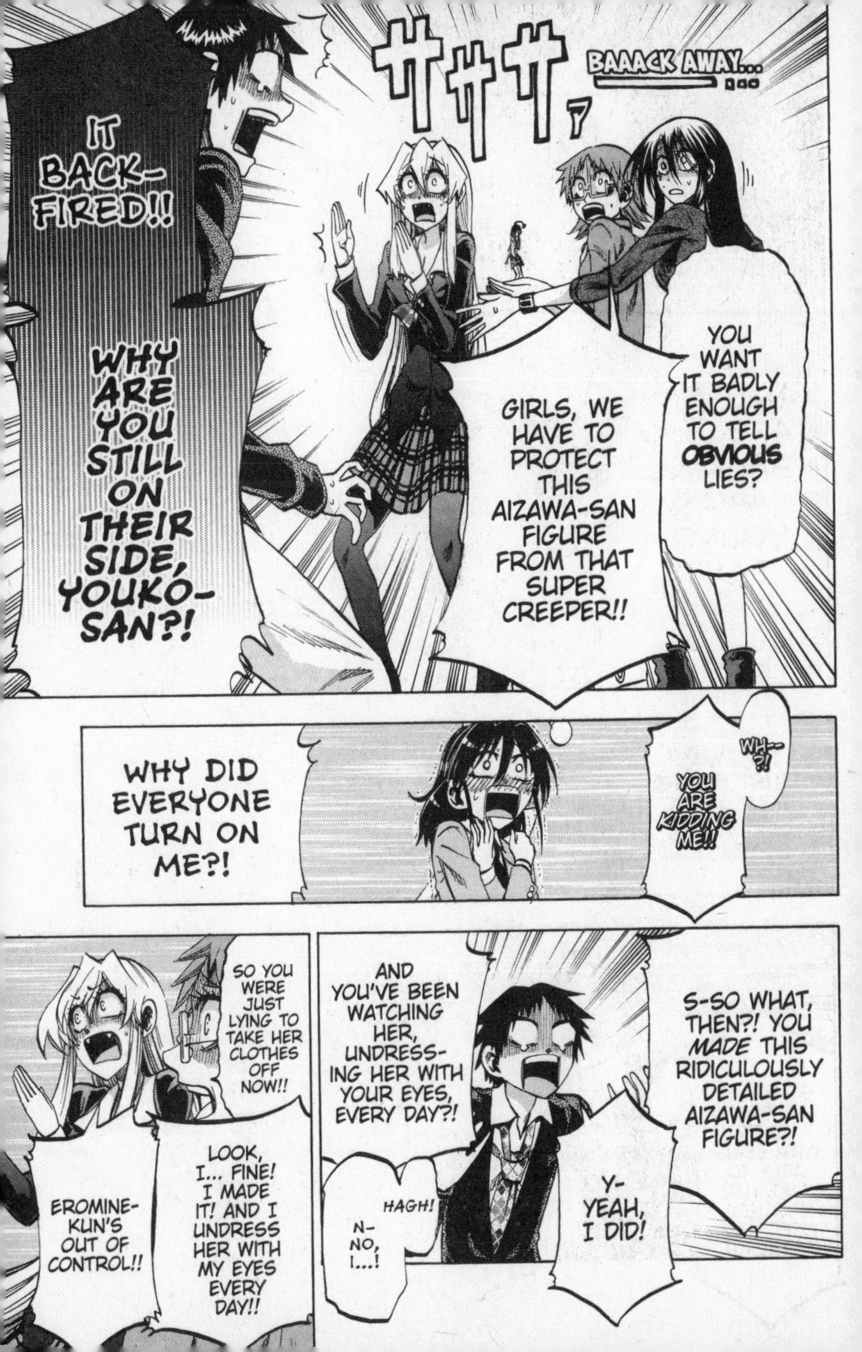
サササァ
BAAACK AWAY...
YOU WANT IT BADLY ENOUGH TO TELL OBVIOUS LIES?
GIRLS, WE HAVE TO PROTECT THIS AIZAWA-SAN FIGURE FROM THAT SUPER CREEPER!!
IT BACK-FIRED!!
WHY ARE YOU STILL ON THEIR SIDE, YOUKO-SAN?!
WH-?!
YOU ARE KIDDING ME!!
WHY DID EVERYONE TURN ON ME?!
S-SO WHAT, THEN?! YOU MADE THIS RIDICULOUSLY DETAILED AIZAWA-SAN FIGURE?!
AND YOU'VE BEEN WATCHING HER, UNDRESSING HER WITH YOUR EYES, EVERY DAY?!
Y-YEAH, I DID!
HAGH!
N-NO, I...!
SO YOU WERE JUST LYING TO TAKE HER CLOTHES OFF NOW!!
LOOK, I... FINE! I MADE IT! AND I UNDRESS HER WITH MY EYES EVERY DAY!!
EROMINE-KUN'S OUT OF CONTROL!!

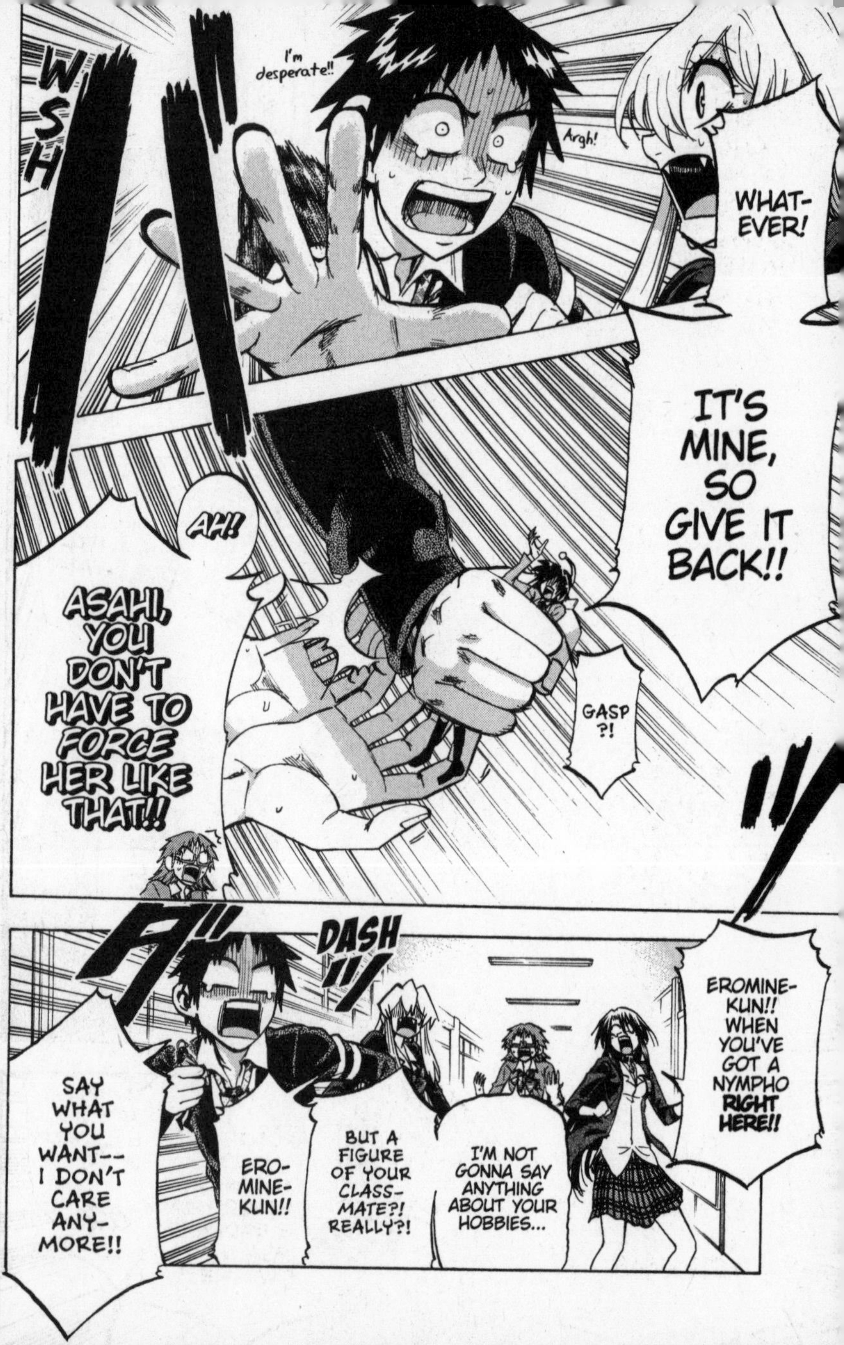
WHAT-EVER!
Argh!
I'm desperate!!
WSH
IT'S MINE, SO GIVE IT BACK!!
AH!
GASP ?!
ASAHI, YOU DON'T HAVE TO FORCE HER LIKE THAT!!
EROMINE-KUN!! WHEN YOU'VE GOT A NYMPHO RIGHT HERE!!
I'M NOT GONNA SAY ANYTHING ABOUT YOUR HOBBIES...
BUT A FIGURE OF YOUR CLASS-MATE?! REALLY?!
ERO-MINE-KUN!!
DASH
SAY WHAT YOU WANT-- I DON'T CARE ANY-MORE!!

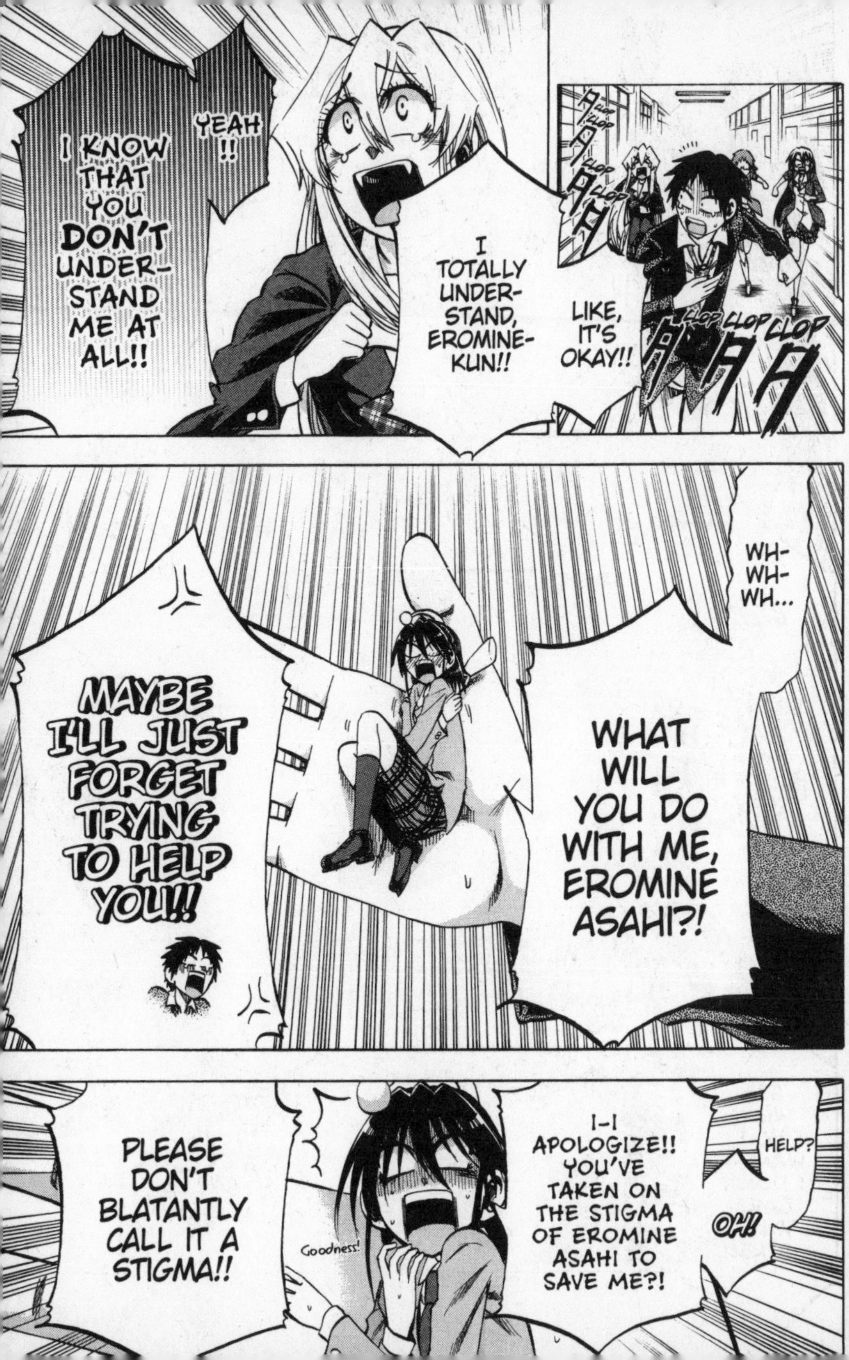
CLOP CLOP
CLOP CLOP
LIKE, IT'S OKAY!!
I TOTALLY UNDER-STAND, EROMINE-KUN!!
CLOP CLOP CLOP
YEAH!!
I KNOW THAT YOU DON'T UNDER-STAND ME AT ALL!!
WH-WH-WH...
WHAT WILL YOU DO WITH ME, EROMINE ASAHI?!
MAYBE I'LL JUST FORGET TRYING TO HELP YOU!!
HELP?
OH!
I-I APOLOGIZE!! YOU'VE TAKEN ON THE STIGMA OF EROMINE ASAHI TO SAVE ME?!
Goodness!
PLEASE DON'T BLATANTLY CALL IT A STIGMA!!

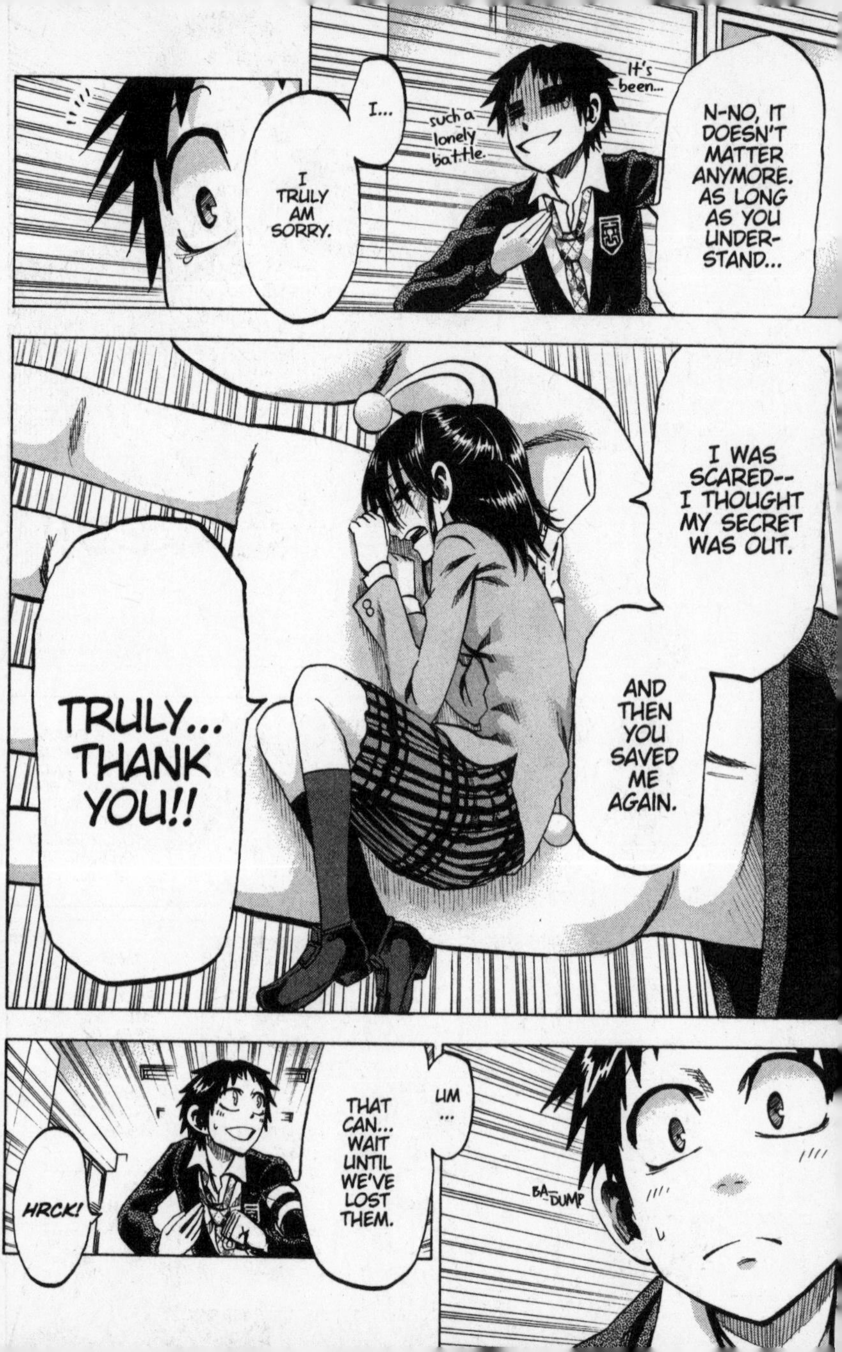
N-NO, IT DOESN'T MATTER ANYMORE. AS LONG AS YOU UNDERSTAND...
It's been...
such a lonely battle.
I...
I TRULY AM SORRY.
I WAS SCARED-- I THOUGHT MY SECRET WAS OUT.
AND THEN YOU SAVED ME AGAIN.
TRULY... THANK YOU!!
BA-DUMP
UM ...
THAT CAN... WAIT UNTIL WE'VE LOST THEM.
HRCK!

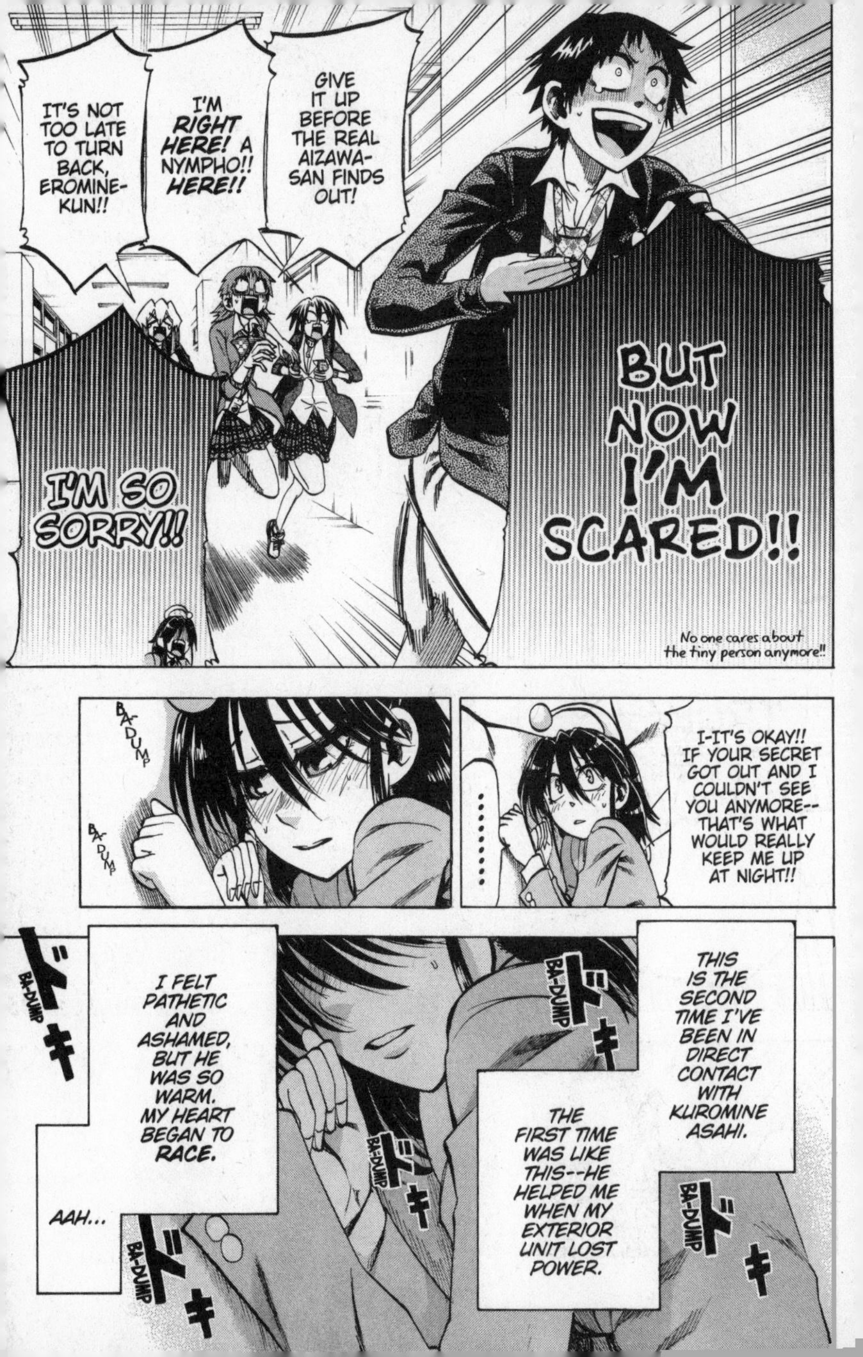
GIVE IT UP BEFORE THE REAL AIZAWA-SAN FINDS OUT!
I'M *RIGHT HERE!* A NYMPHO!! *HERE!!*
IT'S NOT TOO LATE TO TURN BACK, EROMINE-KUN!!
BUT NOW I'M SCARED!!
I'M SO SORRY!!
No one cares about the tiny person anymore!!
I-IT'S OKAY!! IF YOUR SECRET GOT OUT AND I COULDN'T SEE YOU ANYMORE--THAT'S WHAT WOULD REALLY KEEP ME UP AT NIGHT!!
......
BA-DUMP
BA-DUMP
ドキ BA-DUMP
THIS IS THE SECOND TIME I'VE BEEN IN DIRECT CONTACT WITH KUROMINE ASAHI.
ドキ BA-DUMP
THE FIRST TIME WAS LIKE THIS--HE HELPED ME WHEN MY EXTERIOR UNIT LOST POWER.
ドキ BA-DUMP
ドキ BA-DUMP
I FELT PATHETIC AND ASHAMED, BUT HE WAS SO WARM. MY HEART BEGAN TO RACE.
AAH...
ドキ BA-DUMP

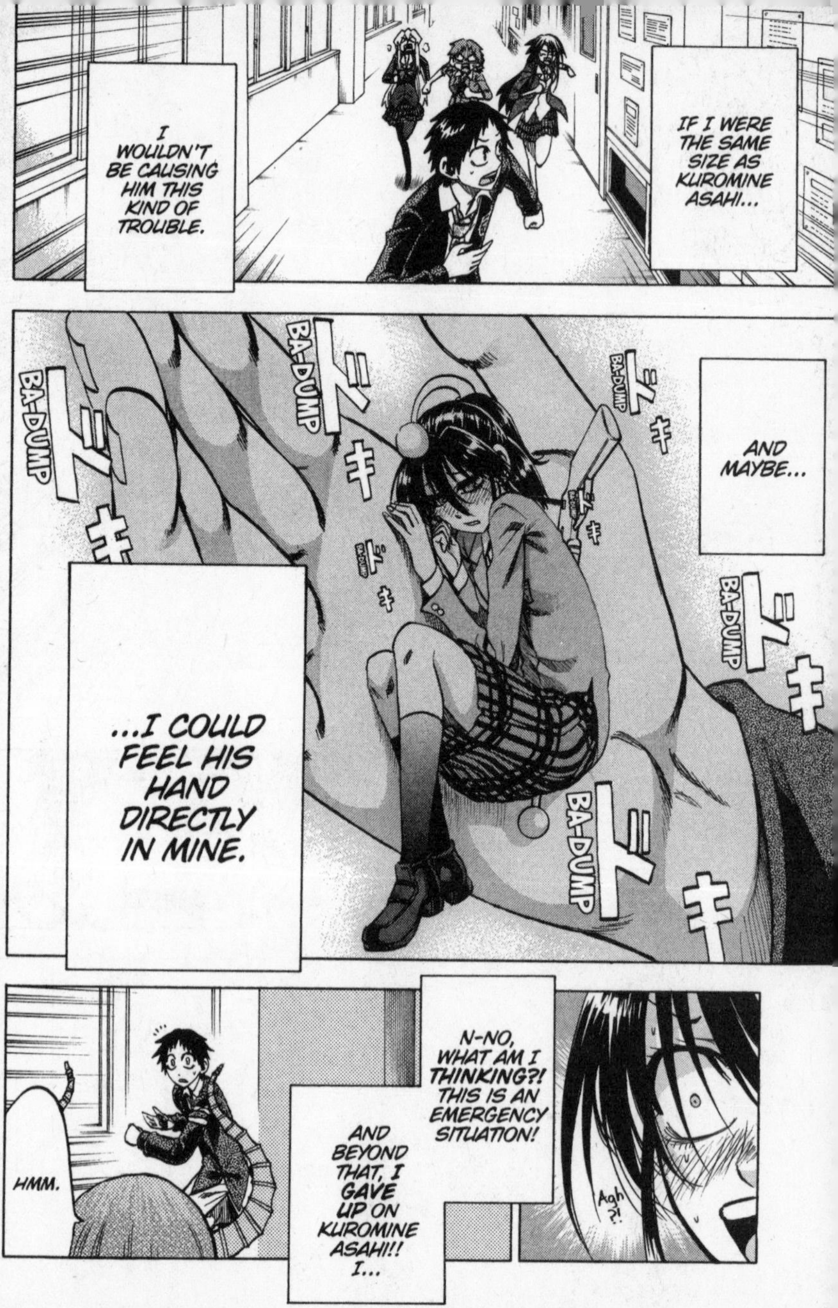
IF I WERE THE SAME SIZE AS KUROMINE ASAHI...
I WOULDN'T BE CAUSING HIM THIS KIND OF TROUBLE.
AND MAYBE...
BA-DUMP
BA-DUMP
BA-DUMP
BA-DUMP
BA-DUMP
...I COULD FEEL HIS HAND DIRECTLY IN MINE.
N-NO, WHAT AM I THINKING?! THIS IS AN EMERGENCY SITUATION!
Agh ?!
AND BEYOND THAT, I GAVE UP ON KUROMINE ASAHI!! I...
HMM.

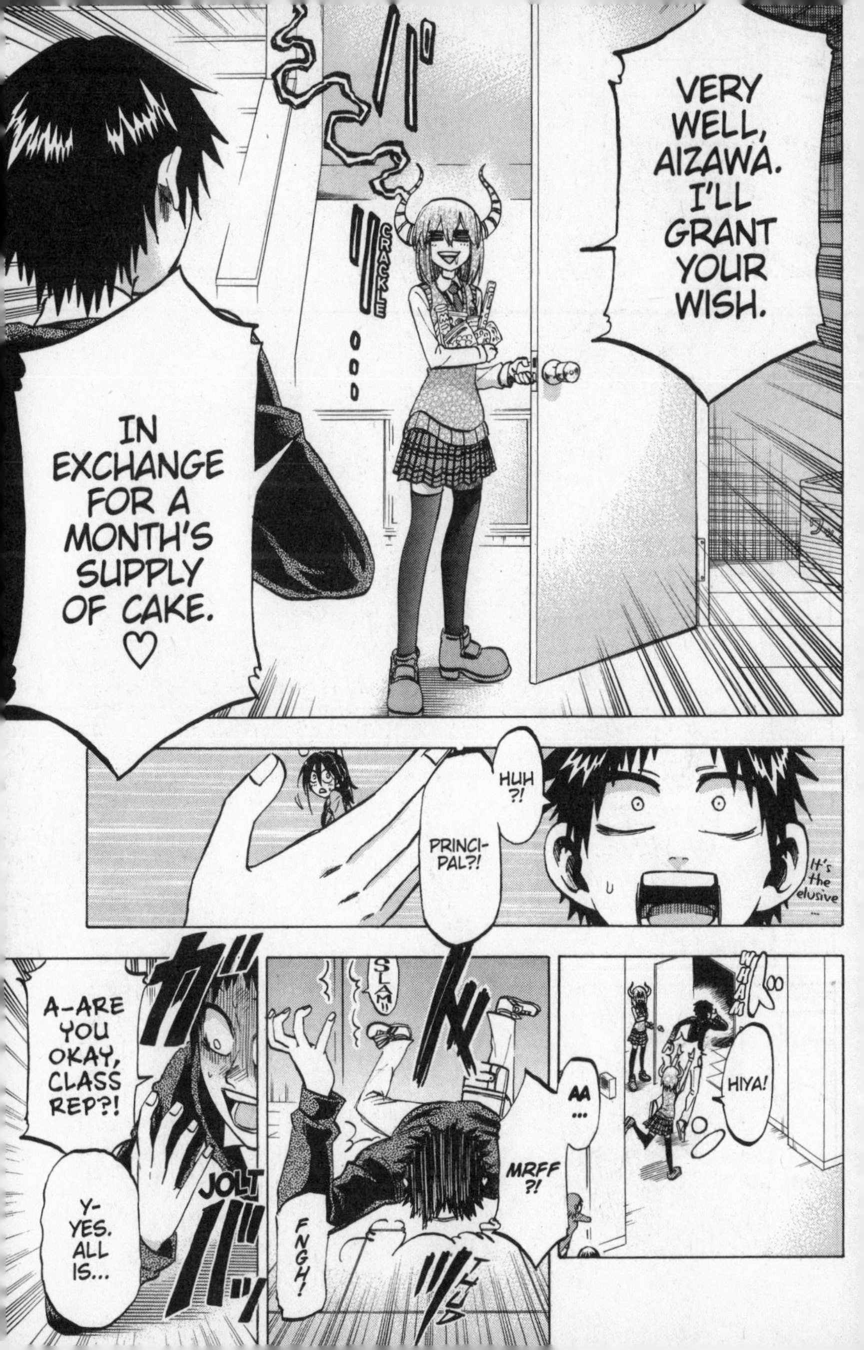
VERY WELL, AIZAWA. I'LL GRANT YOUR WISH.
CRACKLE
IN EXCHANGE FOR A MONTH'S SUPPLY OF CAKE. ♡
HUH ?!
PRINCIPAL?!
It's the elusive ...
WHAM
HIYA!
SLAM!!
AA ...
MRFF ?!
FNGH!
A-ARE YOU OKAY, CLASS REP?!
JOLT
Y-YES. ALL IS...

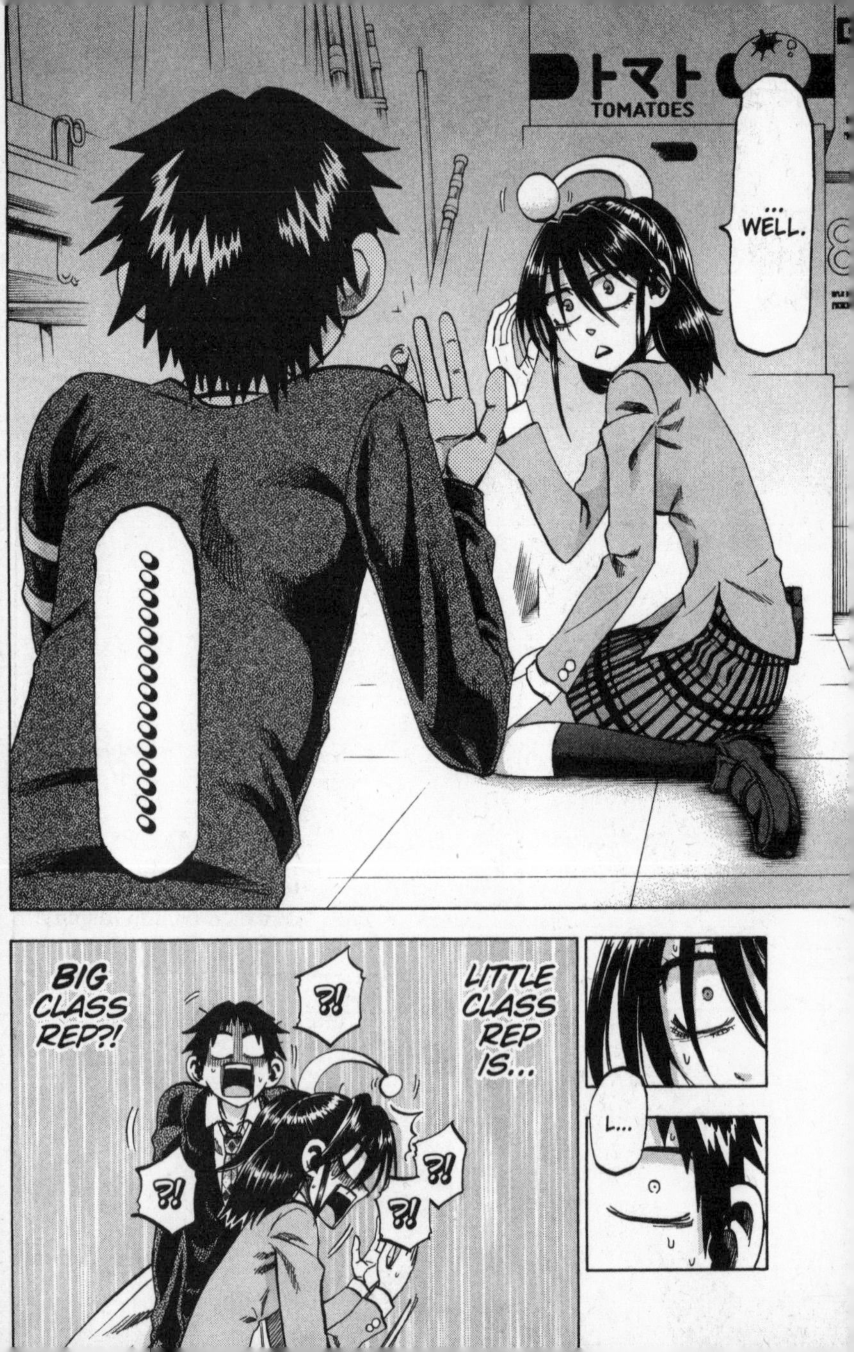
トマト
TOMATOES
...WELL.
OOOOOOOOOOOOOOOOO
L...
LITTLE CLASS REP IS...
?!
BIG CLASS REP?!
?!
?!
?!

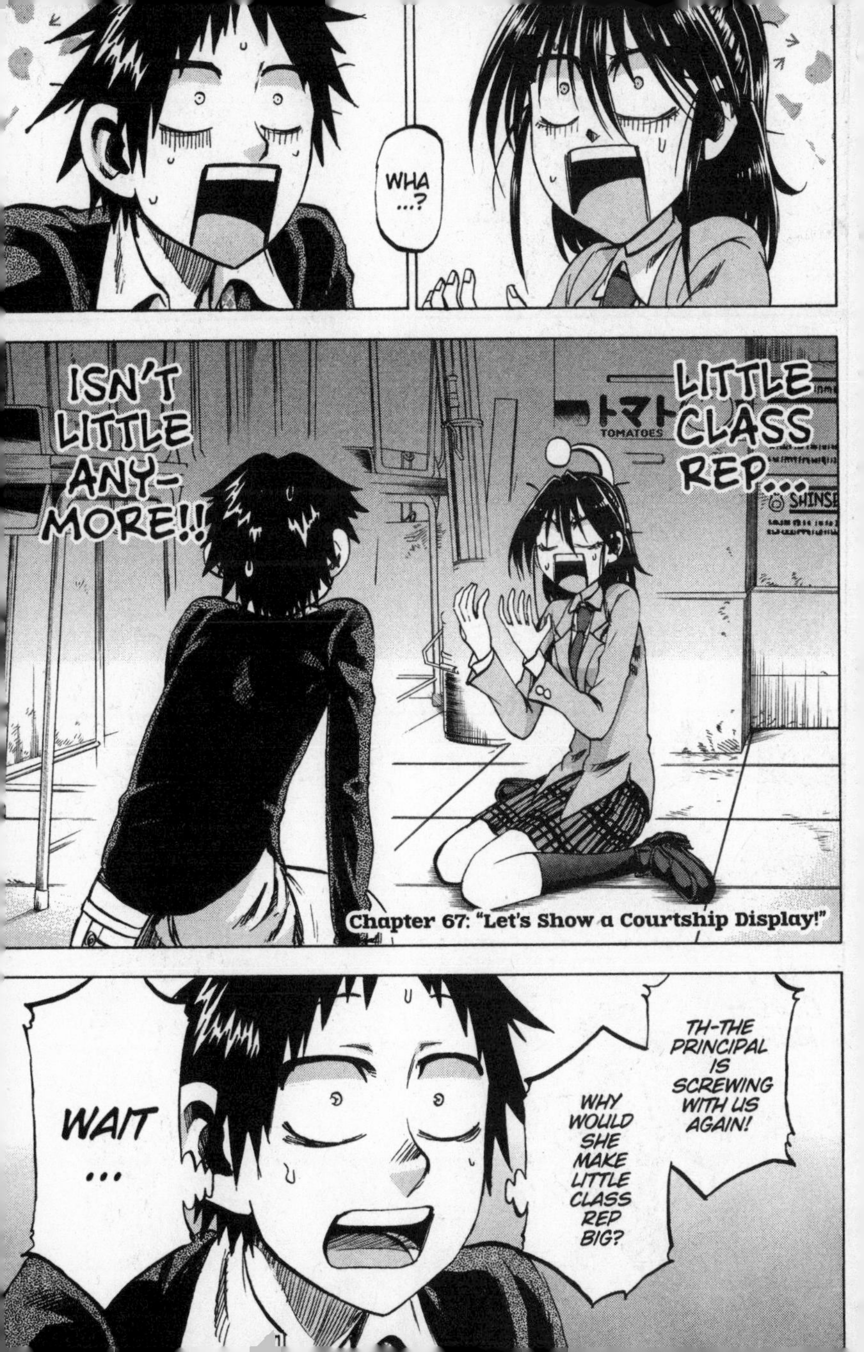
WHA ...?
LITTLE CLASS REP...
トマト
TOMATOES
ISN'T LITTLE ANY-MORE!!
Chapter 67: "Let's Show a Courtship Display!"
TH-THE PRINCIPAL IS SCREWING WITH US AGAIN!
WHY WOULD SHE MAKE LITTLE CLASS REP BIG?
WAIT ...

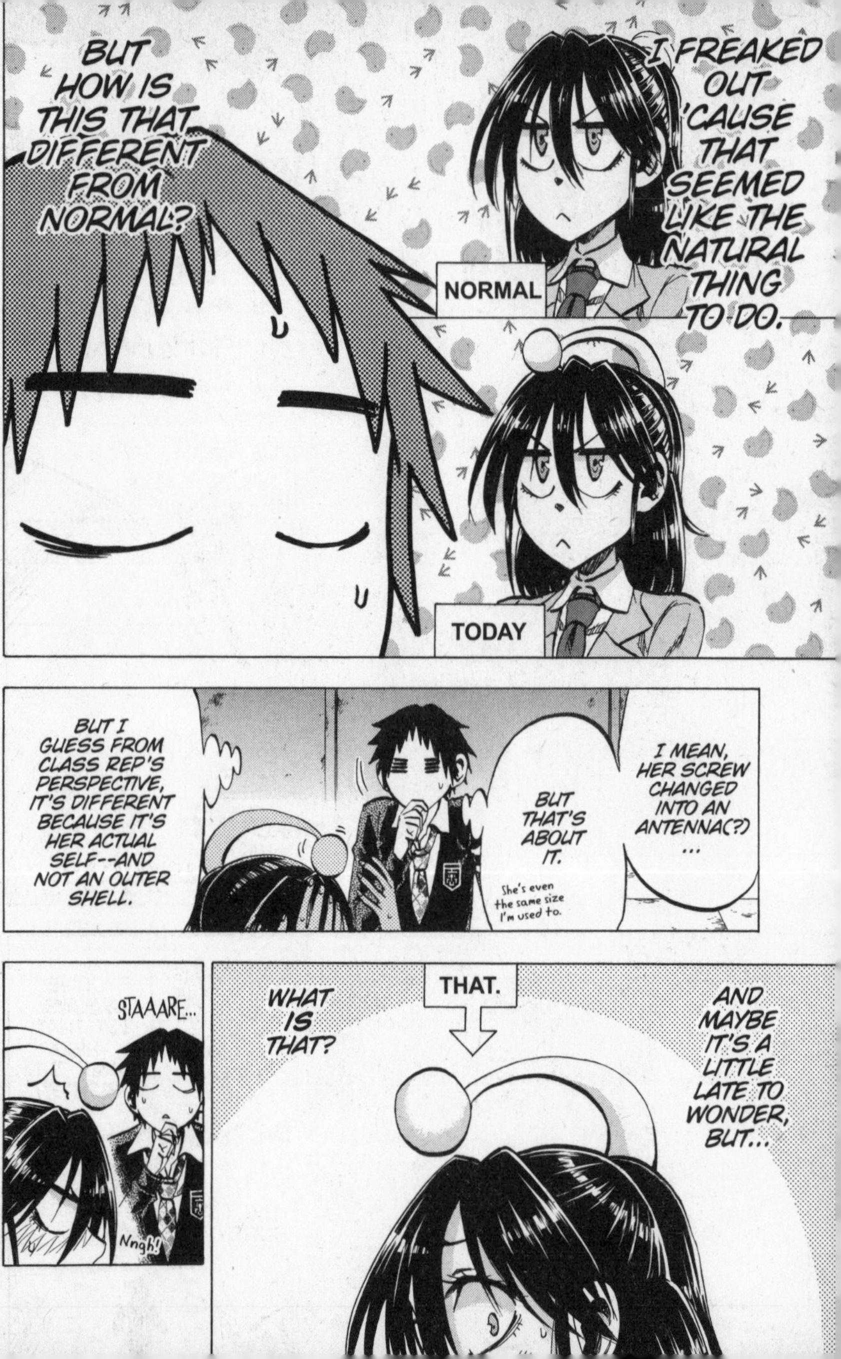
I FREAKED OUT 'CAUSE THAT SEEMED LIKE THE NATURAL THING TO DO.
NORMAL
BUT HOW IS THIS THAT DIFFERENT FROM NORMAL?
TODAY
I MEAN, HER SCREW CHANGED INTO AN ANTENNA(?)...
BUT THAT'S ABOUT IT.
She's even the same size I'm used to.
BUT I GUESS FROM CLASS REP'S PERSPECTIVE, IT'S DIFFERENT BECAUSE IT'S HER ACTUAL SELF--AND NOT AN OUTER SHELL.
AND MAYBE IT'S A LITTLE LATE TO WONDER, BUT...
THAT.
WHAT IS THAT?
STAAARE...
Nngh!

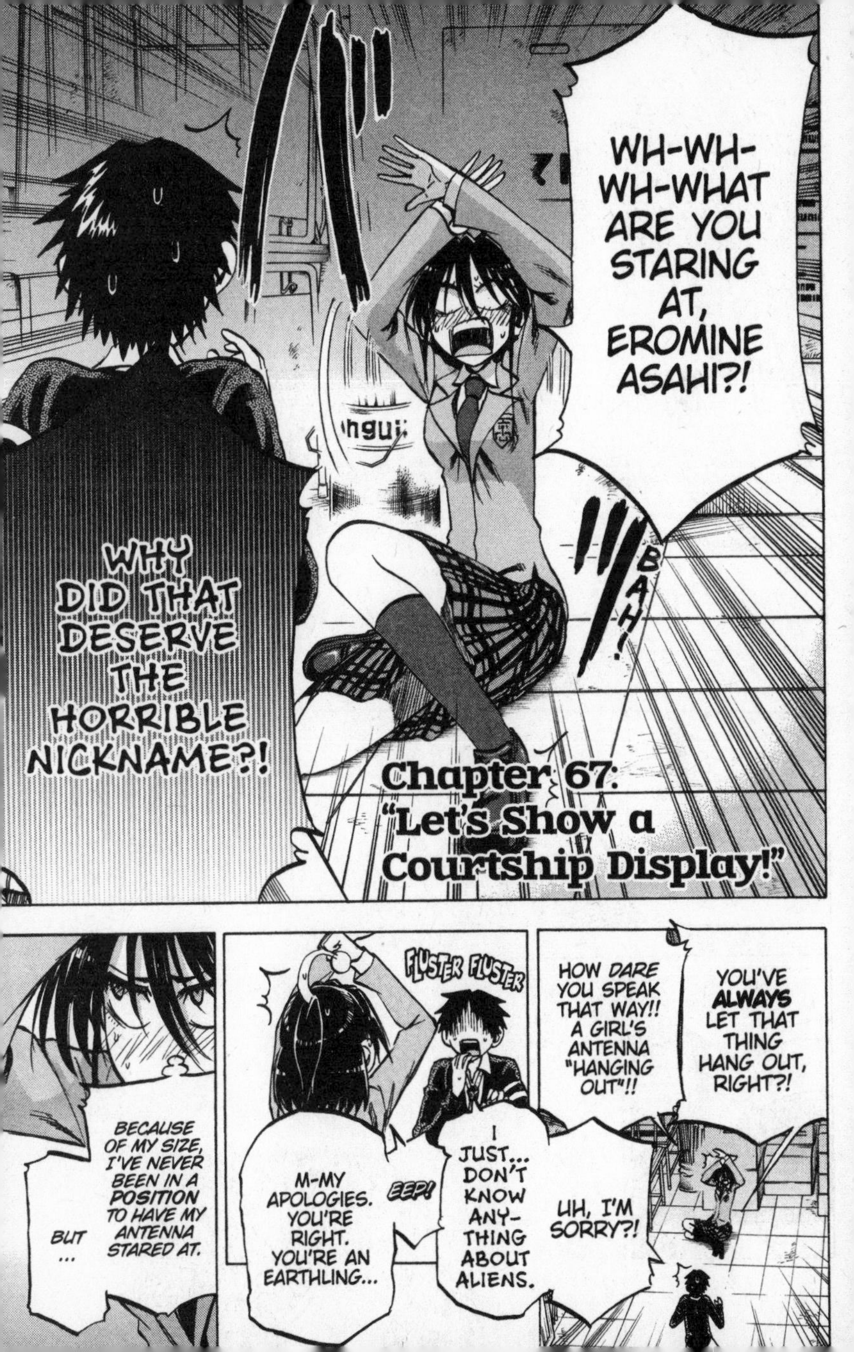
WH-WH-WH-WHAT ARE YOU STARING AT, EROMINE ASAHI?!
BAAH!
WHY DID THAT DESERVE THE HORRIBLE NICKNAME?!
Chapter 67: "Let's Show a Courtship Display!"
YOU'VE ALWAYS LET THAT THING HANG OUT, RIGHT?!
HOW DARE YOU SPEAK THAT WAY!! A GIRL'S ANTENNA "HANGING OUT"!!
UH, I'M SORRY?!
I JUST... DON'T KNOW ANY-THING ABOUT ALIENS.
FLUSTER FLUSTER
EEP!
M-MY APOLOGIES. YOU'RE RIGHT. YOU'RE AN EARTHLING...
BECAUSE OF MY SIZE, I'VE NEVER BEEN IN A POSITION TO HAVE MY ANTENNA STARED AT.
BUT ...

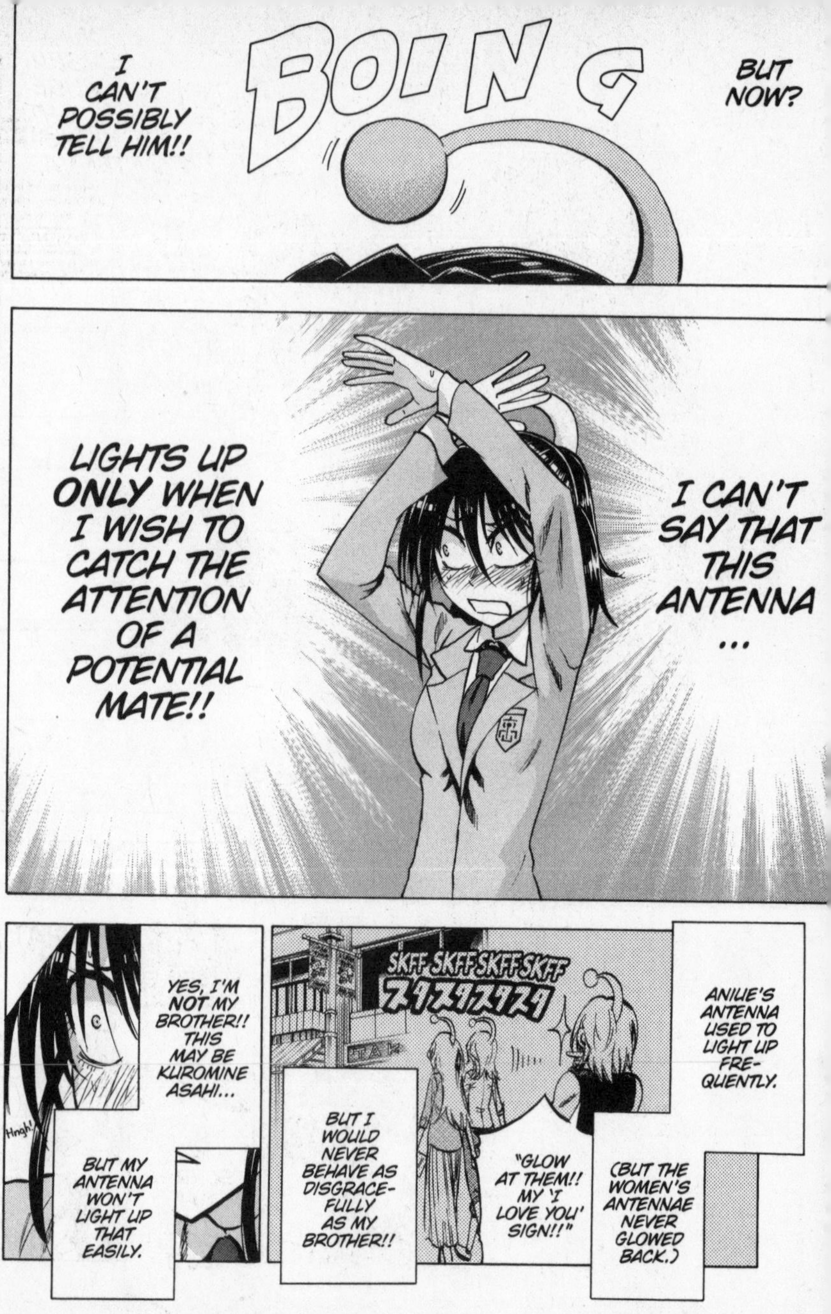
BUT NOW?
BOING
I CAN'T POSSIBLY TELL HIM!!
I CAN'T SAY THAT THIS ANTENNA ...
LIGHTS UP ONLY WHEN I WISH TO CATCH THE ATTENTION OF A POTENTIAL MATE!!
ANIUE'S ANTENNA USED TO LIGHT UP FRE-QUENTLY.
SKFF SKFF SKFF SKFF
"GLOW AT THEM!! MY 'I LOVE YOU' SIGN!!"
(BUT THE WOMEN'S ANTENNAE NEVER GLOWED BACK.)
BUT I WOULD NEVER BEHAVE AS DISGRACE-FULLY AS MY BROTHER!!
YES, I'M NOT MY BROTHER!! THIS MAY BE KUROMINE ASAHI...
Hngh!
BUT MY ANTENNA WON'T LIGHT UP THAT EASILY.

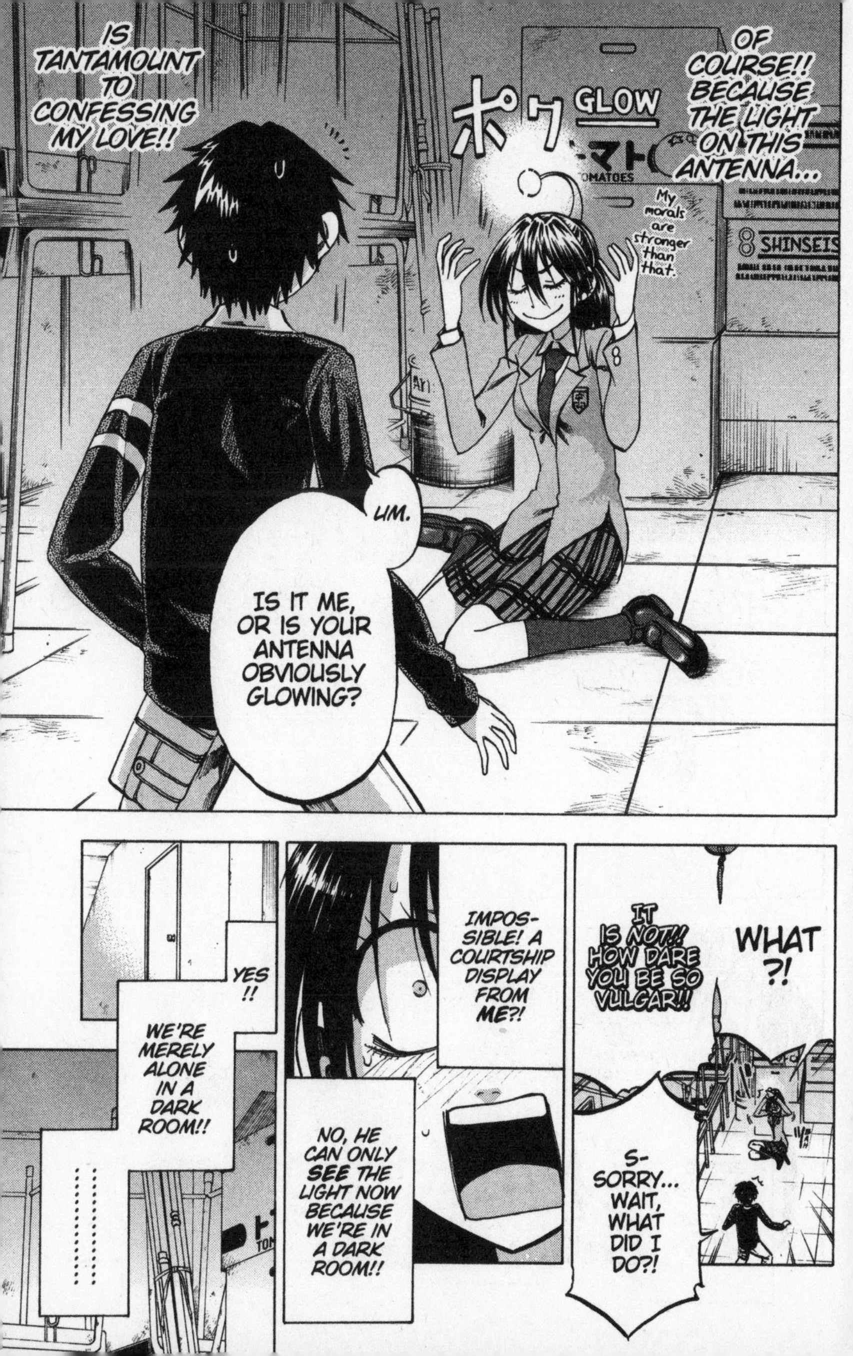
OF COURSE!! BECAUSE THE LIGHT ON THIS ANTENNA...
IS TANTAMOUNT TO CONFESSING MY LOVE!!
ポワ GLOW
TOMATOES
SHINSEIS
My morals are stronger than that.
UM.
IS IT ME, OR IS YOUR ANTENNA OBVIOUSLY GLOWING?
WHAT?!
IT IS NOT!! HOW DARE YOU BE SO VULGAR!!
S-SORRY... WAIT, WHAT DID I DO?!
IMPOSSIBLE! A COURTSHIP DISPLAY FROM ME?!
NO, HE CAN ONLY SEE THE LIGHT NOW BECAUSE WE'RE IN A DARK ROOM!!
YES!!
WE'RE MERELY ALONE IN A DARK ROOM!!
......

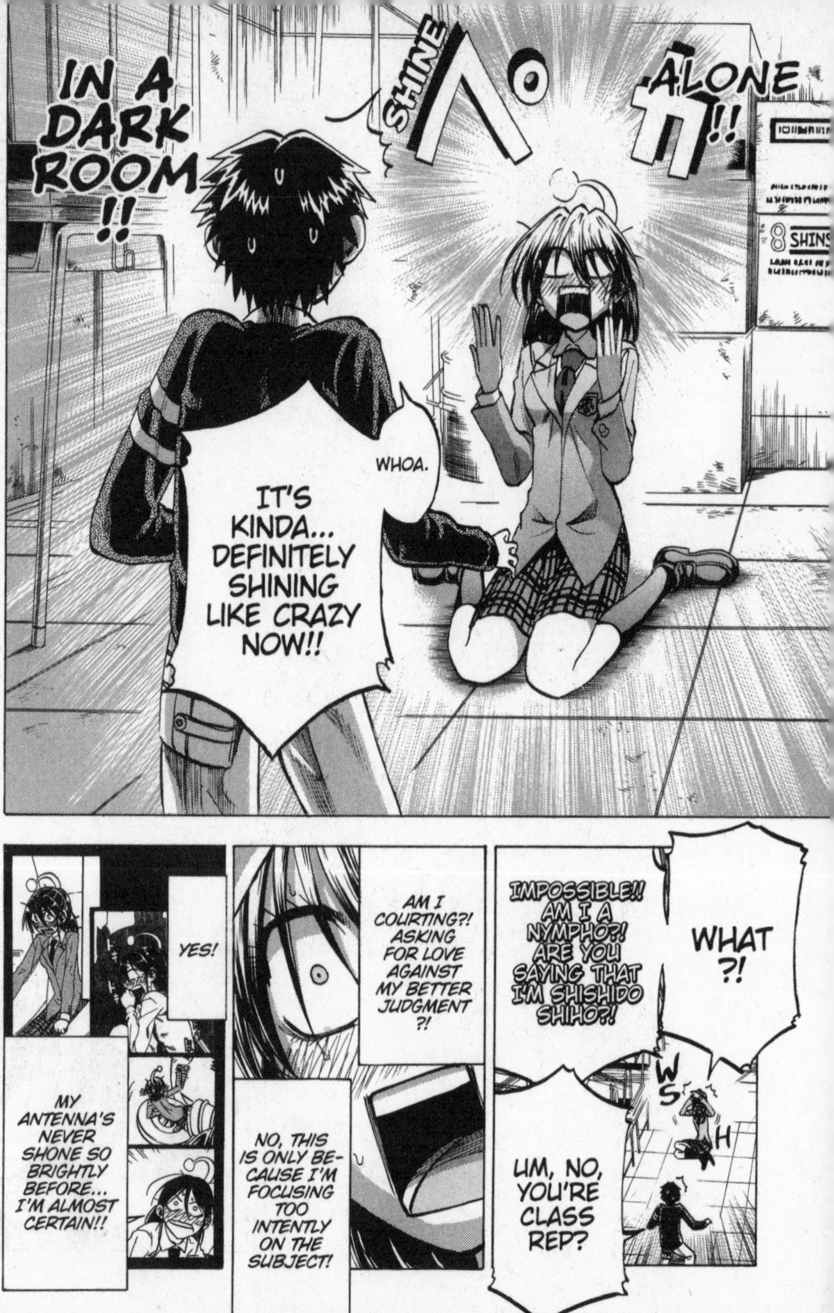
ALONE
!!
SHINE
IN A DARK ROOM!!
WHOA.
IT'S KINDA... DEFINITELY SHINING LIKE CRAZY NOW!!
WHAT ?!
IMPOSSIBLE!! AM I A NYMPHO?! ARE YOU SAYING THAT I'M SHISHIDO SHIHO?!
WSH
UM, NO, YOU'RE CLASS REP?
AM I COURTING?! ASKING FOR LOVE AGAINST MY BETTER JUDGMENT ?!
NO, THIS IS ONLY BE-CAUSE I'M FOCUSING TOO INTENTLY ON THE SUBJECT!
YES!
MY ANTENNA'S NEVER SHONE SO BRIGHTLY BEFORE... I'M ALMOST CERTAIN!!

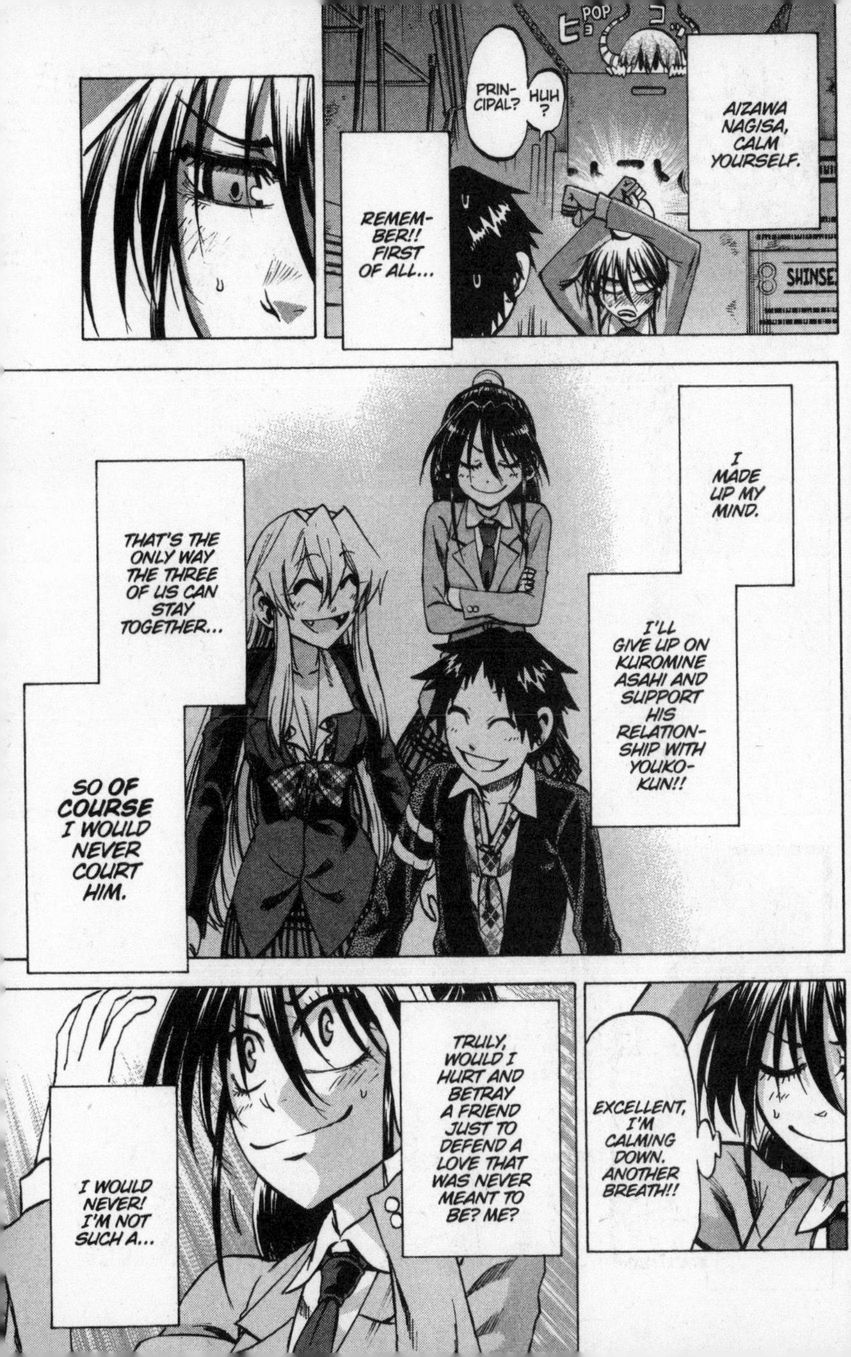
ヒョ
POP
コッ
AIZAWA NAGISA, CALM YOURSELF.
HUH?
PRIN-CIPAL?
SHINSEI
REMEM-BER!! FIRST OF ALL...
I MADE UP MY MIND.
I'LL GIVE UP ON KUROMINE ASAHI AND SUPPORT HIS RELATION-SHIP WITH YOUKO-KUN!!
THAT'S THE ONLY WAY THE THREE OF US CAN STAY TOGETHER...
SO OF COURSE I WOULD NEVER COURT HIM.
EXCELLENT, I'M CALMING DOWN. ANOTHER BREATH!!
TRULY, WOULD I HURT AND BETRAY A FRIEND JUST TO DEFEND A LOVE THAT WAS NEVER MEANT TO BE? ME?
I WOULD NEVER! I'M NOT SUCH A...

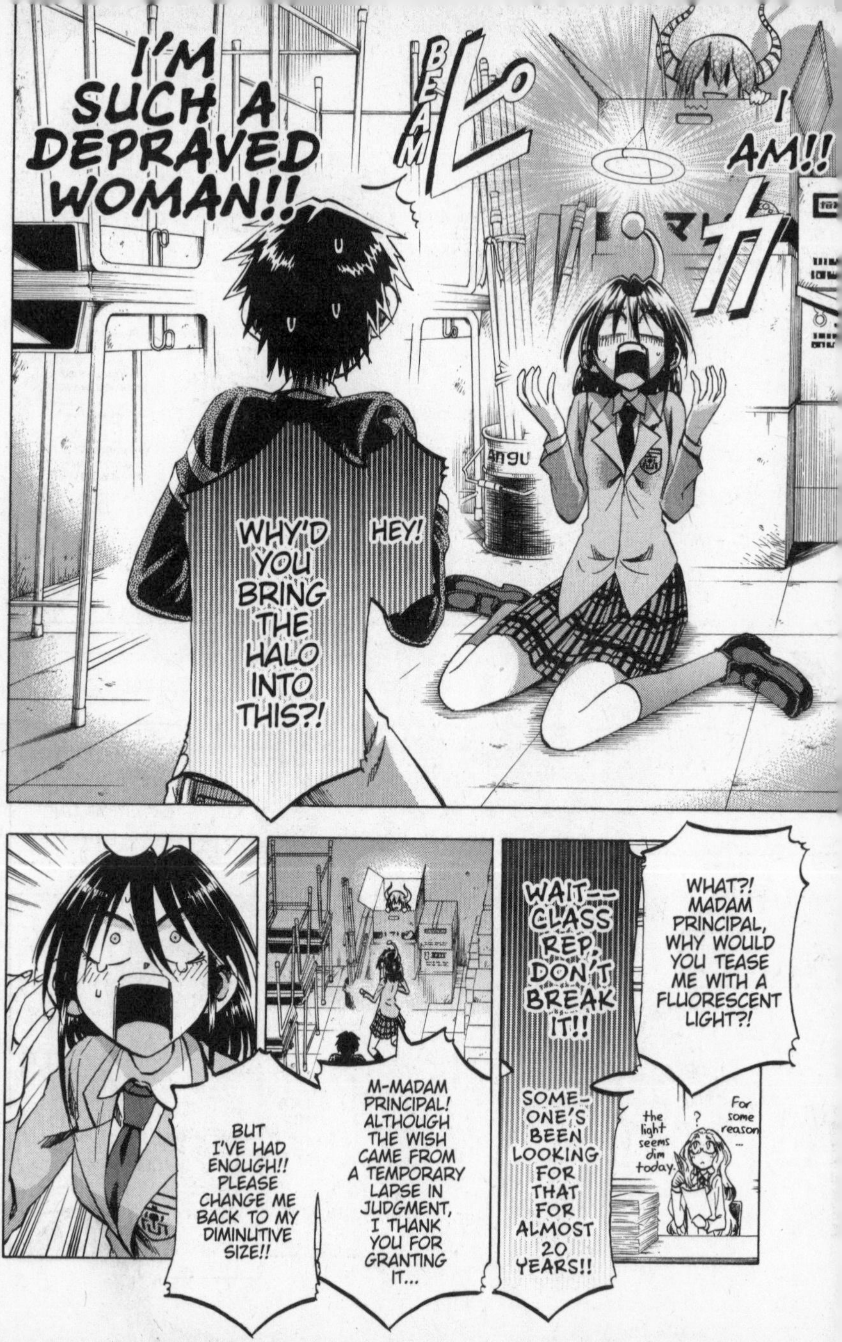
I AM!!
BEAM
I'M SUCH A DEPRAVED WOMAN!!
HEY!
WHY'D YOU BRING THE HALO INTO THIS?!
WHAT?! MADAM PRINCIPAL, WHY WOULD YOU TEASE ME WITH A FLUORESCENT LIGHT?!
For some reason ...
the light seems dim today.
WAIT-- CLASS REP, DON'T BREAK IT!!
SOME-ONE'S BEEN LOOKING FOR THAT FOR ALMOST 20 YEARS!!
M-MADAM PRINCIPAL! ALTHOUGH THE WISH CAME FROM A TEMPORARY LAPSE IN JUDGMENT, I THANK YOU FOR GRANTING IT...
BUT I'VE HAD ENOUGH!! PLEASE CHANGE ME BACK TO MY DIMINUTIVE SIZE!!

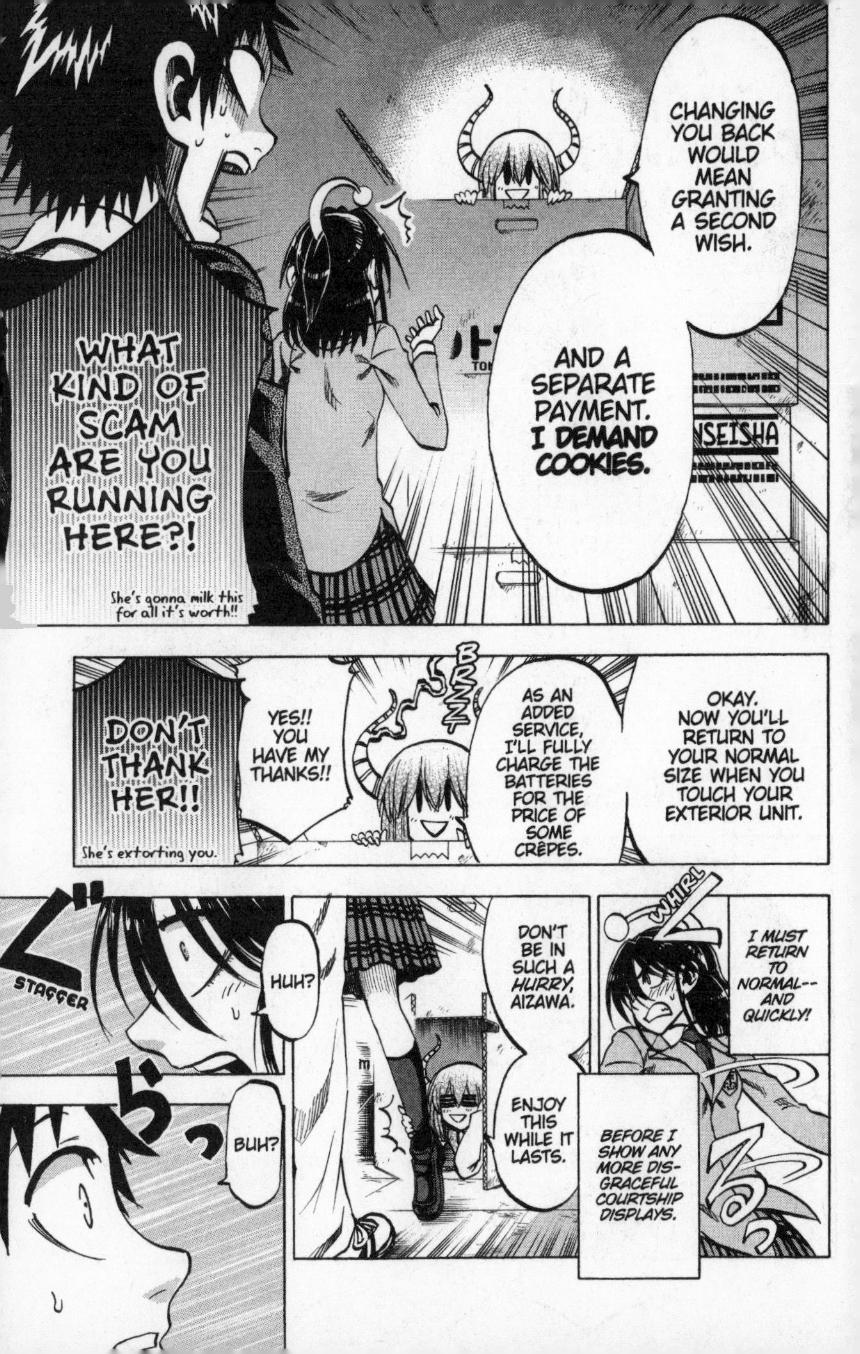
CHANGING YOU BACK WOULD MEAN GRANTING A SECOND WISH.
AND A SEPARATE PAYMENT. I DEMAND COOKIES.
WHAT KIND OF SCAM ARE YOU RUNNING HERE?!
She's gonna milk this for all it's worth!!
OKAY. NOW YOU'LL RETURN TO YOUR NORMAL SIZE WHEN YOU TOUCH YOUR EXTERIOR UNIT.
AS AN ADDED SERVICE, I'LL FULLY CHARGE THE BATTERIES FOR THE PRICE OF SOME CRÊPES.
BRZZT
YES!! YOU HAVE MY THANKS!!
DON'T THANK HER!!
She's extorting you.
WHIRL
I MUST RETURN TO NORMAL-- AND QUICKLY!
BEFORE I SHOW ANY MORE DIS-GRACEFUL COURTSHIP DISPLAYS.
DON'T BE IN SUCH A HURRY, AIZAWA.
ENJOY THIS WHILE IT LASTS.
HUH?
STAGGER
BUH?

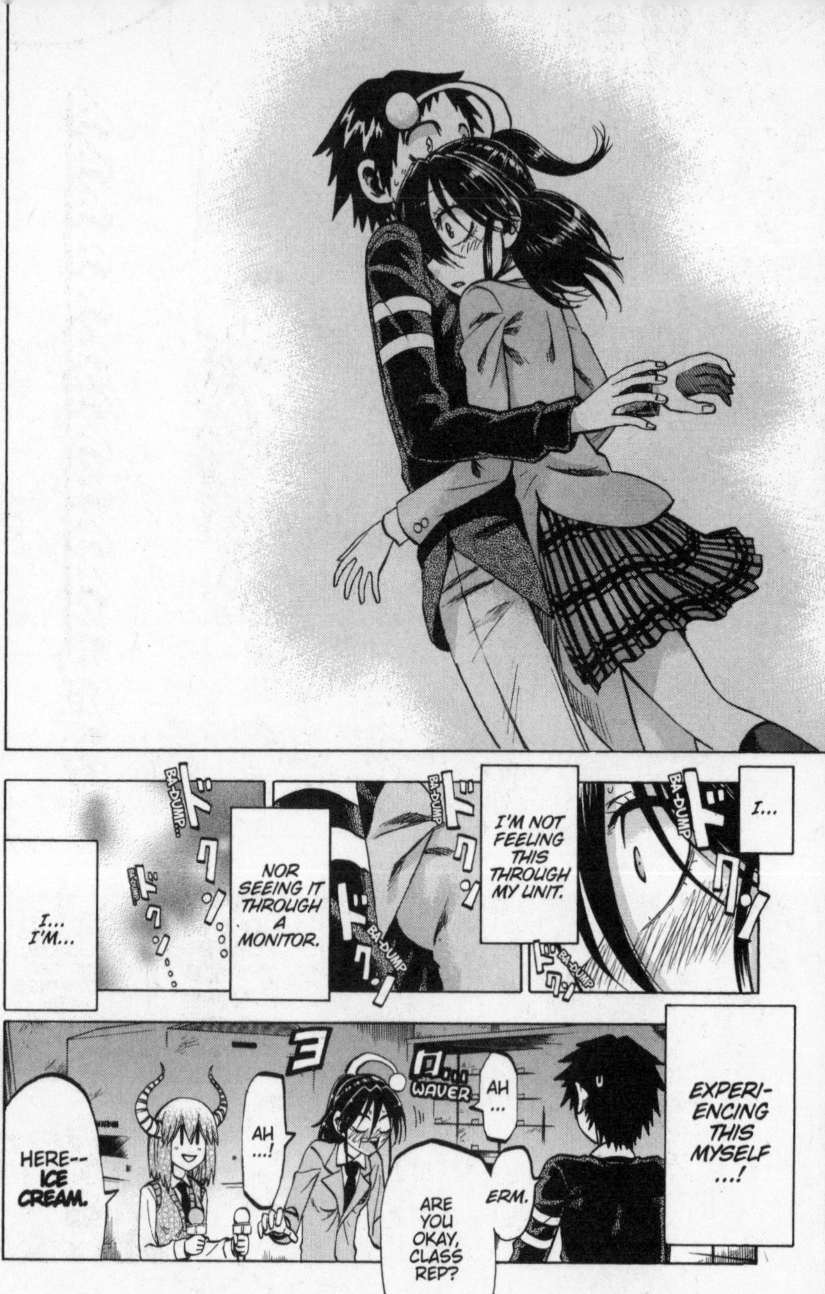
I...
BA-DUMP
BA-DUMP
I'M NOT FEELING THIS THROUGH MY UNIT.
BA-DUMP
BA-DUMP
NOR SEEING IT THROUGH A MONITOR.
BA-DUMP...
I... I'M...
EXPERI-ENCING THIS MYSELF ...!
AH ...
WAVER
ERM.
ARE YOU OKAY, CLASS REP?
AH ...!
HERE-- ICE CREAM.

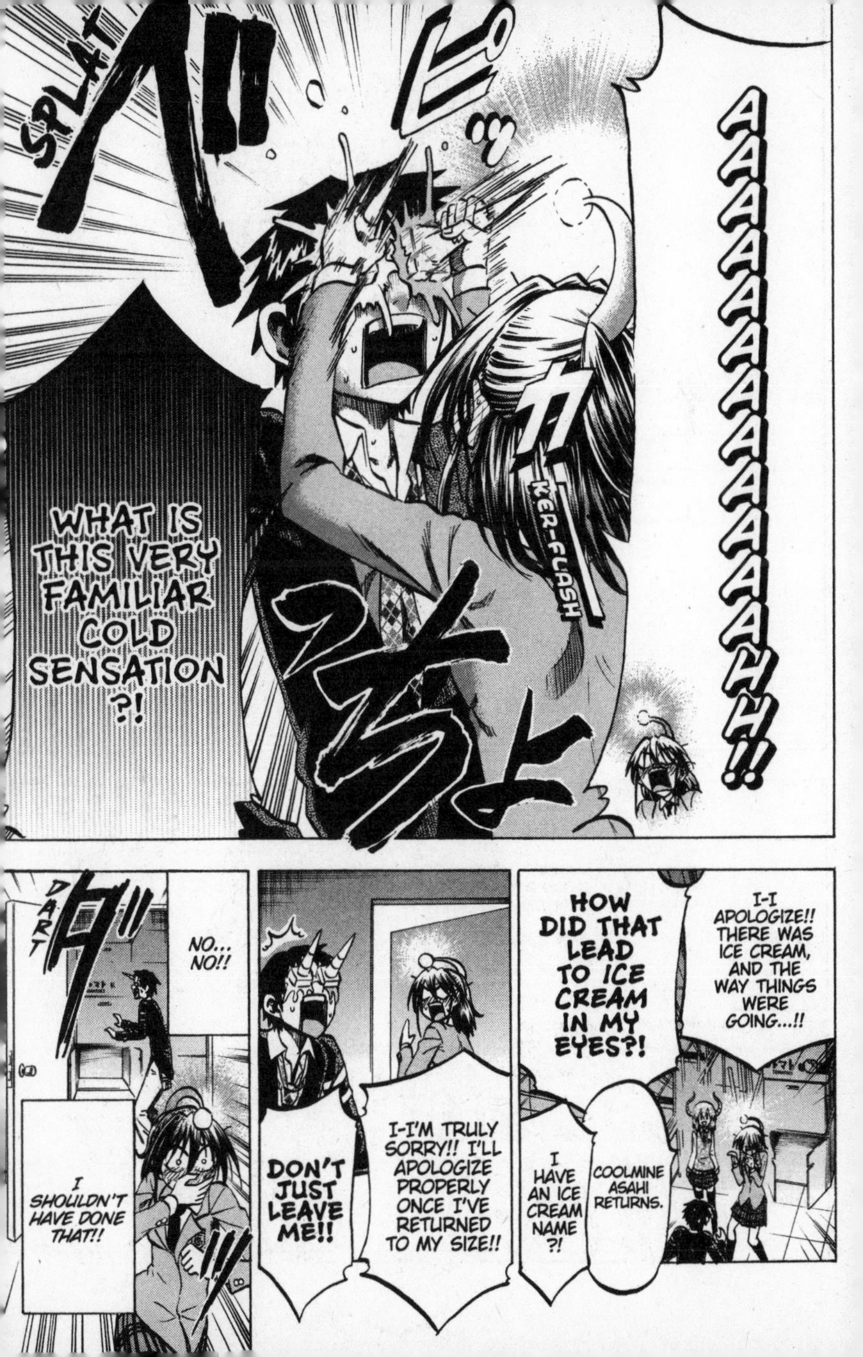
AAAAAAAAAAAAAHH!!
KER-FLASH
SPLAT
WHAT IS THIS VERY FAMILIAR COLD SENSATION ?!
I-I APOLOGIZE!! THERE WAS ICE CREAM, AND THE WAY THINGS WERE GOING...!!
HOW DID THAT LEAD TO ICE CREAM IN MY EYES?!
COOLMINE ASAHI RETURNS.
I HAVE AN ICE CREAM NAME ?!
I-I'M TRULY SORRY!! I'LL APOLOGIZE PROPERLY ONCE I'VE RETURNED TO MY SIZE!!
DON'T JUST LEAVE ME!!
DART
NO... NO!!
I SHOULDN'T HAVE DONE THAT!!

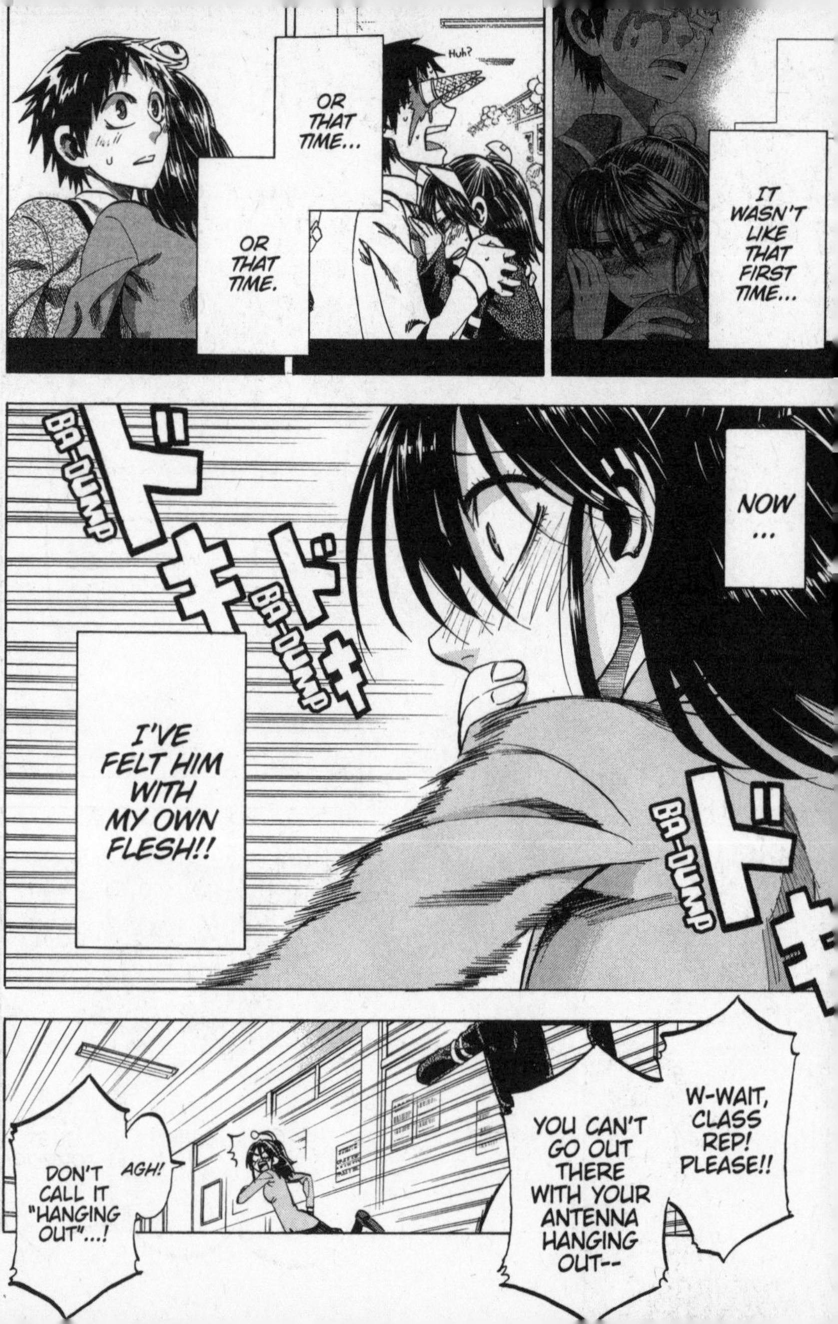
IT WASN'T LIKE THAT FIRST TIME...
Huh?
OR THAT TIME...
OR THAT TIME.
NOW...
BA-DUMP
BA-DUMP
BA-DUMP
I'VE FELT HIM WITH MY OWN FLESH!!
W-WAIT, CLASS REP! PLEASE!!
YOU CAN'T GO OUT THERE WITH YOUR ANTENNA HANGING OUT--
AGH!
DON'T CALL IT "HANGING OUT"...!

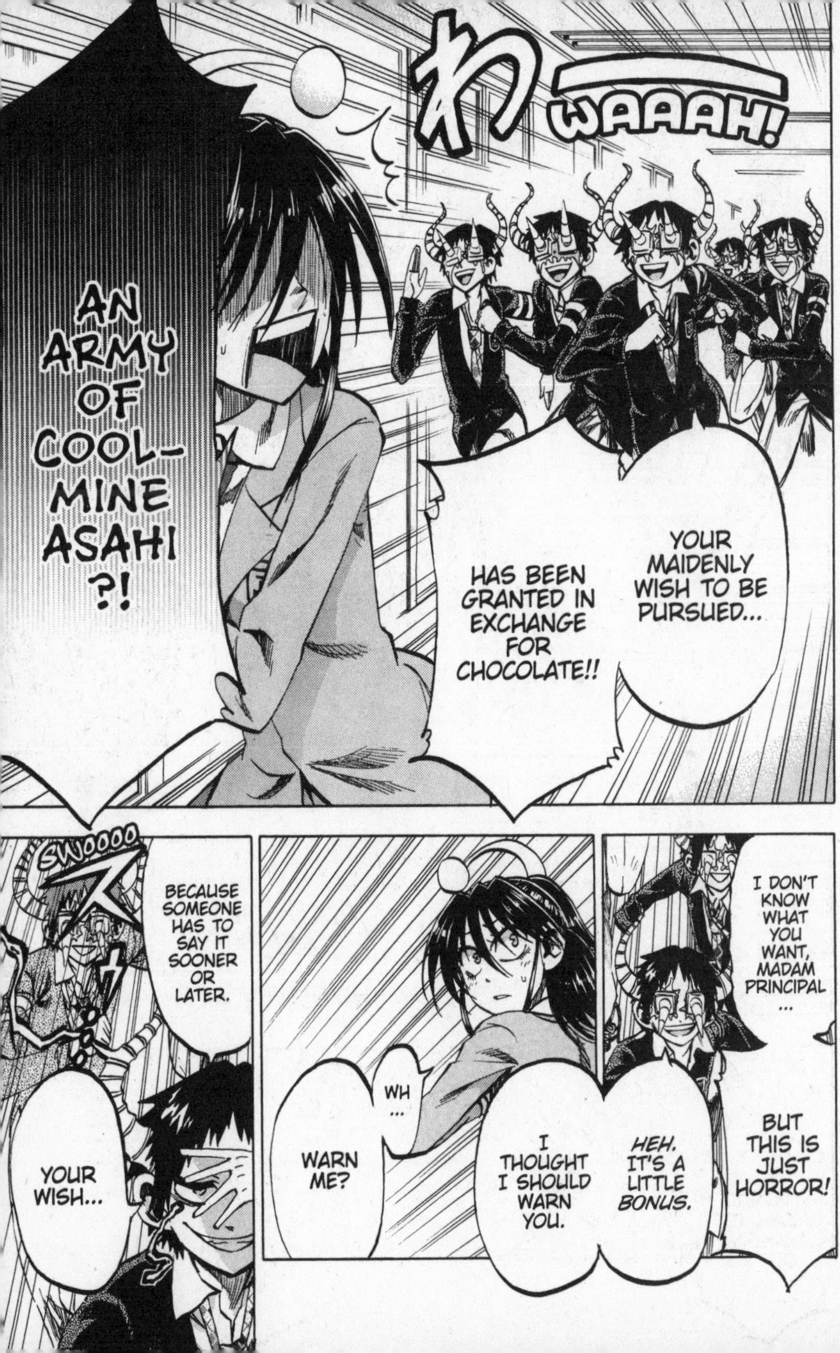
わ
WAAAAH!
YOUR MAIDENLY WISH TO BE PURSUED...
HAS BEEN GRANTED IN EXCHANGE FOR CHOCOLATE!!
AN ARMY OF COOL-MINE ASAHI ?!
I DON'T KNOW WHAT YOU WANT, MADAM PRINCIPAL ...
BUT THIS IS JUST HORROR!
HEH. IT'S A LITTLE BONUS.
I THOUGHT I SHOULD WARN YOU.
WH ...
WARN ME?
SWOOOO
BECAUSE SOMEONE HAS TO SAY IT SOONER OR LATER.
YOUR WISH...

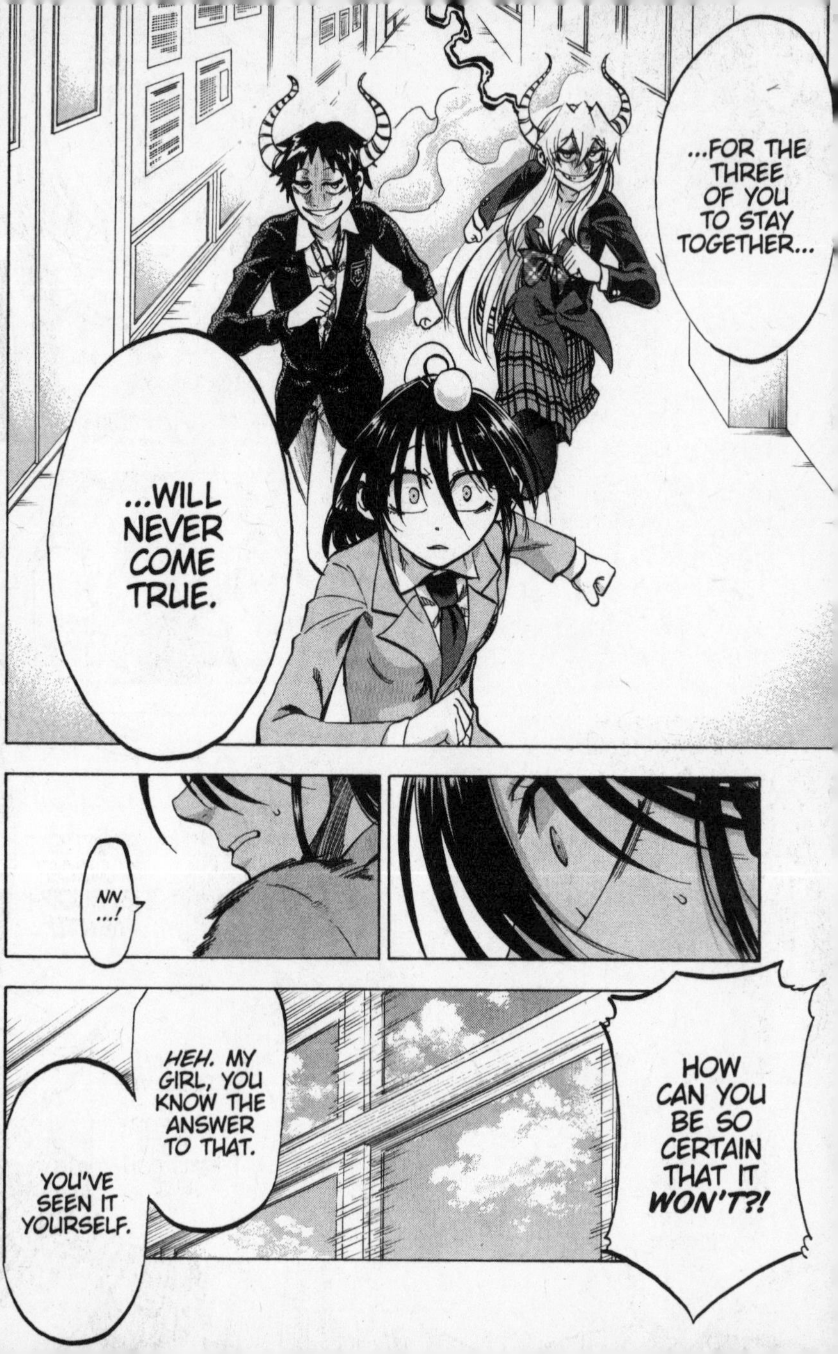
...FOR THE THREE OF YOU TO STAY TOGETHER...
...WILL NEVER COME TRUE.
NN ...!
HOW CAN YOU BE SO CERTAIN THAT IT *WON'T?!*
HEH. MY GIRL, YOU KNOW THE ANSWER TO THAT.
YOU'VE SEEN IT YOURSELF.

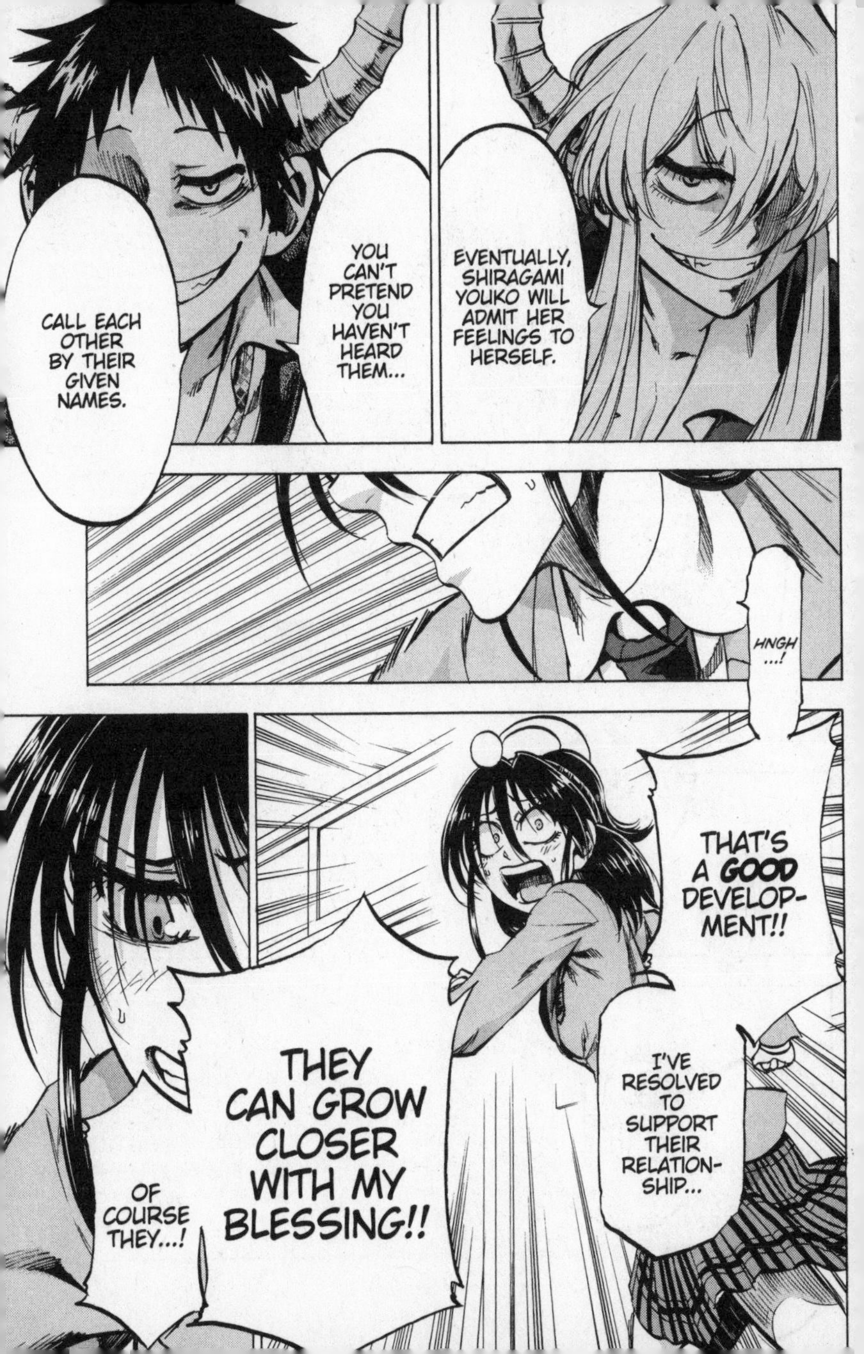
EVENTUALLY, SHIRAGAMI YOUKO WILL ADMIT HER FEELINGS TO HERSELF.
YOU CAN'T PRETEND YOU HAVEN'T HEARD THEM...
CALL EACH OTHER BY THEIR GIVEN NAMES.
HNGH ...!
THAT'S A **GOOD** DEVELOP-MENT!!
I'VE RESOLVED TO SUPPORT THEIR RELATION-SHIP...
THEY CAN GROW CLOSER WITH MY BLESSING!!
OF COURSE THEY...!

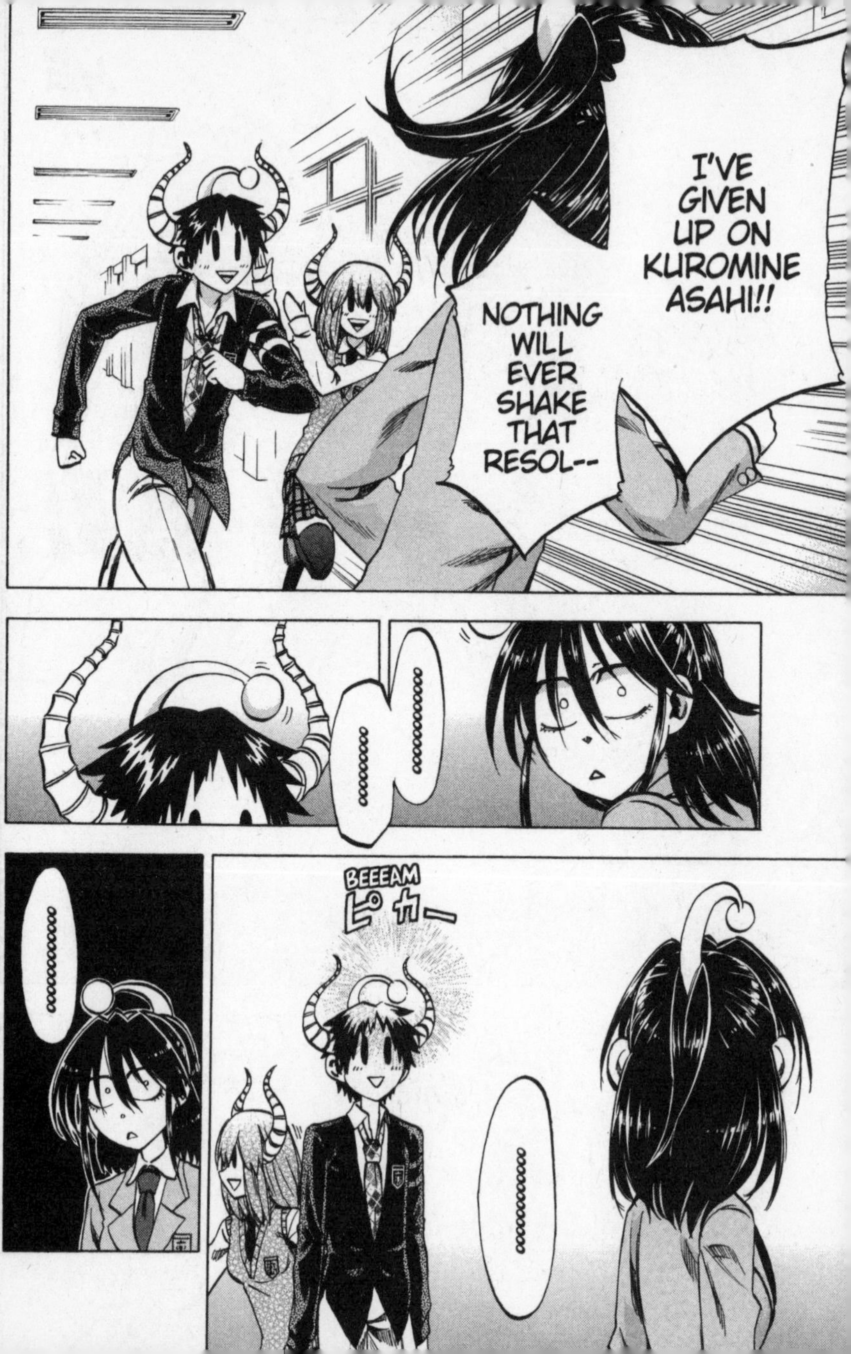
I'VE GIVEN UP ON KUROMINE ASAHI!!
NOTHING WILL EVER SHAKE THAT RESOL--
......
BEEEAM
ピカー
......
......

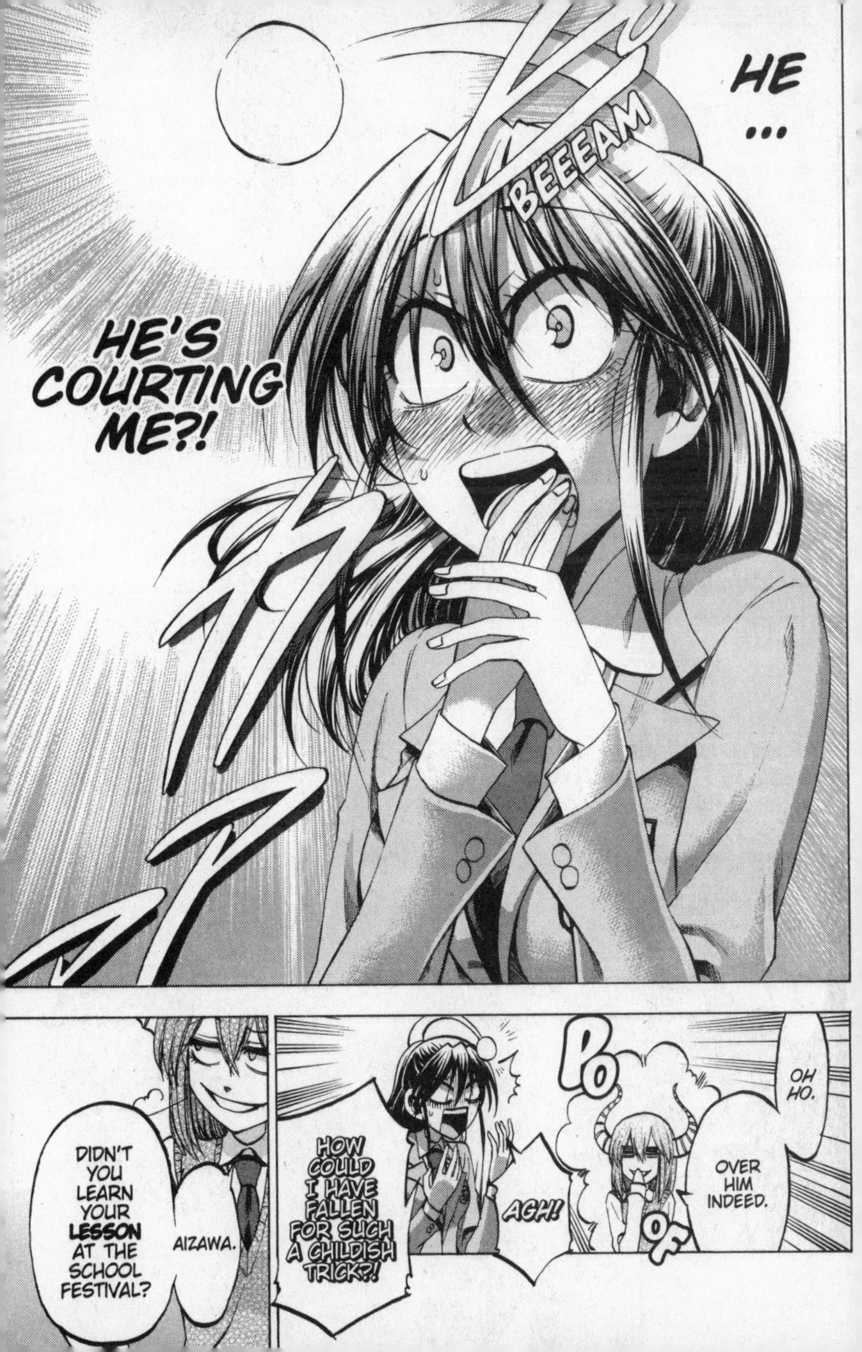
HE ...
BEEEAM
HE'S COURTING ME?!
OH HO.
PO
OVER HIM INDEED.
OF
AGH!
HOW COULD I HAVE FALLEN FOR SUCH A CHILDISH TRICK?!
DIDN'T YOU LEARN YOUR **LESSON** AT THE SCHOOL FESTIVAL?
AIZAWA.

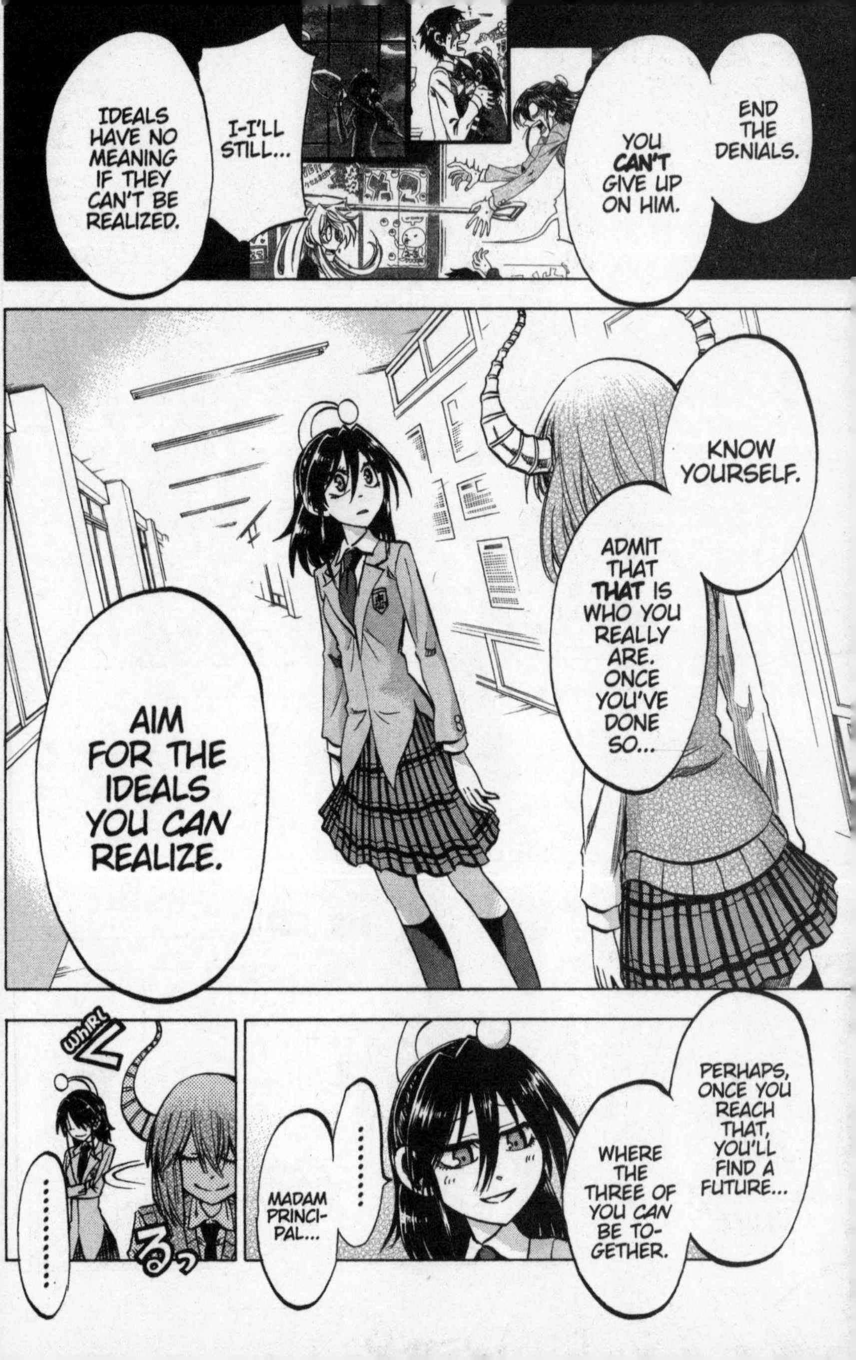
END THE DENIALS.
YOU CAN'T GIVE UP ON HIM.
I-I'LL STILL...
IDEALS HAVE NO MEANING IF THEY CAN'T BE REALIZED.
KNOW YOURSELF.
ADMIT THAT THAT IS WHO YOU REALLY ARE. ONCE YOU'VE DONE SO...
AIM FOR THE IDEALS YOU CAN REALIZE.
PERHAPS, ONCE YOU REACH THAT, YOU'LL FIND A FUTURE...
WHERE THE THREE OF YOU CAN BE TO-GETHER.
......
MADAM PRINCI-PAL...
WHIRL
るっ
......

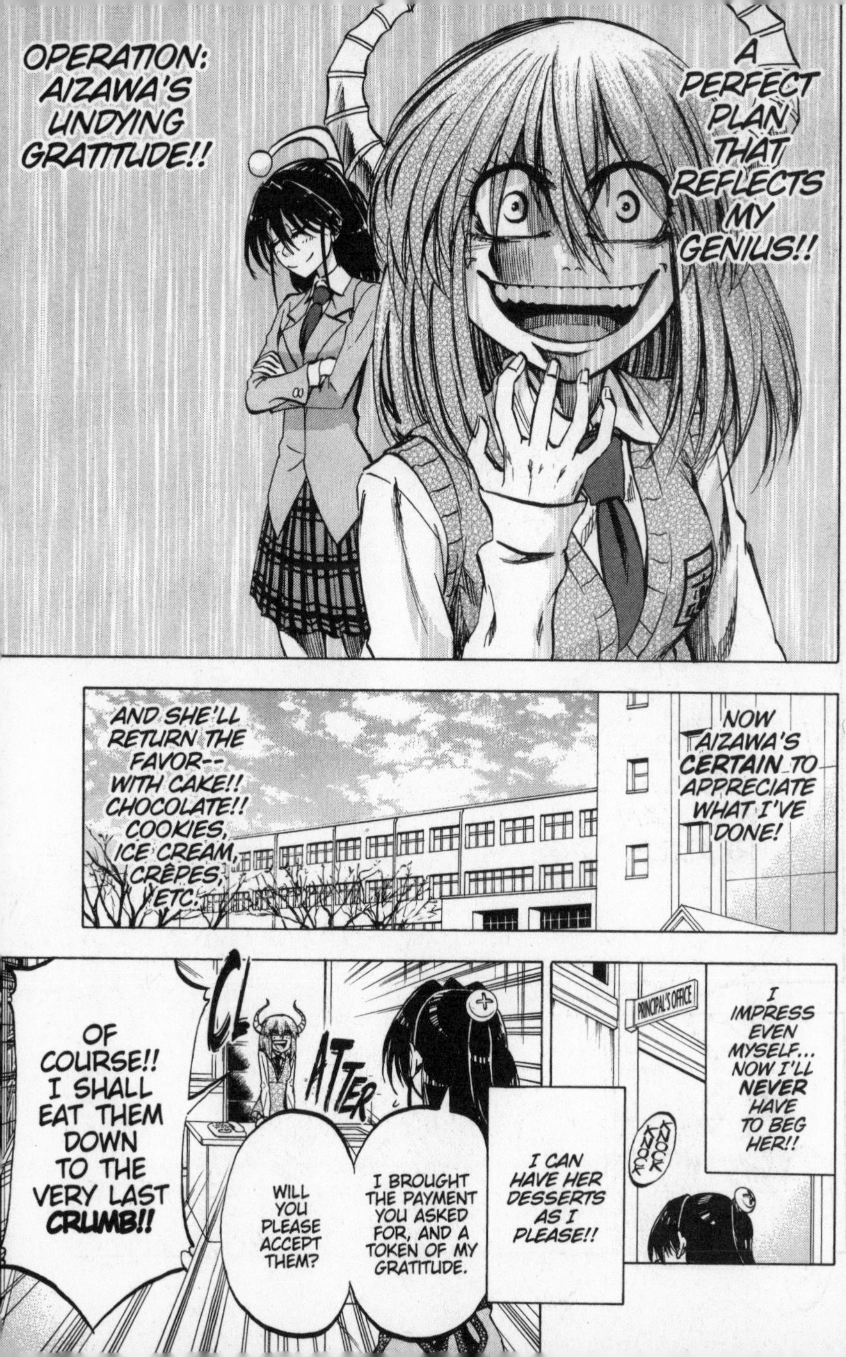
A PERFECT PLAN THAT REFLECTS MY GENIUS!!
OPERATION: AIZAWA'S UNDYING GRATITUDE!!
NOW AIZAWA'S **CERTAIN** TO APPRECIATE WHAT I'VE DONE!
AND SHE'LL RETURN THE FAVOR-- WITH CAKE!! CHOCOLATE!! COOKIES, ICE CREAM, CRÊPES, ETC.
I IMPRESS EVEN MYSELF... NOW I'LL **NEVER** HAVE TO BEG HER!!
PRINCIPAL'S OFFICE
KNOCK KNOCK
I CAN HAVE HER DESSERTS AS I PLEASE!!
I BROUGHT THE PAYMENT YOU ASKED FOR, AND A TOKEN OF MY GRATITUDE.
WILL YOU PLEASE ACCEPT THEM?
CLATTER
OF COURSE!! I SHALL EAT THEM DOWN TO THE VERY LAST **CRUMB!!**

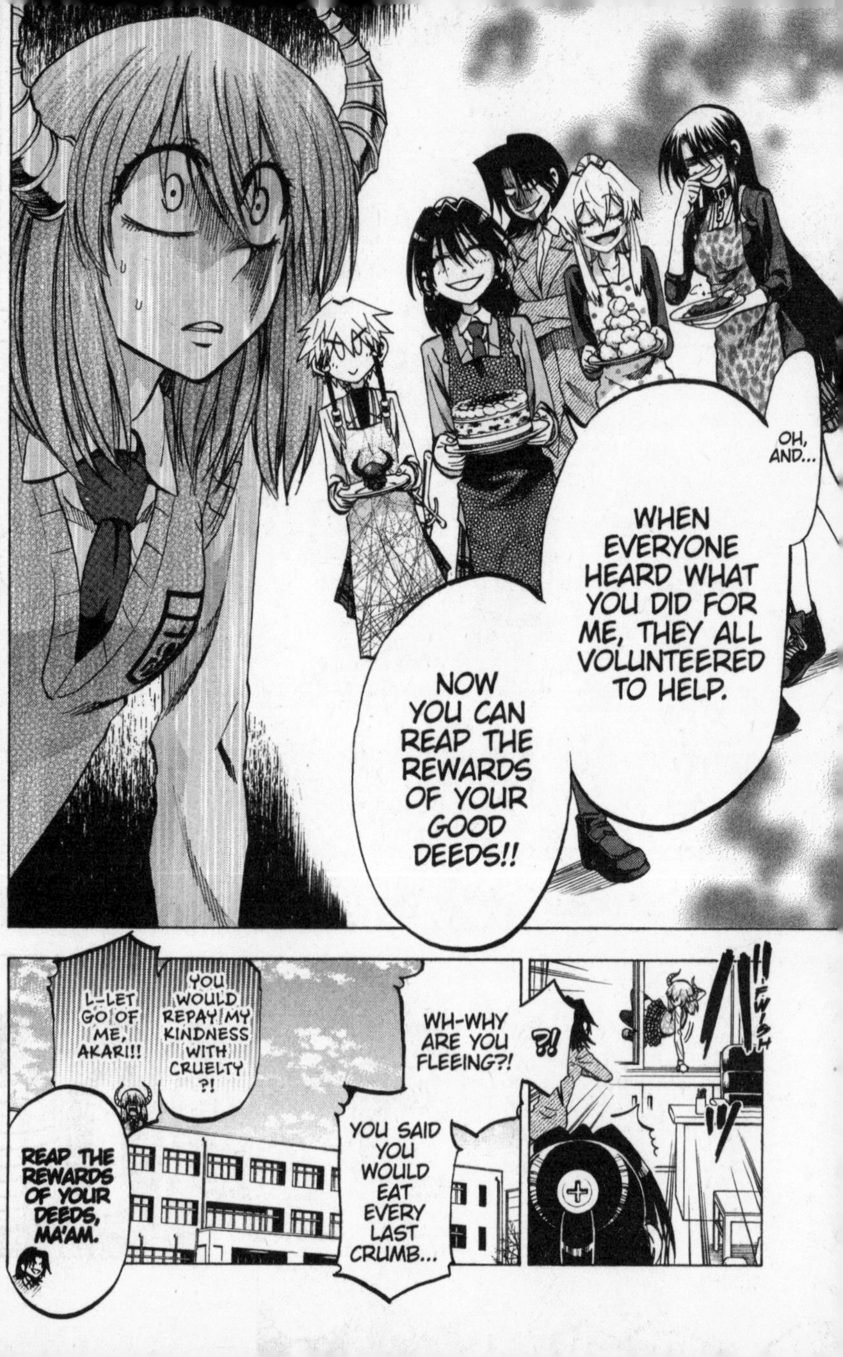
OH, AND...
WHEN EVERYONE HEARD WHAT YOU DID FOR ME, THEY ALL VOLUNTEERED TO HELP.
NOW YOU CAN REAP THE REWARDS OF YOUR GOOD DEEDS!!
FWISH
?!
WH-WHY ARE YOU FLEEING?!
YOU SAID YOU WOULD EAT EVERY LAST CRUMB...
YOU WOULD REPAY MY KINDNESS WITH CRUELTY?!
L-LET GO OF ME, AKARI!!!
REAP THE REWARDS OF YOUR DEEDS, MA'AM.

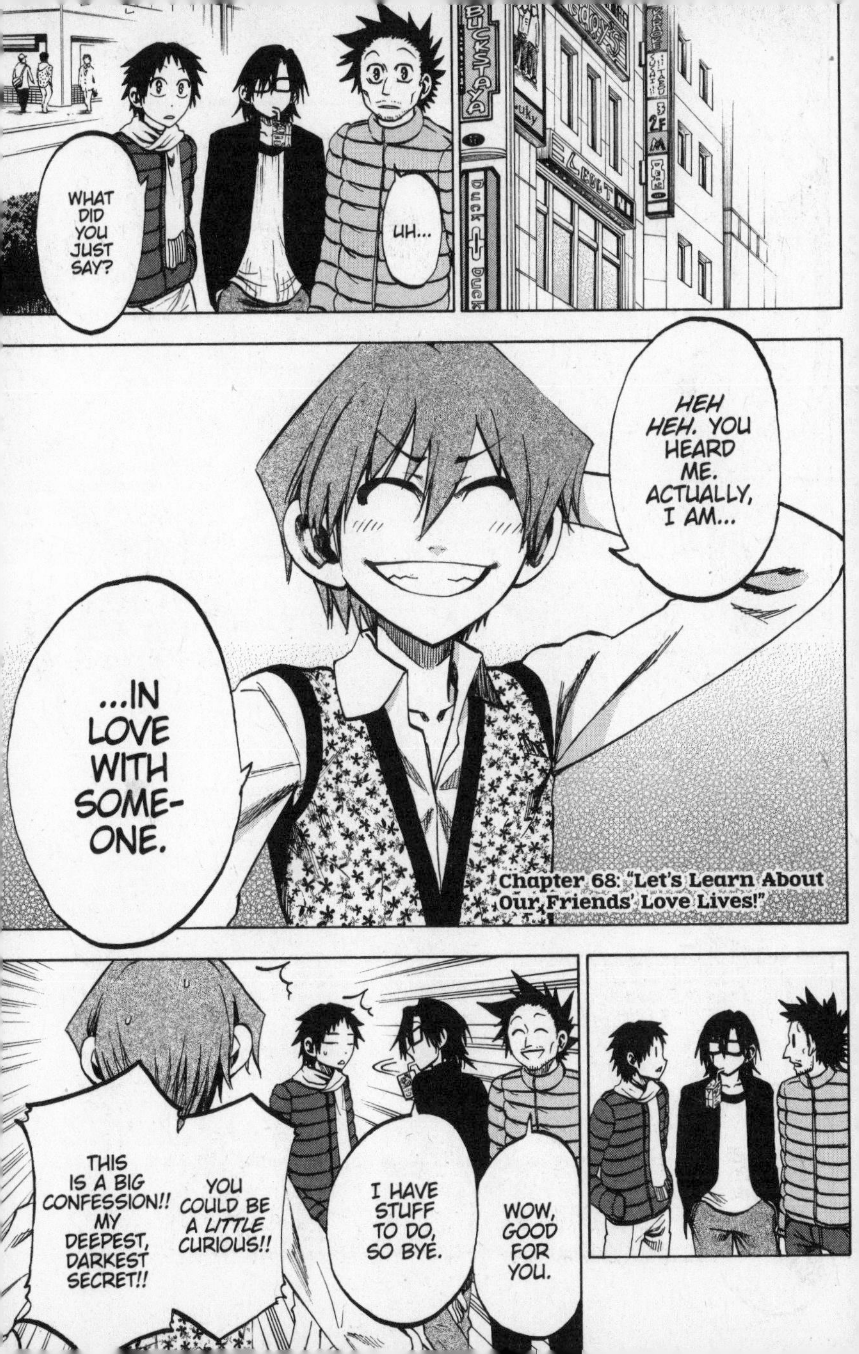
UH...
WHAT DID YOU JUST SAY?
HEH HEH. YOU HEARD ME. ACTUALLY, I AM...
...IN LOVE WITH SOME-ONE.
Chapter 68: "Let's Learn About Our Friends' Love Lives!"
WOW, GOOD FOR YOU.
I HAVE STUFF TO DO, SO BYE.
YOU COULD BE A *LITTLE* CURIOUS!!
THIS IS A BIG CONFESSION!! MY DEEPEST, DARKEST SECRET!!

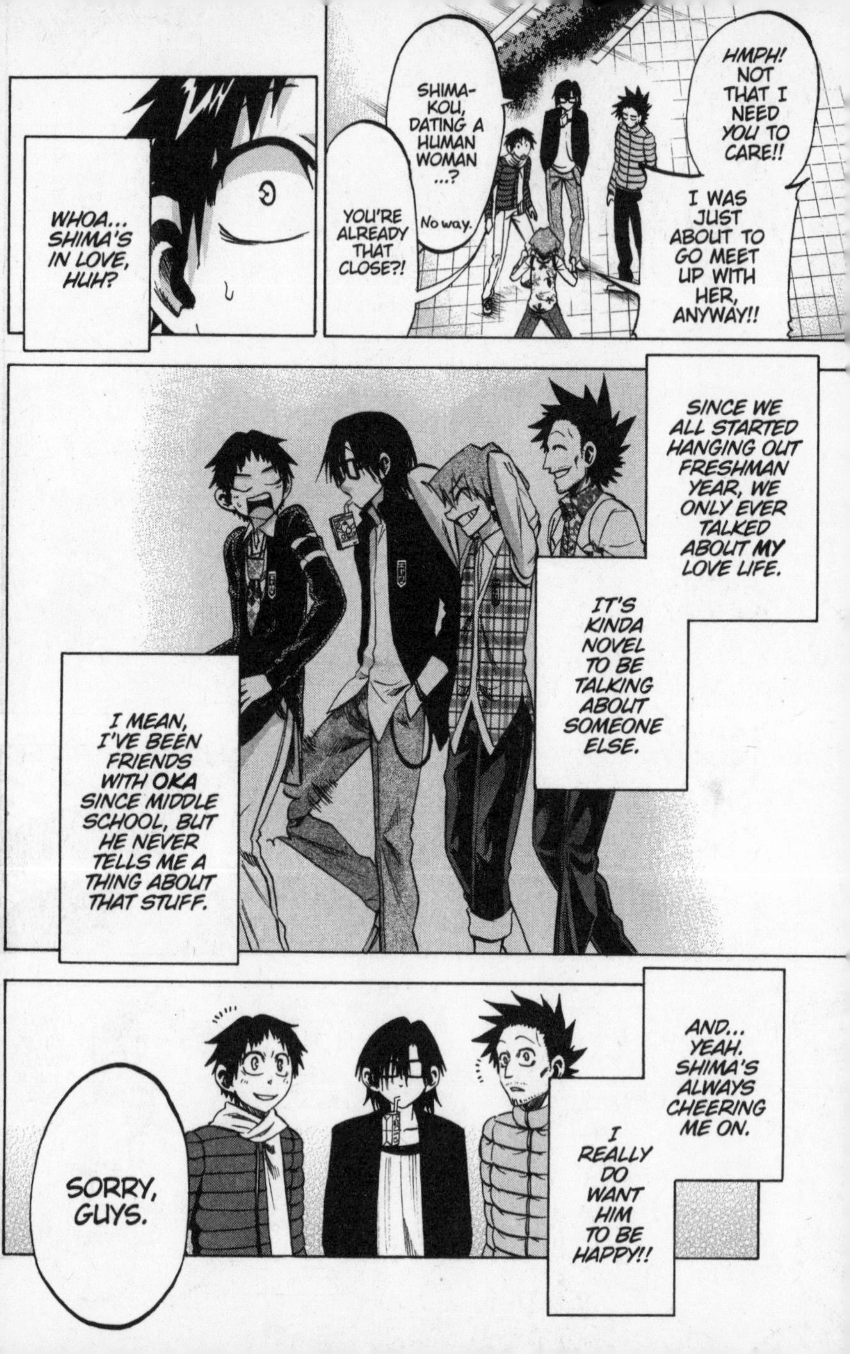
HMPH! NOT THAT I NEED YOU TO CARE!!
I WAS JUST ABOUT TO GO MEET UP WITH HER, ANYWAY!!
SHIMA-KOU, DATING A HUMAN WOMAN ...?
No way.
YOU'RE ALREADY THAT CLOSE?!
WHOA... SHIMA'S IN LOVE, HUH?
SINCE WE ALL STARTED HANGING OUT FRESHMAN YEAR, WE ONLY EVER TALKED ABOUT MY LOVE LIFE.
IT'S KINDA NOVEL TO BE TALKING ABOUT SOMEONE ELSE.
I MEAN, I'VE BEEN FRIENDS WITH OKA SINCE MIDDLE SCHOOL, BUT HE NEVER TELLS ME A THING ABOUT THAT STUFF.
AND... YEAH. SHIMA'S ALWAYS CHEERING ME ON.
I REALLY DO WANT HIM TO BE HAPPY!!
SORRY, GUYS.

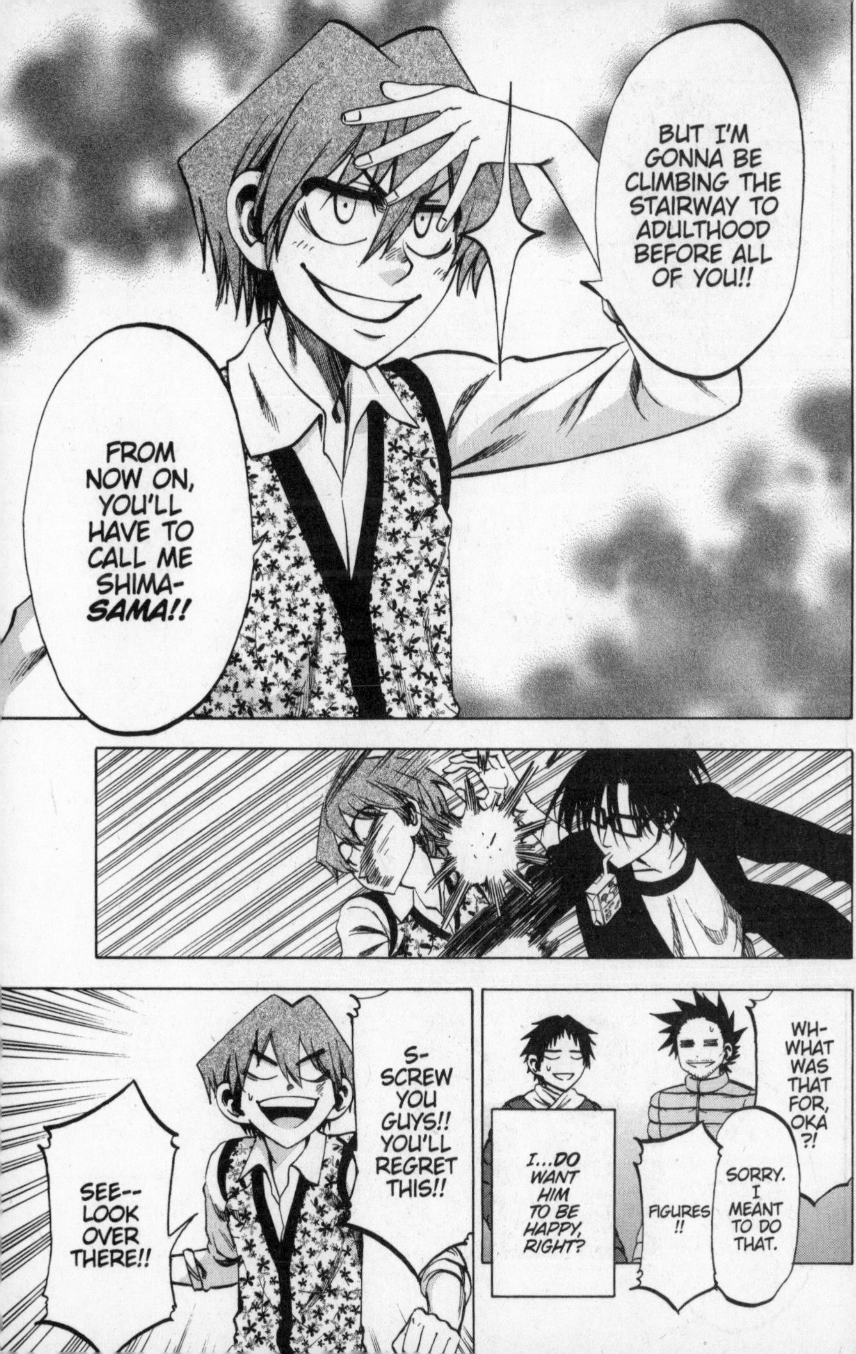
BUT I'M GONNA BE CLIMBING THE STAIRWAY TO ADULTHOOD BEFORE ALL OF YOU!!
FROM NOW ON, YOU'LL HAVE TO CALL ME SHIMA-*SAMA*!!
WH-WHAT WAS THAT FOR, OKA?!
SORRY. I MEANT TO DO THAT.
FIGURES!!
I...DO WANT HIM TO BE HAPPY, RIGHT?
S-SCREW YOU GUYS!! YOU'LL REGRET THIS!!
SEE--LOOK OVER THERE!!

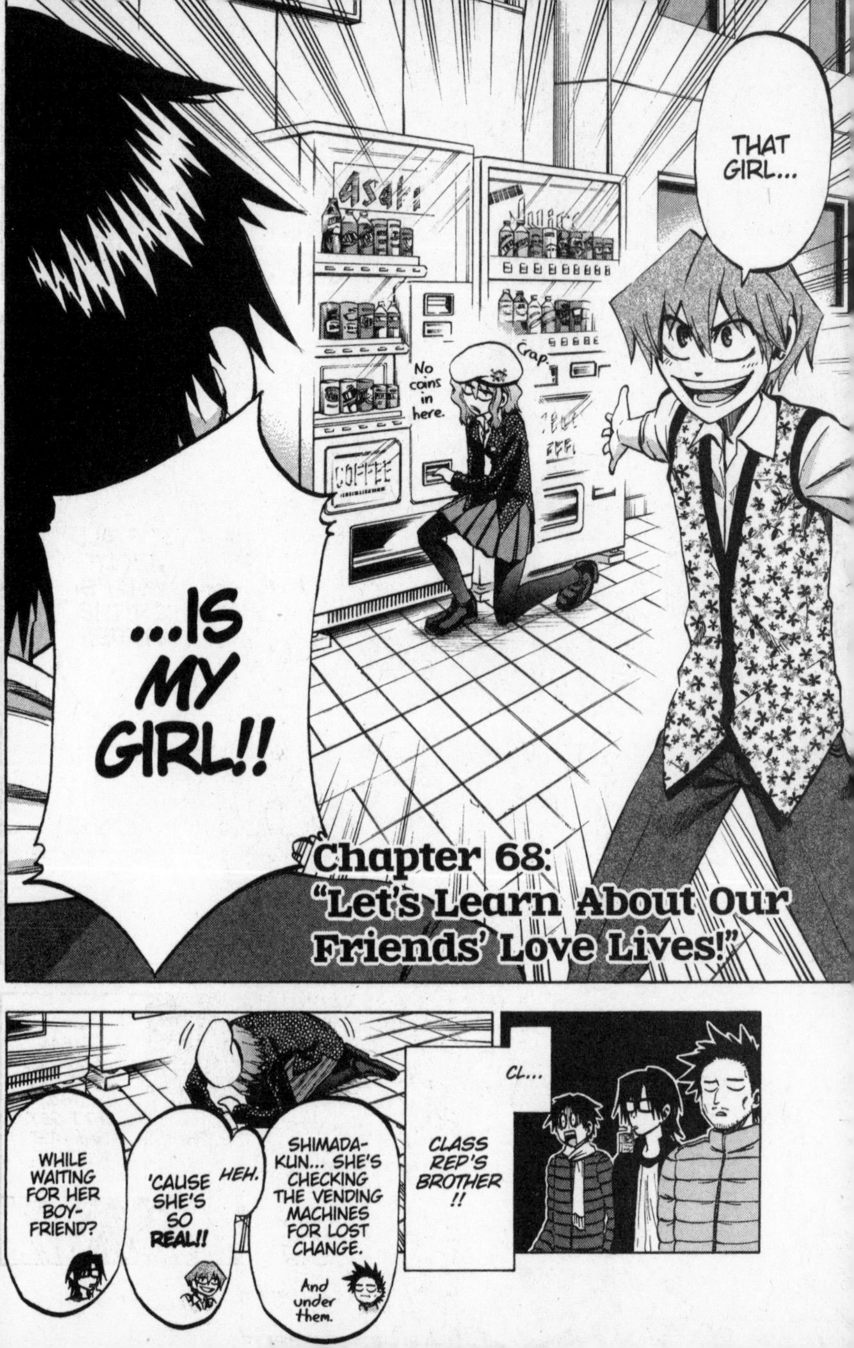
THAT GIRL...
Crap.
No coins in here.
COFFEE
...IS MY GIRL!!
Chapter 68: "Let's Learn About Our Friends' Love Lives!"
CL...
CLASS REP'S BROTHER !!
SHIMADA-KUN... SHE'S CHECKING THE VENDING MACHINES FOR LOST CHANGE.
And under them.
HEH.
'CAUSE SHE'S SO REAL!!
WHILE WAITING FOR HER BOY-FRIEND?

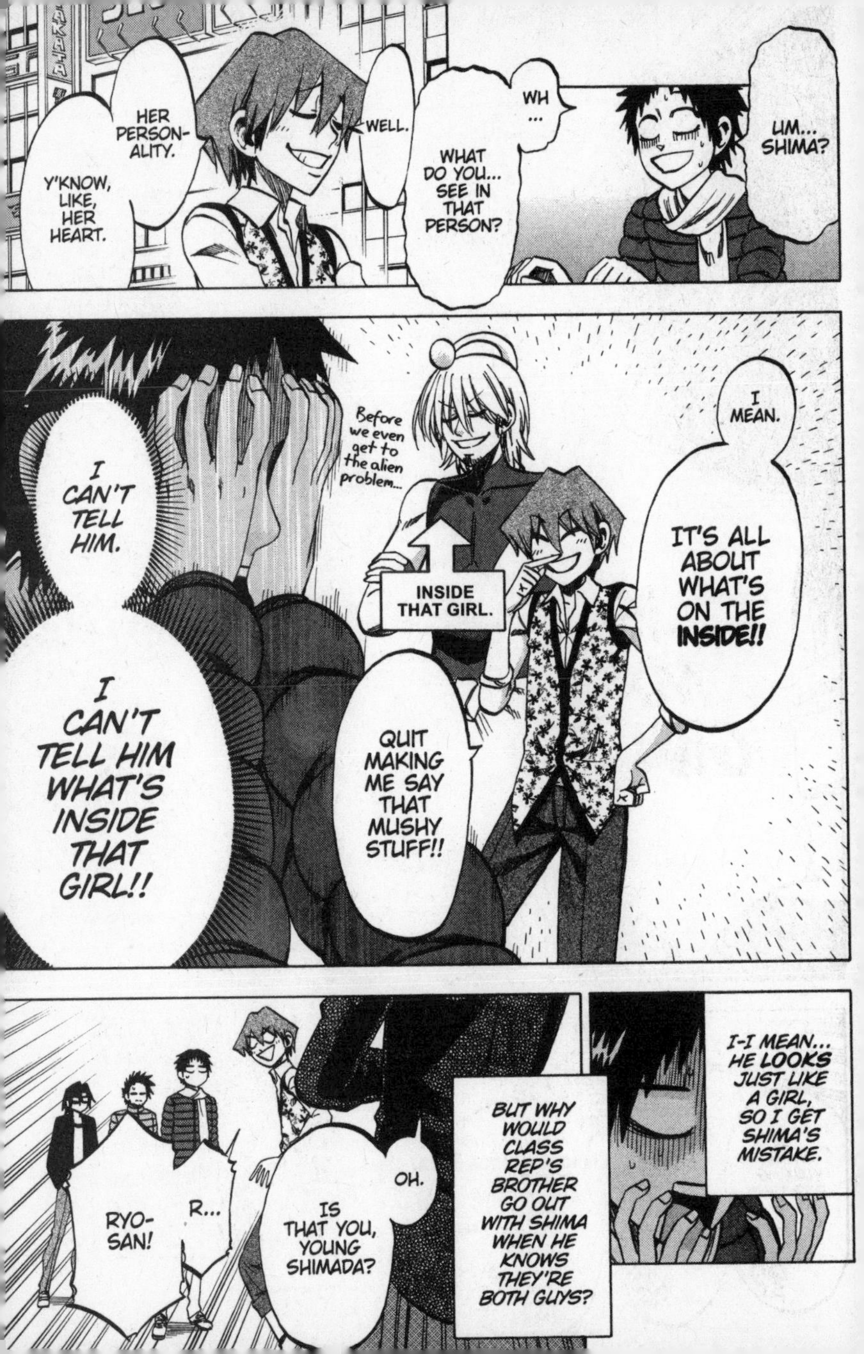
UM... SHIMA?
WH... WHAT DO YOU... SEE IN THAT PERSON?
WELL.
HER PERSONALITY.
Y'KNOW, LIKE, HER HEART.
I MEAN.
IT'S ALL ABOUT WHAT'S ON THE **INSIDE!!**
INSIDE THAT GIRL.
Before we even get to the alien problem...
QUIT MAKING ME SAY THAT MUSHY STUFF!!
I CAN'T TELL HIM.
I CAN'T TELL HIM WHAT'S INSIDE THAT GIRL!!
I-I MEAN... HE LOOKS JUST LIKE A GIRL, SO I GET SHIMA'S MISTAKE.
BUT WHY WOULD CLASS REP'S BROTHER GO OUT WITH SHIMA WHEN HE KNOWS THEY'RE BOTH GUYS?
OH.
IS THAT YOU, YOUNG SHIMADA?
R...
RYO-SAN!

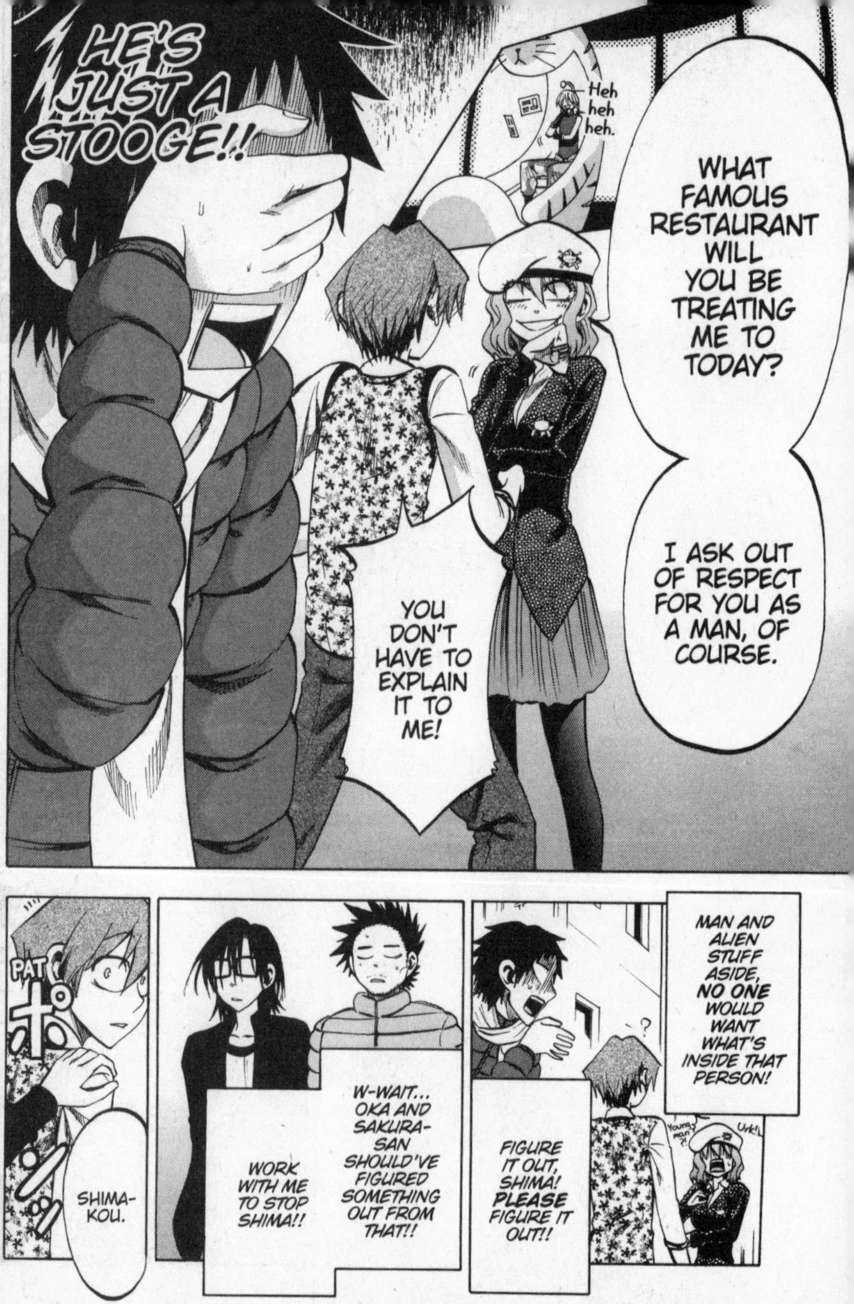
WHAT FAMOUS RESTAURANT WILL YOU BE TREATING ME TO TODAY?
Heh heh heh.
HE'S JUST A STOOGE!!
I ASK OUT OF RESPECT FOR YOU AS A MAN, OF COURSE.
YOU DON'T HAVE TO EXPLAIN IT TO ME!
MAN AND ALIEN STUFF ASIDE, NO ONE WOULD WANT WHAT'S INSIDE THAT PERSON!
?
Urk!!
Young man?!
FIGURE IT OUT, SHIMA! PLEASE FIGURE IT OUT!!
W-WAIT... OKA AND SAKURA-SAN SHOULD'VE FIGURED SOMETHING OUT FROM THAT!!
WORK WITH ME TO STOP SHIMA!!
PAT
SHIMA-KOU.

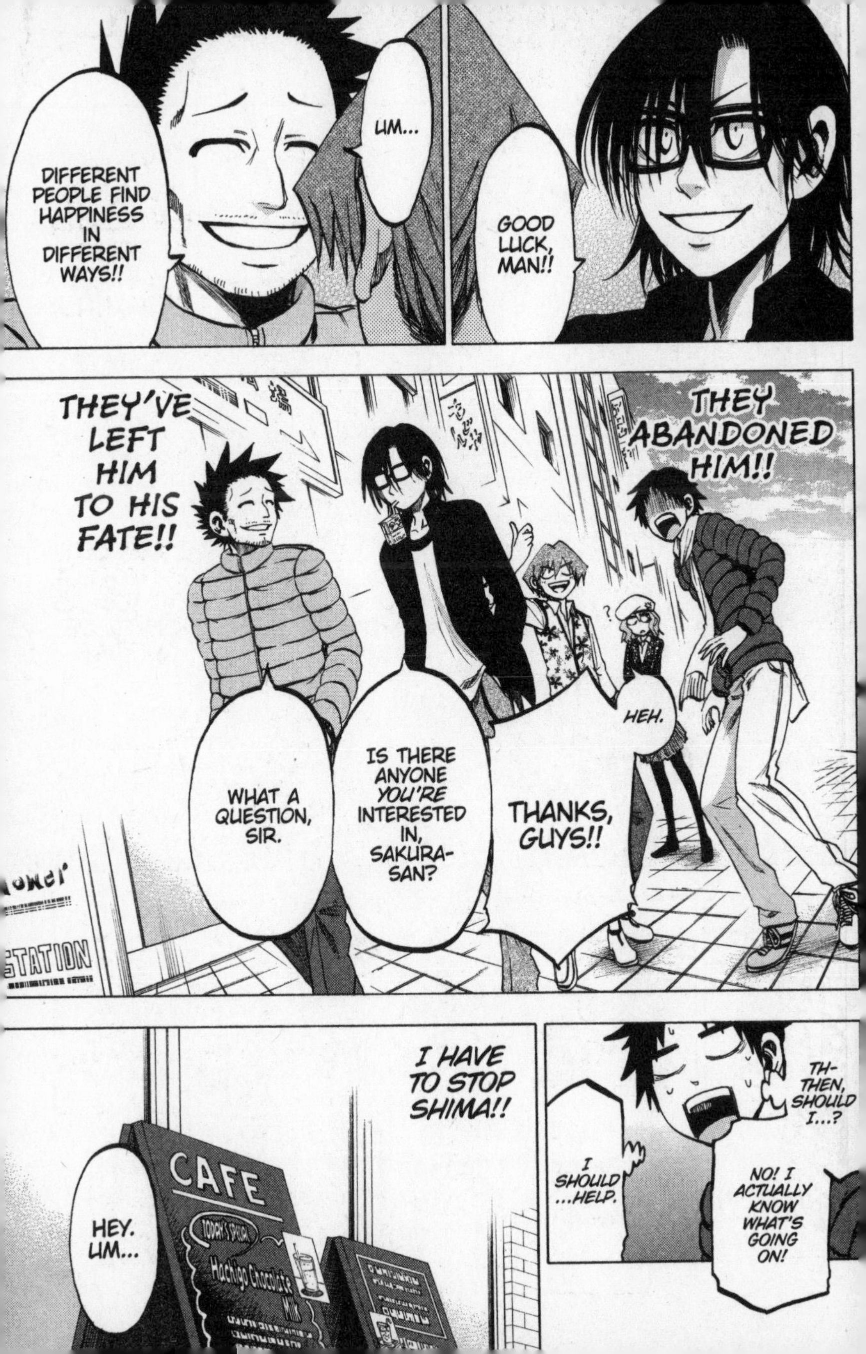
GOOD LUCK, MAN!!
UM...
DIFFERENT PEOPLE FIND HAPPINESS IN DIFFERENT WAYS!!
THEY ABANDONED HIM!!
THEY'VE LEFT HIM TO HIS FATE!!
HEH.
THANKS, GUYS!!
IS THERE ANYONE *YOU'RE* INTERESTED IN, SAKURA-SAN?
WHAT A QUESTION, SIR.
STATION
TH-THEN, SHOULD I...?
NO! I ACTUALLY KNOW WHAT'S GOING ON!
I SHOULD ...HELP.
I HAVE TO STOP SHIMA!!
HEY. UM...
CAFE
TODAY'S SPECIAL
Hachigo Chocolate Milk

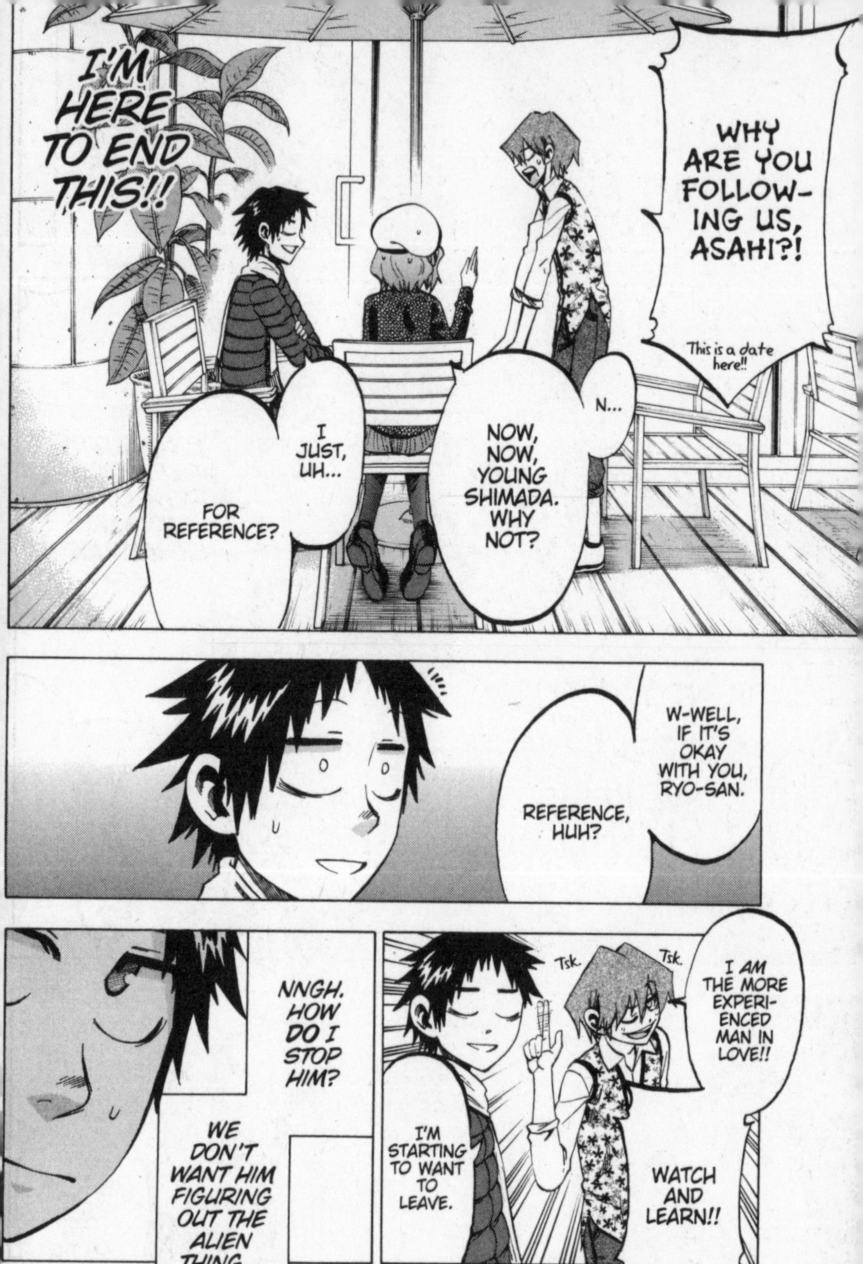
WHY ARE YOU FOLLOWING US, ASAHI?!
This is a date here!!
I'M HERE TO END THIS!!
N...
NOW, NOW, YOUNG SHIMADA. WHY NOT?
I JUST, UH...
FOR REFERENCE?
W-WELL, IF IT'S OKAY WITH YOU, RYO-SAN.
REFERENCE, HUH?
I AM THE MORE EXPERIENCED MAN IN LOVE!!
Tsk.
Tsk.
WATCH AND LEARN!!
I'M STARTING TO WANT TO LEAVE.
NNGH. HOW DO I STOP HIM?
WE DON'T WANT HIM FIGURING OUT THE ALIEN THING...

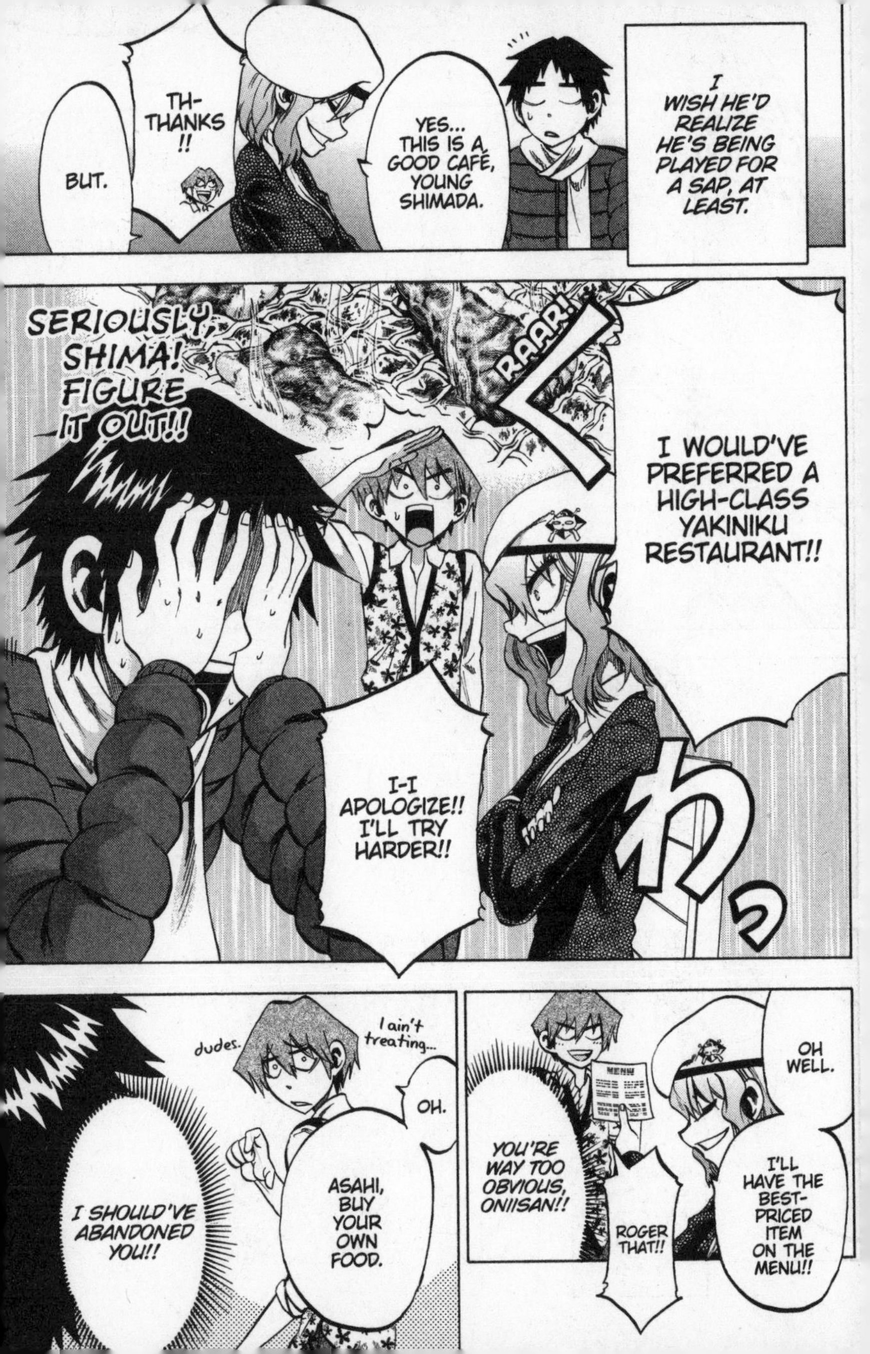
I WISH HE'D REALIZE HE'S BEING PLAYED FOR A SAP, AT LEAST.
YES... THIS IS A GOOD CAFÉ, YOUNG SHIMADA.
TH-THANKS!!
BUT.
I WOULD'VE PREFERRED A HIGH-CLASS YAKINIKU RESTAURANT!!
RAAR!
SERIOUSLY, SHIMA! FIGURE IT OUT!!
I-I APOLOGIZE!! I'LL TRY HARDER!!
わっ
OH WELL.
I'LL HAVE THE BEST-PRICED ITEM ON THE MENU!!
MENU
ROGER THAT!!
YOU'RE WAY TOO OBVIOUS, ONIISAN!!
I ain't treating...
dudes.
OH.
ASAHI, BUY YOUR OWN FOOD.
I SHOULD'VE ABANDONED YOU!!

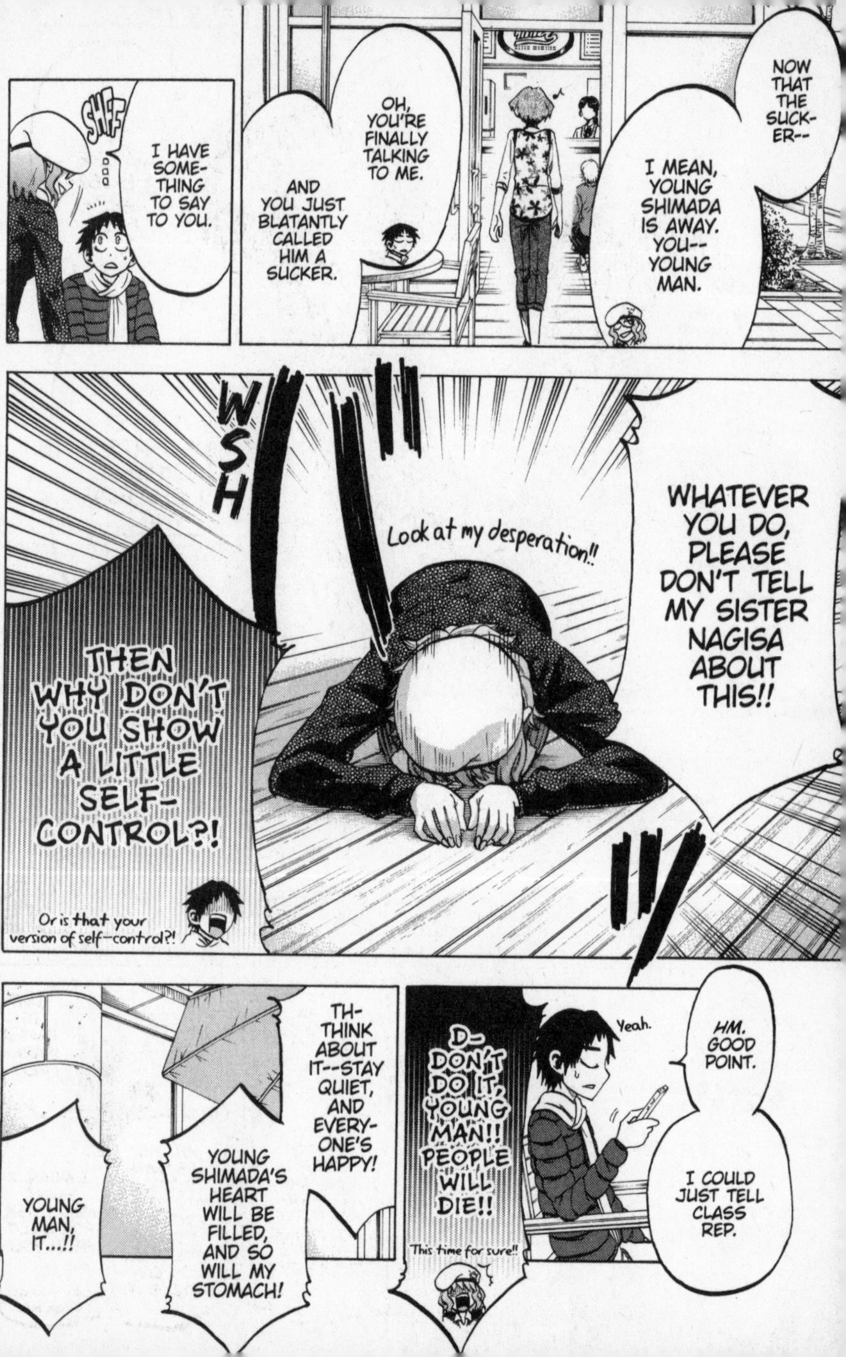
NOW THAT THE SUCK-ER--
I MEAN, YOUNG SHIMADA IS AWAY. YOU--YOUNG MAN.
OH, YOU'RE FINALLY TALKING TO ME.
AND YOU JUST BLATANTLY CALLED HIM A SUCKER.
SHF
I HAVE SOME-THING TO SAY TO YOU.
WHATEVER YOU DO, PLEASE DON'T TELL MY SISTER NAGISA ABOUT THIS!!
WSH
Look at my desperation!!
THEN WHY DON'T YOU SHOW A LITTLE SELF-CONTROL?!
Or is that your version of self-control?!
HM. GOOD POINT.
Yeah.
I COULD JUST TELL CLASS REP.
D-DON'T DO IT, YOUNG MAN!! PEOPLE WILL DIE!!
This time for sure!!
TH-THINK ABOUT IT--STAY QUIET, AND EVERY-ONE'S HAPPY!
YOUNG SHIMADA'S HEART WILL BE FILLED, AND SO WILL MY STOMACH!
YOUNG MAN, IT...!!

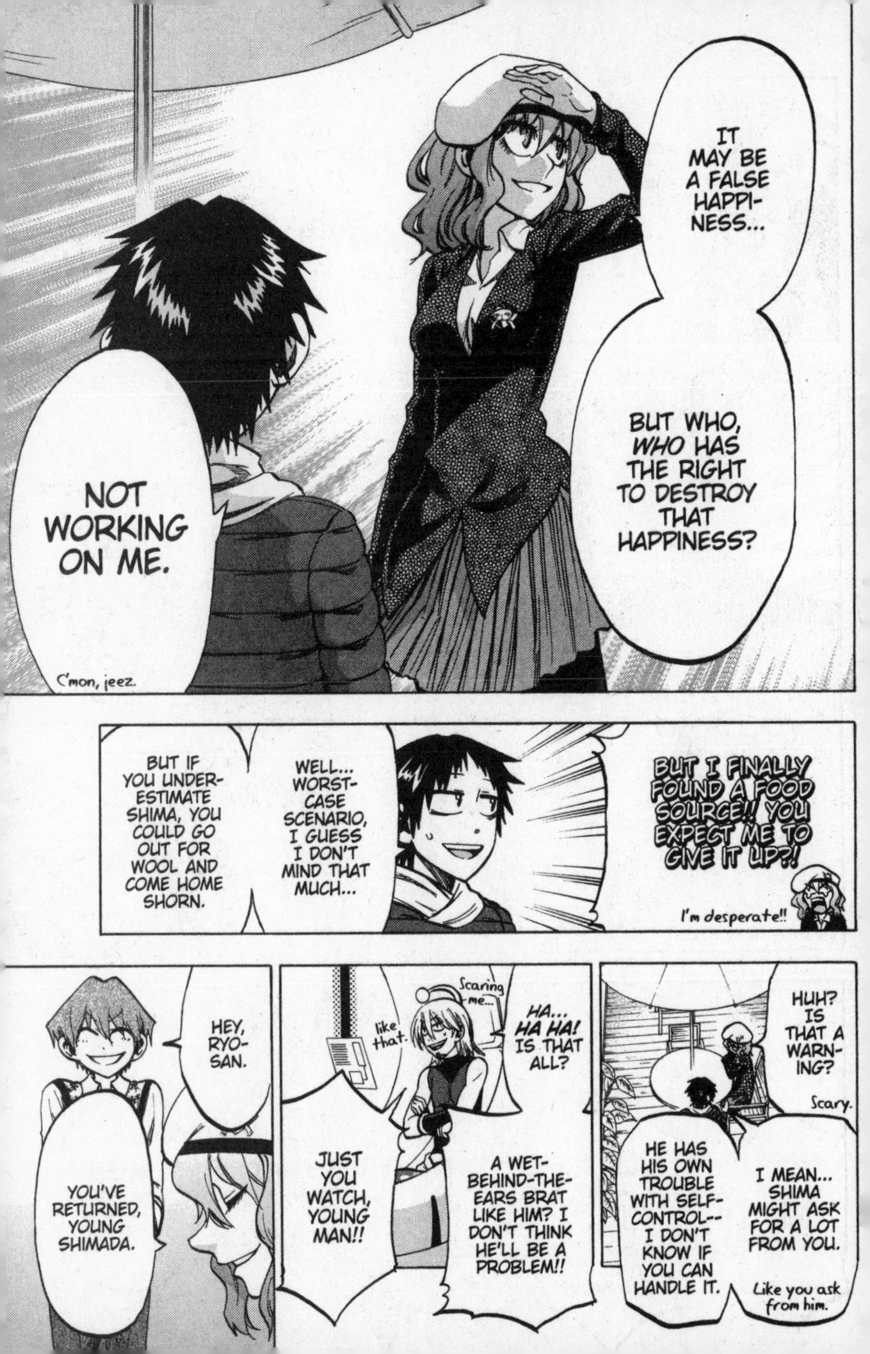
IT MAY BE A FALSE HAPPINESS...
BUT WHO, *WHO* HAS THE RIGHT TO DESTROY THAT HAPPINESS?
NOT WORKING ON ME.
C'mon, jeez.
BUT I FINALLY FOUND A FOOD SOURCE!! YOU EXPECT ME TO GIVE IT UP?!
I'm desperate!!
WELL... WORST-CASE SCENARIO, I GUESS I DON'T MIND THAT MUCH...
BUT IF YOU UNDER-ESTIMATE SHIMA, YOU COULD GO OUT FOR WOOL AND COME HOME SHORN.
HUH? IS THAT A WARNING?
Scary.
I MEAN... SHIMA MIGHT ASK FOR A LOT FROM YOU.
Like you ask from him.
HE HAS HIS OWN TROUBLE WITH SELF-CONTROL-- I DON'T KNOW IF YOU CAN HANDLE IT.
HA... HA HA! IS THAT ALL?
Scaring me... like that.
A WET-BEHIND-THE-EARS BRAT LIKE HIM? I DON'T THINK HE'LL BE A PROBLEM!!
JUST YOU WATCH, YOUNG MAN!!
HEY, RYO-SAN.
YOU'VE RETURNED, YOUNG SHIMADA.

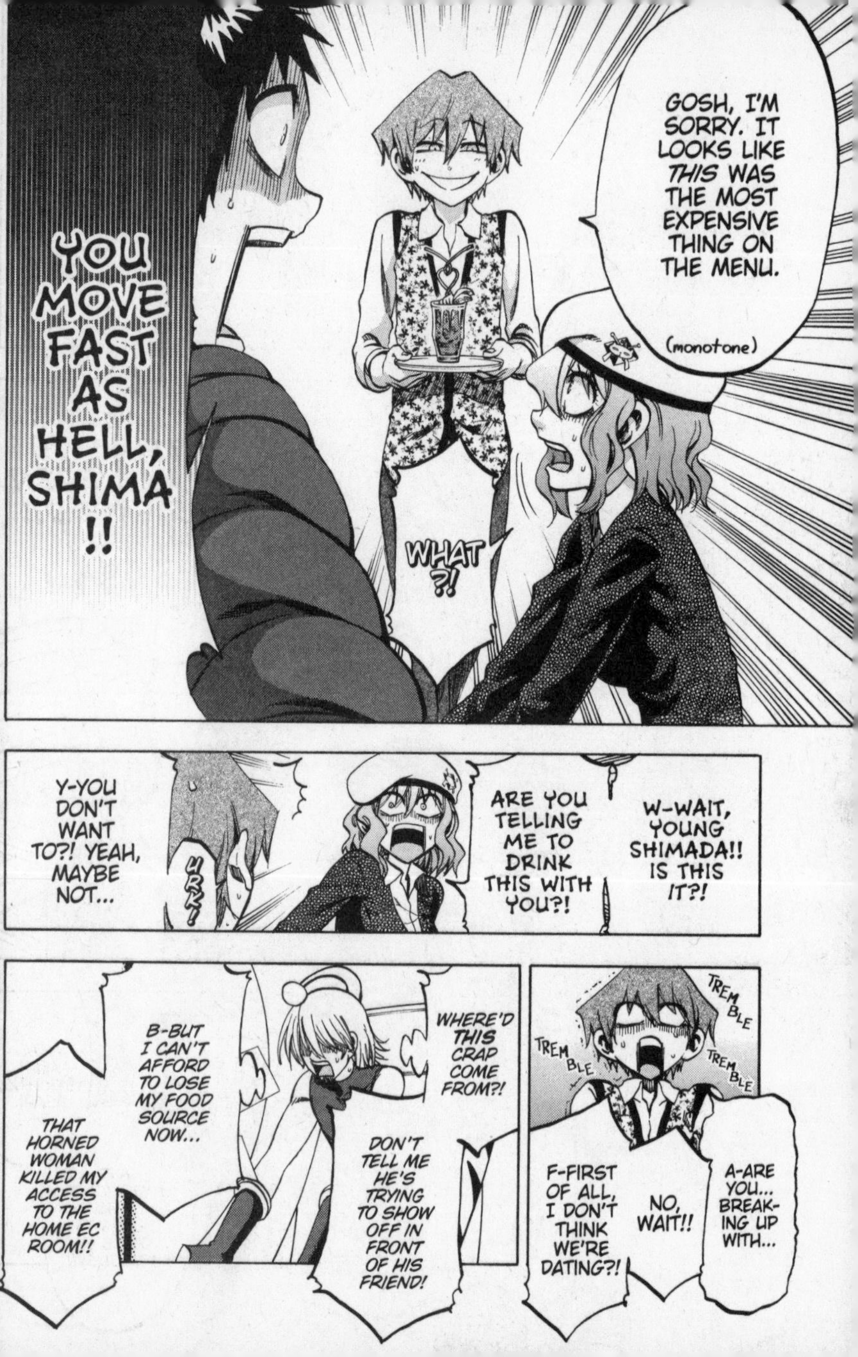
GOSH, I'M SORRY. IT LOOKS LIKE *THIS* WAS THE MOST EXPENSIVE THING ON THE MENU.
(monotone)
WHAT?!
YOU MOVE FAST AS HELL, SHIMA!!
W-WAIT, YOUNG SHIMADA!! IS THIS IT?!
ARE YOU TELLING ME TO DRINK THIS WITH YOU?!
URK!
Y-YOU DON'T WANT TO?! YEAH, MAYBE NOT...
TREMBLE
TREMBLE
TREMBLE
A-ARE YOU... BREAKING UP WITH...
NO, WAIT!!
F-FIRST OF ALL, I DON'T THINK WE'RE DATING?!
WHERE'D **THIS** CRAP COME FROM?!
DON'T TELL ME HE'S TRYING TO SHOW OFF IN FRONT OF HIS FRIEND!
B-BUT I CAN'T AFFORD TO LOSE MY FOOD SOURCE NOW...
THAT HORNED WOMAN KILLED MY ACCESS TO THE HOME EC ROOM!!

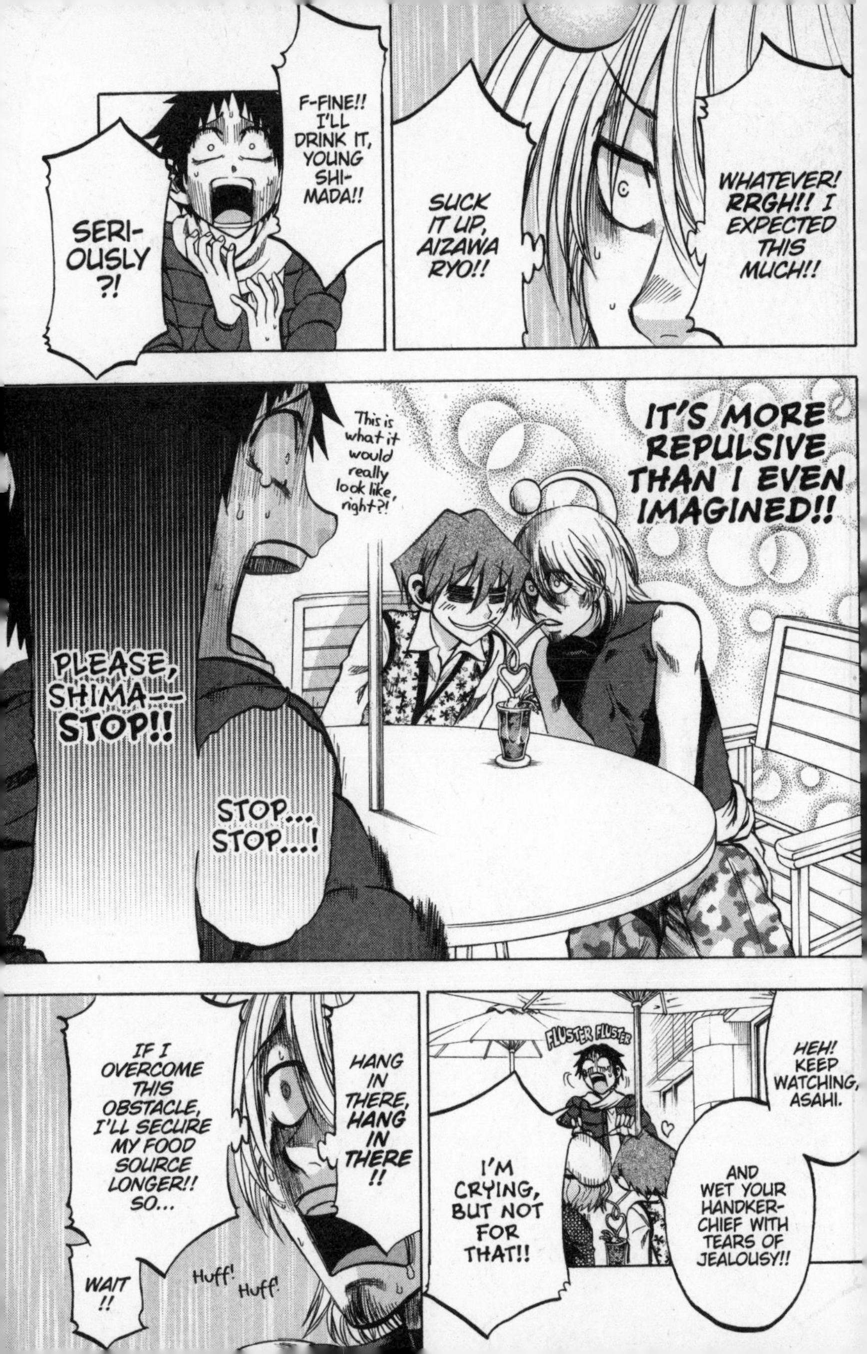
WHATEVER! RRGH!! I EXPECTED THIS MUCH!!
SUCK IT UP, AIZAWA RYO!!
F-FINE!! I'LL DRINK IT, YOUNG SHI-MADA!!
SERI-OUSLY?!
IT'S MORE REPULSIVE THAN I EVEN IMAGINED!!
This is what it would really look like, right?!
PLEASE, SHIMA-- STOP!!
STOP... STOP...!
HEH! KEEP WATCHING, ASAHI.
FLUSTER FLUSTER
AND WET YOUR HANDKER-CHIEF WITH TEARS OF JEALOUSY!!
I'M CRYING, BUT NOT FOR THAT!!
HANG IN THERE, HANG IN THERE!!
IF I OVERCOME THIS OBSTACLE, I'LL SECURE MY FOOD SOURCE LONGER!! SO...
Huff! Huff!
WAIT!!

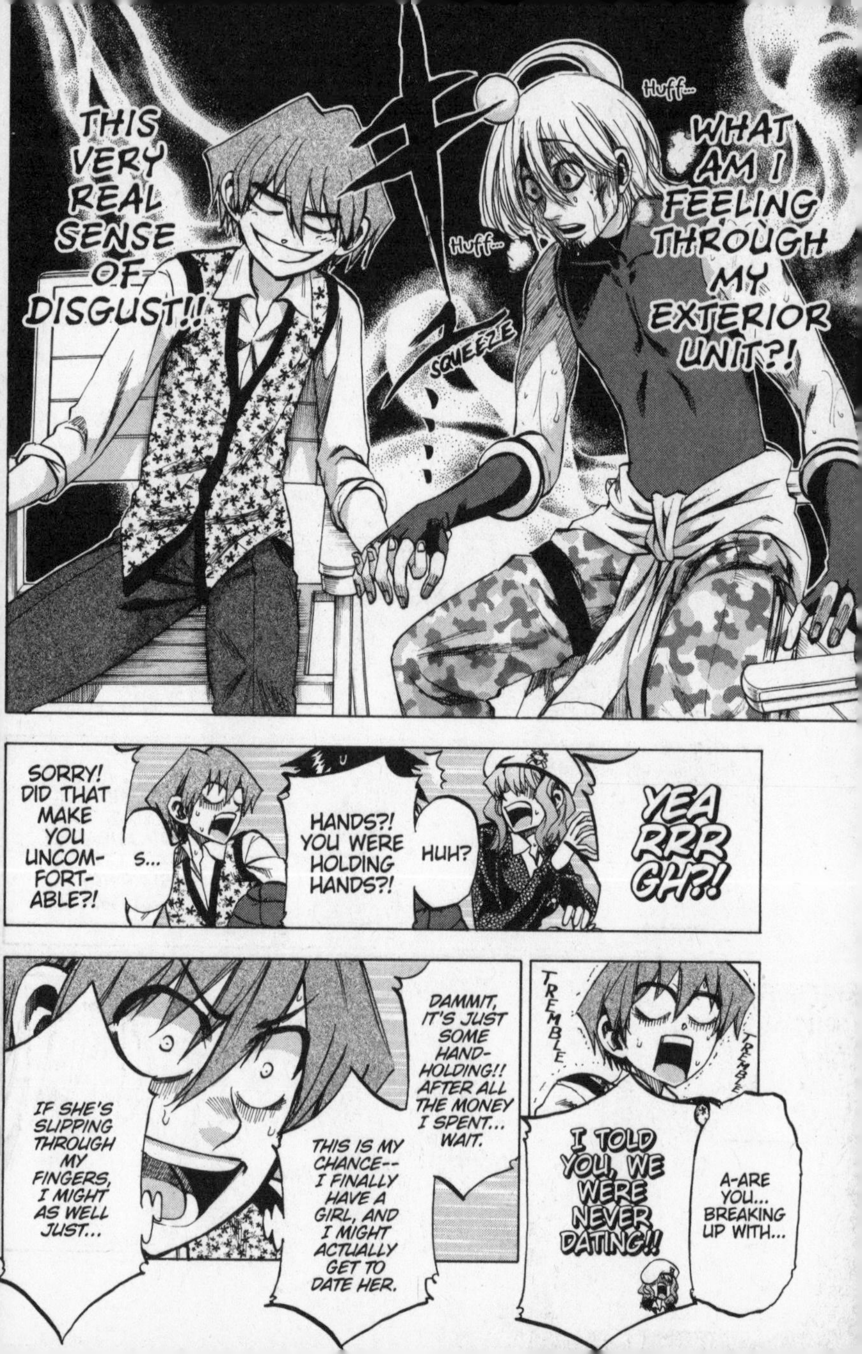
Huff...
WHAT AM I FEELING THROUGH MY EXTERIOR UNIT?!
Huff...
SQUEEZE
THIS VERY REAL SENSE OF DISGUST!!
YEA RRR GH?!
HUH?
HANDS?! YOU WERE HOLDING HANDS?!
S...
SORRY! DID THAT MAKE YOU UNCOM-FORT-ABLE?!
TREMBLE
TREMBLE
A-ARE YOU... BREAKING UP WITH...
I TOLD YOU, WE WERE NEVER DATING!!
DAMMIT, IT'S JUST SOME HAND-HOLDING!! AFTER ALL THE MONEY I SPENT... WAIT.
THIS IS MY CHANCE-- I FINALLY HAVE A GIRL, AND I MIGHT ACTUALLY GET TO DATE HER.
IF SHE'S SLIPPING THROUGH MY FINGERS, I MIGHT AS WELL JUST...

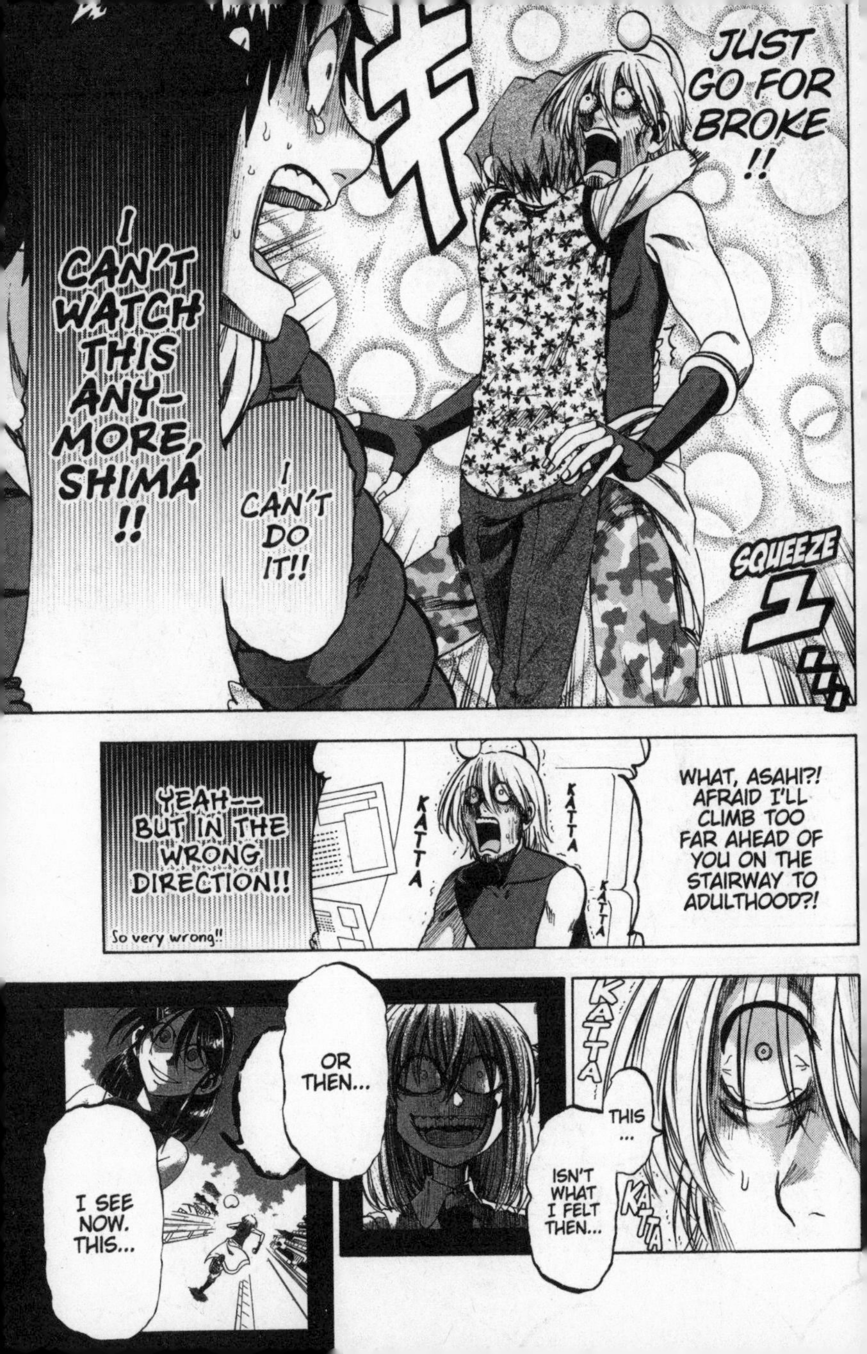
JUST GO FOR BROKE !!
SQUEEZE
I CAN'T DO IT!!
I CAN'T WATCH THIS ANY-MORE, SHIMA !!
WHAT, ASAHI?! AFRAID I'LL CLIMB TOO FAR AHEAD OF YOU ON THE STAIRWAY TO ADULTHOOD?!
KATTA
KATTA
KATTA
KATTA
YEAH-- BUT IN THE WRONG DIRECTION!!
So very wrong!!
KATTA
THIS ...
ISN'T WHAT I FELT THEN...
KATTA
OR THEN...
I SEE NOW. THIS...

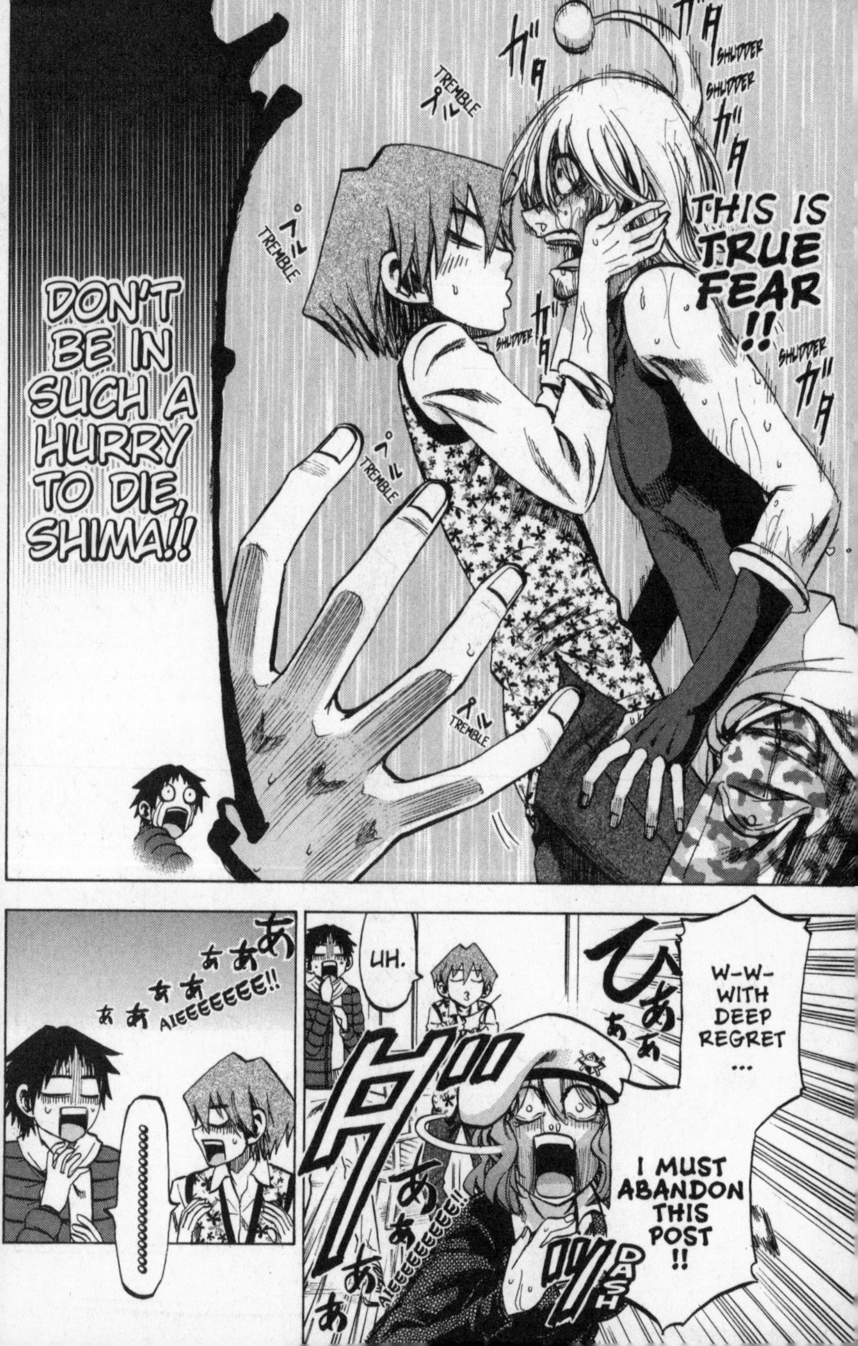
SHUDDER
SHUDDER
TREMBLE
THIS IS TRUE FEAR!!
SHUDDER
SHUDDER
TREMBLE
TREMBLE
TREMBLE
DON'T BE IN SUCH A HURRY TO DIE, SHIMA!!
W-W-WITH DEEP REGRET...
I MUST ABANDON THIS POST!!
AIEEEEEEEEE!!
DASH
UH.
AIEEEEEEE!!
....

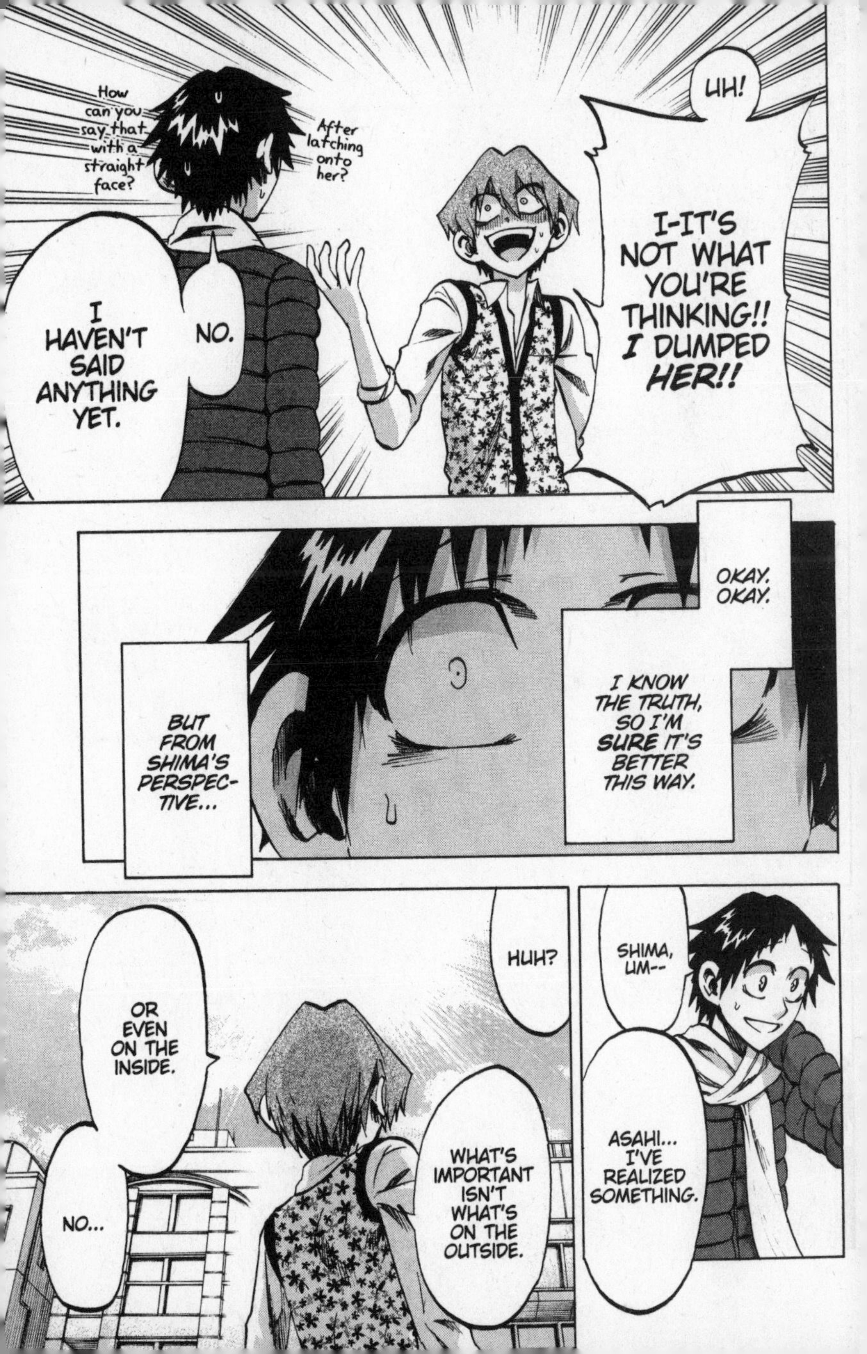
UH!
I-IT'S NOT WHAT YOU'RE THINKING!! I DUMPED HER!!
After latching onto her?
How can you say that with a straight face?
NO.
I HAVEN'T SAID ANYTHING YET.
OKAY. OKAY.
I KNOW THE TRUTH, SO I'M SURE IT'S BETTER THIS WAY.
BUT FROM SHIMA'S PERSPECTIVE...
SHIMA, UM--
ASAHI... I'VE REALIZED SOMETHING.
HUH?
WHAT'S IMPORTANT ISN'T WHAT'S ON THE OUTSIDE.
OR EVEN ON THE INSIDE.
NO...

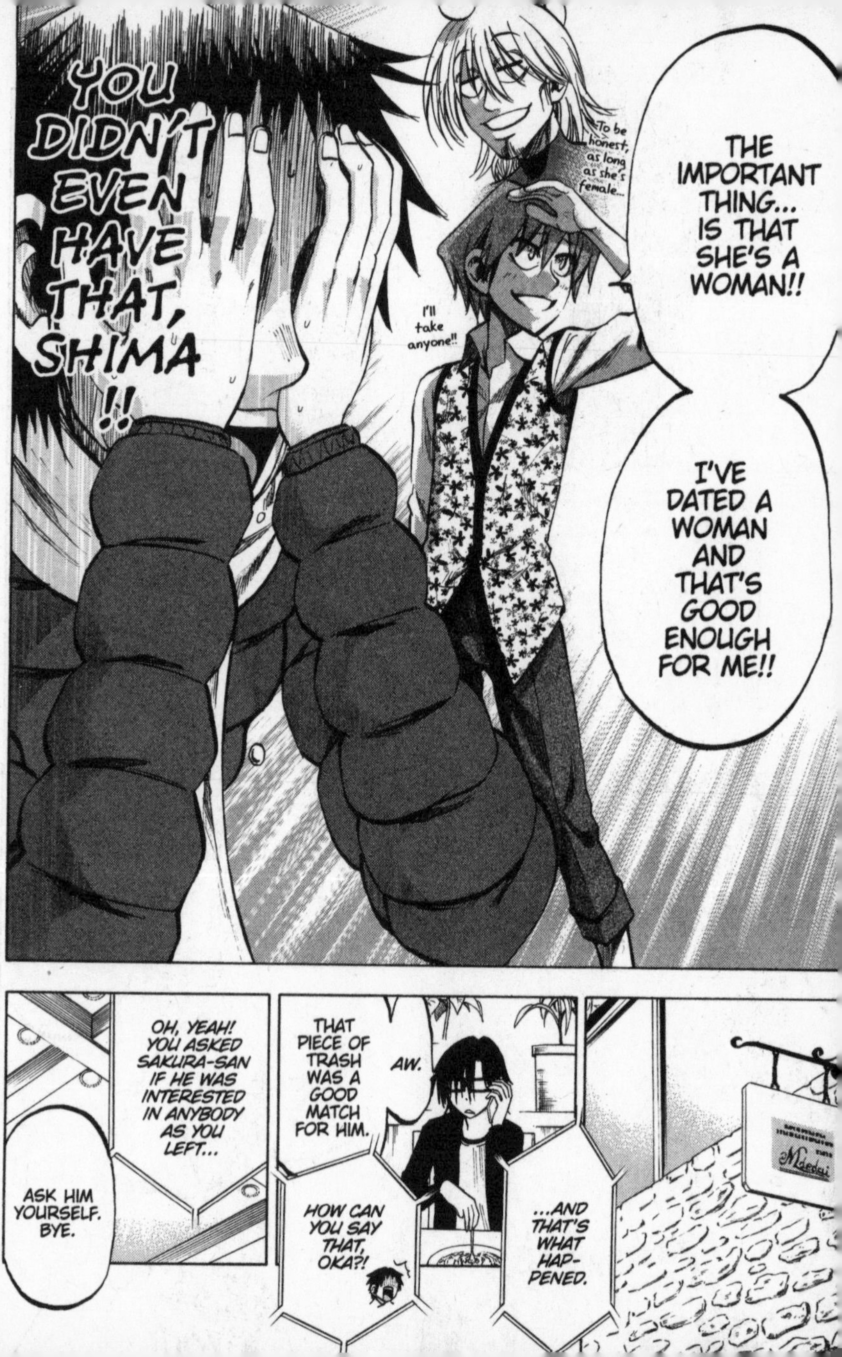
THE IMPORTANT THING... IS THAT SHE'S A WOMAN!!
I'VE DATED A WOMAN AND THAT'S GOOD ENOUGH FOR ME!!
To be honest, as long as she's female...
I'll take anyone!!
YOU DIDN'T EVEN HAVE THAT, SHIMA!!
...AND THAT'S WHAT HAPPENED.
THAT PIECE OF TRASH WAS A GOOD MATCH FOR HIM.
AW.
HOW CAN YOU SAY THAT, OKA?!
OH, YEAH! YOU ASKED SAKURA-SAN IF HE WAS INTERESTED IN ANYBODY AS YOU LEFT...
ASK HIM YOURSELF. BYE.

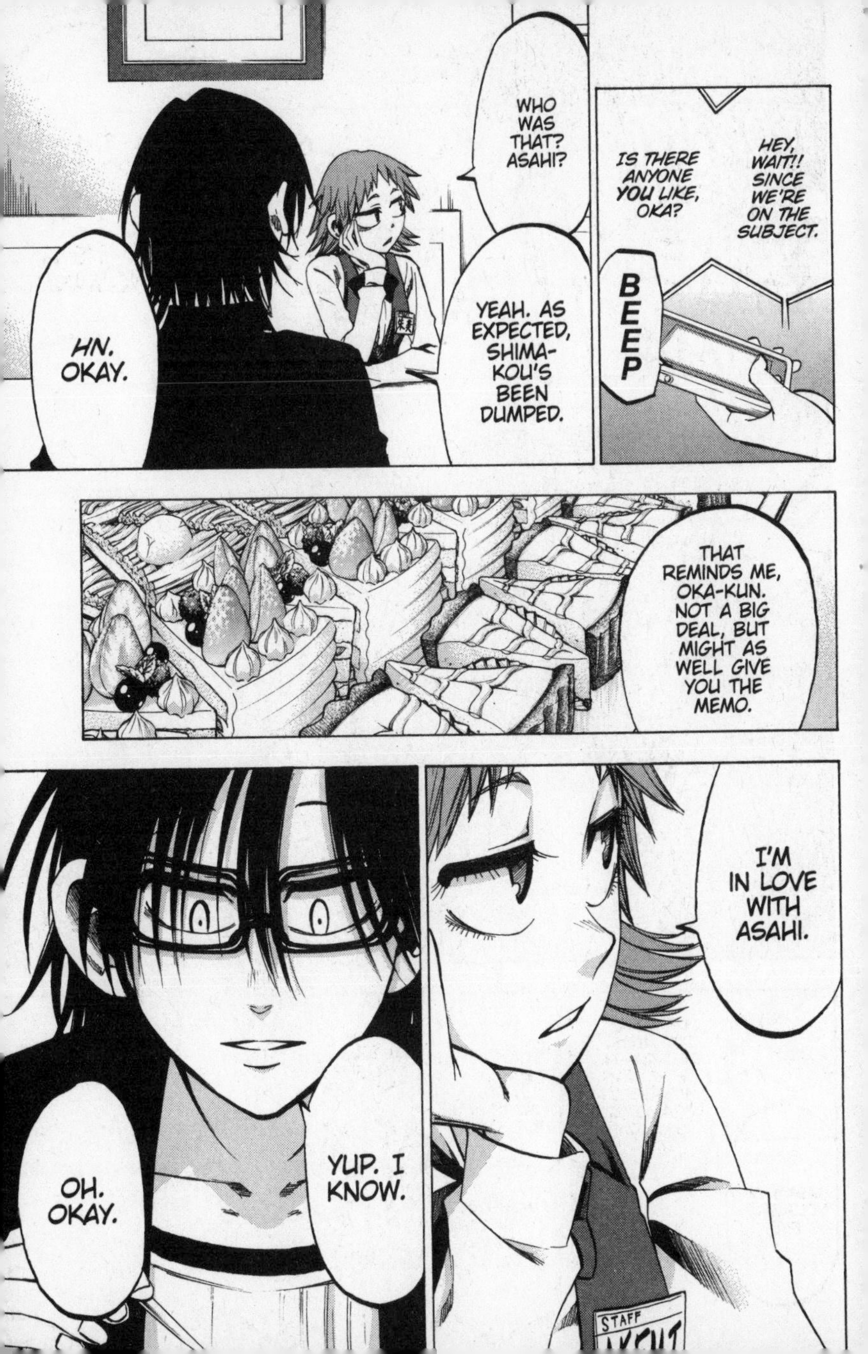
HEY, WAIT!! SINCE WE'RE ON THE SUBJECT.
IS THERE ANYONE YOU LIKE, OKA?
BEEP
WHO WAS THAT? ASAHI?
YEAH. AS EXPECTED, SHIMA-KOU'S BEEN DUMPED.
HN. OKAY.
THAT REMINDS ME, OKA-KUN. NOT A BIG DEAL, BUT MIGHT AS WELL GIVE YOU THE MEMO.
I'M IN LOVE WITH ASAHI.
YUP. I KNOW.
OH. OKAY.
STAFF

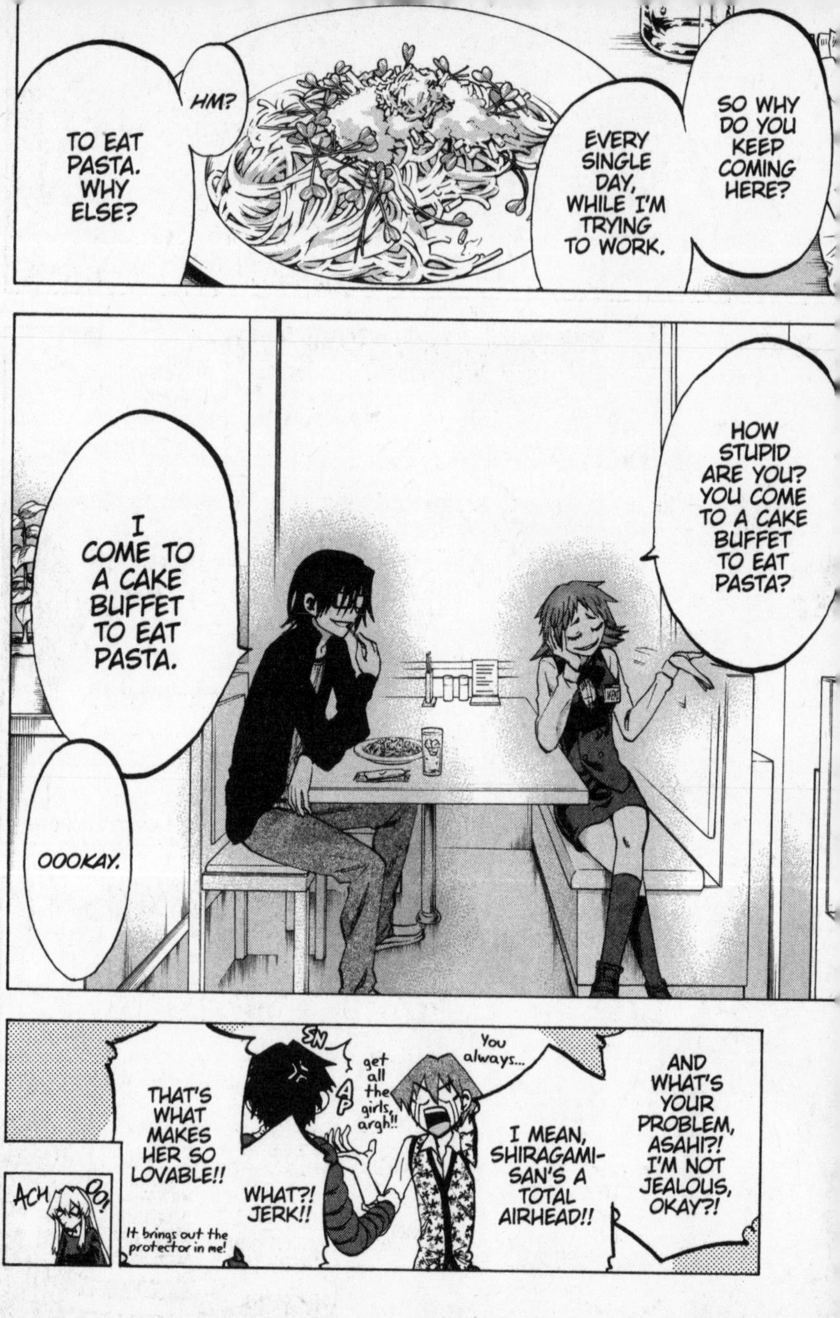
SO WHY DO YOU KEEP COMING HERE?
EVERY SINGLE DAY, WHILE I'M TRYING TO WORK.
HM?
TO EAT PASTA. WHY ELSE?
HOW STUPID ARE YOU? YOU COME TO A CAKE BUFFET TO EAT PASTA?
I COME TO A CAKE BUFFET TO EAT PASTA.
OOOKAY.
AND WHAT'S YOUR PROBLEM, ASAHI?! I'M NOT JEALOUS, OKAY?!
You always...
get all the girls, argh!!
I MEAN, SHIRAGAMI-SAN'S A TOTAL AIRHEAD!!
SNAP
WHAT?! JERK!!
THAT'S WHAT MAKES HER SO LOVABLE!!
It brings out the protector in me!
ACHOO!

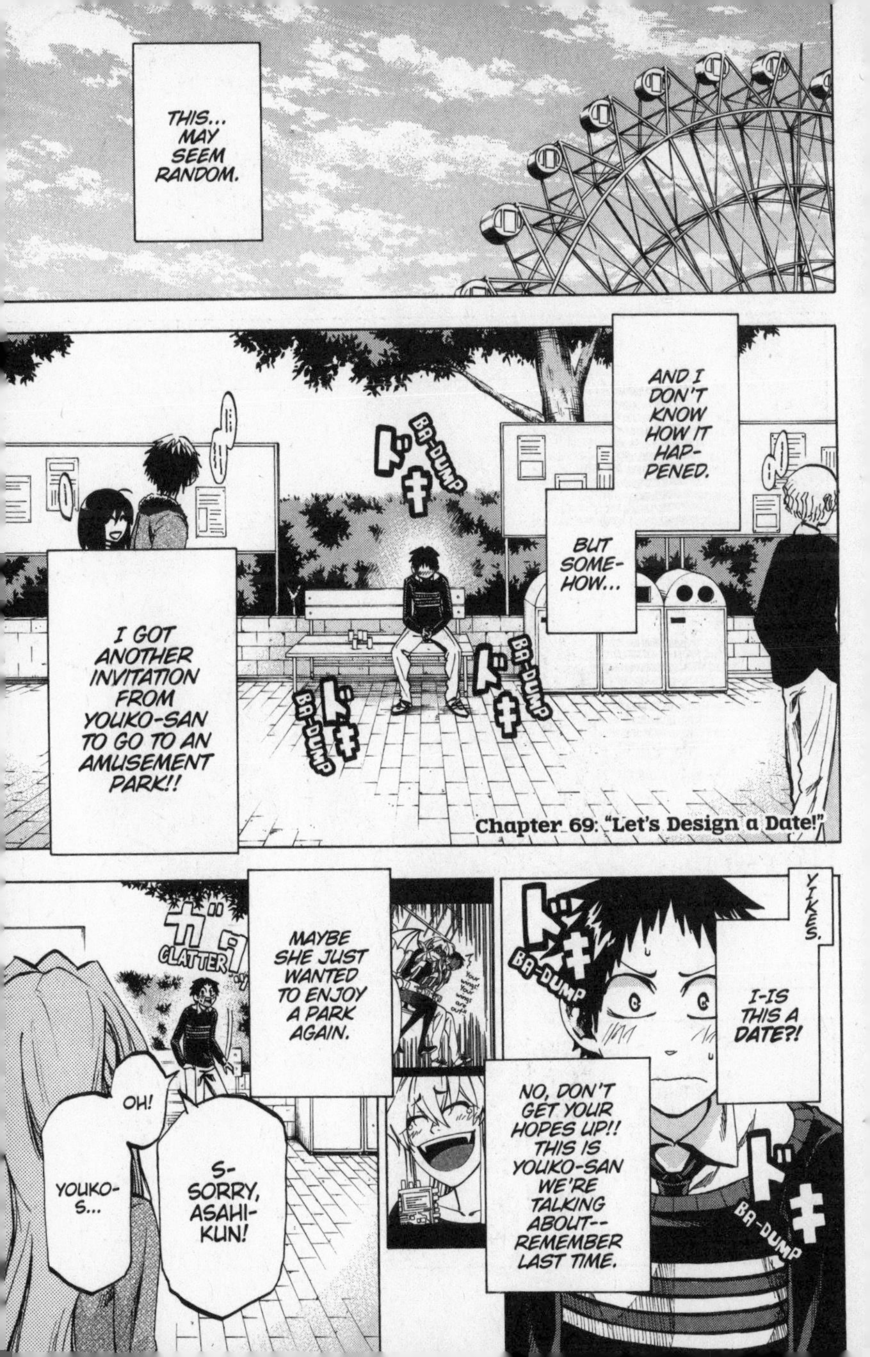
THIS... MAY SEEM RANDOM.
AND I DON'T KNOW HOW IT HAP-PENED.
BUT SOME-HOW...
BA-DUMP
BA-DUMP
BA-DUMP
I GOT ANOTHER INVITATION FROM YOUKO-SAN TO GO TO AN AMUSEMENT PARK!!
Chapter 69: "Let's Design a Date!"
YIKES.
BA-DUMP
I-IS THIS A DATE?!
NO, DON'T GET YOUR HOPES UP!! THIS IS YOUKO-SAN WE'RE TALKING ABOUT-- REMEMBER LAST TIME.
BA-DUMP
MAYBE SHE JUST WANTED TO ENJOY A PARK AGAIN.
Your wings! Your wings are out!
CLATTER
OH!
S-SORRY, ASAHI-KUN!
YOUKO-S...

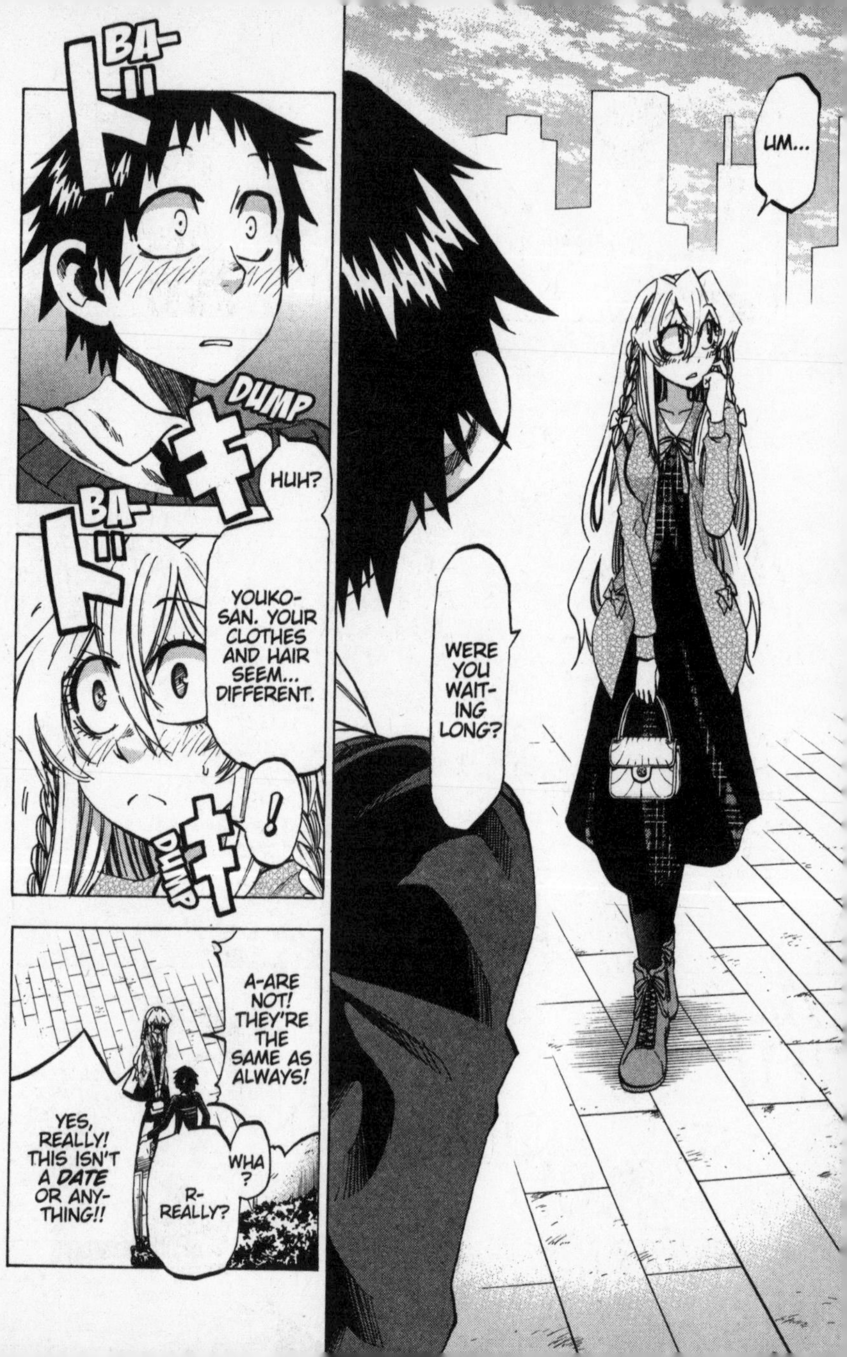
UM...
WERE YOU WAITING LONG?
BA-
DUMP
HUH?
BA-
YOUKO-SAN. YOUR CLOTHES AND HAIR SEEM... DIFFERENT.
!
DUMP
A-ARE NOT! THEY'RE THE SAME AS ALWAYS!
WHA?
R-REALLY?
YES, REALLY! THIS ISN'T A *DATE* OR ANYTHING!!

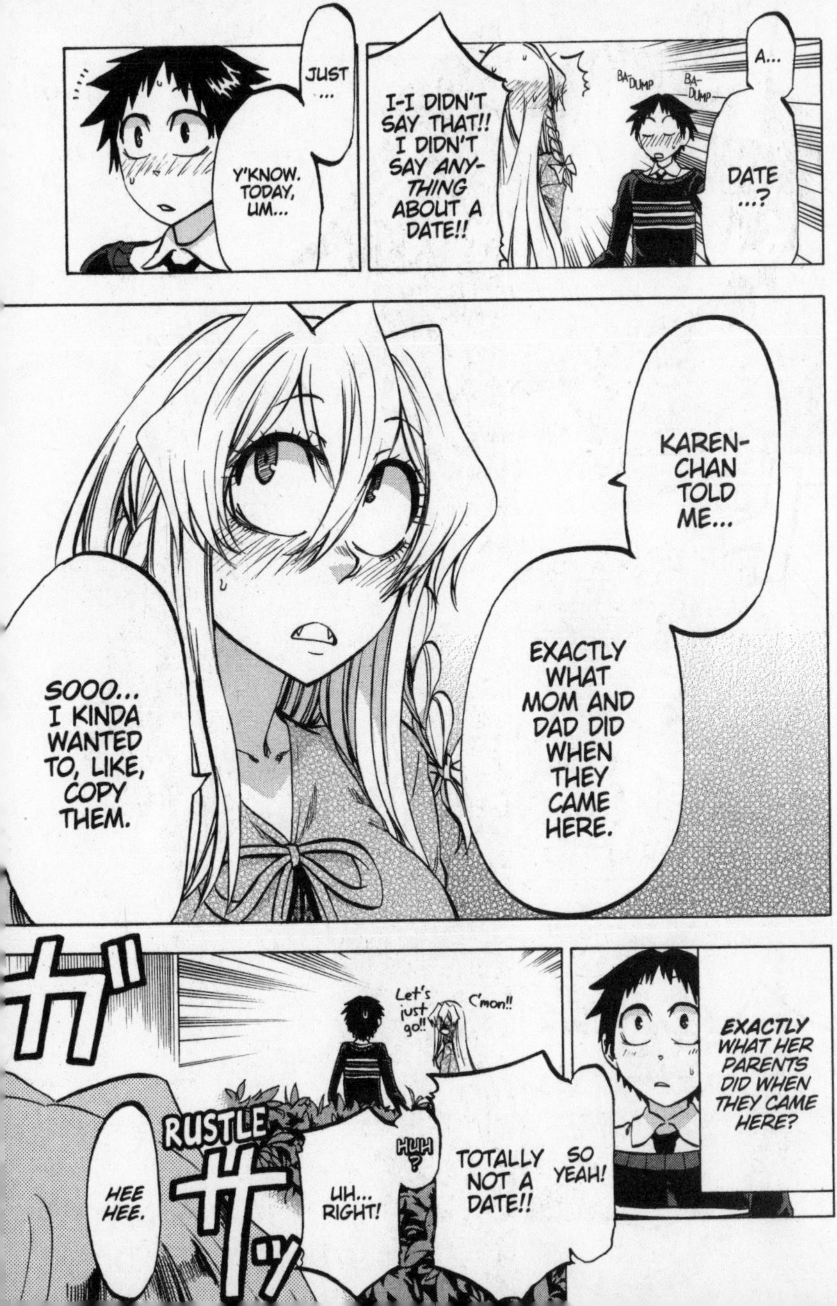
A...
DATE ...?
BA-DUMP
BA-DUMP
I-I DIDN'T SAY THAT!! I DIDN'T SAY ANY-THING ABOUT A DATE!!
JUST ...
Y'KNOW. TODAY, UM...
KAREN-CHAN TOLD ME...
EXACTLY WHAT MOM AND DAD DID WHEN THEY CAME HERE.
SOOO... I KINDA WANTED TO, LIKE, COPY THEM.
EXACTLY WHAT HER PARENTS DID WHEN THEY CAME HERE?
SO YEAH!
TOTALLY NOT A DATE!!
HUH ?
UH... RIGHT!
C'mon!!
Let's just go!!
ガ
RUSTLE
ザッ
HEE HEE.

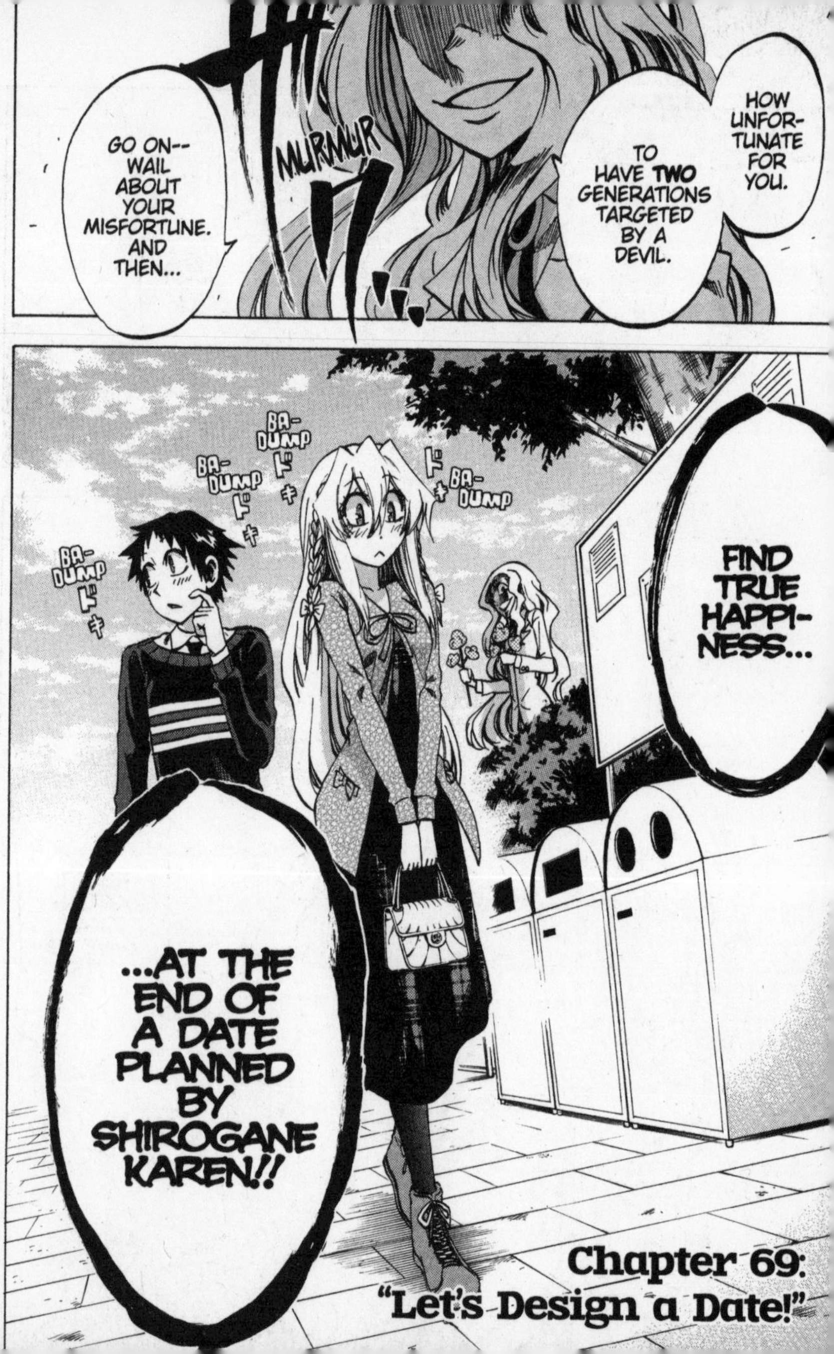
HOW UNFORTUNATE FOR YOU.
TO HAVE **TWO** GENERATIONS TARGETED BY A DEVIL.
MURMUR
GO ON-- WAIL ABOUT YOUR MISFORTUNE. AND THEN...
FIND TRUE HAPPINESS...
BA-DUMP
BA-DUMP
BA-DUMP
BA-DUMP
...AT THE END OF A DATE PLANNED BY SHIROGANE KAREN!!
Chapter 69: "Let's Design a Date!"

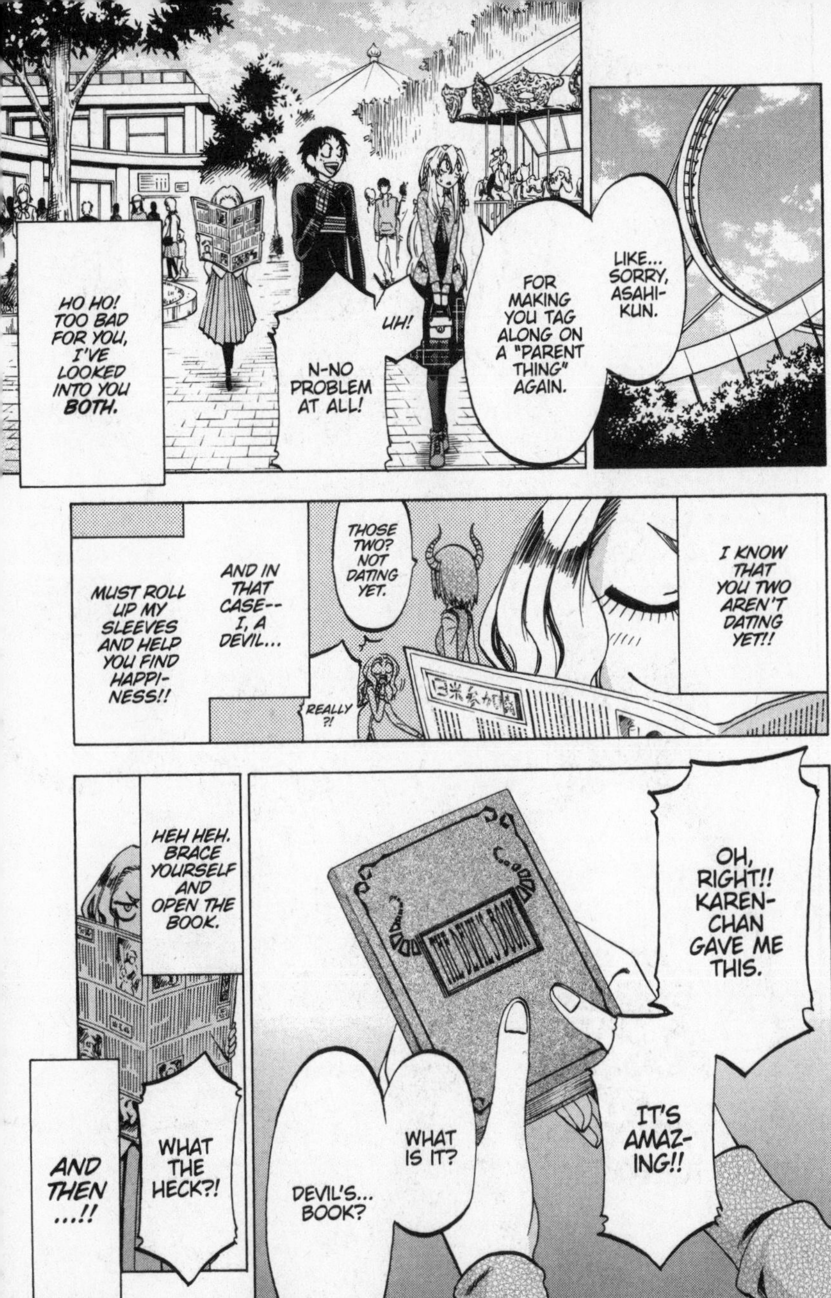
LIKE... SORRY, ASAHI-KUN.
FOR MAKING YOU TAG ALONG ON A "PARENT THING" AGAIN.
UH!
N-NO PROBLEM AT ALL!
HO HO! TOO BAD FOR YOU, I'VE LOOKED INTO YOU BOTH.
I KNOW THAT YOU TWO AREN'T DATING YET!!
THOSE TWO? NOT DATING YET.
REALLY?!
AND IN THAT CASE-- I, A DEVIL...
MUST ROLL UP MY SLEEVES AND HELP YOU FIND HAPPINESS!!
OH, RIGHT!! KAREN-CHAN GAVE ME THIS.
THE DEVIL'S BOOK
IT'S AMAZING!!
WHAT IS IT?
DEVIL'S... BOOK?
HEH HEH. BRACE YOURSELF AND OPEN THE BOOK.
WHAT THE HECK?!
AND THEN ...!!

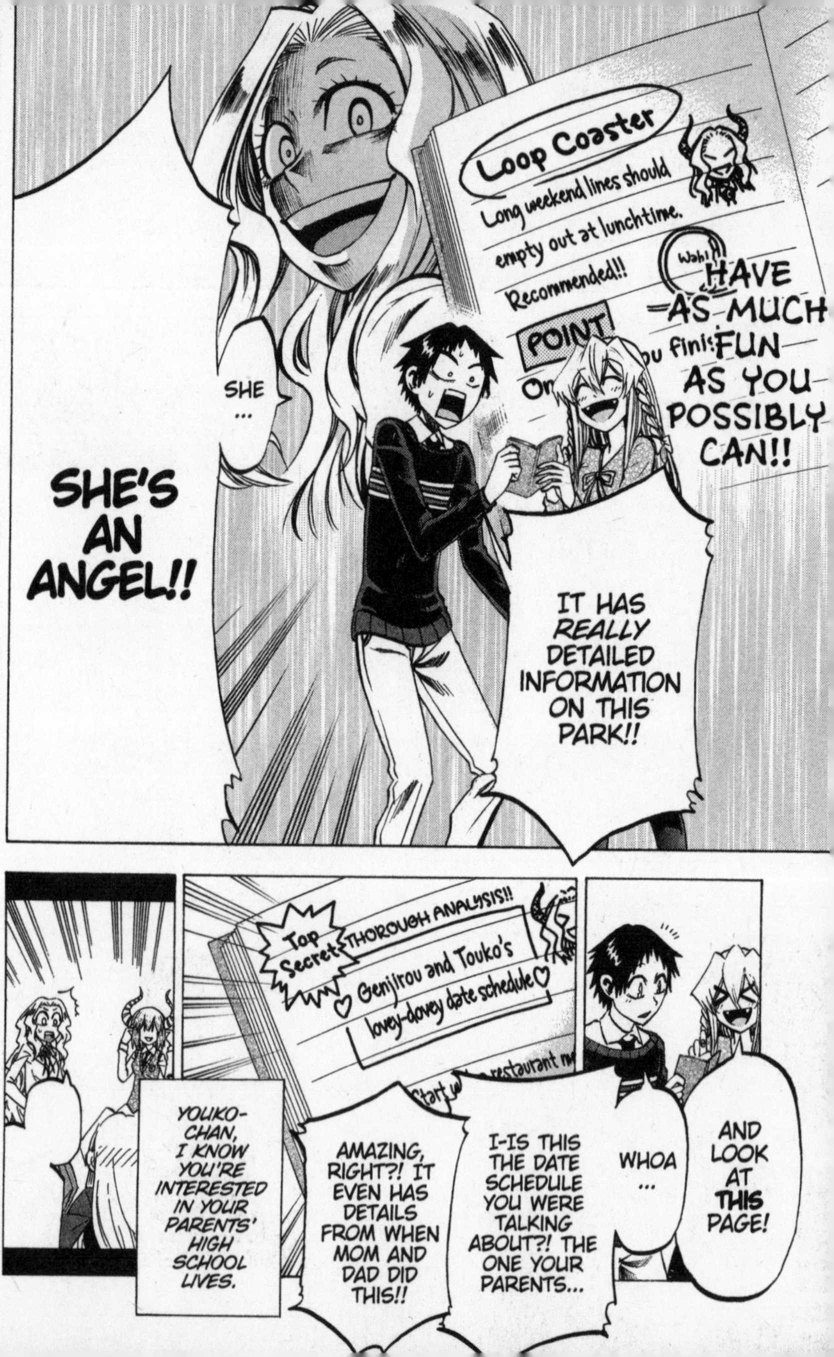
Loop Coaster
Long weekend lines should empty out at lunchtime. Recommended!!
Wah!
POINT
HAVE AS MUCH FUN AS YOU POSSIBLY CAN!!
IT HAS REALLY DETAILED INFORMATION ON THIS PARK!!
SHE ...
SHE'S AN ANGEL!!
AND LOOK AT THIS PAGE!
WHOA ...
Top Secret
THOROUGH ANALYSIS!!
Genjirou and Touko's lovey-dovey date schedule
I-IS THIS THE DATE SCHEDULE YOU WERE TALKING ABOUT?! THE ONE YOUR PARENTS...
AMAZING, RIGHT?! IT EVEN HAS DETAILS FROM WHEN MOM AND DAD DID THIS!!
YOUKO-CHAN, I KNOW YOU'RE INTERESTED IN YOUR PARENTS' HIGH SCHOOL LIVES.

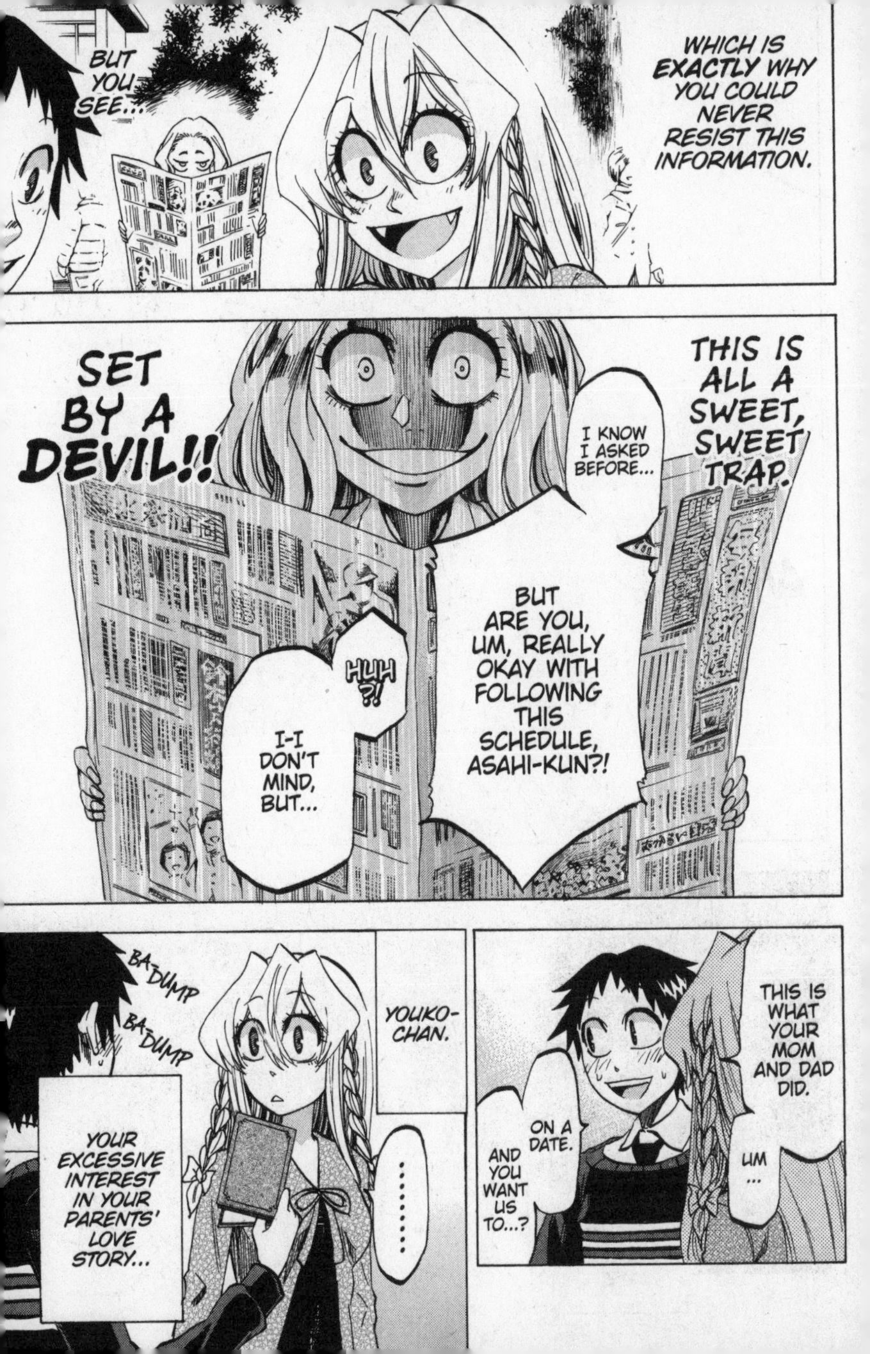
WHICH IS EXACTLY WHY YOU COULD NEVER RESIST THIS INFORMATION.
BUT YOU SEE...
THIS IS ALL A SWEET, SWEET TRAP.
I KNOW I ASKED BEFORE...
BUT ARE YOU, UM, REALLY OKAY WITH FOLLOWING THIS SCHEDULE, ASAHI-KUN?!
HUH?!
I-I DON'T MIND, BUT...
SET BY A DEVIL!!
THIS IS WHAT YOUR MOM AND DAD DID.
UM...
ON A DATE.
AND YOU WANT US TO...?
YOUKO-CHAN.
BA-DUMP
BA-DUMP
......
YOUR EXCESSIVE INTEREST IN YOUR PARENTS' LOVE STORY...

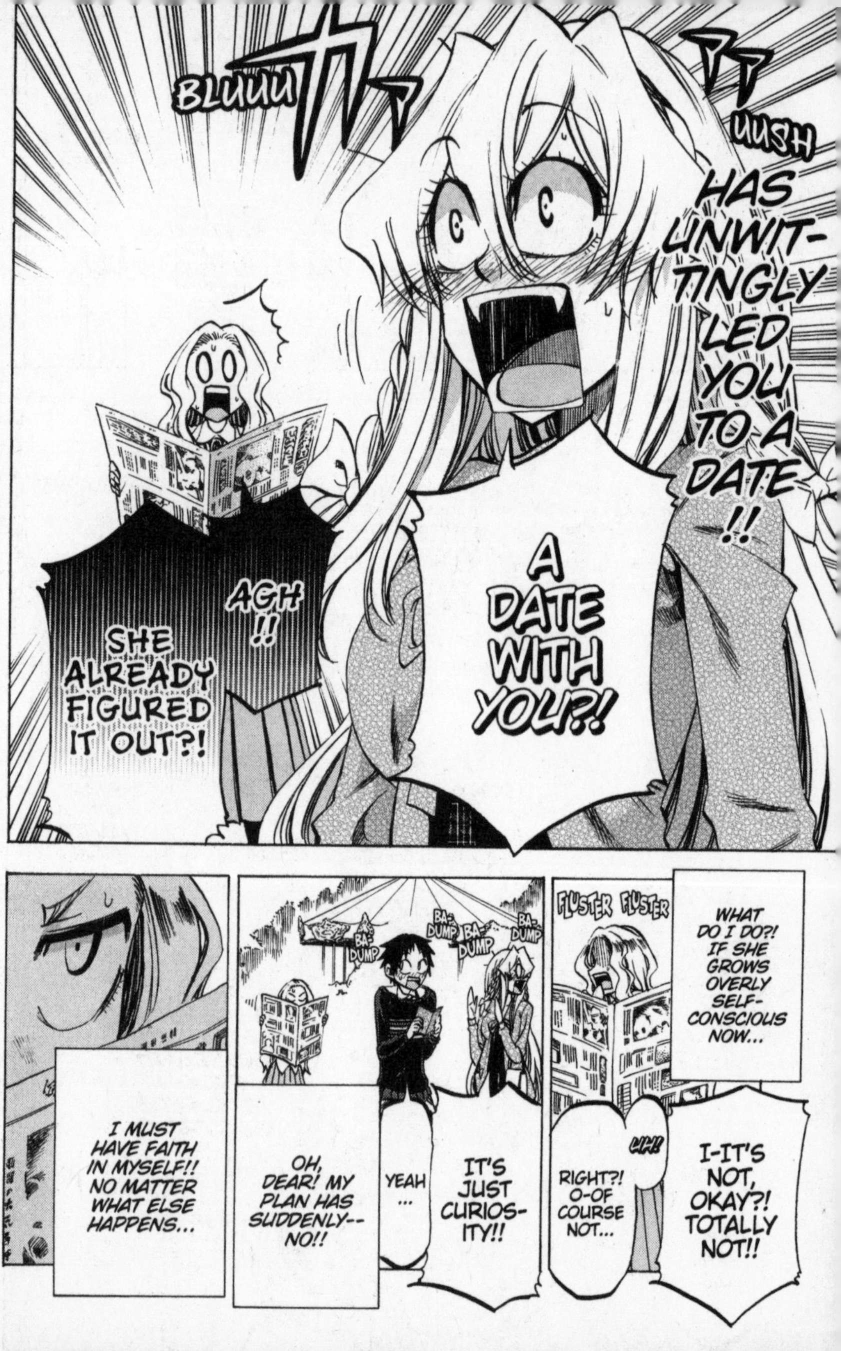
BLUUU
UUSH
HAS UNWITTINGLY LED YOU TO A DATE!!
A DATE WITH YOU?!
AGH!!
SHE ALREADY FIGURED IT OUT?!
FLUSTER FLUSTER
WHAT DO I DO?! IF SHE GROWS OVERLY SELF-CONSCIOUS NOW...
I-IT'S NOT, OKAY?! TOTALLY NOT!!
UH!
RIGHT?! O-OF COURSE NOT...
BA-DUMP
BA-DUMP
BA-DUMP
BA-DUMP
IT'S JUST CURIOSITY!!
YEAH ...
OH, DEAR! MY PLAN HAS SUDDENLY-- NO!!
I MUST HAVE FAITH IN MYSELF!! NO MATTER WHAT ELSE HAPPENS...

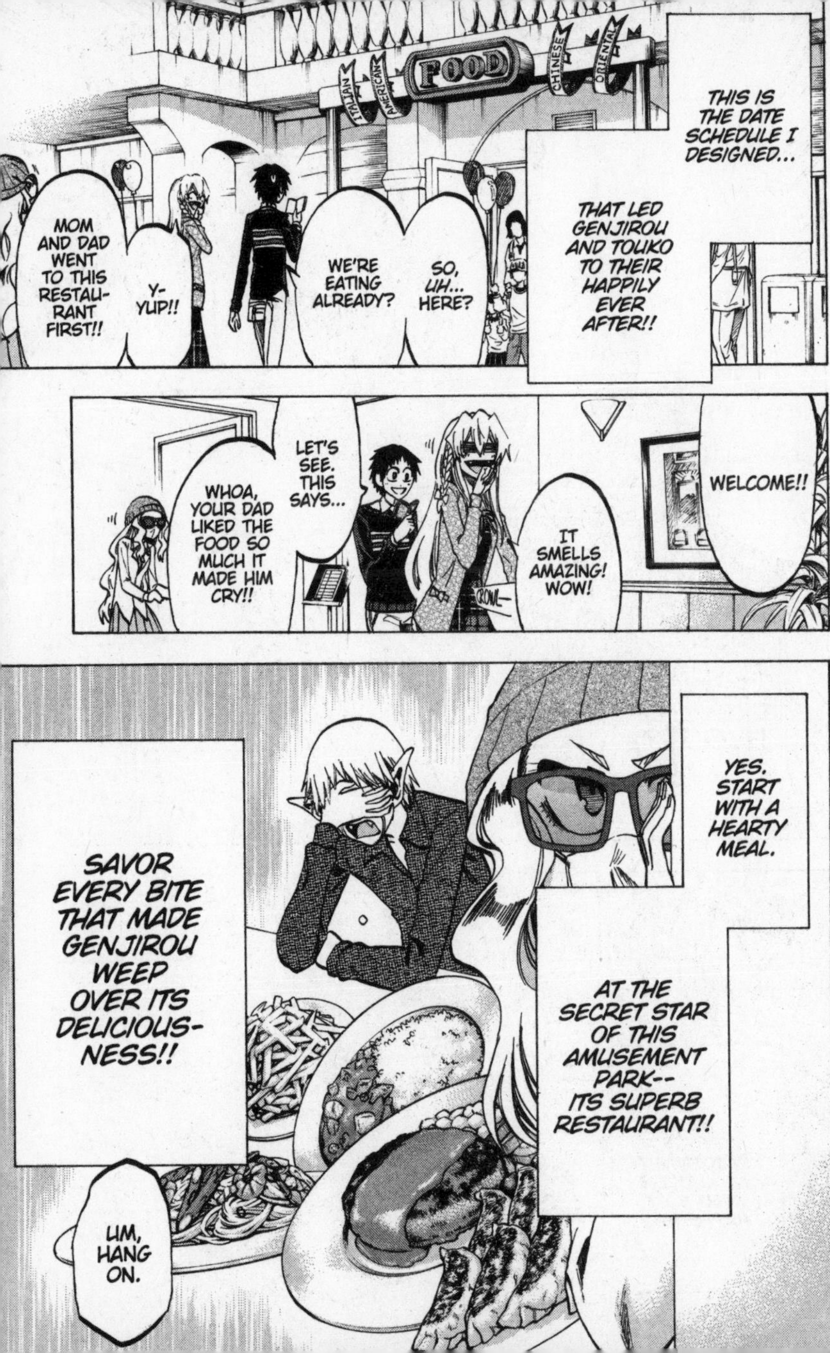
FOOD
ITALIAN
AMERICAN
CHINESE
ORIENTAL
THIS IS THE DATE SCHEDULE I DESIGNED...
THAT LED GENJIROU AND TOUKO TO THEIR HAPPILY EVER AFTER!!
SO, UH... HERE?
WE'RE EATING ALREADY?
Y-YUP!!
MOM AND DAD WENT TO THIS RESTAU-RANT FIRST!!
WELCOME!!
IT SMELLS AMAZING! WOW!
CROWL-
LET'S SEE. THIS SAYS...
WHOA, YOUR DAD LIKED THE FOOD SO MUCH IT MADE HIM CRY!!
YES. START WITH A HEARTY MEAL.
AT THE SECRET STAR OF THIS AMUSEMENT PARK-- ITS SUPERB RESTAURANT!!
SAVOR EVERY BITE THAT MADE GENJIROU WEEP OVER ITS DELICIOUS-NESS!!
UM, HANG ON.

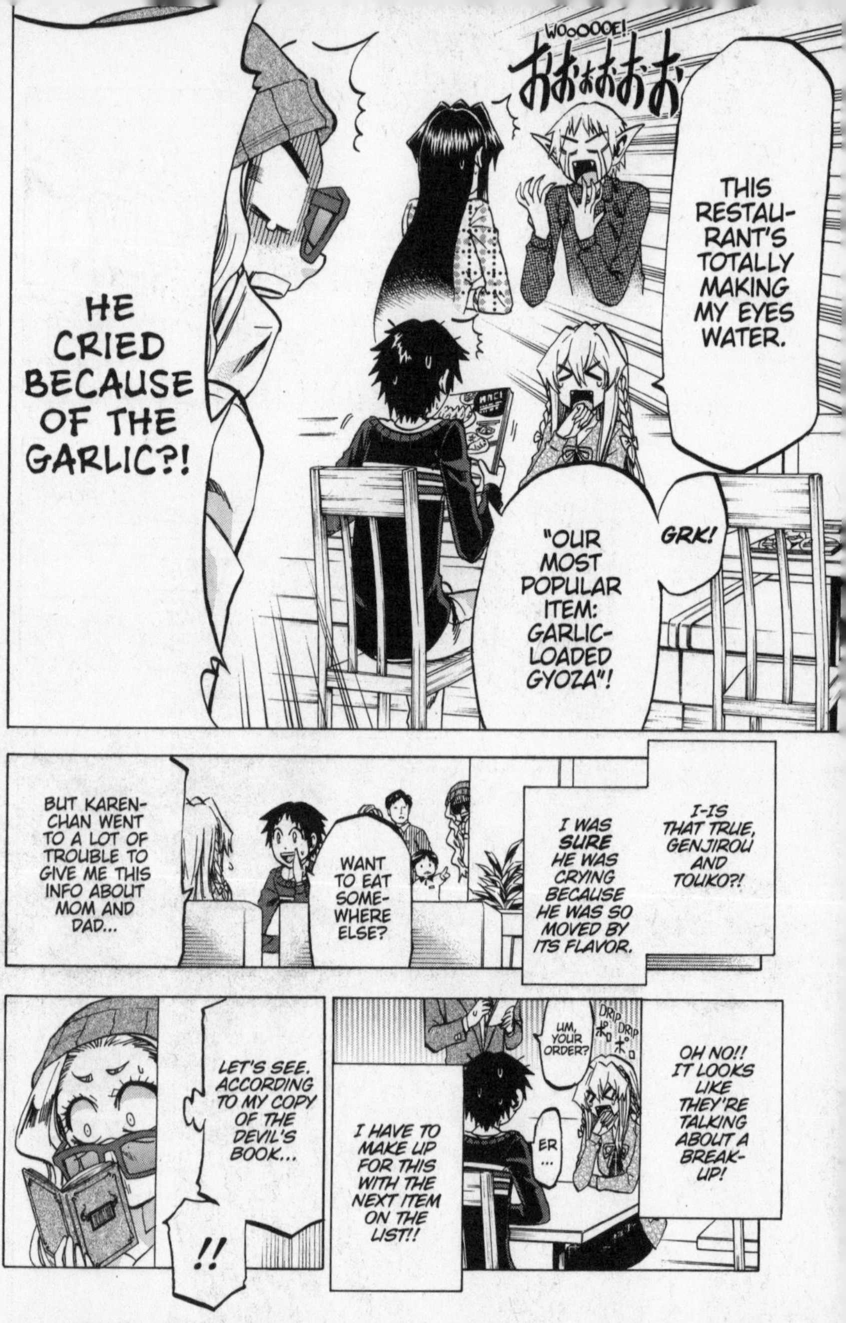
WOOOOOE!
THIS RESTAU-RANT'S TOTALLY MAKING MY EYES WATER.
GRK!
"OUR MOST POPULAR ITEM: GARLIC-LOADED GYOZA"!
HE CRIED BECAUSE OF THE GARLIC?!
I-IS THAT TRUE, GENJIROU AND TOUKO?!
I WAS SURE HE WAS CRYING BECAUSE HE WAS SO MOVED BY ITS FLAVOR.
WANT TO EAT SOME-WHERE ELSE?
BUT KAREN-CHAN WENT TO A LOT OF TROUBLE TO GIVE ME THIS INFO ABOUT MOM AND DAD...
OH NO!! IT LOOKS LIKE THEY'RE TALKING ABOUT A BREAK-UP!
DRIP DRIP
UM, YOUR ORDER?
ER...
I HAVE TO MAKE UP FOR THIS WITH THE NEXT ITEM ON THE LIST!!
LET'S SEE. ACCORDING TO MY COPY OF THE DEVIL'S BOOK...
!!

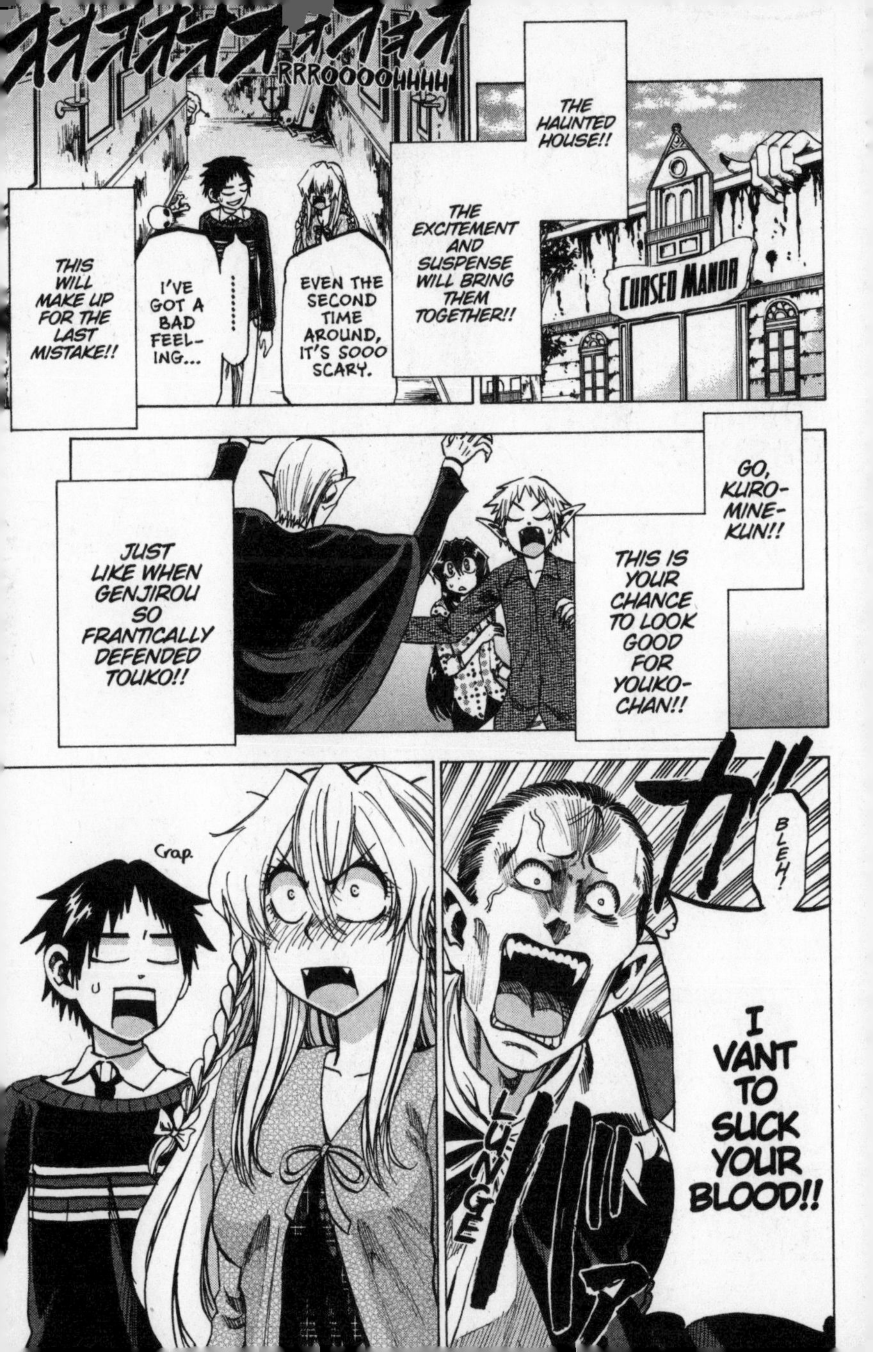
THE HAUNTED HOUSE!!
THE EXCITEMENT AND SUSPENSE WILL BRING THEM TOGETHER!!
CURSED MANOR
オオオオオォォォォォ
RRROOOOHHHH
EVEN THE SECOND TIME AROUND, IT'S SOOO SCARY.
......
I'VE GOT A BAD FEEL-ING...
THIS WILL MAKE UP FOR THE LAST MISTAKE!!
GO, KURO-MINE-KUN!!
THIS IS YOUR CHANCE TO LOOK GOOD FOR YOUKO-CHAN!!
JUST LIKE WHEN GENJIROU SO FRANTICALLY DEFENDED TOUKO!!
ガ!
BLEH!
LUNGE
I VANT TO SUCK YOUR BLOOD!!
Crap.

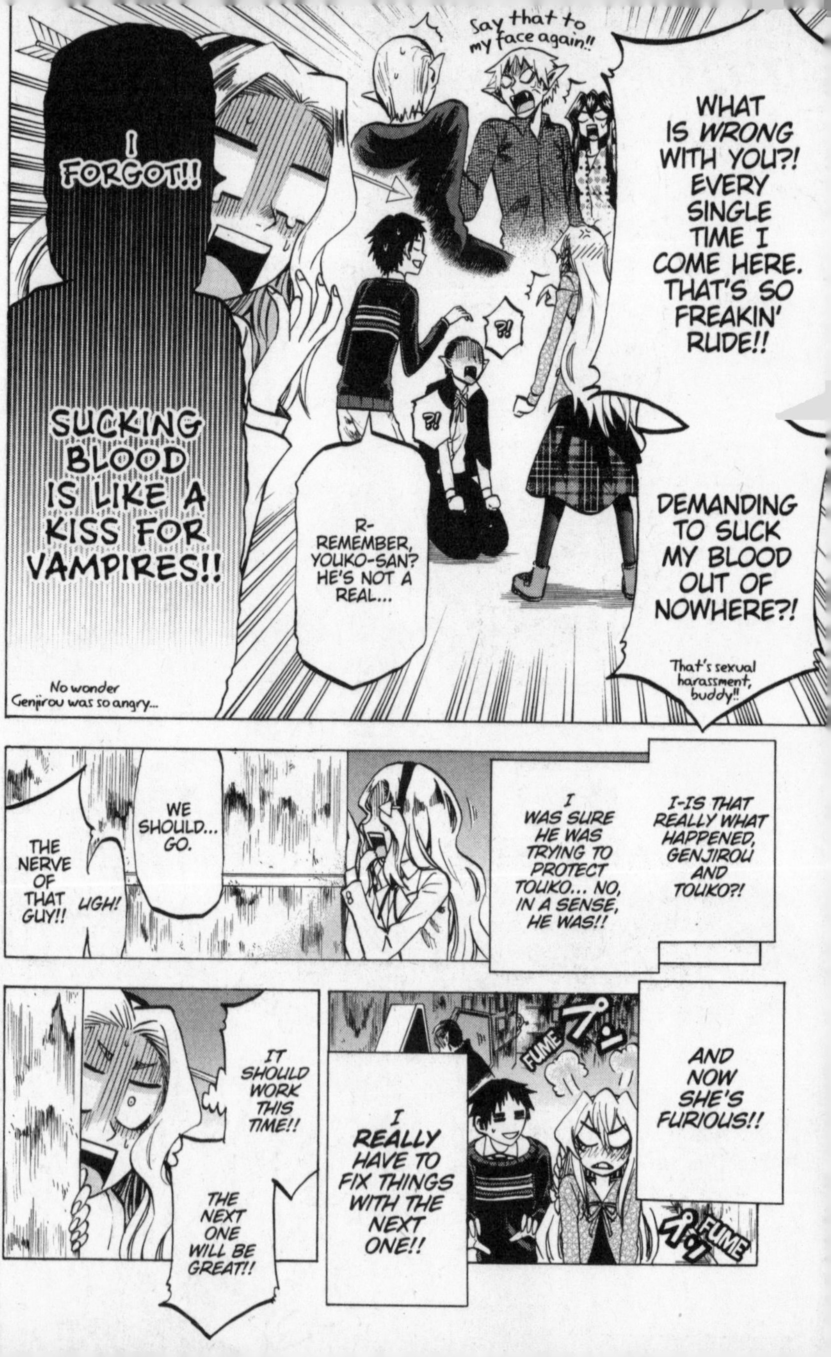
Say that to my face again!!
WHAT IS WRONG WITH YOU?! EVERY SINGLE TIME I COME HERE. THAT'S SO FREAKIN' RUDE!!
?!
DEMANDING TO SUCK MY BLOOD OUT OF NOWHERE?!
That's sexual harassment, buddy!!
?!
R-REMEMBER, YOUKO-SAN? HE'S NOT A REAL...
I FORGOT!!
SUCKING BLOOD IS LIKE A KISS FOR VAMPIRES!!
No wonder Genjirou was so angry...
I-IS THAT REALLY WHAT HAPPENED, GENJIROU AND TOUKO?!
I WAS SURE HE WAS TRYING TO PROTECT TOUKO... NO, IN A SENSE, HE WAS!!
WE SHOULD... GO.
THE NERVE OF THAT GUY!!
UGH!
AND NOW SHE'S FURIOUS!!
FUME
I REALLY HAVE TO FIX THINGS WITH THE NEXT ONE!!
FUME
IT SHOULD WORK THIS TIME!!
THE NEXT ONE WILL BE GREAT!!

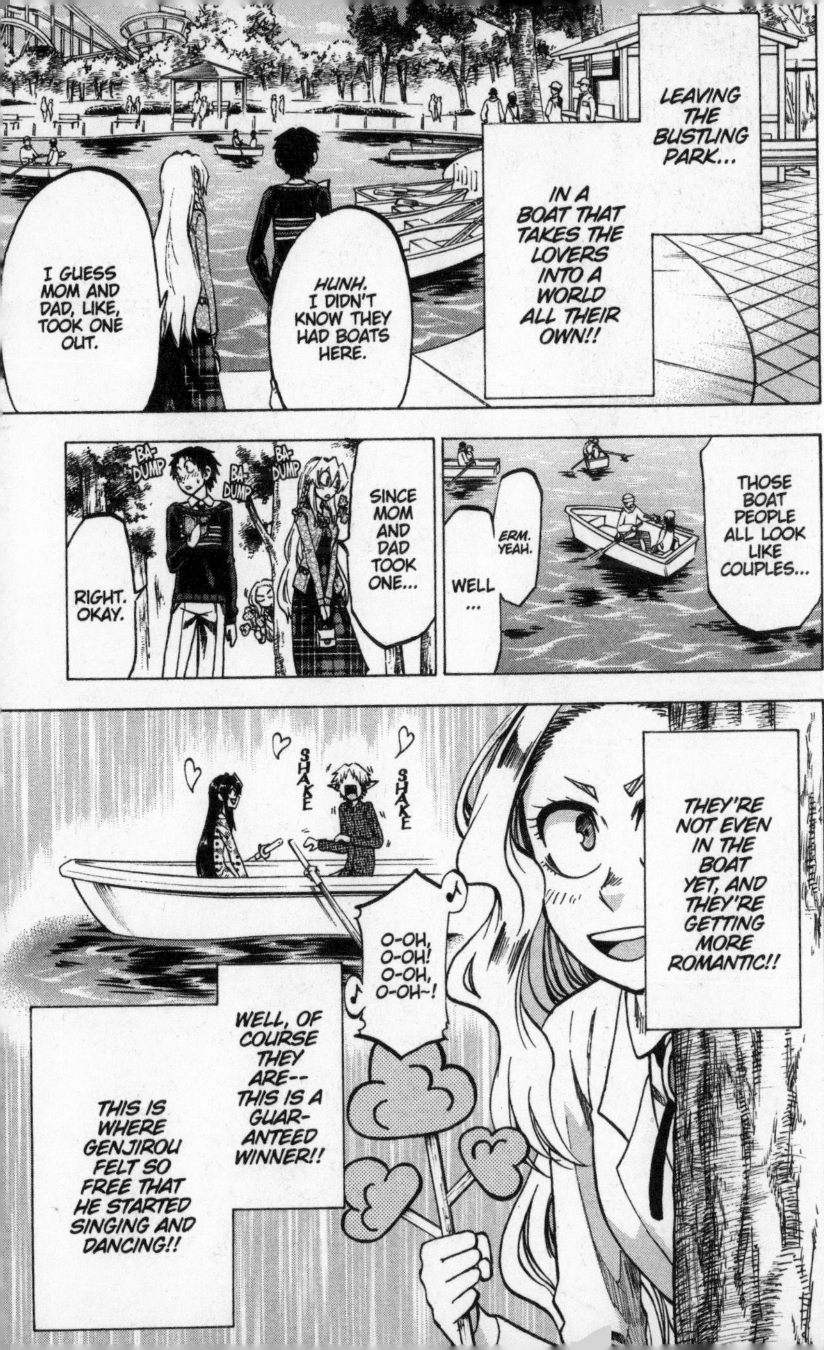
LEAVING THE BUSTLING PARK...
IN A BOAT THAT TAKES THE LOVERS INTO A WORLD ALL THEIR OWN!!
HUNH. I DIDN'T KNOW THEY HAD BOATS HERE.
I GUESS MOM AND DAD, LIKE, TOOK ONE OUT.
THOSE BOAT PEOPLE ALL LOOK LIKE COUPLES...
ERM. YEAH.
WELL ...
SINCE MOM AND DAD TOOK ONE...
BA-DUMP
BA-DUMP
BA-DUMP
RIGHT. OKAY.
THEY'RE NOT EVEN IN THE BOAT YET, AND THEY'RE GETTING MORE ROMANTIC!!
SHAKE
SHAKE
O-OH, O-OH! O-OH, O-OH~!
WELL, OF COURSE THEY ARE-- THIS IS A GUAR-ANTEED WINNER!!
THIS IS WHERE GENJIROU FELT SO FREE THAT HE STARTED SINGING AND DANCING!!

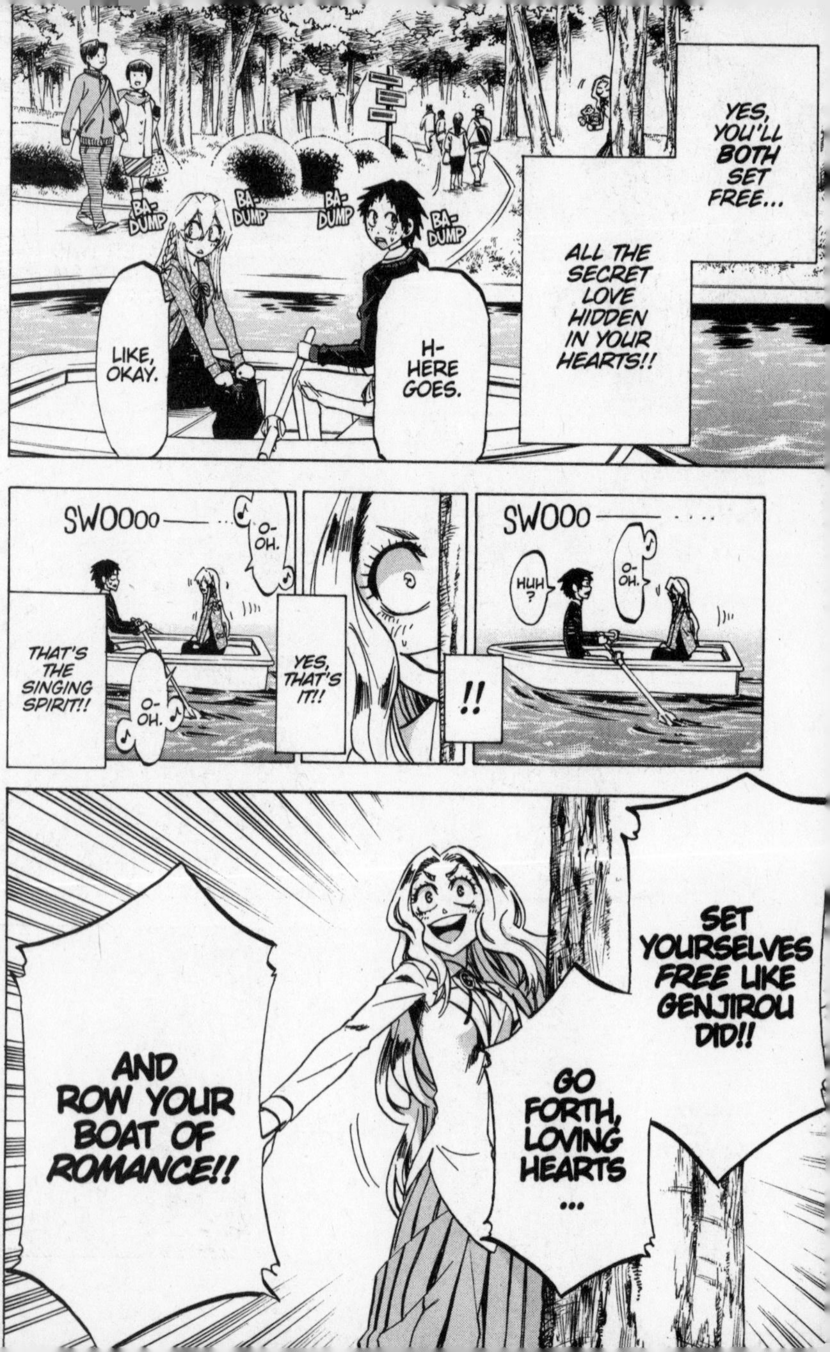
YES, YOU'LL BOTH SET FREE...
ALL THE SECRET LOVE HIDDEN IN YOUR HEARTS!!
BA-DUMP
BA-DUMP
BA-DUMP
BA-DUMP
H-HERE GOES.
LIKE, OKAY.
SWOOO——....
HUH?
O-OH.
!!
YES, THAT'S IT!!
SWOOOO——...
O-OH.
THAT'S THE SINGING SPIRIT!!
O-OH.
SET YOURSELVES FREE LIKE GENJIROU DID!!
GO FORTH, LOVING HEARTS...
AND ROW YOUR BOAT OF ROMANCE!!

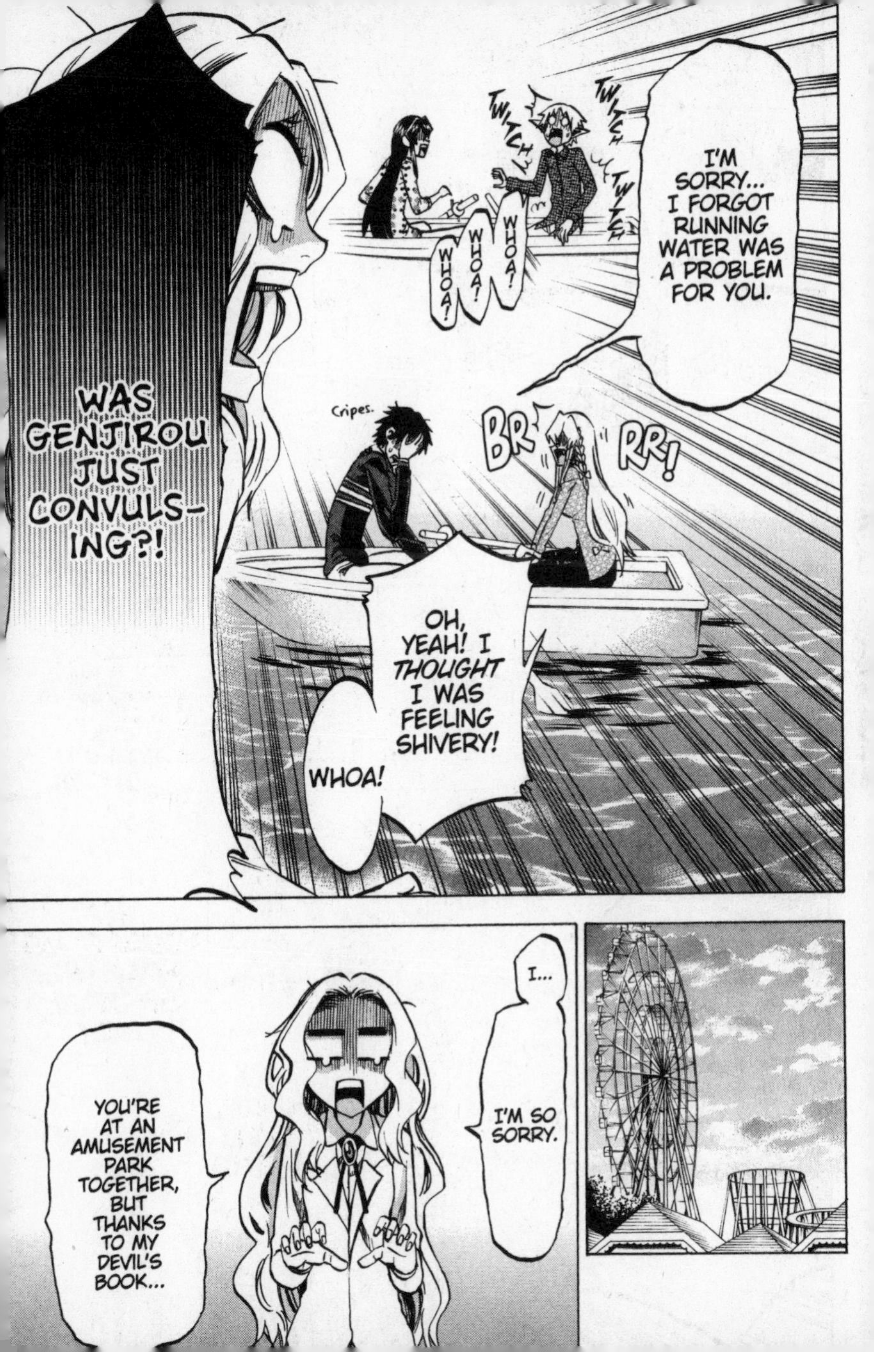
TWITCH
TWITCH
I'M SORRY... I FORGOT RUNNING WATER WAS A PROBLEM FOR YOU.
TWITCH
WHOA!
WHOA!
WHOA!
BRRR!
Cripes.
OH, YEAH! I *THOUGHT* I WAS FEELING SHIVERY!
WHOA!
WAS GENJIROU JUST CONVULS-ING?!
I...
I'M SO SORRY.
YOU'RE AT AN AMUSEMENT PARK TOGETHER, BUT THANKS TO MY DEVIL'S BOOK...

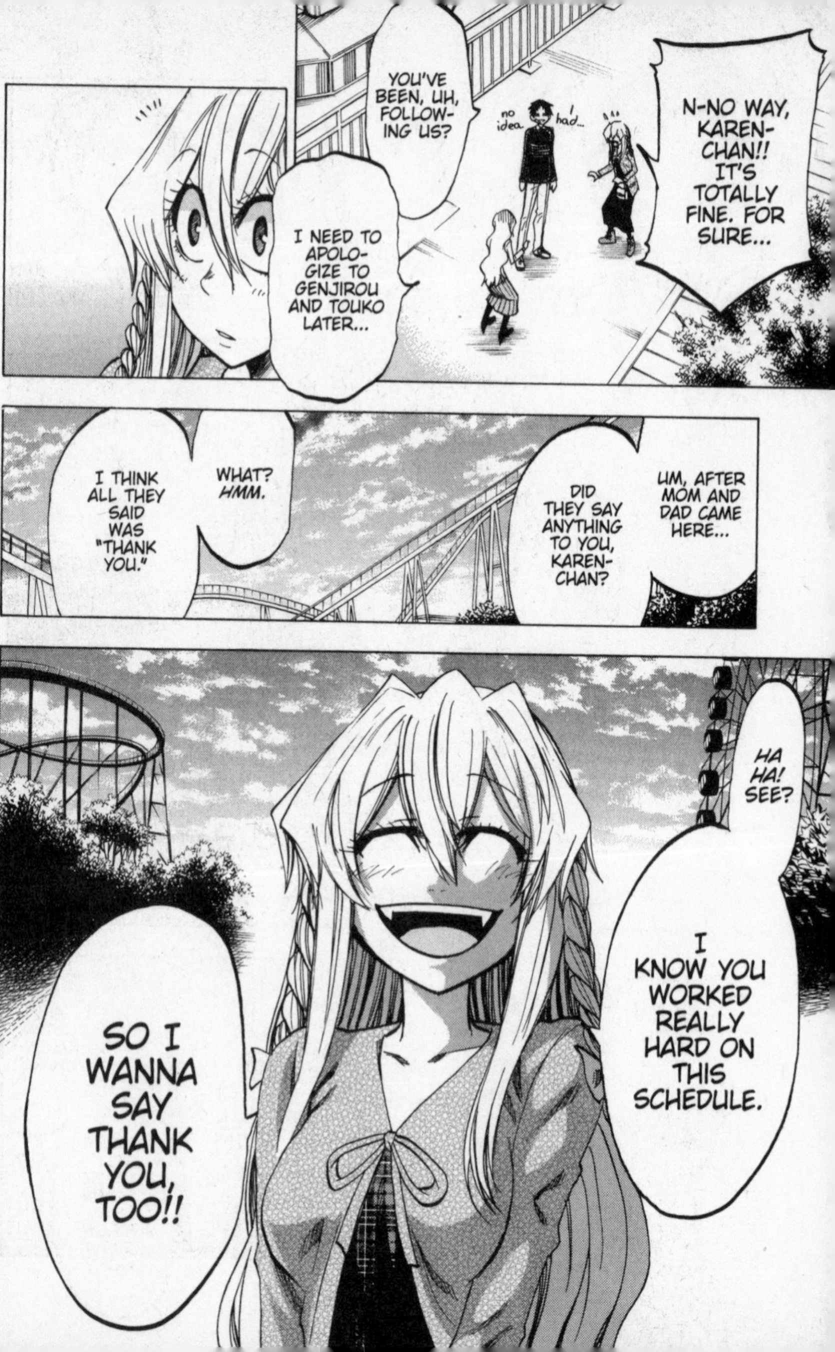
N-NO WAY, KAREN-CHAN!! IT'S TOTALLY FINE. FOR SURE...
I had...
no idea.
YOU'VE BEEN, UH, FOLLOWING US?
I NEED TO APOLOGIZE TO GENJIROU AND TOUKO LATER...
UM, AFTER MOM AND DAD CAME HERE...
DID THEY SAY ANYTHING TO YOU, KAREN-CHAN?
WHAT? HMM.
I THINK ALL THEY SAID WAS "THANK YOU."
HA HA! SEE?
I KNOW YOU WORKED REALLY HARD ON THIS SCHEDULE.
SO I WANNA SAY THANK YOU, TOO!!

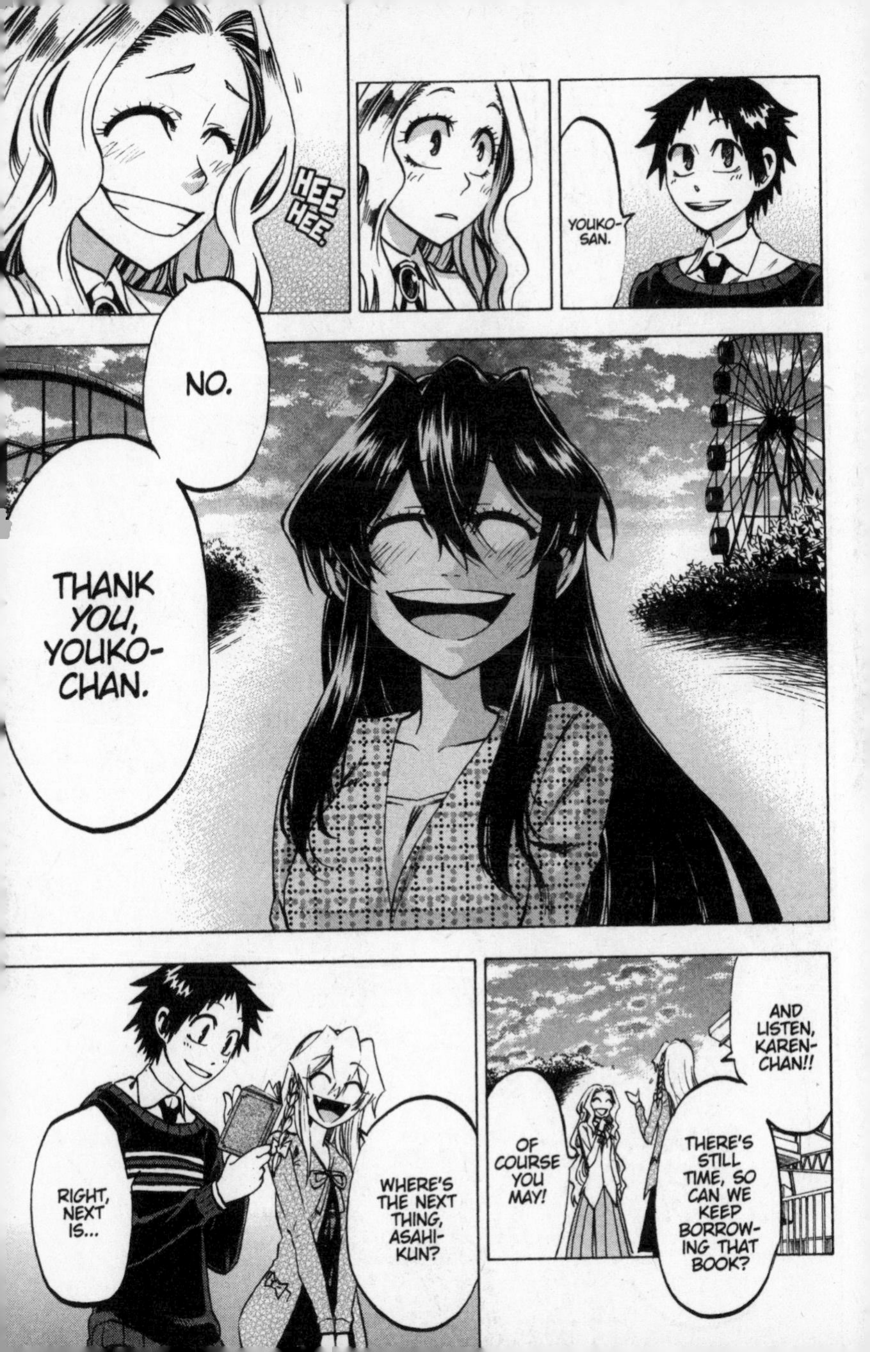
YOUKO-SAN.
HEE HEE.
NO.
THANK YOU, YOUKO-CHAN.
AND LISTEN, KAREN-CHAN!!
THERE'S STILL TIME, SO CAN WE KEEP BORROWING THAT BOOK?
OF COURSE YOU MAY!
WHERE'S THE NEXT THING, ASAHI-KUN?
RIGHT, NEXT IS...

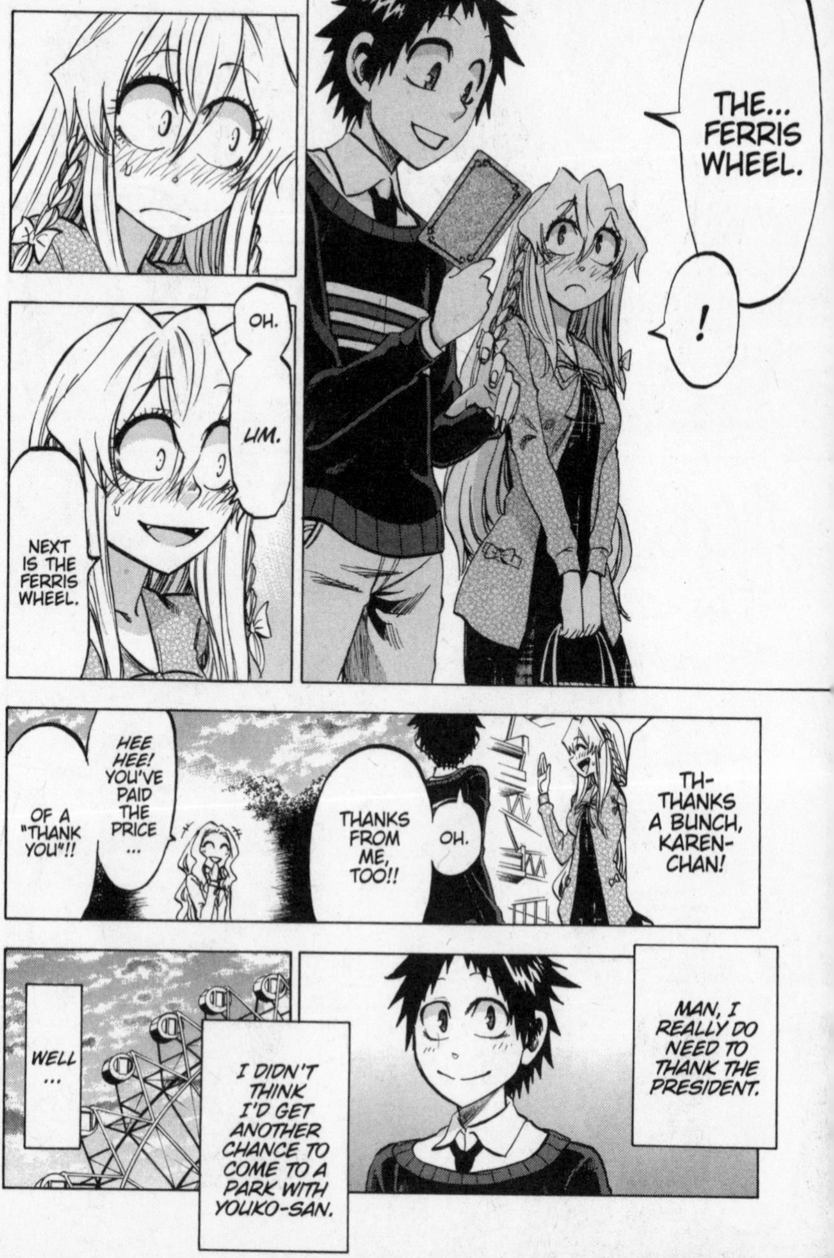
THE... FERRIS WHEEL.
!
OH.
UM.
NEXT IS THE FERRIS WHEEL.
TH- THANKS A BUNCH, KAREN-CHAN!
OH.
THANKS FROM ME, TOO!!
HEE HEE! YOU'VE PAID THE PRICE ...
OF A "THANK YOU"!!
MAN, I REALLY DO NEED TO THANK THE PRESIDENT.
WELL ...
I DIDN'T THINK I'D GET ANOTHER CHANCE TO COME TO A PARK WITH YOUKO-SAN.

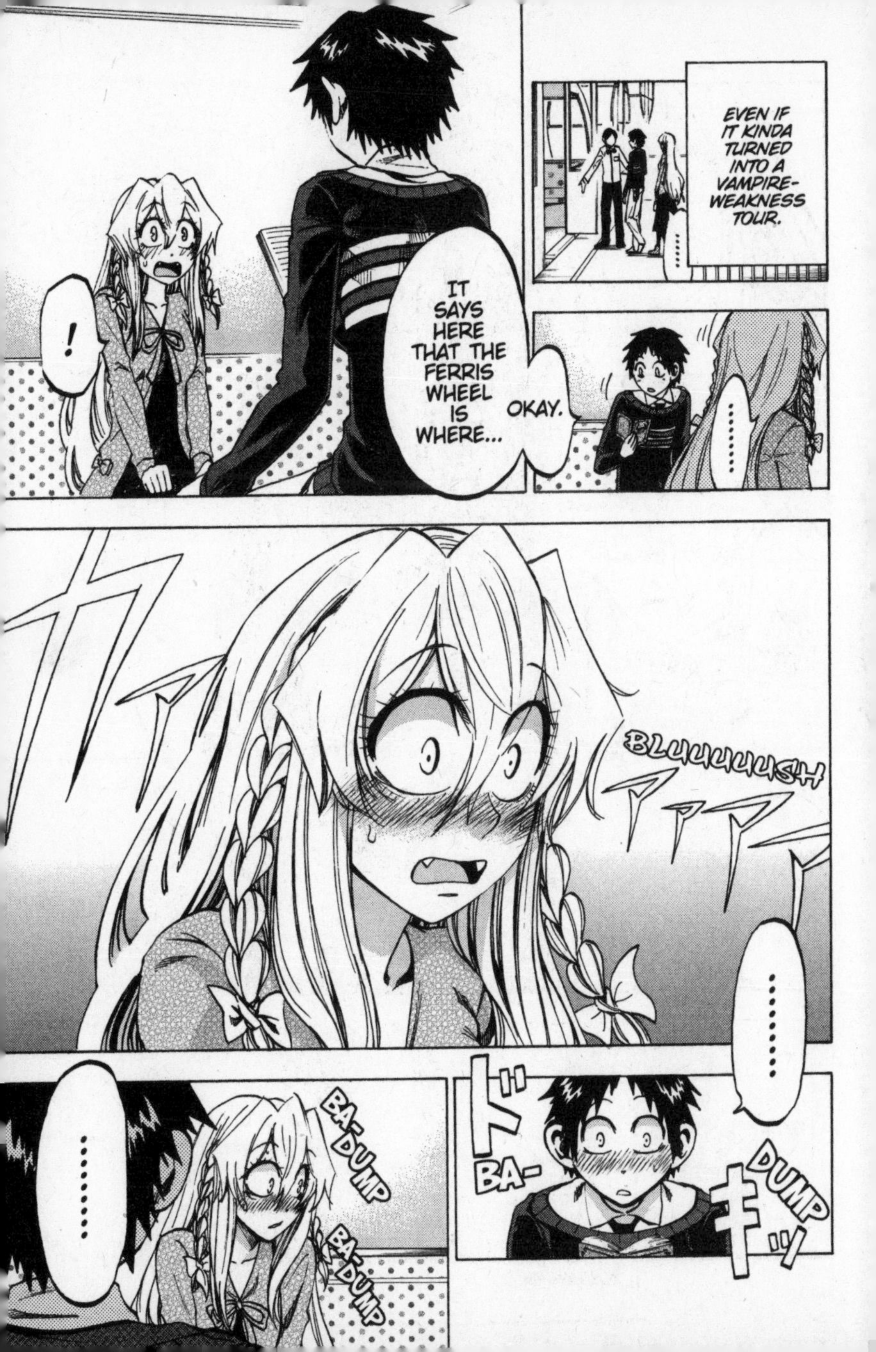
EVEN IF IT KINDA TURNED INTO A VAMPIRE-WEAKNESS TOUR.
......
......
OKAY.
IT SAYS HERE THAT THE FERRIS WHEEL IS WHERE...
!
BLUUUUUSH
......
BA- DUMP
BA-DUMP
BA-DUMP
......

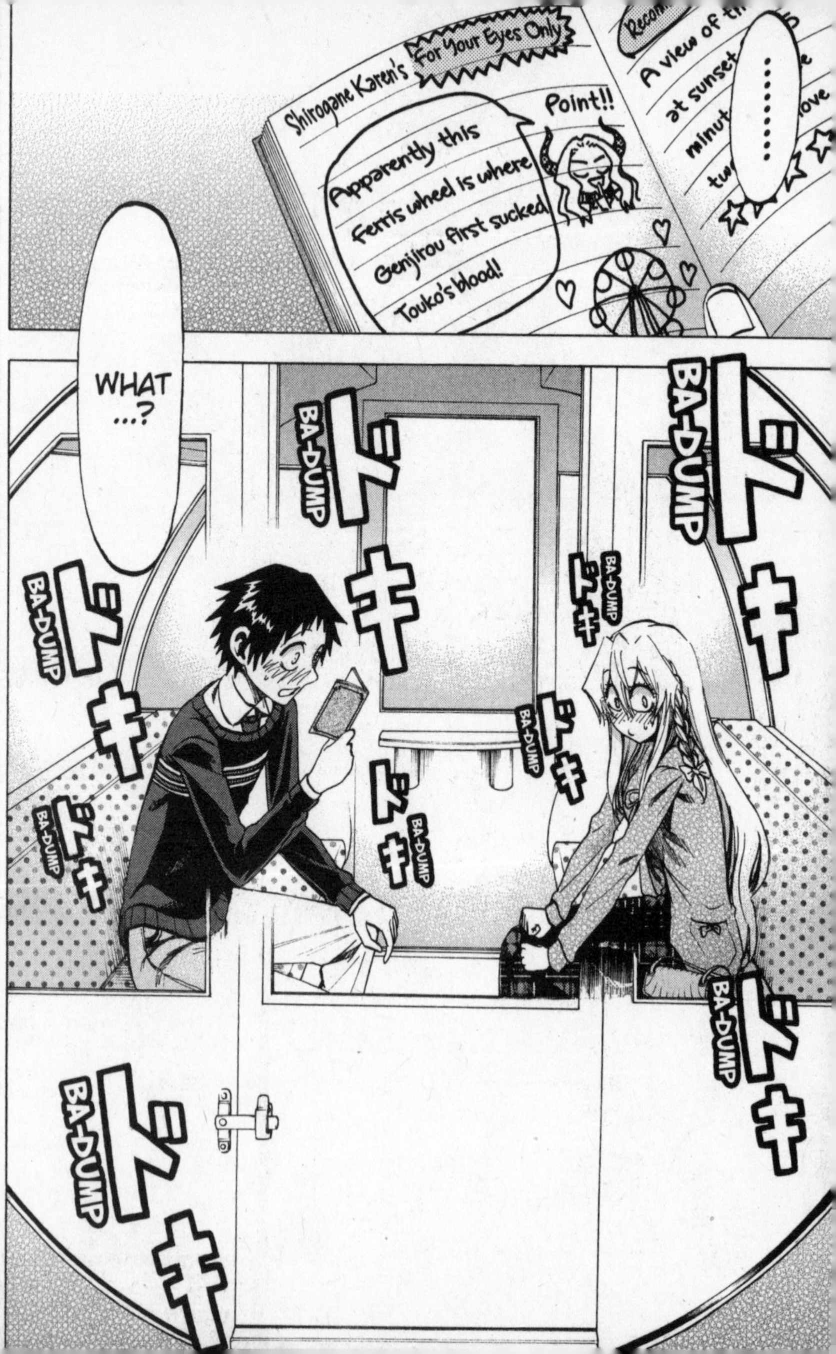

Shirogane Karen's For Your Eyes Only
Point!!
Apparently this Ferris wheel is where Genjirou first sucked Touko's blood!
......
ドキ BA-DUMP
ドキ BA-DUMP
ドキ BA-DUMP
ドキ BA-DUMP
ドキ BA-DUMP
WHAT ...?
ドキ BA-DUMP
ドキ BA-DUMP
ドキ BA-DUMP
ドキ BA-DUMP

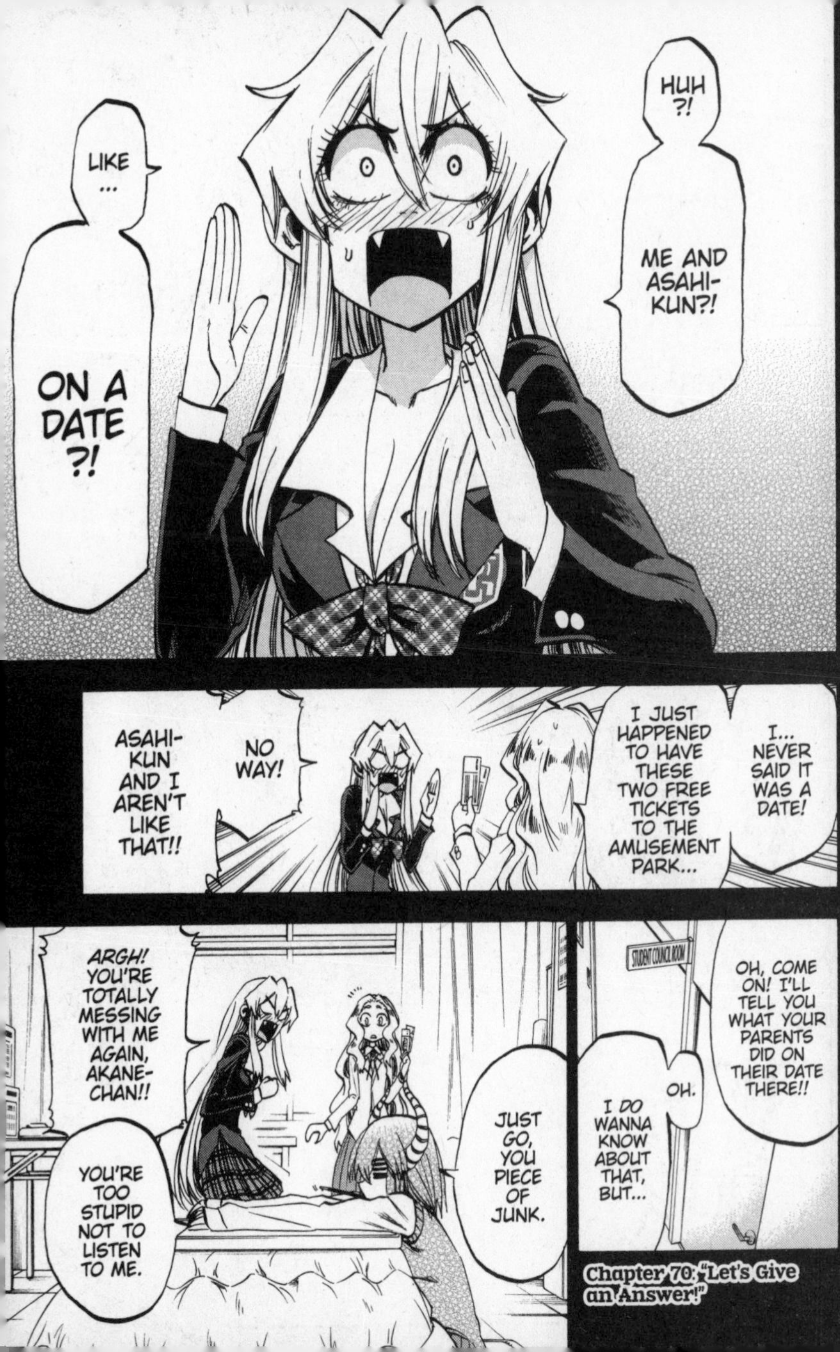
HUH ?!
ME AND ASAHI-KUN?!
LIKE ...
ON A DATE ?!
I... NEVER SAID IT WAS A DATE!
I JUST HAPPENED TO HAVE THESE TWO FREE TICKETS TO THE AMUSEMENT PARK...
NO WAY!
ASAHI-KUN AND I AREN'T LIKE THAT!!
STUDENT COUNCIL ROOM
OH, COME ON! I'LL TELL YOU WHAT YOUR PARENTS DID ON THEIR DATE THERE!!
OH.
I *DO* WANNA KNOW ABOUT THAT, BUT...
ARGH! YOU'RE TOTALLY MESSING WITH ME AGAIN, AKANE-CHAN!!
JUST GO, YOU PIECE OF JUNK.
YOU'RE TOO STUPID NOT TO LISTEN TO ME.

Chapter 70: "Let's Give an Answer!"

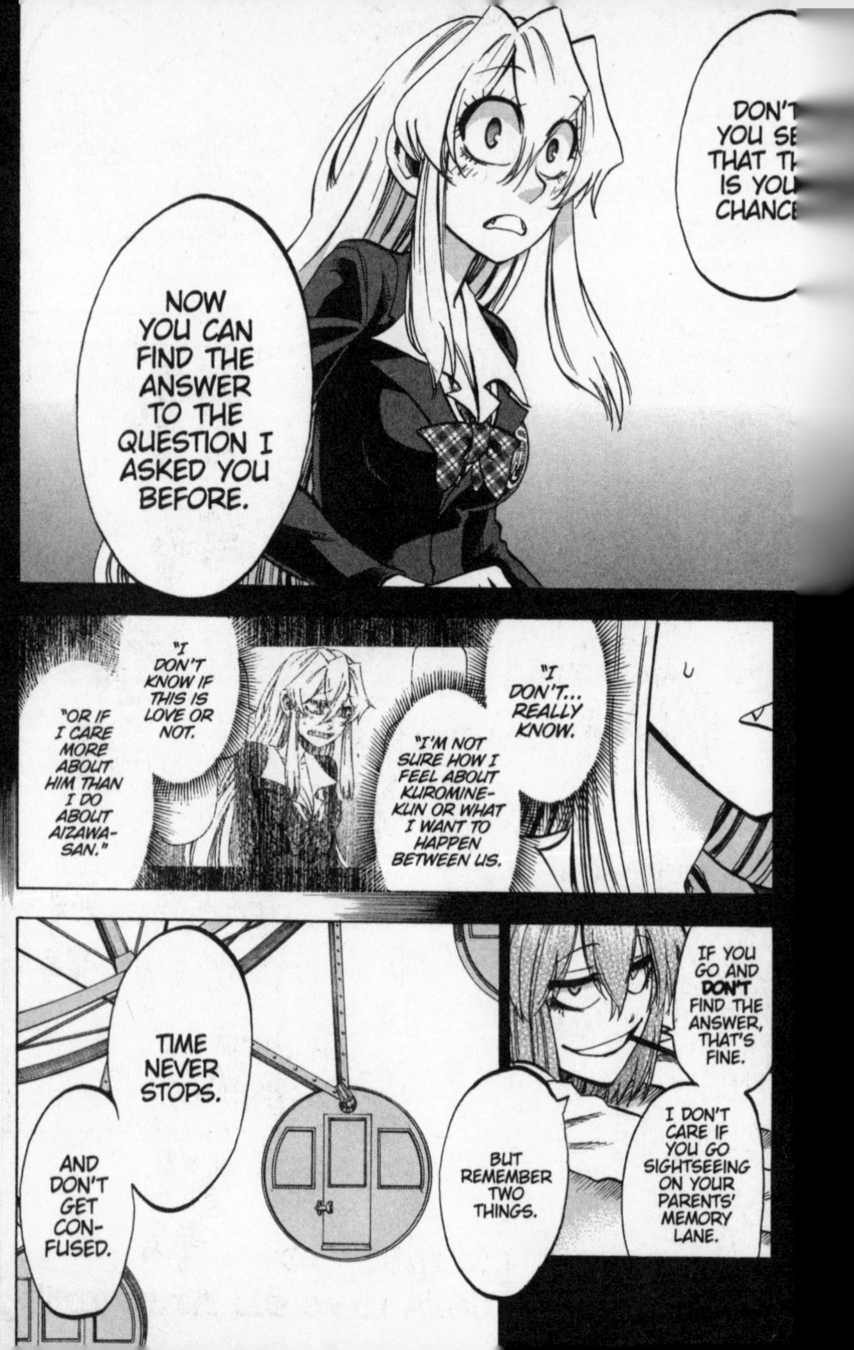
DON'T YOU SE THAT TH IS YOU CHANCE
NOW YOU CAN FIND THE ANSWER TO THE QUESTION I ASKED YOU BEFORE.
"I DON'T... REALLY KNOW.
"I'M NOT SURE HOW I FEEL ABOUT KUROMINE-KUN OR WHAT I WANT TO HAPPEN BETWEEN US.
"I DON'T KNOW IF THIS IS LOVE OR NOT.
"OR IF I CARE MORE ABOUT HIM THAN I DO ABOUT AIZAWA-SAN."
IF YOU GO AND **DON'T** FIND THE ANSWER, THAT'S FINE.
I DON'T CARE IF YOU GO SIGHTSEEING ON YOUR PARENTS' MEMORY LANE.
BUT REMEMBER TWO THINGS.
TIME NEVER STOPS.
AND DON'T GET CON-FUSED.

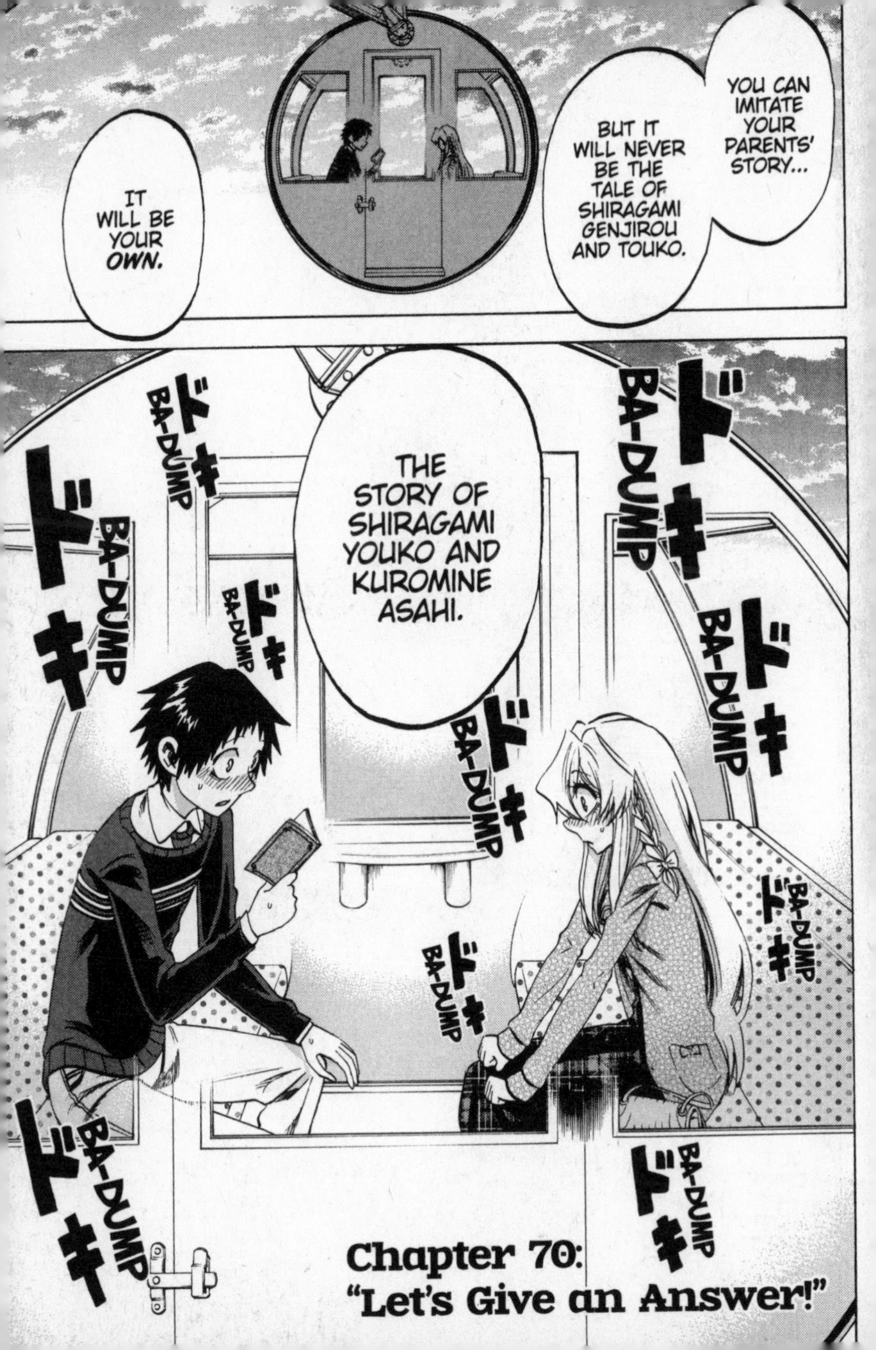
YOU CAN IMITATE YOUR PARENTS' STORY...
BUT IT WILL NEVER BE THE TALE OF SHIRAGAMI GENJIROU AND TOUKO.
IT WILL BE YOUR OWN.
ドキ BA-DUMP
ドキ BA-DUMP
THE STORY OF SHIRAGAMI YOUKO AND KUROMINE ASAHI.
ドキ BA-DUMP
ドキ BA-DUMP
ドキ BA-DUMP
ドキ BA-DUMP
ドキ BA-DUMP
ドキ BA-DUMP
ドキ BA-DUMP
ドキ BA-DUMP
Chapter 70: "Let's Give an Answer!"

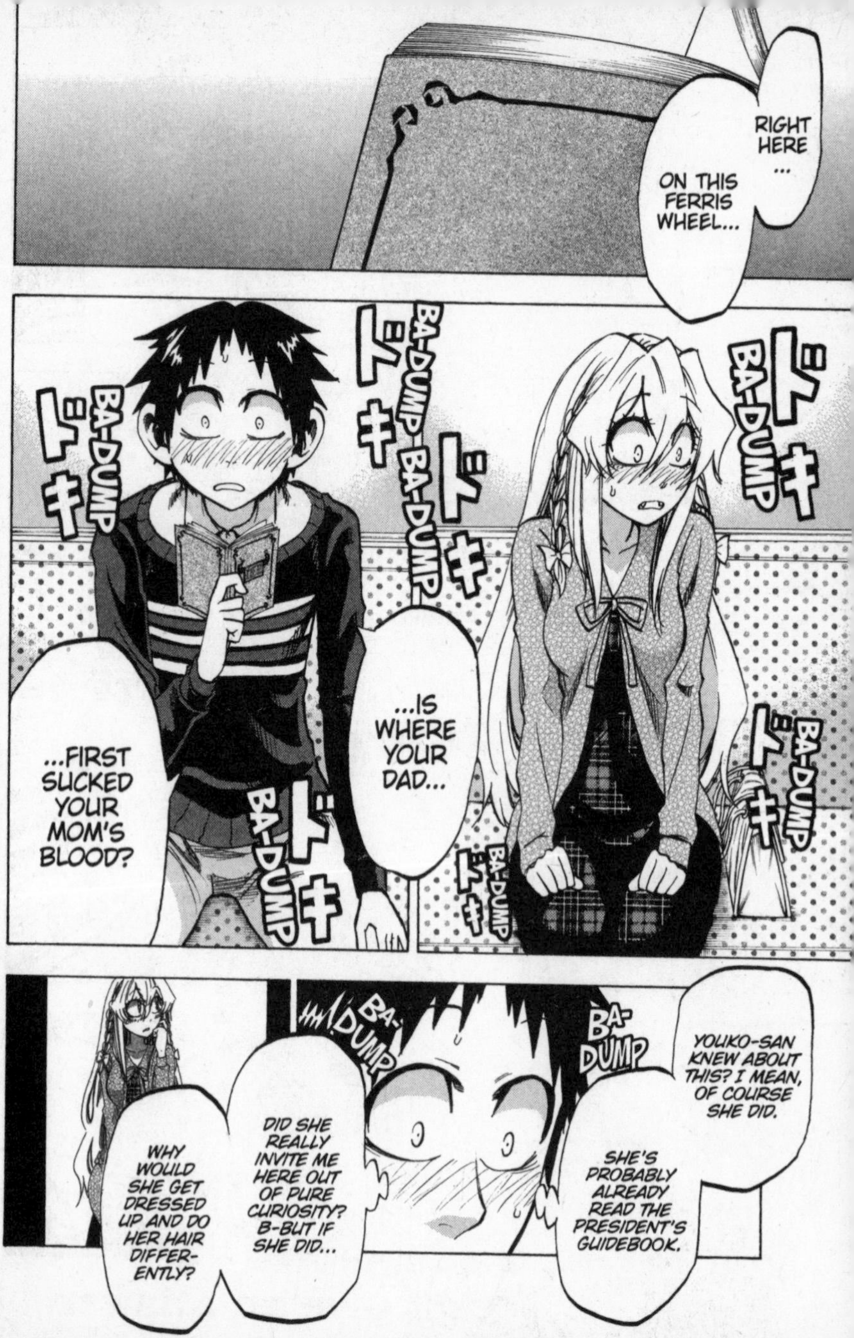
RIGHT HERE ...
ON THIS FERRIS WHEEL...
ドキ BA-DUMP
...IS WHERE YOUR DAD...
ドキ BA-DUMP
ドキ BA-DUMP
ドキ ドキ BA-DUMP-BA-DUMP
ドキ BA-DUMP
...FIRST SUCKED YOUR MOM'S BLOOD?
ドキ BA-DUMP
YOUKO-SAN KNEW ABOUT THIS? I MEAN, OF COURSE SHE DID.
BA-DUMP
SHE'S PROBABLY ALREADY READ THE PRESIDENT'S GUIDEBOOK.
BA-DUMP
DID SHE REALLY INVITE ME HERE OUT OF PURE CURIOSITY? B-BUT IF SHE DID...
WHY WOULD SHE GET DRESSED UP AND DO HER HAIR DIFFER-ENTLY?

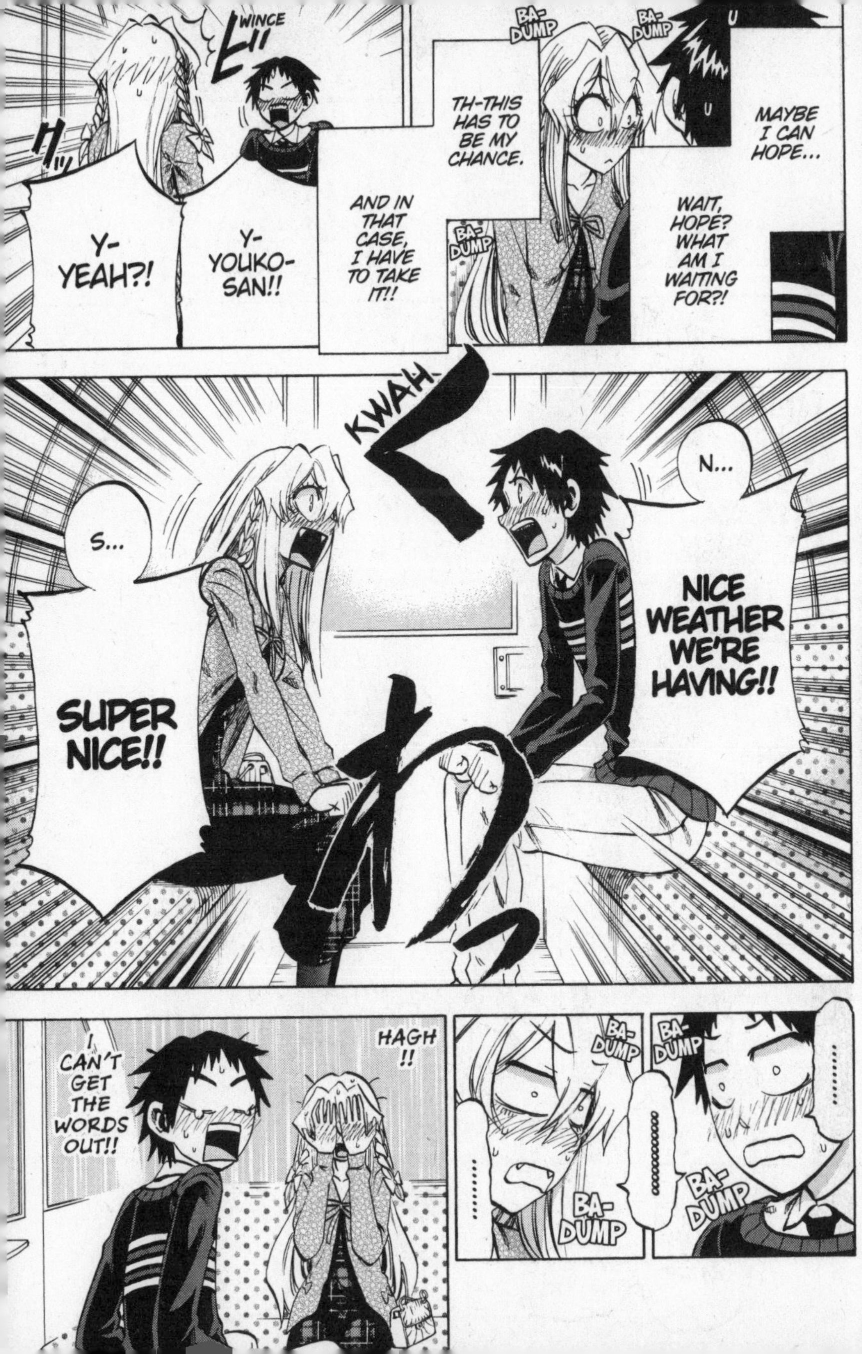
BA-DUMP
BA-DUMP
MAYBE I CAN HOPE...
WAIT, HOPE? WHAT AM I WAITING FOR?!
TH-THIS HAS TO BE MY CHANCE.
BA-DUMP
AND IN THAT CASE, I HAVE TO TAKE IT!!
WINCE
Y-YOUKO-SAN!!
Y-YEAH?!
KWAH
N...
NICE WEATHER WE'RE HAVING!!
S...
SUPER NICE!!
BA-DUMP
BA-DUMP
......
......
......
BA-DUMP
BA-DUMP
HAGH!!
I CAN'T GET THE WORDS OUT!!

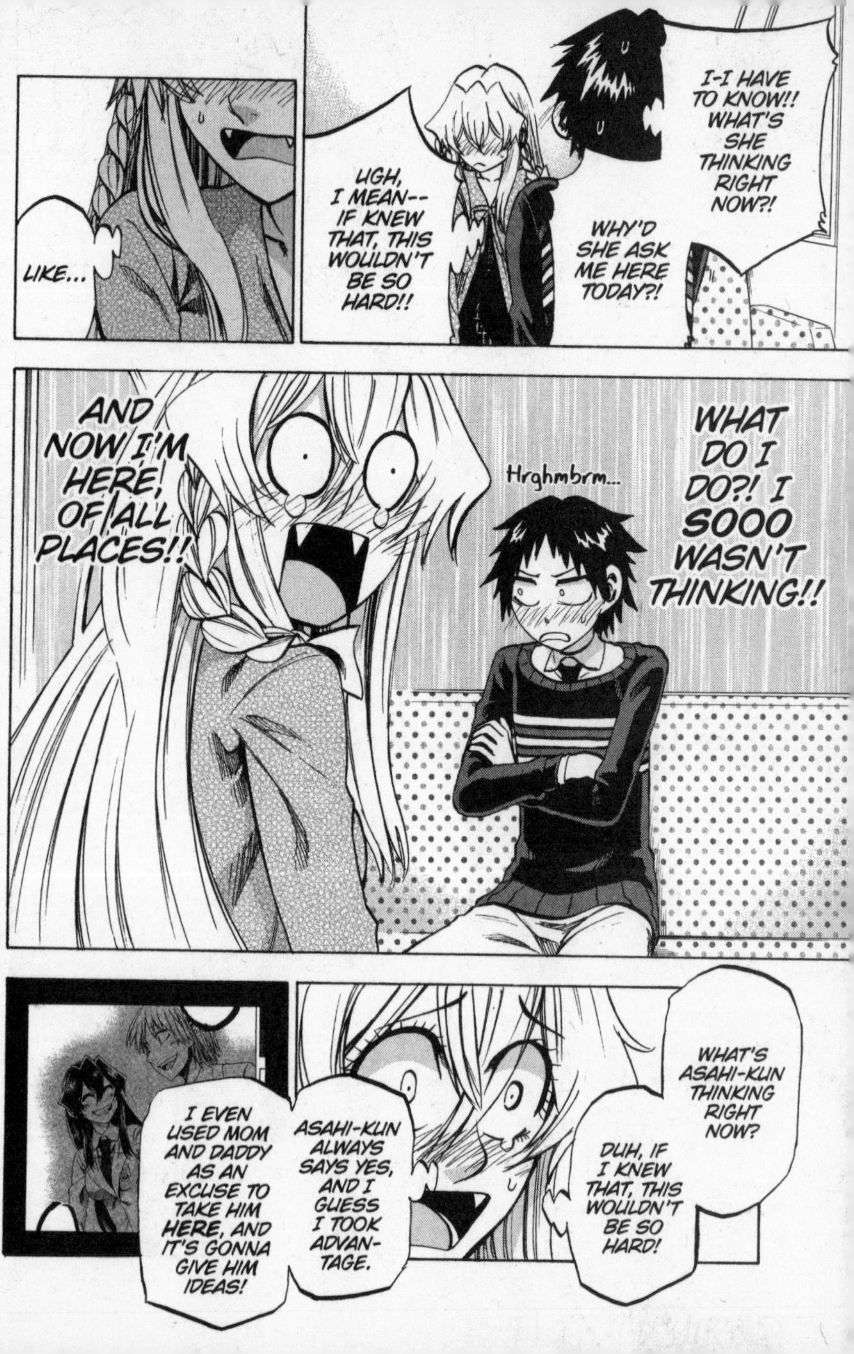
I-I HAVE TO KNOW!! WHAT'S SHE THINKING RIGHT NOW?!
WHY'D SHE ASK ME HERE TODAY?!
UGH, I MEAN-- IF KNEW THAT, THIS WOULDN'T BE SO HARD!!
LIKE...
WHAT DO I DO?! I SOOO WASN'T THINKING!!
Hrghmbrm...
AND NOW I'M HERE, OF ALL PLACES!!
WHAT'S ASAHI-KUN THINKING RIGHT NOW?
DUH, IF I KNEW THAT, THIS WOULDN'T BE SO HARD!
ASAHI-KUN ALWAYS SAYS YES, AND I GUESS I TOOK ADVAN-TAGE.
I EVEN USED MOM AND DADDY AS AN EXCUSE TO TAKE HIM HERE, AND IT'S GONNA GIVE HIM IDEAS!

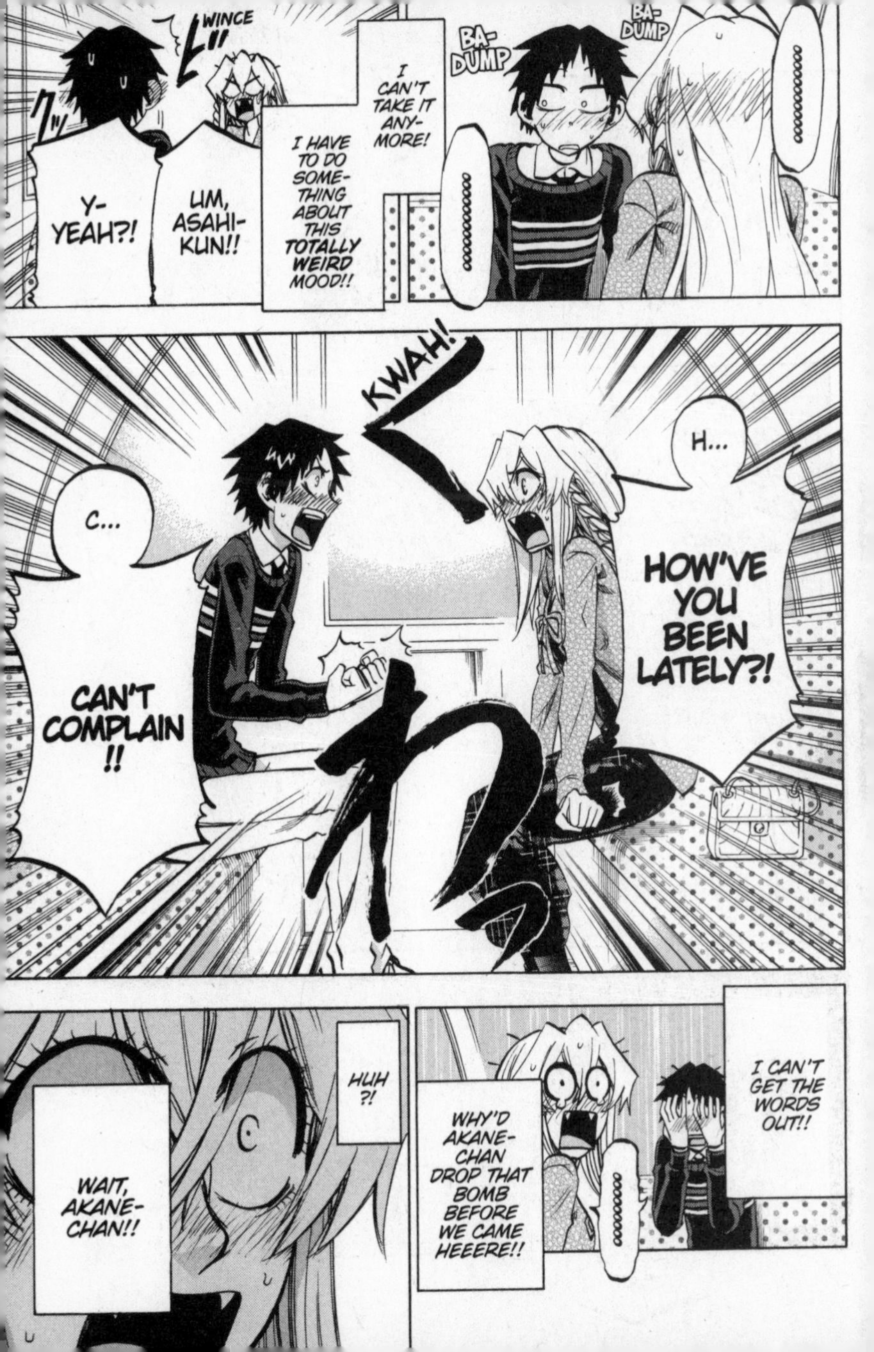
BA-DUMP
BA-DUMP
....
....
I CAN'T TAKE IT ANYMORE!
I HAVE TO DO SOMETHING ABOUT THIS TOTALLY WEIRD MOOD!!
WINCE
UM, ASAHI-KUN!!
Y-YEAH?!
KWAH!
H...
HOW'VE YOU BEEN LATELY?!
C...
CAN'T COMPLAIN!!
I CAN'T GET THE WORDS OUT!!
WHY'D AKANE-CHAN DROP THAT BOMB BEFORE WE CAME HEEERE!!
....
HUH?!
WAIT, AKANE-CHAN!!

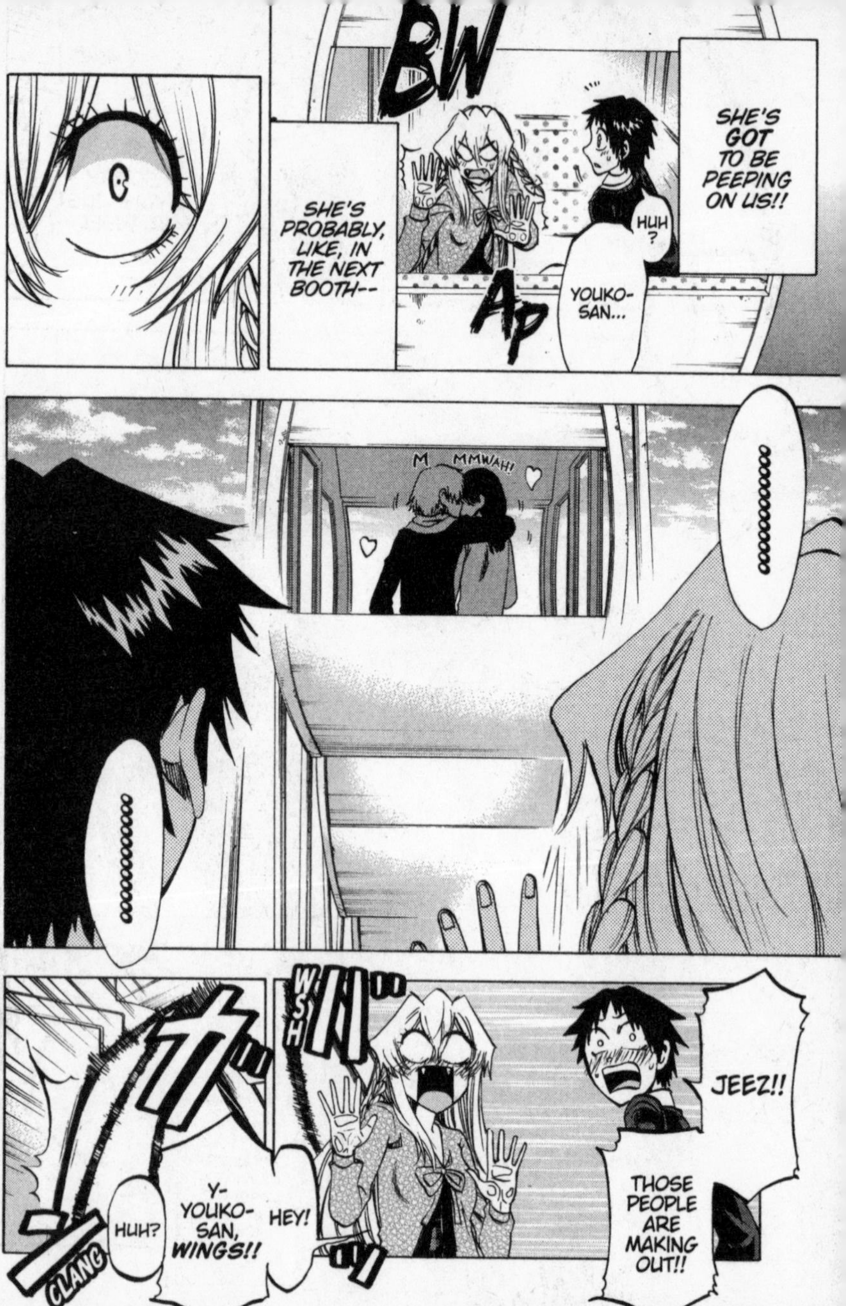
SHE'S GOT TO BE PEEPING ON US!!
HUH?
YOUKO-SAN...
BW
AP
SHE'S PROBABLY, LIKE, IN THE NEXT BOOTH--
....
M
MMWAH!
....
JEEZ!!
THOSE PEOPLE ARE MAKING OUT!!
WSH
HEY!
Y-YOUKO-SAN, WINGS!!
HUH?
CLANG

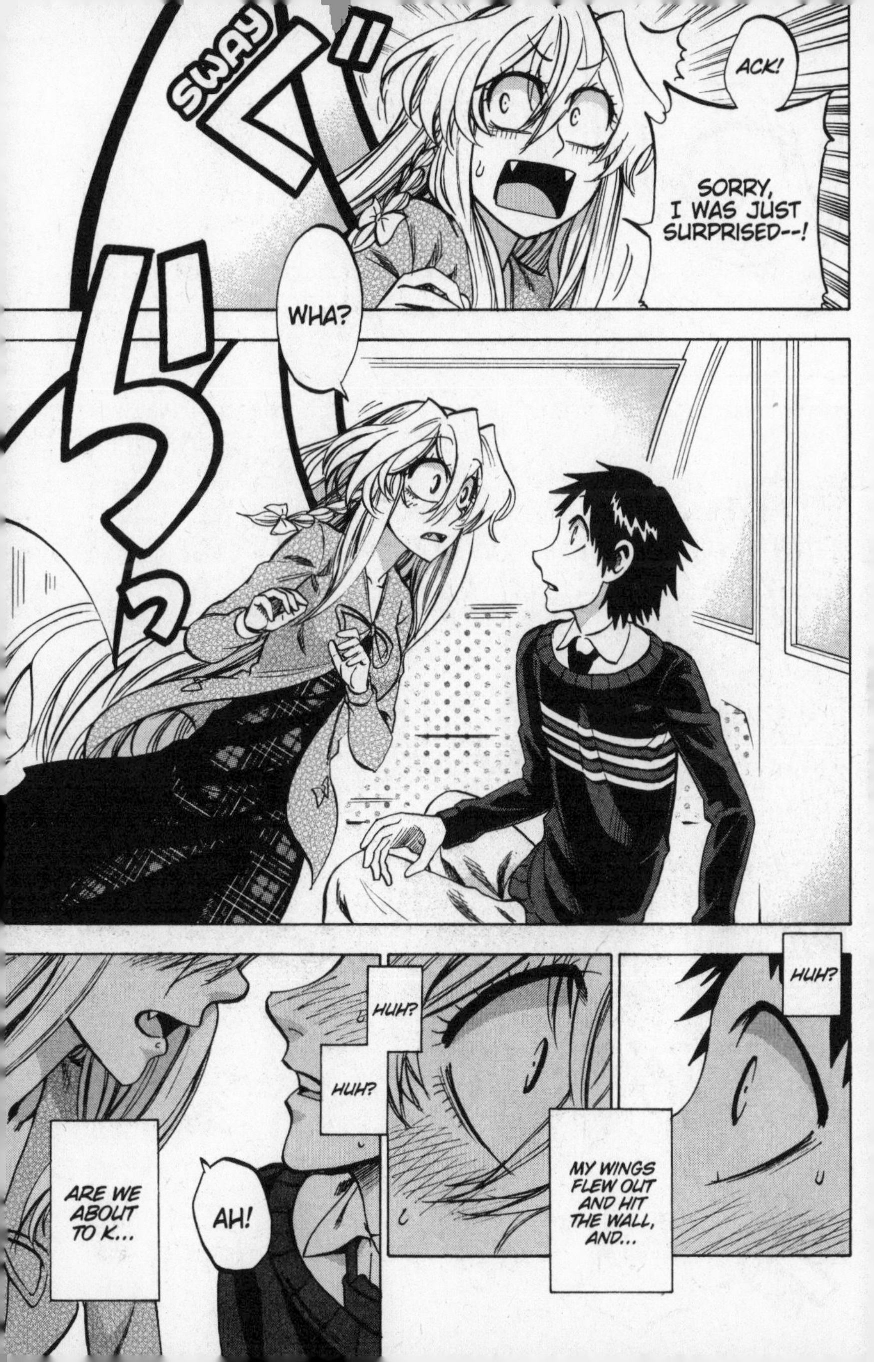
ACK!
SORRY, I WAS JUST SURPRISED--!
SWAY
WHA?
HUH?
MY WINGS FLEW OUT AND HIT THE WALL, AND...
HUH?
HUH?
AH!
ARE WE ABOUT TO K...

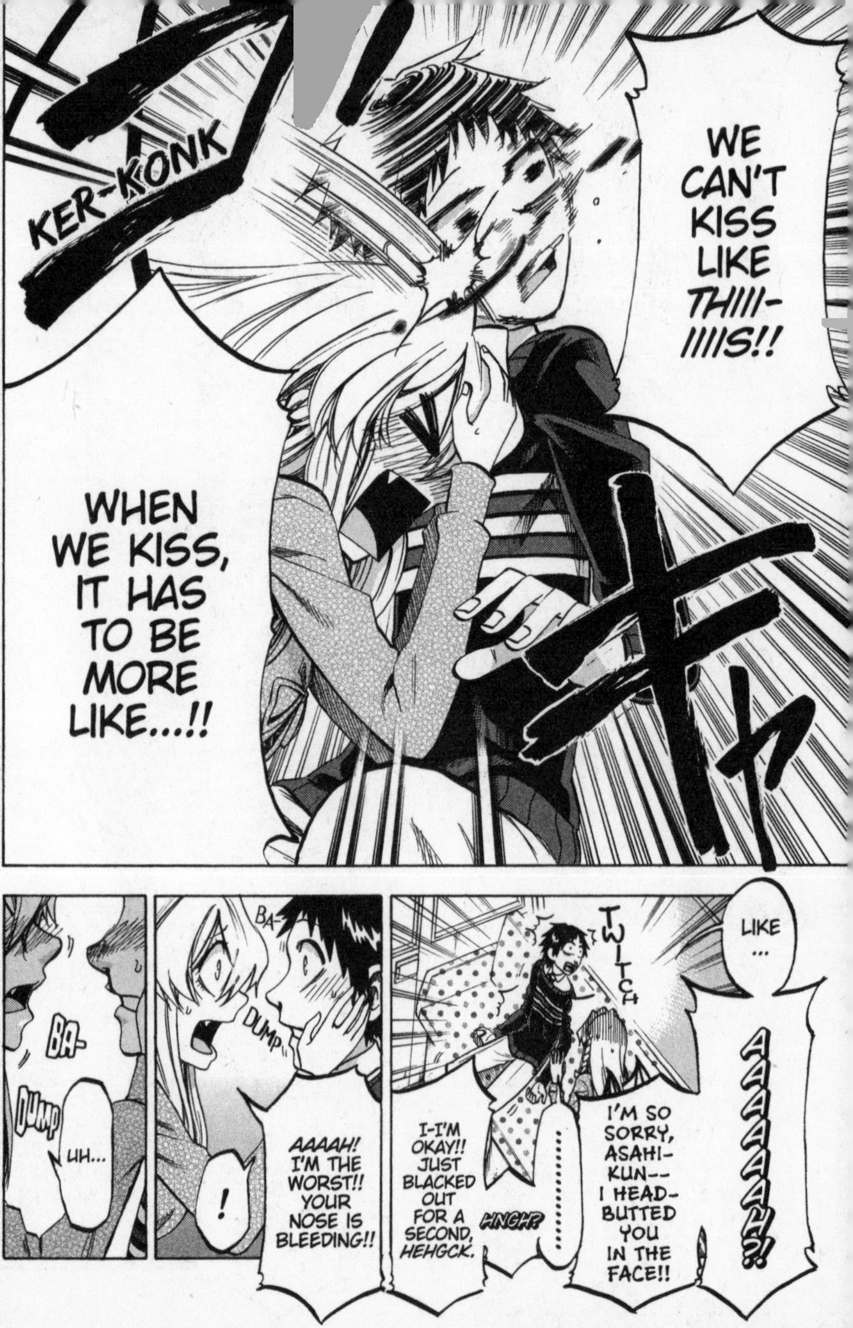
WE CAN'T KISS LIKE THIIII-IIIIS!!
KER-KONK
WHEN WE KISS, IT HAS TO BE MORE LIKE...!!
LIKE ...
AAAAAAAAH?!
TWITCH
I'M SO SORRY, ASAHI-KUN-- I HEAD-BUTTED YOU IN THE FACE!!
......
HNGH?
I-I'M OKAY!! JUST BLACKED OUT FOR A SECOND, HEHGCK.
AAAAH! I'M THE WORST!! YOUR NOSE IS BLEEDING!!
BA-
DUMP
!
BA-
DUMP
UH...

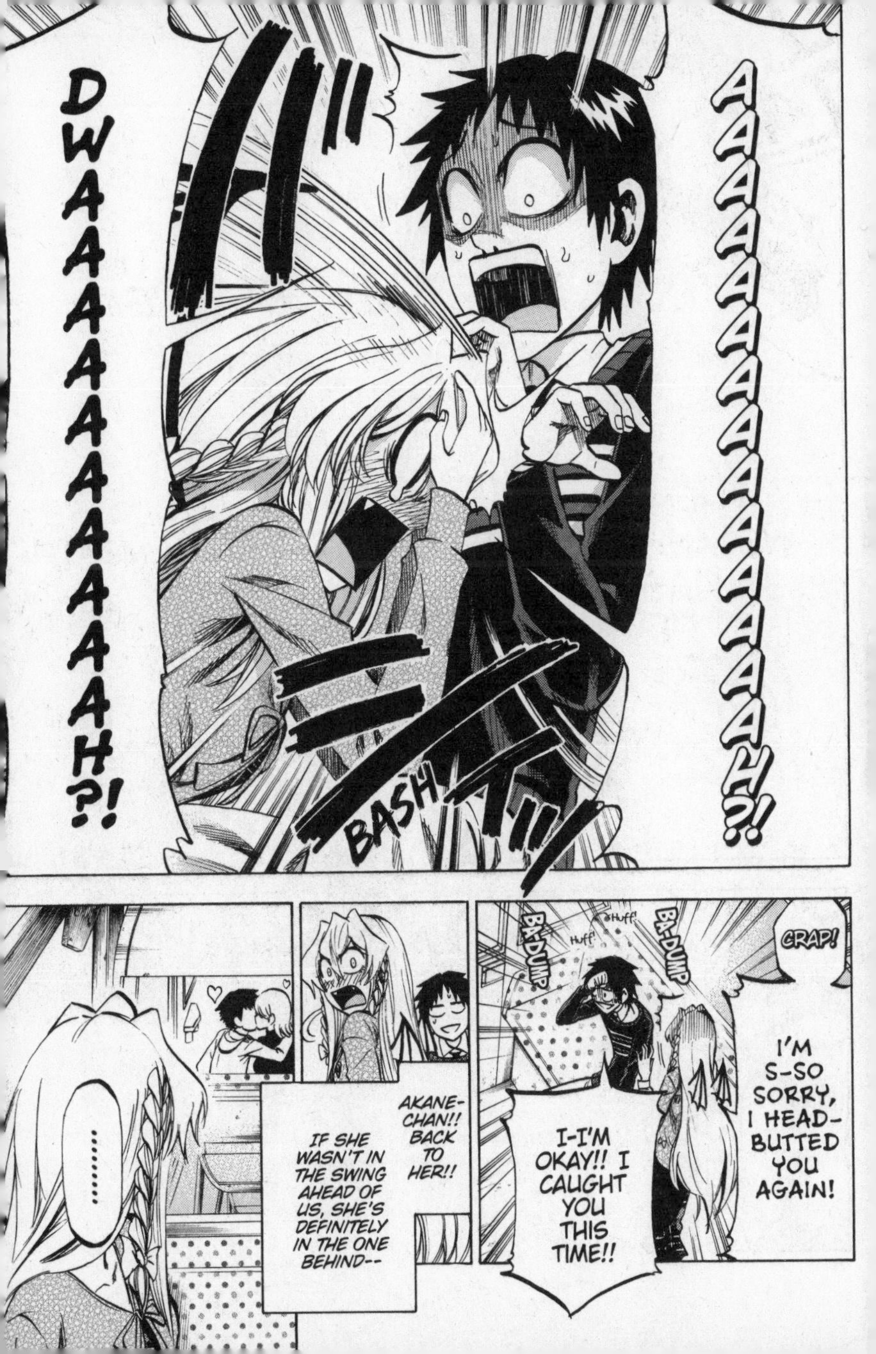
AAAAAAAAAAAAAAAAH?!
BASH
DWAAAAAAAAAAAAH?!
CRAP!
I'M S-SO SORRY, I HEAD-BUTTED YOU AGAIN!
BA-DUMP
Huff!
Huff!
BA-DUMP
I-I'M OKAY!! I CAUGHT YOU THIS TIME!!
AKANE-CHAN!! BACK TO HER!!
IF SHE WASN'T IN THE SWING AHEAD OF US, SHE'S DEFINITELY IN THE ONE BEHIND--
......

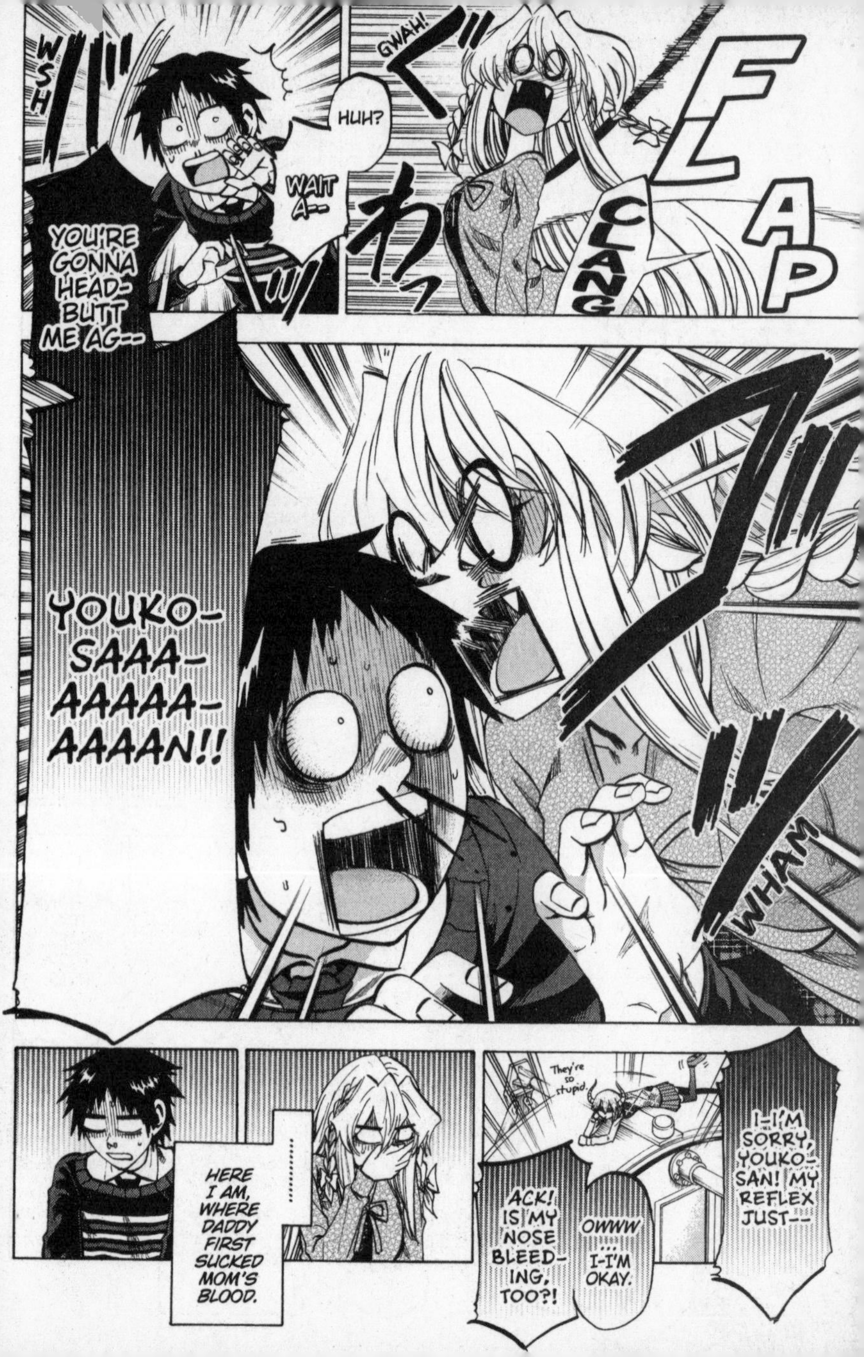
FLAP
CLANG
GWAH!
ぐわっ
HUH?
WAIT A--
YOU'RE GONNA HEAD-BUTT ME AG--
WSH
YOUKO-SAAAAAAAAAAAAN!!
WHAM
I-I'M SORRY, YOUKO-SAN! MY REFLEX JUST--
They're so stupid.
OWWW.... I-I'M OKAY.
ACK! IS MY NOSE BLEEDING, TOO?!
....
HERE I AM, WHERE DADDY FIRST SUCKED MOM'S BLOOD.

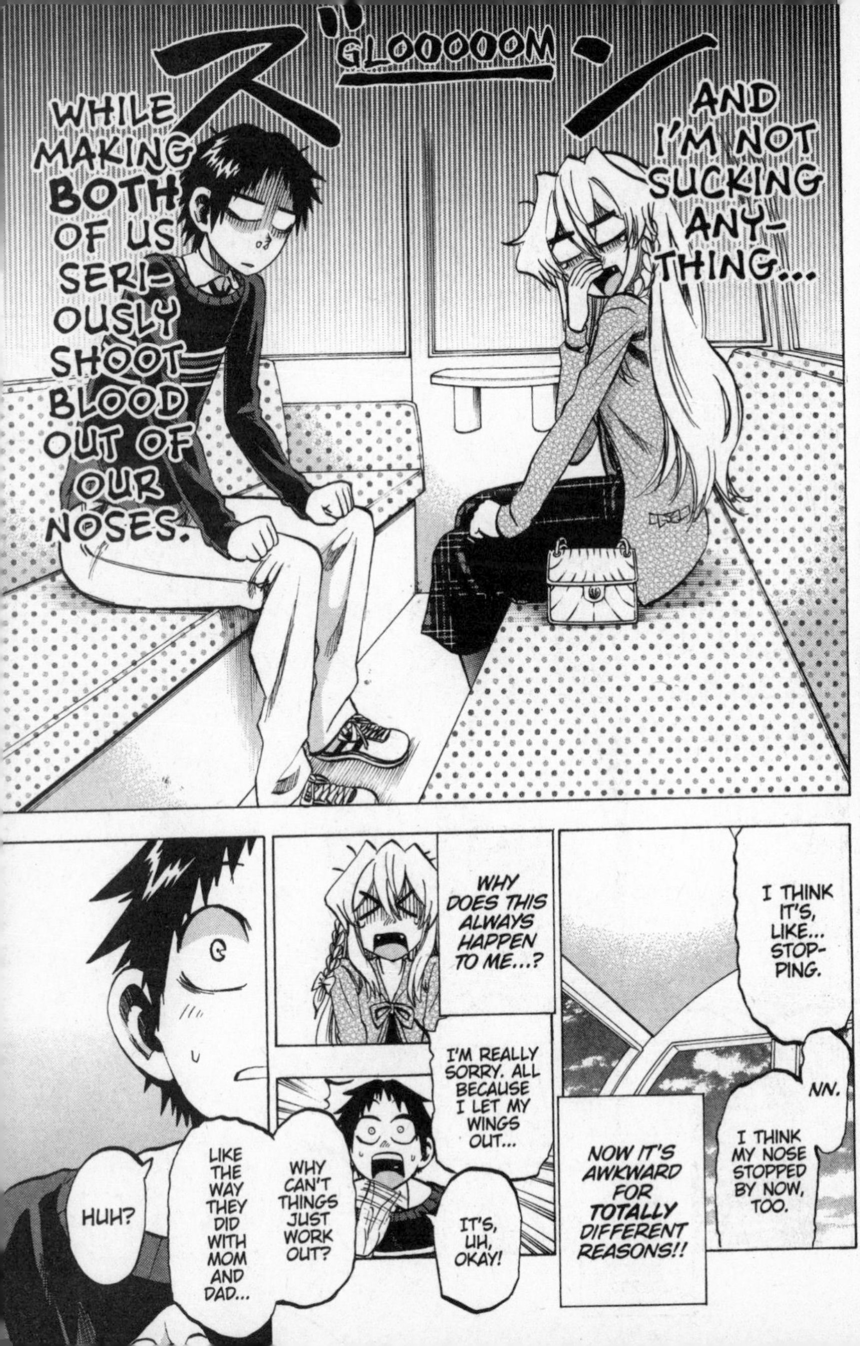
GLOOOOOM
AND I'M NOT SUCKING ANYTHING...
WHILE MAKING BOTH OF US SERIOUSLY SHOOT BLOOD OUT OF OUR NOSES.
I THINK IT'S, LIKE... STOPPING.
NN.
I THINK MY NOSE STOPPED BY NOW, TOO.
NOW IT'S AWKWARD FOR TOTALLY DIFFERENT REASONS!!
WHY DOES THIS ALWAYS HAPPEN TO ME...?
I'M REALLY SORRY. ALL BECAUSE I LET MY WINGS OUT...
IT'S, UH, OKAY!
WHY CAN'T THINGS JUST WORK OUT?
LIKE THE WAY THEY DID WITH MOM AND DAD...
HUH?

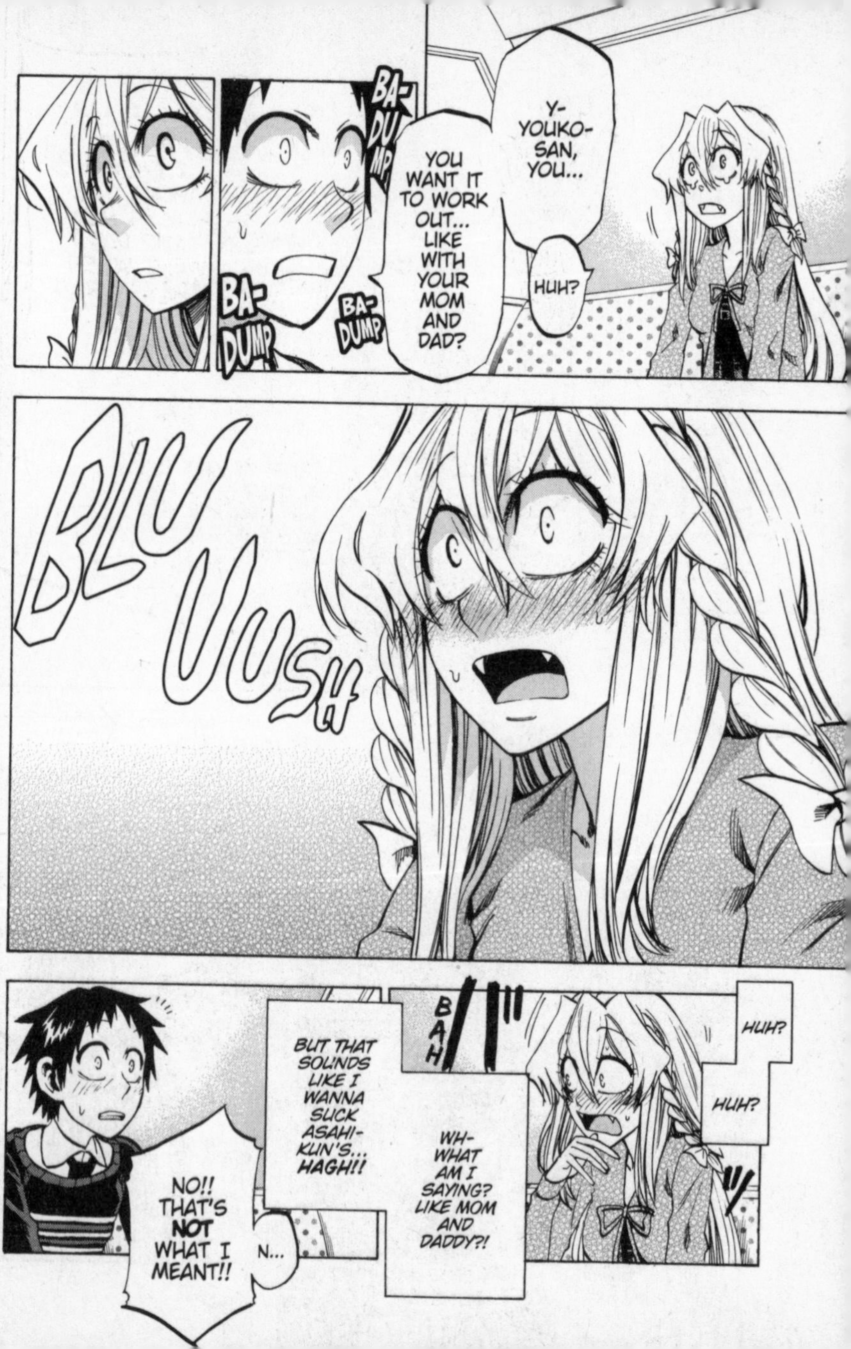
Y-YOUKO-SAN, YOU...
HUH?
YOU WANT IT TO WORK OUT... LIKE WITH YOUR MOM AND DAD?
BA-DUMP
BA-DUMP
BA-DUMP
BLUUUSH
HUH?
HUH?
BAH
WH-WHAT AM I SAYING? LIKE MOM AND DADDY?!
BUT THAT SOUNDS LIKE I WANNA SUCK ASAHI-KUN'S... HAGH!!
N...
NO!! THAT'S **NOT** WHAT I MEANT!!

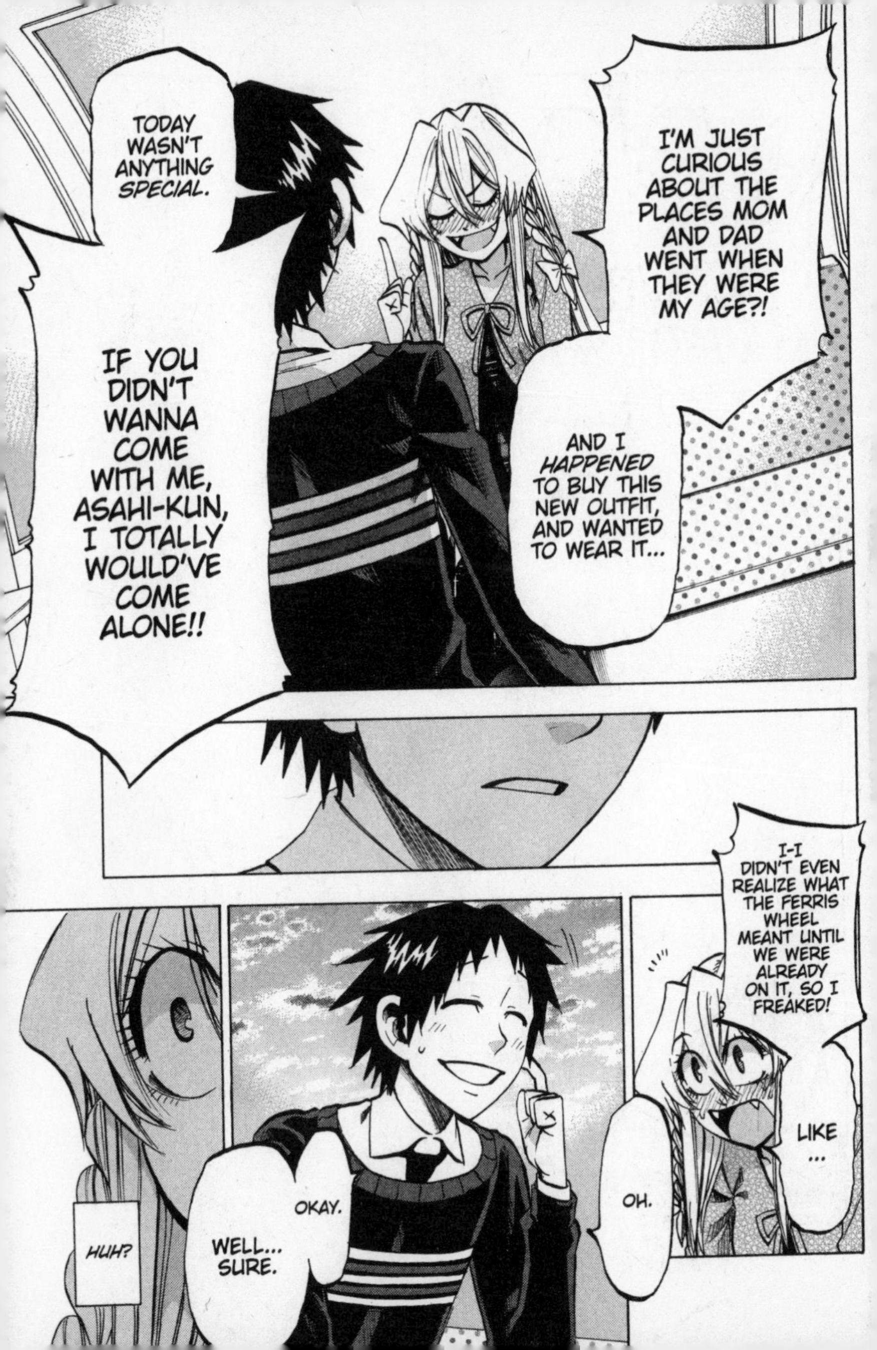
I'M JUST CURIOUS ABOUT THE PLACES MOM AND DAD WENT WHEN THEY WERE MY AGE?!
TODAY WASN'T ANYTHING SPECIAL.
AND I HAPPENED TO BUY THIS NEW OUTFIT, AND WANTED TO WEAR IT...
IF YOU DIDN'T WANNA COME WITH ME, ASAHI-KUN, I TOTALLY WOULD'VE COME ALONE!!
I-I DIDN'T EVEN REALIZE WHAT THE FERRIS WHEEL MEANT UNTIL WE WERE ALREADY ON IT, SO I FREAKED!
LIKE ...
OH.
OKAY.
WELL... SURE.
HUH?

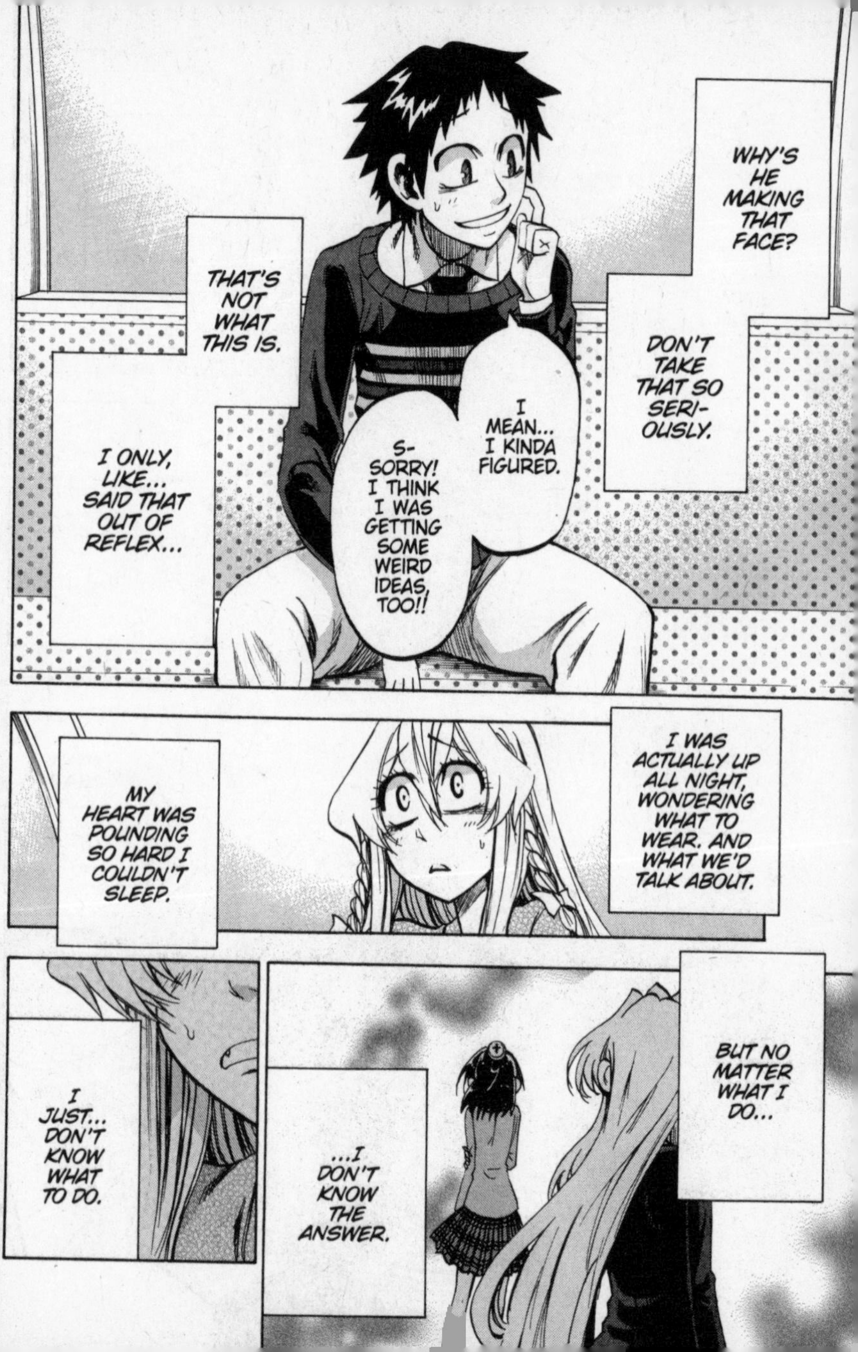
WHY'S HE MAKING THAT FACE?
DON'T TAKE THAT SO SERI-OUSLY.
I MEAN... I KINDA FIGURED.
S-SORRY! I THINK I WAS GETTING SOME WEIRD IDEAS, TOO!!
THAT'S NOT WHAT THIS IS.
I ONLY, LIKE... SAID THAT OUT OF REFLEX...
I WAS ACTUALLY UP ALL NIGHT, WONDERING WHAT TO WEAR. AND WHAT WE'D TALK ABOUT.
MY HEART WAS POUNDING SO HARD I COULDN'T SLEEP.
BUT NO MATTER WHAT I DO...
...I DON'T KNOW THE ANSWER.
I JUST... DON'T KNOW WHAT TO DO.

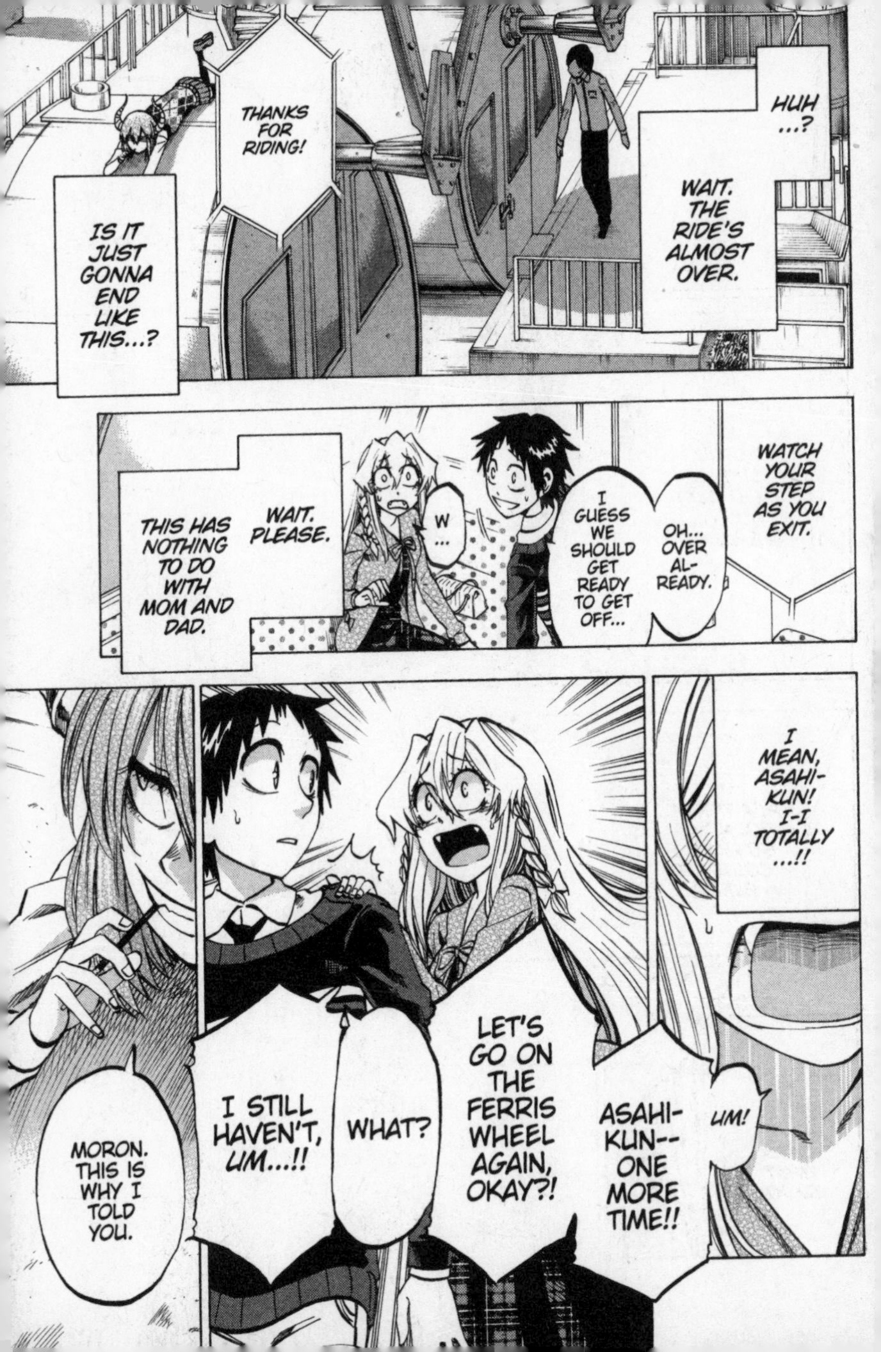
HUH ...?
WAIT. THE RIDE'S ALMOST OVER.
THANKS FOR RIDING!
IS IT JUST GONNA END LIKE THIS...?
WATCH YOUR STEP AS YOU EXIT.
OH... OVER AL-READY.
I GUESS WE SHOULD GET READY TO GET OFF...
W ...
WAIT. PLEASE.
THIS HAS NOTHING TO DO WITH MOM AND DAD.
I MEAN, ASAHI-KUN! I-I TOTALLY ...!!
UM!
ASAHI-KUN-- ONE MORE TIME!!
LET'S GO ON THE FERRIS WHEEL AGAIN, OKAY?!
WHAT?
I STILL HAVEN'T, UM...!!
MORON. THIS IS WHY I TOLD YOU.

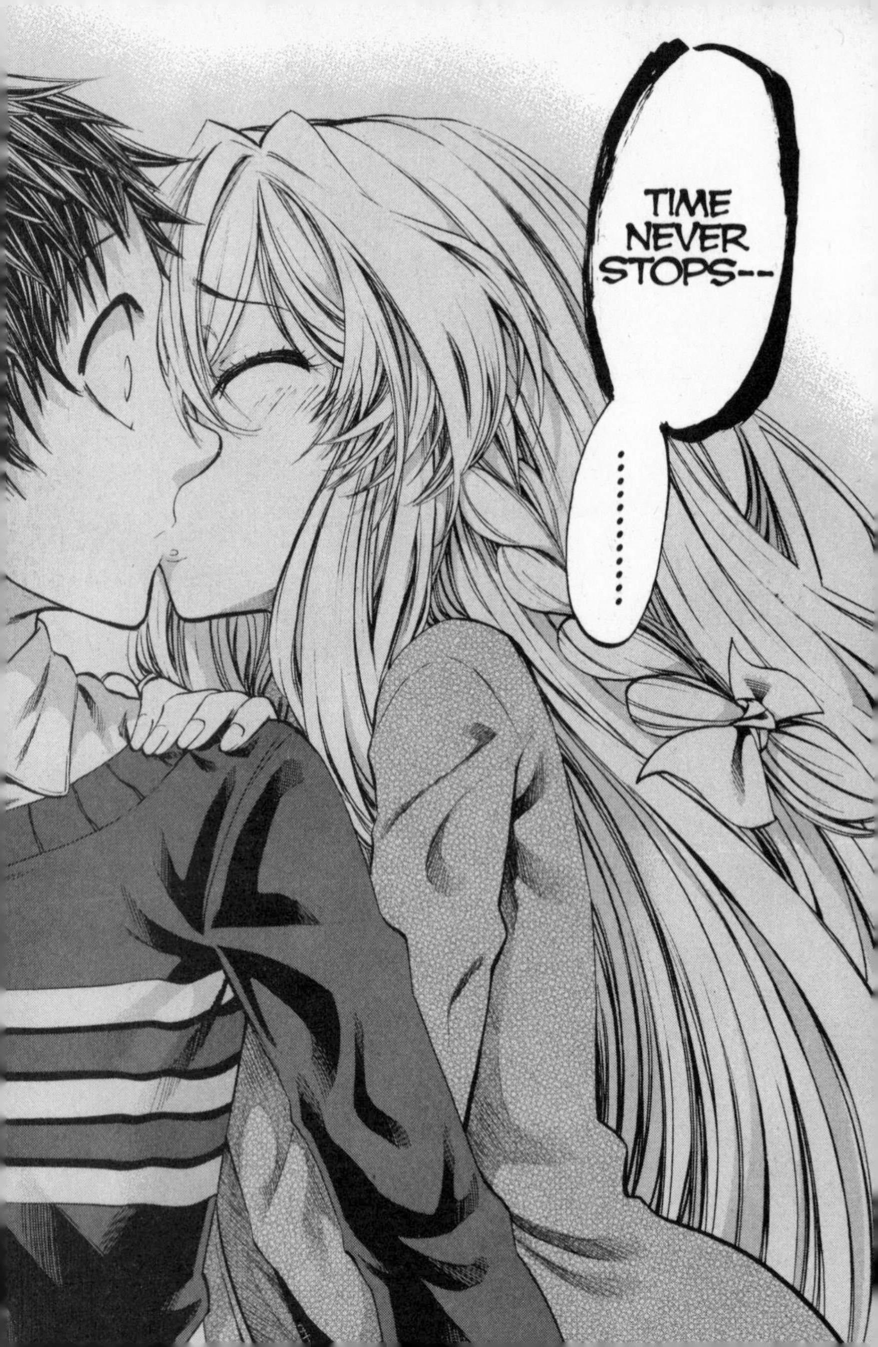
TIME NEVER STOPS--
......

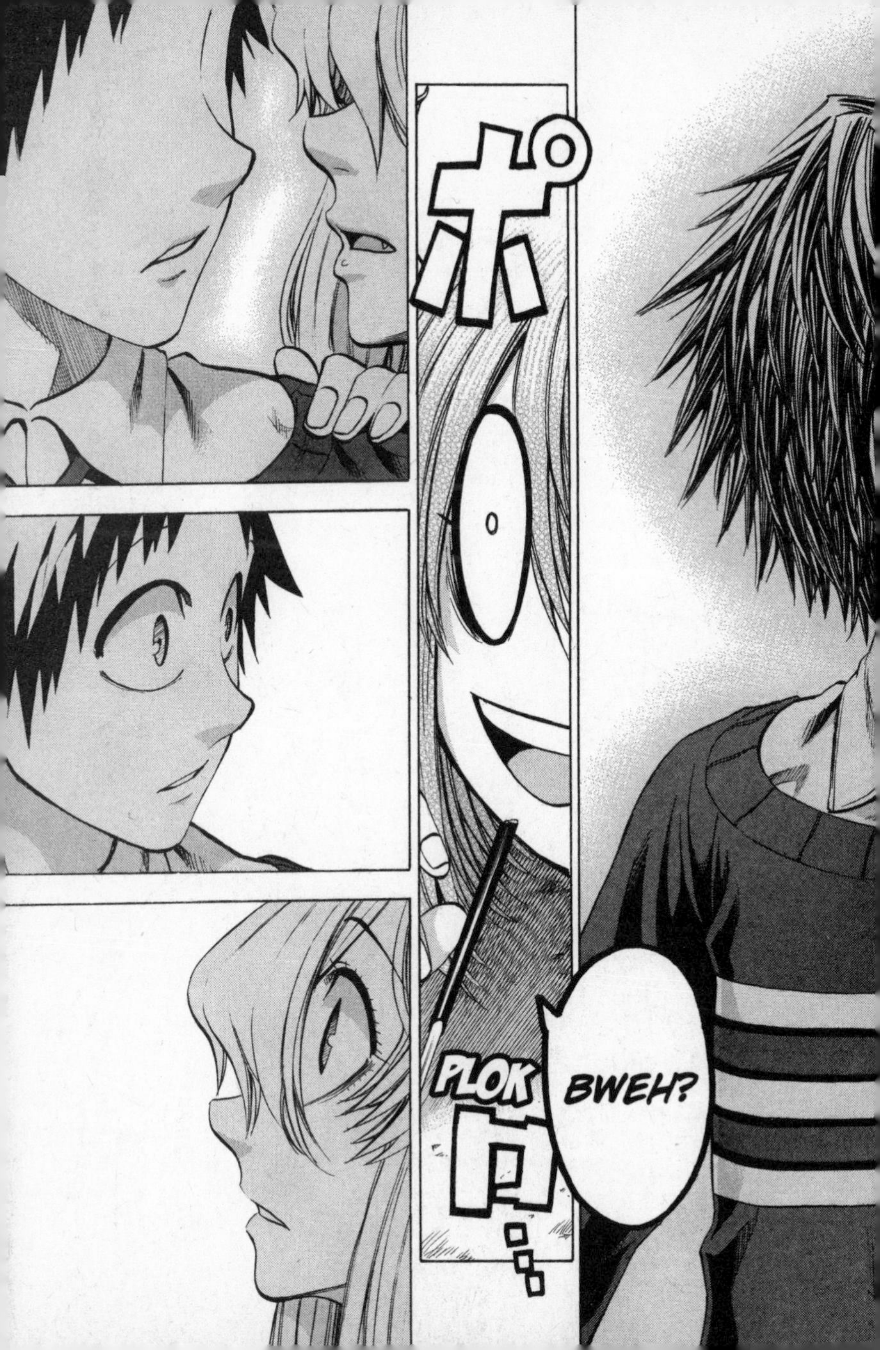
ポ
PLOK
BWEH?

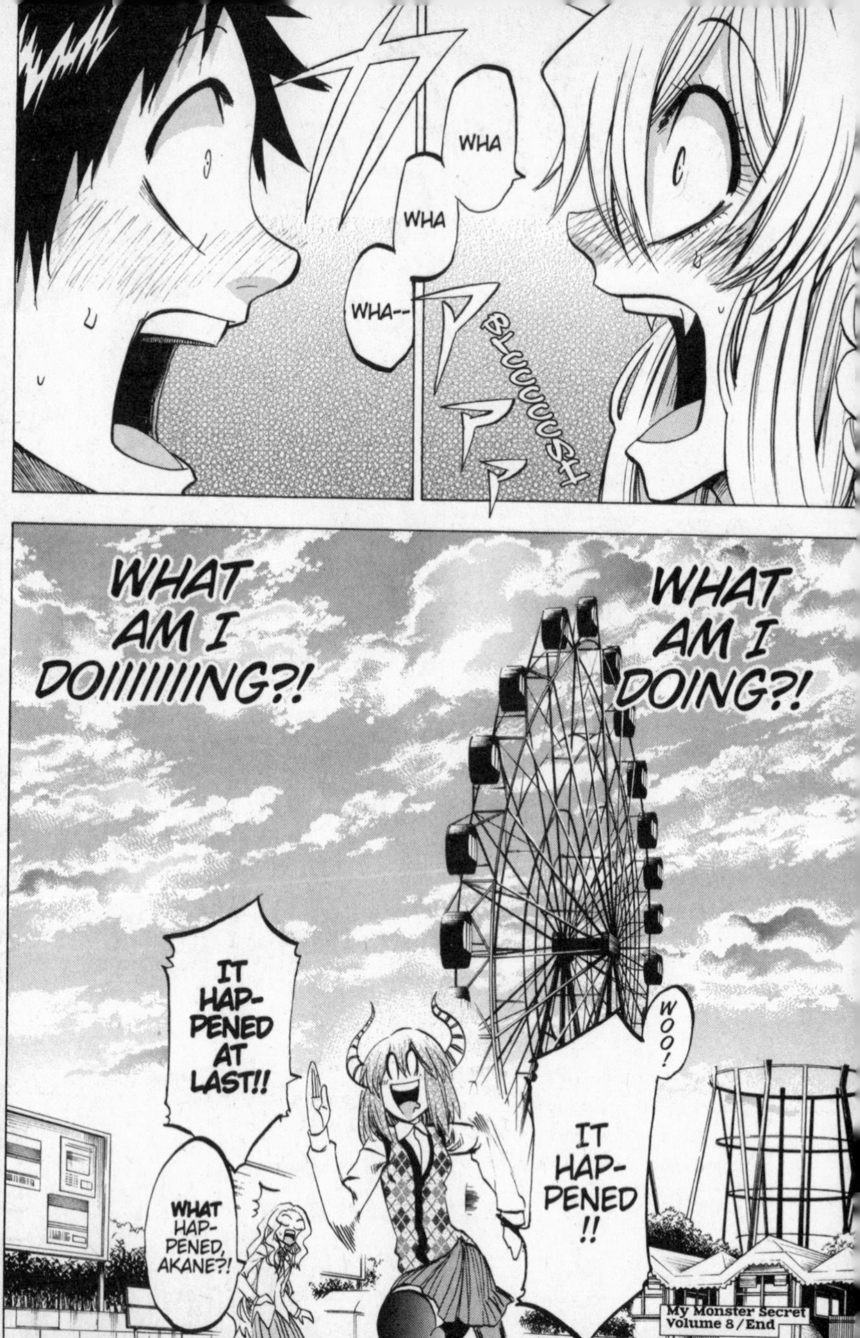
WHA
WHA
WHA--
BLUUUUSH
WHAT AM I DOING?!
WHAT AM I DOIIIIIIING?!
WOO!
IT HAP-PENED AT LAST!!
IT HAP-PENED!!
WHAT HAP-PENED, AKANE?!
My Monster Secret Volume 8 / End

Memories that cannot be related without tears.

STAFF.

- Garage Okada-san
- Shuumeigiku-san
- Seijun Suzuki-san
- Rie Hayashi-san
- Haruki Mana-san
- Hiroki Minemura-san

(in syllabary order)

SPECIAL THANKS.

- Kouki Nakashima-san
- Jirou Yamada-san

Editor: Mukawa-san, Otsuka-san

I give my thanks to those of you holding this book right now and everyone who let me and this work be a part of their lives.

Eiji Masuda

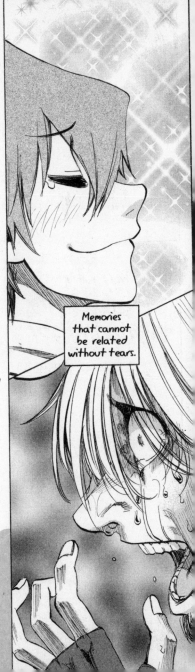

I am 8...

Angel Feathers

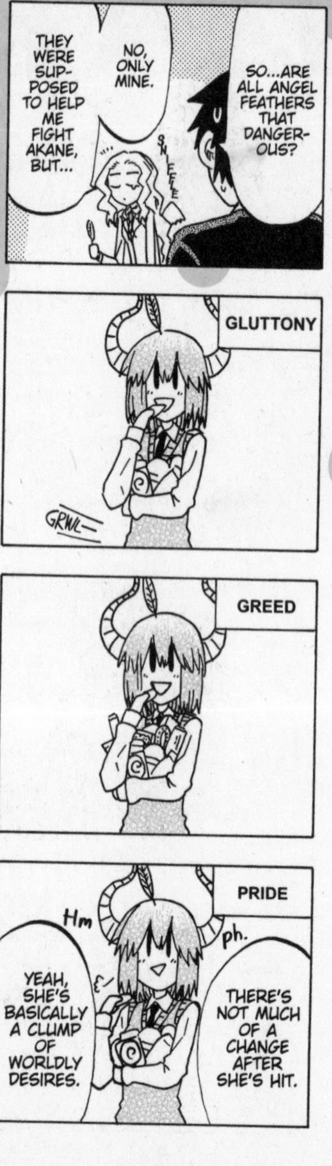
SO...ARE ALL ANGEL FEATHERS THAT DANGER-OUS?
NO, ONLY MINE.
THEY WERE SUP-POSED TO HELP ME FIGHT AKANE, BUT...
SNIFFLE
GLUTTONY
GRWL
GREED
PRIDE
ph.
Hm
THERE'S NOT MUCH OF A CHANGE AFTER SHE'S HIT.
YEAH, SHE'S BASICALLY A CLUMP OF WORLDLY DESIRES.

Birthday

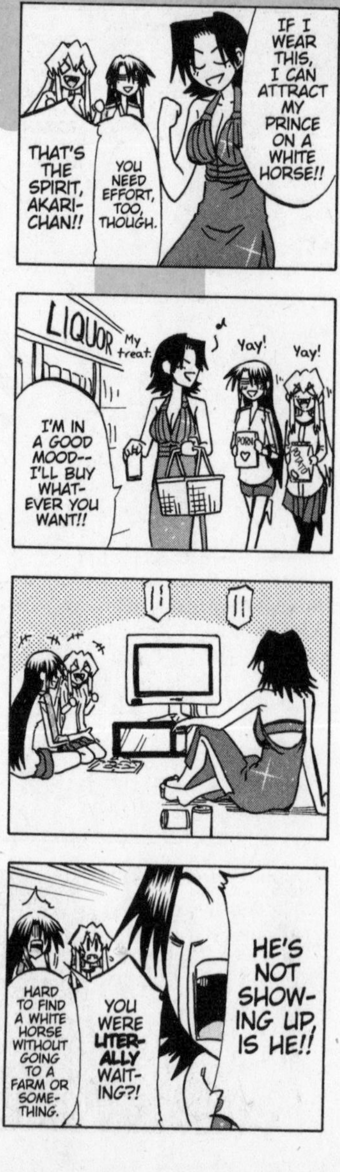
IF I WEAR THIS, I CAN ATTRACT MY PRINCE ON A WHITE HORSE!!
YOU NEED EFFORT, TOO, THOUGH.
THAT'S THE SPIRIT, AKARI-CHAN!!
Yay!
Yay!
My treat.
LIQUOR
I'M IN A GOOD MOOD--I'LL BUY WHAT-EVER YOU WANT!!
POTATO
PORN
HE'S NOT SHOW-ING UP, IS HE!!
YOU WERE LITER-ALLY WAIT-ING?!
HARD TO FIND A WHITE HORSE WITHOUT GOING TO A FARM OR SOME-THING.